AFRICAN CANADIAN LEADERSHIP

Continuity, Transition, and Transformation

Challenging the myth of African Canadian leadership "in crisis," this book opens a broad vista of enquiry into the many and dynamic ways leadership practices occur in African Canadian communities. Exploring topics including Black women's contributions to leadership initiatives, the Black Lives Matter movement, Black LGBTQ activism, HIV/AIDS advocacy, motherhood and grieving, mentoring, and anti-racism, contributors evaluate the complex history and contemporary reality of Blackness and leadership in Canada.

With Canada recognized as a complex site of Black diasporas, contributors offer an account of multiple forms of leadership and suggest that the practices and visions of self-determined Black leadership are incompatible with, and threatening to, White "structures" of power in Canada. As a whole, *African Canadian Leadership* offers perspectives that are complex and in critical conversation with class, gender, health, religion, sexuality, politics, and other matters that are of central concern to African Canadian communities.

TAMARI KITOSSA is an associate professor in the Department of Sociology at Brock University.

ERICA S. LAWSON is an associate professor in the Department of Women's Studies and Feminist Research at the University of Western Ontario.

PHILIP S.S. HOWARD is an assistant professor in the Department of Integrated Studies in Education at McGill University.

African Canadian Leadership

Continuity, Transition, and Transformation

EDITED BY TAMARI KITOSSA,
ERICA S. LAWSON, AND PHILIP S.S. HOWARD

UNIVERSITY OF TORONTO PRESS
Toronto Buffalo London

Toronto Buffalo London
utorontopress.com

ISBN 978-1-4875-0504-2 (cloth) ISBN 978-1-4875-2366-4 (paper)

Library and Archives Canada Cataloguing in Publication

Title: African Canadian leadership: continuity, transition, and transformation / edited by Tamari Kitossa, Erica S. Lawson, and Philip S.S. Howard.
Names: Kitossa, Tamari, editor. | Lawson, Erica S., 1967–, editor. | Howard, Philip S.S., 1964–, editor.
Description: Includes bibliographical references and index.
Identifiers: Canadiana 20190090278 | ISBN 9781487523664 (softcover) | ISBN 9781487505042 (hardcover)
Subjects: LCSH: Leadership – Canada. | LCSH: Blacks – Canada – Social conditions. | LCSH: Canada – Race relations. | CSH: Black Canadians – Social conditions.
Classification: LCC HM1261 .A37 2019 | DDC 303.3/408996071 – dc23

This book has been published with the help of a grant from the Federation for the Humanities and Social Sciences, through the Awards to Scholarly Publications Program, using funds provided by the Social Sciences and Humanities Research Council of Canada.

University of Toronto Press acknowledges the financial assistance to its publishing program of the Canada Council for the Arts and the Ontario Arts Council, an agency of the Government of Ontario.

Canada Council for the Arts Conseil des Arts du Canada

Funded by the Government of Canada | Financé par le gouvernement du Canada | Canada

Contents

Foreword

CECIL FOSTER

What is leadership and how does it manifest itself in Black Canada? These are troubling questions for several reasons. As this anthology suggests, these questions are at the heart of the very things we are supposed to be talking about, concepts that are identified separately as Black community, Canada, and even leadership. When we put them all together conceptually we can end up with a smorgasbord of meaning, something that might not provide any guidance to us if we started out thinking, stereotypically, that there might be one answer or formula for understanding the Black experience in Canada. For one of the great difficulties of scholarship is how to come up with explanations that are broad enough to account for the way people live, how they express their human dignity, and how, whether as individuals or collectively, they assert themselves fully as members of humanity: usually, this can't be done absolutely. Having stated this challenge, I will now ignore my own advice and offer my own conception of leadership in the Black communities across Canada.

Traditionally, leadership has been associated with the notion of greatness: leaders were great people, and greater people were leaders. But how did anyone become great? Those of us familiar with the seminal literature on leadership and greatness have encountered the suggestion that a great person supposedly rises up out of history on the horns of competing dialectical forces and becomes the person who reconciles these differences. The great person was an embodiment of the spirit of the times. Having found the truth of their times, these enlightened persons, because they were articulate interlocutors of a shared experience, oriented others to this truth and in the process became recognized as greater leaders.

This is the story of the Great Men and Women of the Times – a theory that long resonated in Black communities worldwide in recognition of the so-called Race Men and Race Women: those who were considered a credit to the race and were lauded for their achievements. Traditionally, they were the first to be recognized as Black persons of merit to break down barriers against Black inclusion in the wider society. They were the pioneers, those who broke into the mainstream and securely planted a flag of Blackness – setting a new benchmark for all Black people to follow and against which the wider society could then evaluate Black achievements. It is why to this day, even in a moment of multiculturalism and reconciliation, we still tend to take note of the Black person who becomes the first to do or to achieve what members of other groups had long thought was exclusively their due. It is why to this day other groups allege that members of Black communities are neither good mentors nor role models for their youths; this is a criticism that is hardly ever levelled at those ethnic groups that now make up the social mainstream. Under this scenario, each time the flag of Black achievement was planted it represented a higher level of greatness, signifying that a new leader had pointed the way and from this spot was "passing on the baton."

But two things are central to this theorizing. The first is that greatness was achieved unconsciously. Nobody could wake up on a given morning and say, "Today is when I will be great," and then go out and achieve greatness as planned in their imagination. For it was only in the heat of a given battle for justice that greatness was forged, often unbeknown to the soon-to-be Great One and usually recognized only at battle's end. Importantly, then, greatness is earned and conferred by others. The same can be said for organic leadership. But as we know, life as *history* is more like a war[1] than a single skirmish – but a series of them each supposedly capable of producing its own heroes and adding to those across time. The second point is that greatness often portends either the actual or ritual death of the individual. Indeed, it is in the self-sacrificing for others that greatness is achieved. Maybe this explains why nobody gets up in the morning and plans to be great, as to do so would be to openly court physical and symbolic destruction or self-immolation. It also explains why to this day we recognize those who fell in battle as heroes, something that resonates among Black people, who have always had to tell the heroic stories of a leader cut down in the struggle for justice through the machinations of the white power elites and state minions. It should be noted here that assassinations of Black leaders, be it in character or body, are virtually unique among non-white groups, thus signifying that allegations of the failures of Black leadership go to the heart of positioning the oppression of Black communities as a metric for the progress of others into the mainstream.

With the foregoing in mind, I believe there is one thing in particular that makes the quest for understanding leadership and Blackness enigmatic, and it is also why I see issues of leadership and Blackness as matters of social ethics and morality. Unlike for any other branch of humanity, leadership and Blackness always come together on a social battlefield for dignity, respect, and resources shaped by race, racism, and the specificity of anti-Blackness. This is where greatness is achieved, for the history of Black people in this part of the world is one of having every aspect of their lived reality shaped by the racialized gaze of those who claim social superiority. There is no escaping. It is often why critics outside the Black community lament that there is no leadership among Black people, except for when it is expressed politically as a power struggle against Black suppression. As I have shown in *"They Call Me George": The Untold Story of Black Train Porters and the Birth of Modern Canada* (2019), it is in the setting against oppression and the struggle for justice that, across time, Black women – often very much in the lead as a given in the Black reality – and men have sought to assert not so much their greatness but their humanity. Through acts of agency, both past and present, Black leaders speak to the greater need for freedom of their own group and for others as well. This is why in the nineteenth and early twentieth centuries they were always called Race Men and Race Women.

Leadership is about demanding full recognition in social relationships that cumulatively make up the wider social order, and it is morality at work where, either as an individual or as like-minded associates, people fight for what they believe to be good and right. Black leadership for me is about every aspect of the social order in which individuals live and play and enjoy their humanity to the fullest. It is seeing a need, addressing a denial or an obstruction to freedom, and doing something about it whether alone or in concert with others. It is social consciousness. Put this way, leadership is about self-assertiveness, even when there is no thought about greatness but simply about overcoming obstacles to full human acceptance, participation, and rewards. In this context, when the oppression must overcome by any means necessary, improvisation and rhetoric become weapons of struggle in the same way the badly outgunned resort to throwing rocks and sticks in an unfair fight. But just as there is a time for war, there must always ever be a time to beat weapons into ploughshares, evident in caring and the love of self and others as social beings.

The foregoing has been my experience living as a Black man in North America and claiming a sense of belonging for decades in Canada. As a student of this living, I have noticed how acts of leadership are carried out daily by people who have been demeaned and marginalized in some way or another. Leadership takes a multiplicity of forms manifest in Black assertiveness and resistance. And I have noticed that, whether articulated in groups such as trade unions, church associations, high school alumni, or even the lone voices in a particular workplace, Black people have always had to be leaders, first for themselves, with and for the benefit of others. Similarly, I have seen how quickly members of the Canadian Black communities reject people anointed and offered to them as "leaders" by the power elites of the white mainstream. They seem to have a detector that always ferrets out Black leadership being foisted on them, particularly when it comes in the form of handpicked leaders vetted and selected by the power elites of mainstream society. Such leadership is not organically produced by the complicated and fraught proving ground for the development and legitimation of informal authority in Black communities, which alone reserve the right to confer the status of greatness upon their publicly activist members. In the world of civil society, genuine leadership among oppressed groups is democratic enough to demand a choice in determining leaders.

So, in this sense, leadership manifests itself in as many different ways as people need to be free. There is no single method or battlefield *per se*, for as this anthology shows, wherever there are people yearning to be free and to demand an equitable share in the tangible and intangible goods due to all, they will individually or collectively fight to achieve these ends. Leadership in the Black communities across Canada has been more than how *not* to be a deprived and racialized object, but also how to be free and resourced to achieve the fullest expression of one's humanity like any other member of society. Morally, that is the proper way for a human to exist. As the authors in this anthology demonstrate, leadership among Black people in Canada is about proving that Black lives matter in every aspect and every walk of life, and that Black people have the right to assert that their lives matter. And for this reason, the contributors have established new benchmarks for greatness by doing what they were theorizing. As we go forward, discussions on Blackness and leadership will no longer be the same. For one thing, the very creation of this book demonstrates a uniqueness that comes from trying to be a socially conscious Black subject in this part of the world. In contextualizing and recognizing great individual leaders, the contributors to this collection also apprehend that in the everydayness of ordinary Black people's struggle there are many small acts of greatness and many forms of leadership that must be acknowledged and celebrated. For Black people, I believe leadership is simply about ethically and morally living with themselves and with their differences, working towards social uplift for all and resisting the social forces of destruction. That is the kind of *game-changer*, indeed paradigm shift, these authors give us to take forward in any discussion on leadership and Black communities, and in fact on leaders and the world. While the immediate impact of their effort might first be felt in academia, where the majority of them make their living, much would be lost to the social good if what they are saying is not taken up in the wider society, for that is where they live as citizens and humans.

NOTE

1 It is not coincidental that the discourse about leadership and Blackness is dominated by the dreaded rhetoric of blood and gore. I purposely invoke conflict metaphors such as "battles" and "wars" to signify that Black leadership, as with the Black experience from slavery to the present, is about the dominant culture's physical and psychological intentions to limit the horizons of and even destroy Black people. The mainstream has declared war on Blackness and Black leadership precisely because both are sites of difference representing a substantive political challenge to the authority and taken-for-granted dominance of the status quo. My utilization of war metaphors, then, is not endorsement, but a highlighted recognition of the reality of the Black experience in mainstream society. Indeed, such thinking is embedded in discussions via such terms as "clash" and "battle to the death" between cultures and nations in the work of Samuel Huntington (*The Clash of Civilizations and the Remaking of the World Order*), Dinesh D'Souza (*The End of Racism*), and their acolytes throughout North America.

REFERENCES

D'Souza, D. 1995. *The end of racism: Principles for a multiracial society*. New York: Free Press.

Foster, C. 2019. *"They call me George": The untold story of the black train porters and the birth of modern Canada*. Windsor: Biblioasis.

Huntington, S. 1996. *The clash of civilizations and the remaking of the world order*. New York: Simon & Schuster.

AFRICAN CANADIAN LEADERSHIP

Continuity, Transition, and Transformation

Introduction
Interrogating the Notion of Crisis in African Canadian Leadership

TAMARI KITOSSA, PHILIP S.S. HOWARD, AND ERICA S. LAWSON

Across place, space, and time, this book explores African Canadian leadership through the interests, voices, and perspectives of diverse African Canadian intellectuals. The purpose of the collection is to examine and theorize the multiple ways that leadership(s) is/are practised by and within African Canadian communities. It explores individual, community, and institutional contexts from which leadership emanates and assesses their impact on African Canadian communities and the larger Canadian society. The complexity of the making and continued unfolding of Blackness in Canada, which forms the background to this book, opens it to critical engagement with the implications of diasporism and transnationalism on leadership forms, ideologies, and practices. Fully apprised of the complex history and contemporary reality of Blackness in Canada, contributors to this collection explore a range of issues and desirable outcomes for African Canadians. Recognizing that difference among African Canadians does not preclude common goals, contributors are also aware of the heterogeneity, openness, and dynamism of African Canadian or Black communities.

A number of authors in this volume (James, Williams, and Kitossa) critique the strategic ambivalence of White Canadian elites towards African Canadian leaders. They demonstrate that on one hand White elites displace homegrown African Canadian leadership by inviting African American leaders, principally clergymen, as expert knowers in moments of crisis. There is an unmistakable irony here. While White Canadian elites implicitly enable the cultural imperialism of a segment of the Black American elite, where radical Black leaders in both countries (from the Black United Front and the Black Panther Party to the Black Lives Matter organization) make common cause across the symbolic solidity of the forty-ninth parallel, this is criticized as a tutelage and strained importation of radical African American politics. The effect is to raise emotional alarm about the danger non-conforming African Canadian leaders ostensibly pose to the Canadian "fabric," thereby rationalizing their *a priori* exposure to an intensive regime of state surveillance (Austin, 2013).

Yet drawing on historical evidence, a range of African Canadian scholars call the solidity of the border into question and simultaneously assert the distinctive aspirations, types, and qualities of African Canadian leadership in Canada as compared to the United States. They demonstrate that from the period of slavery in both countries to the present, the border has ever been a porous circulation of bodies, experiences, and ideas that, under a range of specific contexts, have "travelled" across national, regional, and political boundaries to reinforce a common awareness of the parallel manifestations of anti-Blackness under White racial domination in the Americas. Indeed, where Blackness is concerned, the histories of the forty-ninth parallel, the Atlantic, the Caribbean, and Iberian America reveal borders to be porous – at once imagined and real (Austin, 2013; Frost & Tucker, 2016; McKittrick, 2006; Shadd, Cooper, & Frost, 2009; Shepard, 1997; Thomson, 1979).

The Context of African Canadian Leadership

The bounded-unboundedness of this book's explicit engagement with Black leadership(s), and its implicit engagement with Black identity/ies in Canada, serves in part as challenge, contextualization, and point of departure from which to critique the discourse of a "crisis" of Black leadership (see Lalonde, 2016; Winsa, 2015). Informed by these always (and properly) unfixed parameters, this notion of crisis means different things to different political actors, and, in fact, *does* different things. For the state and White opinion makers in Canada, the African Canadian presence troubles White racial hegemony and its iterations of what it means to be, and who is considered, "Canadian" at different moments in the life of the nation (Clarke, 2004; C. Foster, 1996, 2019; Henry, 2010; Stewart, 2014; Walcott, 2001). Of course, because African Canadians are not fully imagined as citizens in the fullest sense of entitlements and rights conferred on White Canadians, leadership by and for them is always subject to challenge, questioning, and selective validation in the White imaginary. A simple dualism is effected between "good" and "bad" Black leaders in which the discourse of crisis is both arbiter, shadow, and weapon used to manage conflicts arising from African Canadian encounters with White supremacy and the White racial state.

Indeed, in Canada, the national mythologies that reproduce a discourse of the nation as inherently and unquestionably racially transcendent depend, in part, upon hegemonic narrations of its relationship to Blackness. These include Underground Railroad narratives and erasures and silences around other more ignominious aspects of this relationship, such as transatlantic slavery and Jim Crow (Cooper, 2006; C. Foster, 2019; Walker, 2012). The result is a particularly adverse reaction to African Canadian leadership where it confronts and exposes the sham of Canadian liberal mythologies and their foundational, unacknowledged, unaddressed, and persistent anti-Blackness (Howard, 2018; Kitossa, 2005; Lawson, 2002). With persistent character assassination and maligning, the ruling White Canadian powers displace responsibility for the disorganization, misery, and poverty they impose on African Canadian communities onto those who undertake critical forms of leadership.

Along with our contributors, we note that the practice and visions of radical, self-determined Black leadership(s) are incompatible with, and threatening to, White "structures"[1] of power. These structures blame non-compliant Black leaders for creating "social disorganization" and fostering their communities' "failings" instead of identifying the overarching, morally indifferent, and repressive structures against which these leaders contend. Indeed, as with Dudley Laws, for example, radical Black leaders are blamed for fomenting ungracious dissatisfaction with Canada's largesse rather than "whipping" their followers into shape. Yet it is to fearless leaders such as Hugh Burnett, Viola Desmond, and Dudley Laws that Canadians owe the foundations of human rights legislation and in Ontario the Special Investigations Unit and the Ontario Independent Police Review Directorate. Such leaders are viewed as transgressing the normative practices and responsibilities associated with citizenship. Indeed, radical Black leaders have paid, and continue to pay, the price of actual and ritualized destruction for challenging the contradictions and inequities of the ableist, capitalist, colonialist, heteronormative, patriarchal, and racist liberal democratic state. The reality is that the edifice of White power seeks to eliminate or tarnish revolutionary leaders, block collective change, and appropriate hard-fought victories within and against liberalism (Austin, 2013; L. Foster, 2003). Additionally, a variety of authors consider the ways that the impositions of state organizational and broader ruling relations constrain, disfigure, and distort Black leadership, resulting in bizarre formations that are then blamed on Black communities themselves.

In a parallel manner, Black leaders who operate within the confines of liberal approaches to leadership are viewed as the ones most competent to represent "the community" in dialogue with the Canadian state. They are recruited to cooperate with state-sponsored strategies that do little to disrupt the status quo which sustains the social problems confronting African Canadians. Paradoxically, as Carl James and Chris Williams note in this volume, these African Canadian (neo-liberal) leaders, whose bootstrap interventions constitute accommodations to anti-Blackness, are ultimately also blamed for their communities' presumed failure to grasp, en masse, the ostensibly abundant opportunities offered by Canadian society. We have seen this occur within law enforcement organizations and political institutions, for example, where a few African Canadians become the toast of the White establishment. These self-serving leaders, palatable and accommodating to the White structures that promote them, quickly reveal the limits of their utility to White power, as well as the limits of their capacity to mobilize African Canadians in their defence when they become an embarrassment to the ruling White powers.

In complicated and nuanced ways, these conservative/neo-liberal forms of leadership are often exercised by members of the upwardly mobile African Canadian middle class. As Kevin Gosine notes in this volume, their education, privileged discourse, and strategic locations in the private and public sectors often position them in paradoxical ways to the communities they claim to represent. This fraction of the Black elite is made suspect by their dependence on the legitimacy of the ruling relations of Whiteness and the lack of legitimacy of their claims to leadership of large segments of African Canadian communities. No matter how persuasive a levelling view of this class fraction may be on its face, quite aside from the implied disparagement, its plausibility in the absolute is dubious. As with the racial uplift movement among conservative Black elites in the late nineteenth and early twentieth centuries (i.e., the early W.E.B. Du Bois), conservative Black elites play fundamental roles in forwarding the Black agenda for equity and justice. Some among them have even provided strong but quiet support for Black radicals such as Dudley Laws and the Black Action Defence Committee (BADC) in times of personal and organizational need (Cooper, personal communication, May 2015). We would do well also to recognize that class privilege does not shield African Canadians from the damaging effects of White supremacy (Black Experience Project, 2017).

Beyond Charismatic Leaders and "Crisis" Framing

In addition to critically engaging with the implications of the discourse of crisis, this book empirically and theoretically deconstructs the tendency to see leadership in hegemonic ways – most evident in the top-down interventions of "gifted and charismatic" (often male) individuals – and the problem and possibilities for how Black communities might mobilize leadership without coercion. In the opinion of the editors and many contributors, the notion of the solitary, gifted, charismatic Black leader is and always has been an erroneous construct. Charismatic leadership is one type of leadership, though it tends to be overvalued in historical and theoretical accounts of Black leadership. Despite whatever oratory and organizational giftedness particular individuals demonstrate, and despite the accidents of history that drive them forward, the platform upon which "charismatic leaders" stand is not possible without a conscious, disciplined, and organized critical mass of like-minded comrades who push them towards greatness. Problematically, the construction of charismatic leadership tends to valorize male leaders. But from slave revolts, civil rights movements, and Black liberation to Black Lives Matter, women have always been front and centre in Black leadership in addition to playing supportive roles within organizations, often making possible the work of the charismatic male leaders (Brown 1993).

In this vein, the examination of women's roles in Black leadership situates the emergence of Black Lives Matter (BLM)[2] and the prominent role of women and LGBTQ as a recent iteration of Black activism that is inclusive and that defies easy categorization and classification. Leaderless and at once leaderful, Black Lives Matter both confirms and pushes against the fact that Black lives have never mattered to the White capitalist heteropatriarchal state – something that Afropessimists have been telling us for some time now (Hartman, 1997; Wilderson, 2003). But inasmuch as BLM is built on its predecessors, *now* is clearly a different time. The fact that the cry is no longer for access through civil rights, where full inclusion has proven elusive, and no longer for "Black power" (clearly signifying how battered the movement for Black liberation has been, not to mention its gendered and other limitations) reflects a novel reality, demanding different strategies for leadership and liberation. In the United States, United Kingdom, Canada, and elsewhere, BLM is challenging orthodoxies about leadership and social movements, even as it experiments with acephalous, bottom-up, circular, lateral, margin-to-centre, and participatory democracy regimes. It is not accidental that BLM is widely discredited in the American and Canadian racial states, as reflected in trite and condescending slogans such as "all lives matter." Indeed, BLM in Canada is dismissed as merely mimicking events in the United States (e.g., "Protest rally insensitive," 2015) against which Canadian racist practices are measured and deemed either to be not as bad or non-existent. Responses that dismiss important contemporary Black leadership initiatives demonstrate the defining, though erroneous, national view that Canada is beyond race (or post-racial). The strategic negation of Blackness constructs

Canada as a post-racialist state formation in which the salience of race is made unspeakable while state practices continue to be unapologetically racially and colonially informed (see Goldberg, 2009, 2015; Howard, 2018). Indeed, Rinaldo Walcott (2014), who has undertaken a leadership role in the academy as a Black scholar-activist, puts the lie to the notion that Blackness is limited within the parameters of national boundaries. He recognizes that Black Canada is a complex articulation of multiple Black diasporas across time, place, and space, insisting that "Black Canadian life is best understood through the logics of diaspora ... Black Canadian life takes its formation, its politics and its intellectual traditions, its cultural expressions, its contributions and consciousness in concert with other forms of global blackness" (p. 277). In conversation with this position, focusing on the ways the identities and identification of African Canadians born on the African continent complicate Blackness, Handel Kashope Wright (2015) asserts that "Continental Africans currently living in the diaspora ... constitute an interesting wrinkle on black identity, being both continental and diasporic and always in the process of rendering both categories more complex" (p. 12).

Thus it is with these complexities in mind that the current iteration of Black leadership is being experienced and re/written, with its roots in transatlantic slave rebellions, international slave abolition movements, the anti-lynching campaign, global civil rights struggles, and the Black radical tradition (Richmond, 2017). With a clear "intersectional" politics, accounts of leadership are cognizant of the borderless spectrum of Black identities (women, men, queer, trans, disabled, etc.) that have always constituted Black leadership, and affirm the value of Blackness in all the diverse ways in which it is lived.

In recognizing diversity, "intersectionality," and liminality within Black leadership styles, we seek to situate the greatness of individual leaders as both contextual and provisional and to recognize the broader dynamic of Black liberation as a social movement from below. To this end, taking a broad scope, we suggest that African Canadian leadership has never been more vibrant than it is now. For such a counter-discourse to be compelling, however, empirical evidence and alternative theoretical reasoning are required.

To date, unfortunately, research enquiry and scholarly theorizing about African Canadian leadership are greatly impoverished. What does exist is dated, such as the espionage expert Robin Winks's *The Blacks in Canada* (1997 [1971]) or Paula McClain's *Alienation and Resistance* (1979), both of which usefully demonstrate that *things have to change in order to stay the same.* Curiously, the study of African Canadian leadership is driven by historians (cf. Austin, 2013; Bristow et al., 1994; de b'Beri, Reid-Maroney, & Wright, 2014; Henry, 2010; C. Foster, 2019;

Smardz Frost, 2008; Jones & Walker, 2016; Walker, 2012). This may well be because historians, responding to the erasure of African Canadians, seek to map the experience, contributions, and realities of African Canadians in the economic, cultural, social, and political life before and after Confederation. By identifying charismatic historical personalities and a vast array of organizations ranging from militant to accommodationist, this scholarship provides a rich social history of community life and the internal struggles of conflict and contradiction of various organizations, and identifies metrics for successes in challenging the exclusion of African Canadians.

While historical work offers the basis for assessing both practice and theory in African Canadian leadership, more fine-grained work of the sort undertaken by Cecil Foster (2019), Rocky Jones and James Walker (2016), David Austin (2013), Barrington Walker (2014), and Carmela Marano (2010) demonstrates that African Canadian leadership has always been complex, multidirectional, and multifaceted. These works take us into the inner dynamics of organizations and the fraught relationships and personalities aspiring to achieve well-intentioned goals on behalf of Black communities. Historical perspective is unquestionably important; for with one eye to the past and another on the present, we can achieve a theoretical accounting in support of contemporary actions that shape the future. To use another metaphor: hindsight also affords the convenience of seeing fully the outline of the elephant, which proximity in the here and now does not allow. Yet more and other disciplinary approaches are needed to expand the range of empirical evidence and theoretical perspective useful to assess and identify form, scale, and quality of practice measured by outcomes.

Overview of This Book

The contributors to this book go beyond the discourse of the crisis of African Canadian leadership. They undertake empirical and theoretical analysis of African Canadian leadership from within and between disciplines. They agree on the spuriousness of a Black leadership crisis, criticize and qualify the discourse of the solitary and charismatic male leader, and, finally, assert the need to imagine and recover innovative forms of leadership for the future. Yet, the variety of ways they identify and engage (or not), emphasize (or not), and sideline (or not) various permutations of these concerns makes for a rich collection. No doubt the variety and methods of their approaches are informed by the inter- and multidisciplinarity of their backgrounds and theoretical orientations, but also by the multiple, overlapping, yet heterodox ways in which they come to be positioned as Black or African Canadian persons.

Part 1, "Models and Theories," chapters 1 to 4, is devoted to theorizing African Canadian leadership(s). Distinctive to his chapter, Carl James (chapter 1) usefully devises a working typology of Black leadership styles that are expressive of complexity and the criss-crossing, contradictory nature of social and political allegiance found among African Canadian organizational leaders and political elites. The diversity in substance and style of these forms of leadership seeks to clarify the different ways and degrees to which Black leaders are dis/connected from the interests of class fractions in African Canadian communities and appease or resist power structures instantiated through what he calls "White logic." Complementing though departing from James's typologies, Christopher Williams (chapter 2) examines the implications of the White power structure's intervening in Black political expression. Using African Canadians' resistance to police violence, Williams demonstrates that through the "hierarchy of credibility" White power elites mobilize media and other power resources to discredit the authority of radical leaders while seeking to legitimate state-centric narratives of "good" Black leaders that are compliant with White authority.

Whereas James and Williams typify and situate Black leadership in contention with the state and community aspirations, Tamari Kitossa (chapter 3) reviews the contributions of the limited sociological work on Black leadership for how it opens opportunities for contemporary theorizing of authority and African Canadian leadership. Relying on historical scholarship, an epistemic deconstruction of "crisis theory," and Gramscian social theory to assesses two leadership projects in contemporary Toronto, and to comment on BLM, he suggests that the discourse of the "crisis of Black leadership" is both recursive and productive for leadership formation and political action. In chapter 4, Amoaba Gooden explores African Canadian leadership from a historical sociology of pan-African ideology. Gooden reveals the salient role that women played in establishing cultural and social bridges in 1950s Ontario between endogenous African Canadians and those from Africa and the Caribbean. Revealing the existence of a largely unknown and unheralded dimension of pan-African history in Canada, she traces the genesis of Caribana to pan-African collaborations in 1950s Ontario.

Part 2, "Women and Leadership," chapters 5 to 7, explicates the role of African Canadian women in leadership. An accurate and comprehensive consideration of African Canadian leadership is simply impossible without highlighting the often understated and invisibilized work of African Canadian women. To this end, rosalind hampton and Désirée Rochat (chapter 5) highlight the ways in which Black women in twentieth-century Montreal exercised effective leadership independently of charismatic male figures. The women in their study focused squarely on promoting the practical survival of their communities while they sought to build (albeit imperfect) solidarities across linguistic, class, cultural, and even racial lines. In so doing, they highlight the importance of a focus on the *process* of leadership, rather than solely on its ends.

In contradistinction to public Black leadership, there are times when that leadership is hidden within the institutional walls of the workplace. Annette Henry (chapter 6) exemplifies the complex practice of leadership for African Canadian in the academy. As a distinguished African Canadian academic, she writes to and about the strategies for African Canadian women to thrive in a milieu often antithetical to their existence within it – least of all, as leaders. Erica Lawson's account of African Canadian mothers grieving the loss of their children through gun violence (chapter 7) explicates the intersections of private and public leadership practice in ways that transcend class. Without reifying the broken Black body as spectacle, Lawson demonstrates that since slavery, Black mothers have transformed loss into a mode of resistance to institutionalized White supremacy and a critique of internalized racism.

Part 3, "Organizing and Mobilizing," chapters 8 to 10, involves empirical studies of Black leadership. Without offering a taxonomy of leadership, Philip Howard (chapter 8) identifies a range of ways that Black professionals exercise agency in the context of the normative gendered White supremacy of predominantly White institutions to achieve equity for racialized communities broadly, and for African Canadians in particular. Keeping in full view the very real constraints of these contexts, the chapter enjoins us to resist Manichean notions of good/progressive versus bad/regressive African Canadian leadership. Kevin Gosine (chapter 9) demonstrates that the Black middle-class project of "race uplift" in the nineteenth century has given way to the individualistic practice of mentoring in the neo-liberal context. His chapter examines the complex ways that upwardly mobile African Canadians negotiate Blackness, their professional success, and accommodation to the individualistic ethos of neo-liberalism. He demonstrates that among upwardly mobile Black Canadians there is a sense of racial responsibility that manifests itself in the discourse and practice of "giving back," often rooted in petty bourgeois moralism and accommodation to the "race-neutral" ethos of neo-liberalism. Shamara Baidoobonso (chapter 10) reveals that HIV/AIDS activism in particular, and Black health activism more generally, is a vital locus from which to explicate the ways that everyday/night "organic intellectuals" mobilize to sustain the health of the community, especially those suffering from HIV/AIDS.

Essays in Part 4, "The Politics of the Personal," chapters 11 and 12, demonstrate how auto-ethnography and biography can explicate the challenges, joys, and visions of African Canadian leadership. Wesley Crichlow (chapter 11) undertakes an autoethnography of Black LGBTQ contributions to African Canadian leadership in Toronto. He reveals that Black LGBTQ persons were critical voices in the city's anti-apartheid movement and in resistance to the *Into the Heart of Africa* exhibit at the ROM. Paul Banahene Adjei (chapter 12) offers a critical reappraisal of the historic social justice mission of the Black church in the transatlantic circuit from West Africa to Canada. Centering attention on the "prosperity gospel," he exposes the crass materialism of a circuit of Black transnational capitalist clergymen. Finally, in Part 5, "Black Intellectuals," George Dei (chapter 13) takes an activist and constructivist approach to African Canadian leadership. Dei encourages and challenges African Canadian intellectuals to (a) undertake a rigorous process of indigenizing their minds through an inclusive Africentrism and pan-Africanism, and (b) direct their research expertise to working for, with, and on behalf of Canada's Black communities. Finally, Sam Tecle and David Austin (chapter 14) critically reflect on Black intellectuals' contribution to leadership, both as participants in social movements and as theorists. By reflecting on the production of ideas by intellectuals such as C.L.R. James and Sylvia Wynter, they critically assess the role of intellectuals in Black leadership and how this form of Black leadership takes shape.[3]

The Story of This Book

Every book has a creation story. Along the way to its completion it can take a meandering path. For editors and contributors alike, this manuscript has been a labour of love as much as of soul searching to make sense of an experience with profound implications for their lives and that of their communities. As editors, we invited the participation of scholars from across Canada and internationally who would address leadership in heterodoxic contexts and forms in Canada. We sought to include a wide range of perspectives from an equally broad range of scholars with differing approaches and theoretical perspectives and who are at varying stages of their careers. We aimed for gender parity and the inclusion of sexual orientation and religious commitment. Despite our efforts, not everyone we appealed to expressed interest or responded. A number of the scholars we contacted were interested, but because of other commitments they were unable to contribute to this project. Indicating that Black scholars are generally over-committed, there were others who had intended to submit chapters but were unable to fulfil their submission commitments, and the work had to proceed without them.

We give this background not as a *mea culpa*, but for two reasons we believe important. First, we think it important to emphasize that inasmuch as issues concerning African Canadian leadership are explored, deconstructed, and theorized within these pages, this is not a "how-to" guide. To offer something so grandiose as *a* solution for the real and imagined crisis of African Canadian leadership would be to commit ourselves to the error of a proposition we think requires rethinking. Second, we have not aimed for anything approaching exhaustiveness. There is much to debate and critique in this text; hence the aim is to open dialogue, invite analysis, and encourage research. Inevitably there are topics and issues that if explored could have expanded thinking beyond the perspectives included in this volume. Given that scholarship on African Canadian leadership is a burgeoning area, a short list of what also requires attention might include: Islam, anti-Black Islamophobia, and African Canadian leadership; Indigenous and African Canadian relations; leadership in cross-race coalition-building and solidarities; African Canadians' party affiliation and political representation; Black youth leadership; the role of social media in contemporary leadership practices; and the intersections of dis/ability in the ways that African Canadians both theorize and participate in leadership. While it could go on, this enumeration of possibilities illustrates the breadth of issues and topics awaiting enquiry. Rather than being the last word, this list is intended to promote the continuity of conversations and interest in building a robust body of research into African Canadian leadership.

NOTES

1 See Kitossa, this volume, note 3.

2 In this volume, Kitossa offers a critical assessment of BLM.

3 Various African Canadian academics have taken a direct role in undertaking leadership to challenge anti-Blackness in Canadian academia and to open more spaces for Black academics. Among African Canadian scholars undertaking leadership advocacy through their scholarship are George Dei (e.g., 2000), Annette Henry (e.g., 2015), Carl James (e.g., 2011, co-author of Henry et al., 2017), Malinda Smith (2017, co-author of Henry et al, 2017), and Rinaldo Walcott (e.g., 2014).

REFERENCES

Austin, D. (2013). *Fear of a black nation: Race, sex, and security in sixties Montreal*. Toronto: Between the Lines.

Black Experience Project (BEP). (2017). *Black Experience Project in the GTA: Overview report.* Retrieved from https://www.theblackexperienceproject.ca/wp-content/uploads/2017/07/Black-Experience-Project-GTA-OVERVIEW-REPORT-4.pdf

Bristow, P., Brand, D., Carty, L., Cooper, A., Hamilton, B., & Shadd, A. (1994). *We're rooted here and they can't pull us up: Essays in African Canadian women's history.* Toronto: University of Toronto Press.

Brown, E. (1993). *A taste of power: A black woman's story.* New York: Anchor.

Clarke, G. (2004). Raising raced and eraced executions in Canada: Or, unearthing Angélique. In C. Nelson & C. Nelson (Eds.), *Racism eh?: A critical inter-disciplinary anthology of race and racism in Canada* (pp. 65–84). Toronto: Captus.

Cooper, A. (2006). *The hanging of Angelique: The untold story of Canadian slavery and the burning of Old Montreal.* Toronto: HarperCollins.

Cose, E. (1994). *The rage of a privileged class: Why do prosperous blacks still have the blues?* New York: Harper Perennial.

de b'Beri, B., Reid-Maroney, N., & Wright, H. (2014). *The promised land: History and historiography of the black experience in Chatham-Kent's settlements and beyond.* Toronto: University of Toronto Press.

Dei, G.J.S. (2000). Rethinking the role of indigenous knowledges in the academy. *International Journal of Inclusive Education, 4*(2), 111–32. https://doi.org/10.1080/136031100284849

Foster, C. (1996). *A place called heaven: The meaning of being black in Canada.* Toronto: HarperCollins.

Foster, C. (2019). *"They call me George": The untold story of the Black train porters and the birth of modern Canada.* Windsor: Biblioasis.

Foster, L. (2003). Social control of our black leaders. *Share,26*(23).

Frost, K.S. (2008). *I've got a home in glory land: A lost tale of the Underground Railroad.* New York: Farrar, Straus and Giroux.

Frost, K.S., & Tucker, V. (Eds.). 2016. *A fluid frontier: Slavery, resistance, and the Underground Railroad in the Detroit River borderland.* Detroit: Wayne State University Press.

Goldberg, D.T. (2009). *The threat of race: Reflections on racial neoliberalism.* Malden: Blackwell.

Goldberg, D.T. (2015). *Are we all postracial yet?* Malden: Polity.

Hartman, S. (1997). *Scenes of subjection: Terror, slavery, and self-making in nineteenth-century America.* New York: Oxford University Press.

Henry, A. (2015). "We especially welcome applications from visible minorities": Reflections on race, gender and life at three universities. *Race, Ethnicity and Education, 18*(5), 589–610. https://doi.org/10.1080/13613324.2015.1023787

Henry, F., Dua, E., James, C.E., Kobayashi, A., Li, P., Ramos, H., & Smith, M.S. (2017). *The equity myth: Racialization and indigeneity at Canadian universities.* Vancouver: UBC Press.

Henry, N. (2010). *Emancipation day: Celebrating freedom in Canada.* Toronto: Dundurn.

Howard, P.S.S. (2018). On the back of blackness: Contemporary Canadian blackface and the consumptive production of post-racialist, white Canadian subjects. *Social Identities, 24*(1), 87–103. Retrieved from https://doi.org/10.1080/13504630.2017.1281113

James, C. (2011, 29 April). Welcoming "visible minorities": Paradoxes of equity hiring in Canadian universities. Retrieved from https://www.ideas-idees.ca/blog/welcoming-visible-minorities-paradoxes-equity-hiring-canadian-universities

Jones, B.R., & Walker, J.W.St.G. (2016). *Burnley Rocky Jones: Revolutionary.* Halifax: Roseway/Fernwood.

Kitossa, T. (2005). *Malleus Maleficarum Africanus*: The criminalization of African Canadians and "due process" as a property of whiteness. In L. Visano (Ed.), *Law and criminal justice: A critical inquiry* (pp. 153–72). Toronto: APF Press.

Lalonde, M. (2016, 24 February). Do black lives matter in Montreal? *Montreal Gazette.* Retrieved from http://montrealgazette.com/news/local-news/in-an-era-of-black-lives-matter-montreal-has-been-curiously-quiet-where-are-the-young-black-activists

Lawson, E. (2002). Images in black: Black women, media and the mythology of an orderly society. In N. Wane, D. Deliovsky, & E. Lawson (Eds.), *Back to the drawing board: African Canadian feminisms* (pp. 199–222). Toronto: Sumach.

McClain, P. (1979). *Alienation and resistance: The political behavior of Afro-Canadians.* Palo Alto: R & E Research Associates.

McKittrick, K. (2006). *Demonic grounds: Black women and the cartographies of struggle.* Minneapolis: University of Minnesota Press.

Marano, C. (2010). "Rising strongly and rapidly": The Universal Negro Improvement Association in Canada, 1919–1940. *Canadian Historical Review, 91*(2), 233–59. https://doi.org/10.1353/can.0.0309

Protest rally insensitive to real victims. (2015, 30 July). *Moose Jaw Times Herald.* Retrieved from http://www.mjtimes.sk.ca/Opinion/Editorials/2015-07-30/article-4231198/Protest-rally-insensitive-to-real-victims/1

Richmond, N.O. (2017). The untold story of the black radical tradition in Canada. Retrieved from http://panafricannews.blogspot.ca/2017/01/the-untold-story-of-black-radical.html

Shadd, A., Cooper, A., & Frost, K. (2009). *The Underground Railroad: Next stop, Toronto!* Toronto: National Heritage Books.

Shepard, R. (1997). *Deemed unsuitable: Blacks from Oklahoma move to the Canadian prairies in search of equality in the early 20th century only to find racism in their new home.* Toronto: Umbrella.

Smith, M.S. (2017). The diversity gap. Retrieved from https://uofaawa.wordpress.com/awa-diversity-gap-campaign/the-diversity-gap-in-university-leadership-2017/

Stewart, A. (2014). *Visitor: My life in Canada.* Halifax: Fernwood.

Thomson, C. (1979). *Blacks in deep snow: Black pioneers in Canada.* Toronto: Dent.

Walcott, R. (2001). Caribbean pop culture in Canada: Or, the impossibility of belonging to the nation. *Small Axe: A Caribbean Journal of Criticism, 5*(1), 123–39. https://doi.org/10.1353/smx.2001.0011

Walcott, R. (2014). Shame: A polemic. *CLR James Journal, 20*(1–2), 275–9. https://doi.org/10.5840/clrjames201492318

Walker, B. (2012). *Race on trial: Black defendants in Ontario's criminal courts, 1858–1958.* Toronto: University of Toronto Press.

Wilderson III, F. (2003). Gramsci's black Marx: Whither the slave in civil society? *Social Identities, 9*(2), 225–40. https://doi.org/10.1080/1350463032000101579

Winks, R. 1997 [1971]. *The blacks in Canada: A history.* Montreal/Kingston: McGill-Queen's University Press.

Winsa, P. (2015). Searching for Toronto's next generation of black leaders. *Toronto Star.* Retrieved from https://www.thestar.com/news/insight/2015/03/21/searching-for-torontos-next-generation-of-black-leaders.html

Wright, H.K. (2015). Stuart Hall's relevance for the study of African blackness. *International Journal of Cultural Studies,* 19(1), 85–99. https://doi.org/10.1177%2F1367877915599613

PART ONE

Models and Theories

1 Black Leadership and White Logic: Models of Community Engagement

CARL E. JAMES

In this chapter, I explore Black leadership in Canada with particular reference to Toronto. While I will refer to historical occurrences, much of the discussion will focus on leadership in the twenty-first century, building on my observations and the activities in which I have been involved since the 1970s. Significant to the discussion is the fact that, as a racialized group in Canada, Black leadership exists in relation to the racial hierarchy of society and is shaped by the historical, political, economic, and cultural contexts of the time. This racial hierarchy in which whites dominate through mechanisms such as immigration, settlement, social, educational, and policing policies and practices is framed by multiculturalism, which aims to control the presence, activities, and behaviours of subordinate communities. So too is the leadership of minoritized communities subjected to the patriarchal and racial power and related logic of the white dominant group. I argue that the leadership of the African community is both structured by, and at times resistant to, a "white logic" that is deeply rooted in the politics of common sense, universalism, colonialism, patriarchy, and neo-liberalism, and in the ambivalence of our presence in Canada from colonial days to today when we are constructed as foreigners or immigrants. Given that construction as "foreigners" and unlearned naïve people (unaccustomed to disciplinary practices of authority), Black leadership in the white imagination will be doubtful unless modelled on white structures and sanctioned accordingly.

In the section that follows, I elaborate on the tenets of whiteness and white logic before discussing the constructs of Black leadership in today's Canada, particularly Toronto. I offer five interchangeable ways in which African Canadian leadership has been constructed and enacted: as role models, corrective agents, arbitrators, change agents, and cultural curators. I conclude by suggesting that there is a need for education that provides insights into these issues and prepares community members to understand and engage with the dynamics of Black leadership and "followership" (Wyper, 2014) in a society where our marginalization is an ever-present reality.

Setting the Context

During 2013 Black History Month CTV, on its *Canada AM* program, featured a segment titled "The State of Black Leadership in Canada."[1] Co-host Marcia MacMillan started the conversation with the question:

> Last November Barack Obama was elected for a second term as US president. And while his leadership has been welcomed by the Black community, it's made the absence of a similar strong Black presence in Canada all too evident ... Is Black leadership lacking in this country? Is it hard to find?

The host's reference to President Obama to start the conversation is instructive; it represents the tendency to imagine – or frame – "Black leadership" through a US lens – with Obama, particularly in white imagination, being the model of Black leadership, along with, as guest Linton Kwesi Johnson mentioned, "Martin [Luther King] and Malcolm [X]." Notwithstanding the heteronormative male paradigm of identifiable black leadership (see Henry, Gooden, and hampton and Rochat in this volume), the reference to the United States – or using the United States as a starting point – tends to symbolize the shadow that the country casts on Blackness in Canada,[2] and the ahistorical reading by Canadians of Blacks' presence and contributions to Canada's development. In such a context, then, it is the absence, as MacMillan claims, rather than the presence of "strong Black" Canadian leadership that is more likely to be "evident." In responding to the host's question, the guests on the program – signalling that as a panel, they represented Black leadership in Canada – argued that it was not that there was an absence of Black leadership, but rather a failure of community members "coming together" on issues pertaining to "our community."

This discourse of unity as a necessary means of addressing the presumed deficits of African Canadians was also evident in a *Toronto Star* newspaper article by reporter Patty Winsa (2015) that was headlined "Searching for Toronto's next generation of black leaders." Winsa writes of meetings convened by three Black organizations in "a desperate call to action from an older generation of leaders who want to create a unified front of African and Caribbean people in the GTA to combat the 'severe crisis' they see in the community: Over-representation of blacks in school suspensions, the criminal justice system and prisons." She goes on to say that the "town halls are also about succession planning"[3] – seemingly implying that this too was a crisis since activists who have been working "in the community for decades can't see a generation behind them to pass the baton to ... [They do not] know who the young leaders are." This older generation seems to be looking for a generation of "young leaders" in the fashion of "Dudley Laws, Charles Roach, Sherona Hall and Lennox Farrell," who were named in the article as having founded the Black Action Defence Committee.[4] But as Winsa notes, young people such as Dena Henry, coordinator of a research project into Black experience, suggest that "times have changed" and that "the older generation needs to pass that baton, they need to let go and allow the young people to take their place." The young leaders claimed to be working differently – that is, they are working on local issues in their local communities and, where and when necessary, they take advantage of opportunities in established organizations and institutions to "tackle" issues of concern. As well, in their professional roles, they advocate for the community and engage in mentoring activities (see also Gosine in this volume; Maroon, 2014; Walker, Brady, & Hardward, 2015).

Unsurprisingly, there are generational differences in how older (over fifty years) and younger (less than thirty-five – particularly the millennial) members of the community both view and engage in leadership. The older members, according to Valerie Steele, a community leader, "believe that in the last few years there's too much silence and not enough activism, not enough holding certain entities accountable for what is happening" (Winsa, 2015). If Ms Steele is representative, it seems that for the older generation of Black members, activism and related leadership must be visible and representative of "a unified front." This, it is believed, should be evident in public display or organized opposition and challenge to the "entities" or institutions that are responsible for, as community member Kingsley Gilliam noted, today's "decline in the black community's material condition" (Winsa, 2015). Some young people justifiably claim that times have changed, and as young leaders, they are working "collaboratively" to create programs that will generate change. Referencing the activities of young leaders, Annette Walker and her colleagues (2015) write that "there is an impressive group of emerging leaders who not only work for the community's marginalized youth, but *with* them" (emphasis in original); and very often these leaders are marginalized youth themselves.

The assertions by young people alert us not only to generational differences but also to the contextual and dynamic realities of the diverse Black/African communities with which leaders must contend. There has never been, nor will there ever be, a "unified" community with a single approach to leadership. Nevertheless, in varying ways, past and present generations of leaders and activists (some doing better than others) have managed to navigate the societal structures of inequity, racism, and discrimination that have led to the material conditions of today's communities. However, there is much more work to be done if today's leaders are to effectively address the problems – or as some contend, the crisis[5] – within our communities. To this end, it is useful to critically reflect on the various approaches to leadership that account for the situation in which we find ourselves today, and with the purpose of doing activism differently in order to gain the needed social change.

Leadership, Whiteness, Canadian Multiculturalism, and White Logic

Leadership is largely conceived of as the capability and skills that individuals possess to identify the needs or assets of a group or community, and to inspire and mobilize others to join with them in addressing the needs or mobilizing the assets. And having a vision for the group or community, leaders are expected to work with others to set priorities and engage in activities that enable achievement of the vision. Hence, leaders need to have a belief in the worthiness of the endeavours in which they engage, a determination to contribute to the greater good or goals of the community, and a willingness at times to put the interests and goals of the community ahead of their own ambitions. Essentially, leaders are people who have the ability to make things happen; and their exercise of power is not value neutral, but based on a value system informed by their social circumstances, lived experiences, and acquired ideologies – all of which mediate the integrity, humility, shared goals, and capacity to make tough decisions on which leadership roles are to be built. Accordingly, the performance of leadership is contextual, relational, and circumstantial (see "Leadership development," 2019.; Torkornoo, 2015). In their "working definition" of leadership, *Leadership Now* 2019 suggests that "leadership is about shared values, vision and results. It is exemplified through the work people do, the attitudes they adopt and the potential they realize. But it all begins with an intention to influence others ... Leadership is intentional influence" ("Leadership development," 2019).

Day and Antonakis (2012) argue that our understanding and expectations of leadership – and the standards by which effective or good leadership is decided – tend to be premised on Western thinking, which often ignores the contextual realities of the culture that gives shape and meaning to styles, orientation, and performance of leadership. Within this Eurocentric frame, whiteness – an ideology with "a set of assumptions, beliefs, and practices that place the interests and perspectives of

White people at the center of what is considered normal and everyday" (Gillborn, 2015, p. 278) – operates to influence decisions about who is assigned or takes up leadership. And as Harris (1993) points out, asserting or practising forms of leaderships rooted in traditions and ways of knowing other than whiteness is akin to trespassing on private property because it undermines and challenges the supremacy of whiteness. Whiteness is not simply about White bodies, but is the articulation and enactment of the principles of leadership that operate more in the interests of Whites than minoritized or racialized groups. Inherent in the hegemonic discourse of whiteness is Christianity, which as Gilroy (2013) proffers, "supports the generalization of neoliberal ideas" (p. 30),[6] as well as the moral standards by which individuals are judged, expectations established, and leadership procured and maintained. So too, the "white-cultural gaze" not only serves to promote heteronormative, patriarchal, and upward mobility messaging, but also narrows and delegitimizes "the sociopolitical, cultural, and philosophical offerings of communities of color" (Edwards, 2013, p. 148). Into this "racial cosmology" (Leonardo & Broderick, 2011, p. 2209) of whiteness, and enticed by the power and promise of privileges afforded by their leadership, racialized individuals emerge and are recruited to become leaders. They are expected to help address the problems of "their" group or community members, be a representative of "their" group or community, and "speak" on their behalf.

A common expectation is that leaders will be smart, and as such, able to lead others towards producing tangible outcomes. What constitutes smartness is informed by a white orthodoxy that holds some individuals to be intellectually superior to others, resulting in their gaining the cultural capital, social status, and material rewards "that such an identity generally affords" (see Leonardo & Broderick, 2011, p. 2214). Furthermore, in a neo-liberal societal context in which smartness or intelligence – structured by the hegemonic culture of whiteness – is deemed an integral component of leadership, only those individuals who are judged as smart and willingly use their abilities in the service of whiteness will be legitimately entitled to become leaders. Others will be marked as innately deficient in this desirable trait – for example, "radicals" who will be castigated – and thus unqualified to lead. But as Leonardo and Broderick (2011) point out, "'Smartness' is not an inherent physical feature of individual brains, not a 'stuff' or a 'quantity' that some people have more than others, no more than 'Whiteness' is an inherent physical feature of white bodies" (p. 2227). Therefore, smartness or intelligence entangled in whiteness continues to be one of those oppressive arbitrary attributes or tools that is used to exclude from leadership those deemed "not smart."

In her work on whiteness, DiAngelo (2011) argues that whites, especially upper- and middle-class whites, engage in processes of whiteness in which they protect and insulate themselves from race-based stress that comes from challenges to the structures of racism that afford them unequal benefits. According to DiAngelo, one attribute of whiteness and its effect is "white fragility," which is conceptualized as "a state in which even a minimum amount of racial stress becomes intolerable, triggering a range of defensive moves ... [including] outward display of emotions such as anger, fear, and guilt, and behaviors such as argumentation, silence, and leaving the stress-inducing situation" (p. 57). Resulting from a disruption to that which is racially familiar to whites, these reactions can stem from, among other sources, having to deal with racialized people in leadership positions, which situation could be perceived as a "challenge to white authority" (p. 57). In such a context, in their exercise of leadership racialized leaders – if they are to attain and/or maintain leadership and, concomitantly, the power and privilege – are expected to attend to the fragility of whites by keeping whites' interests and perspectives central, and to shelter them from discomfort – something that in effect is unattainable or elusive for the leaders, since, as DiAngelo writes, "In the dominant position, whites are almost always racially comfortable and thus have developed unchallenged expectations to remain so" (p. 60).[7]

In Canada, whiteness is made elusive and invisible through the seductive neo-liberal discourse of multiculturalism and, concomitantly, colour blindness, meritocracy, and equality of opportunity (as opposed to equity). This discourse obscures the dominance and ideological power of whiteness in Canadian society where culture is ascribed to "foreign" (read, non-white) bodies and used as a synecdoche to explain the circumstances and station in life of "foreign Others." In other words, racial disparities are explained and understood as cultural and moral deficiencies specific to racialized groups (regardless of their generations in Canada) and a direct reflection of their individuals' efforts. Bannerji (1996) asserts that Canada is an "imagined community" where racialized people "remain an ambiguous presence" and their "existence a question mark." Nevertheless they "continue to live here as outsider-insiders of the nation which offers a proudly multicultural profile to the international community" (p. 105; see also Haque, 2012; James, 2010; Walcott, 1997). This ambiguous presence of racialized Canadians fosters an ambivalent and paradoxical relationship with racial difference – that is, difference is denied ("we don't see race") as it is re-inscribed – and in so doing scaffolds a pretention of Canada, compared to the United States, as having long been a "non-racial" society bolstered by its multicultural policy (1971) and Canadian Multiculturalism Act (1988).

In addition to being Canada's southern "next-door" neighbour and its historical reference for why racialized immigration (specifically of Blacks) should be controlled, the United States has exerted an influence on race narratives and practices in Canada that cannot be overestimated.[8] In Canada as in the United States, the enslavement and later the selective immigration of Africans are not unrelated to today's predominantly Black neighbourhoods being plagued by poverty, scarce social amenities, and limited educational supports (James, 2010; Walker, 2010). And as in the United States, Canada has produced Black leaders who have advocated for human rights, equity, and social justice (Austin, 2013; Gooden, 2008). But in a society that claims to be colour-blind and inclusive, recognizing Black or African Canadian leadership that does not conform with the logics of multiculturalism and whiteness would be antithetical to its claims. It is understandable, then (the US publishing machinery notwithstanding), that African American icons would not only become more known in Canada, but become Canadian icons as well.[9] And the fact that African Canadians would look to the United States for leadership (especially political and educational leadership), or for models of leadership that they might employ in Canada, reflects how whiteness as practised in Canada functions in the development of leadership framed by essentialist racial affiliation that is inconsistent with the Canadian colour-blind ethos.[10] As Lorne Foster (2011) states: in the "collective consciousness" of Canadians, Black community members and their leaders are devalued and trivialized "as fringe players in history and in [today's] society."

What emerges regarding Black leadership that is framed by whiteness is a logic by which it is imagined and understood by individuals, and expected to be performed in ways that appeal to white Canada. And, embedded in Canada's neo-liberal ethos of multiculturalism and, relatedly, cultural democracy, personal responsibility, and equality of opportunity, the logic holds that the opportunity structure meritoriously serves all communities – "none more than the other," to borrow from Prime Minister Pierre Trudeau's speech in putting forth the multicultural policy in 1971 (cited in James, 2010, p. 137). Hence, it follows that the role of leadership in the African Canadian community is to strengthen or culturally amplify the state's message of accommodation, and help to build and maintain harmonious relationships between the state and "the community." The use of the singular or essentialist form of "community" is deliberate, in that in the presented logic, each minoritized community is constructed as a single community with a single leader who is expected to serve as its representative and spokesperson taking up members' interests and concerns. But communities are diverse in terms of ethnic or regional origin, generational status or years in Canada, country or island of origin, political affiliation and, of course, age, skin colour, class, gender, language, education, occupation, and so on. This diversity has implications for the multiple forms of Black leadership that exist in Canada and its various regions and cities. Consider also the ideological differences informed by numerous political and educational experiences.

There has never been and will never be one Black leader – it is inconceivable for one person, no matter how charismatic, to represent any community. The prevailing logic of forging some form of "unity" (as we observed in the CTV panel discussion mentioned above) is premised on the notion of fear that the differences or variations among communities or community members will be exploited by governments, media, and others to justify and maintain the status quo, thereby negating the concerns against which Blacks have been struggling. In what follows, I discuss the five forms – role models, corrective agents, arbitrators, change agents, and cultural curators – that Black leadership tends to take with regard to the logic of whiteness, noting the role that dominant social values and expectations play in structuring and inventing leadership for the communities, and how the communities invent, cultivate, and respond to the various leadership forms. These leadership forms are not mutually exclusive, but are dynamic, contextual, and relational to the social and cultural situation at the time.

Constructs of Black Leadership

Role Models

One of the most prominent characteristics or expectations of a leader is to be a role model or mentor – someone who has the experiences, knowledge, attributes, and desire to provide guidance and support to others or subordinates, or be a reference (someone to look up to, or "become like") – in ways that will enable his or her "charges" to effectively navigate and negotiate the structures of society and attain their aspirations. In other words, "role models and mentors are understood to be people who know what it means to take advantage of the opportunities and possibilities in life through individual efforts" (James, 2012, p. 77). Typically, role models are given, chosen, named, or identified as such because they are believed to have the moral values and integrity to be "successful" in a valued aspect of society's social, cultural, economic, and political project. In the context of a neo-liberal society where there is a need to demonstrate that social inequity is not a barrier to becoming a leader, racialized leaders – whether invented, elected, awarded, or named through ethnic community involvement or the hegemonic political apparatus – become useful "evidence" that hurdles or barriers need not prevent them from attaining influential positions in society or "their" communities. What is important is that individuals observe the ethics of leadership: hard work, commitment to "your" community, and advocacy pertaining to the norms, values, and aspirations of the society. Any failure in leadership is seen as a product not only of individual attitudes, morals, actions, and sense of purpose but also of a lack of community support, cooperation, and harmony.

No doubt conscious of the white gaze and logic of leadership, Black leaders engage in discourse and actions in the community that demonstrate their leadership skills in working to establish a "unified" community whose members, through the leader's help or support, can expect to, and will, participate in various institutions in the society. On this point, the CTV leadership panel (see note 1) offered the following:

MEREDITH:[11] We've got leadership in high positions. We need to begin to be in ... banking, government ... [I'm the] fourth African Canadian in the Senate in 146 years of this country ... So, we now have leaders who are in positions to be able to bring other leadership and strengthen that capacity. So our young people can see and be mentored by that leadership. That's critical. But we need to begin to build this internal capacity so that the next generation coming after us can see that we are coming together ... I think one of the critical things within leadership, within our community, is that there is still a divisiveness ... We need to come together as leaders. We can't be divisive on these issues that are so important to the well-being of our youth in this country.

IEN: Is that easier said than done though? – to come together?

JOHNSON: I had a conversation with a good friend of mine about this panel and he said, you know, you can put one hundred individuals of African Canadian descent in positions of power, that doesn't make them Black leaders. For me, the definition of a Black leader is someone that is using their abilities to transform, to build, to maintain the communities and the social and physical world in and around them, and someone who inspires others to do the same. So, in essence, if we have those types of characteristics that are in our leaders ...

CLEMONS: Well said ... There has been a call to leadership in Toronto ... There is a void in leadership. So, in many ways our community is a microcosm of its larger society. (Winsa, 2015)

What transpires in this conversation is that, for these leaders, being able to participate within the existing structures is paramount, and education is seen as a means towards this end. And while it is understood that Black leaders will be role models and mentors who will use "their abilities to transform [and] to build" a sense of unity and sameness, there is no engaging with the realities of the diversity and differences (politically, ideologically, and otherwise) within the community and the fact that, as Foster (2011) notes, Black leaders are "systematically miniaturized," leading to a "crisis that has wreaked untold havoc and damage on the Black community."

With reference to role modeling in another instance, I reasoned elsewhere that

> having Black mentors and role models is not all that is needed within a society where inequity, marginalization and racialization exist, and where racism, now couched in cultural terms, obscures the fact that it is not simply individual disposition or community cultural ethos that are responsible for Black and other minoritized people's life circumstance. The liberal notions of colour-blindness and individualism articulated by media, educators, human service agents and State institutions would have us believe that equity has been established and everyone has the same quality of living and experiencing society. The evidence points otherwise. (James, 2012, p. 90)

Sylvia Ann Hewlett's (2013) argument on the advantage of sponsors compared to mentors is a valuable reference here. With reference to women, Hewlett writes that "a sponsor – a powerfully positioned champion" or advocate – is what is needed to get ahead. Mentors, she says, might "act as a sounding board ... offering advice as needed and support and guidance as requested; they expect very little in return. Sponsors, in contrast, are much more vested in their protégés, offering guidance and critical feedback because they believe in them." Further, sponsorship is a two-way relationship built on trust and interdependence. "It is in this area of trust," Hewlett writes, "that women and minorities often fail to get the help they need. When it comes to figuring out whom to sponsor, senior leaders – typically white men – most readily turn to the people they feel most comfortable with. Most often, that means other white men."

Furthermore, I have argued that inasmuch as role models and mentors are named or given to help Black youth, particularly males, address their educational, social, and cultural problems, they can more accurately be identified as, to borrow Patrick Shannon's (1998) term, "corrective agents" (James, 2012). This term is similarly relevant here, as I will show in the following section.

Corrective Agents

The case can be made that just as Black youth – especially so-termed fatherless young men – are perceived to need father-figures in the form of Black role models and mentors, more aptly they also need corrective agents who will provide discipline, structure, and moral guidance enabling young men to fit into the ways of society. And insofar as the "Black community" is perceived to be homogenous, and populated by foreigners, troublemakers, complainers, and "divisive" factions, the logic tends to be that the "community" (singular) similarly needs corrective agents who will help address the community's needs and problems. In their role as corrective agents, Black leaders are expected to "unite" the members of the various Black communities around one issue, goal, or ambition, for division among members of "the community" is viewed as an impediment to progress. Hence, the leaders call for a "unified" community that, as leaders, they expect to bring about. This raises the questions: How is division or divisiveness understood? And what would a "unified" community look like? Is it possible that divisiveness is confused with diversity: the cultural, regional, national, generational, status, political, or ideological differences that are to be found among members of the Black community, or indeed any community or society? Furthermore, it is understandable that these differences[12] will find expression in the disagreements and dissenting opinions that are voiced by members of the community. To believe that "the community" (conceived of as singular) needs to "come together" or be "unified" is to concede to the logic of minoritized communities as homogeneous, and that as such its members follow the lead of one person and have a common purpose or approach to addressing their needs and issues. The idea of homogeneity gives leaders the illusion that they know, represent, and speak for "their community" and are in a position to get the community to do their bidding – therefore fulfilling the expectations of governments, regulating agencies, and society's power elite.

To cajole the community into a homogeneous predisposition, corrective agents engage in a discourse of comparison by which they draw attention to how well other communities are doing "compared to us, the Black community." The assumption is that these other communities "come together," support each other financially, socially, and otherwise, have identifiable leaders whom all members support, are actively engaged in party politics, and support the electoral political ambitions of "their own" (presumably supporting the same political parties). Corrective agents would also draw attention to the political and financial supports that other communities obtain, claiming that these other communities have identifiable leaders with clear aspirational agendas for their communities – including active participation in political party activities that gains them representation in governments. The message from these Black corrective agents is that it is only through collective efforts and regulated leadership that the "Black community" will be able to become socially respectable (see James, 2012; Shannon, 1998; and Williams in this volume).

Basically, corrective agents, adhering to white, middle-class, patriarchal, heteronormative forms of leadership, play regulatory roles in maintaining social responsibility and compliance in the community. As leaders, they re-inscribe the liberalist ideals of multiculturalism that hold that the challenges, problems, and failures of the members of the community are the result of individual deficits – accounting for deficits in the community – rather than a reflection of societal impediments. This ideological understanding helps to frame the ways in which these leaders conceive of their positions as role models and mentors who, oblivious to the diversity of the communities, are there to "correct" the problems that debilitate the community and its members. Oftentimes, the media's pathologizing representation of "the Black community" (ignoring its complexity and diversity) and call for Black leaders to take responsibility for addressing the ills that plague the community contribute to these leaders' perceptions and assessments of the community as culturally deficient, apathetic, dysfunctional, and lacking initiative and moral integrity. In responding to media and other opinion makers, these Black leaders not only reference African American leaders as models for their work in the Canadian context,[13] they also invite African Americans to Canada – both to bolster their own leadership influence (showing they have connections to international Black stars) and to have the visitors "tell" community members what they should be doing.

For example, Reverend Eugene Rivers, an African American Christian minister from Boston who was heralded as a leader and expert in helping "lost young men," was brought to Toronto to help "diagnose" and "correct" the problems of our young Black men and boys. Interviewed on a local CBC radio program from his US base, Rivers was able to spread his word, which was consistent with that of his Canadian religious counterparts, the media, governments, and others. He claimed that "there is a high correlation between father absence, single parent households and criminal behaviour particularly on the part of young males" that was an internal matter for "the community" to address (cited in James, 2012, p. 87). And he also insisted that

> Canada's black community faces a crisis. A generation of poor, predominantly black youth is in violent rebellion against their fatherlessness and, by logical extension, against the law and order established by middle-class

> black leadership that purport to speak for them ... Internally, the black community has to make a decision that it will move beyond excuses, asking for funding to do programs which can be initiated without funding. (p. 87; see also Alcoba, 2006; Black, 2006; "Pastor preaches hope," 2006; Wells, 2006)

It is instructive that a number of corrective agents are religious people and police officers for whom their religion and the culture of "law and order" provide a moral ethos that they bring to their understanding of the type of leadership the community needs. This perspective gives little to no meaningful consideration to the social and political structures that are the basis of the persistent problems and that cannot be simply fixed through an attitudinal shift or individual behaviours.

Arbitrators

Rev. Rivers and his Canadian counterparts could also be considered arbitrators – leaders who take it upon themselves, or are called upon by community members or social or state authorities, to intervene or mediate matters affecting "their" community. Typically, arbitrators, like Rivers, tend to focus largely on "what's wrong with the community," or on the problems that the community ostensibly brought onto itself rather than on the role that social inequity or the opportunity structures might have played in creating problems faced by the community.[14] These leaders act with the notion that the community is a singular entity and their role is to promote consensus, negotiate discords, arbitrate conflicts, and pacify troublemakers. What Meredith had to say about his role in helping to address a violent situation is revealing.

> In 2002 violence erupted in this city. I took leadership of that with respect to other leaders that came around to work together on that particular issue. The media came around and supported what we were trying to do. Again, eradicate violence in the city of Toronto ... We have leadership who, again, join forces. Pinball, you were very front and centre in that with respect to the foundation money granted by the ministry. We clearly have this leadership. And I think it's important that we recognize the leadership and respect the leadership that's there within the communities. We galvanize around certain issues, whether it be violence, whether it be employment issues. We need to begin to support those leaders who speak for sort of the larger and broader community. And I think it's important that Canadians start recognizing that there is leadership and that we're not in void of leadership within this country. There are leaders who are standing up for these types of issues.

Arbitrators are the ones more inclined to respond to concerns raised by civic leaders and other power brokers about lack of leadership in the community and the inability or unwillingness of community leaders to take control of crises within the community – and more specifically, to rein in young Black men who have long been seen as an unpredictable, volatile group in society (see Fine, 1990). It is arbitrators who will take seriously and work to execute advice such as that articulated by Robert Payne in the community newspaper *Share* many years ago. Payne advised in 1990 that leaders in the "Black community" needed "to develop strategies and structures that will ultimately win over the white middle class and civic and business leaders ... This includes: forming a strong, broad-based organization able to deal with concerns responsibly and with integrity" (cited in Fine, 1990, p. A11). Such advice is not merely intended to help these Black leaders effectively address the concerns of "the community," but advises them to keep the interests and perspectives of white folks central, and to free whites, as DiAngelo (2011) puts it, "from carrying the psychic burden of race" (p. 63). The idea is that whites "lack of racial stamina" – they are "fragile" on issues of race (DiAngelo 2011, p. 56); hence it is in the interest of Black leaders to help them live psychically comfortable lives without fear of the unpredictable elements of society.

An attempt to arbitrate white comfort versus Black need for voice was displayed in a 2014 Toronto mayoral debate in the Jane and Finch community. Writing about the incident, which he refers to as a "rude act" – "the ways marginalized and displaced Black youth interrupt, interject and intrude into social and political debates" – Tecle (2015) tells of how a young Black woman and mayoral candidate, D!ONNE Renée, intervened in the proceedings to get heard and, in doing so, annoyed – if not embarrassed – the host, a young Black leader, Antonius Clarke. Renée insisted that she should be invited to the stage with the three other candidates. No invitation was extended; nevertheless, she took the vacant seat on stage (that of Doug Ford), whereupon Clarke asked "authorities" to remove her. This did not happen, and seemingly frustrated with the disquiet in the audience, some of whom supported Renée, Clarke said: "Excuse me, please keep the peace. This is not a circus. You guys are acting like you're not adults. Please have maturity here. We have a problem and we are trying to rectify it. Give us a moment please. Thank you." And to Renée, he said:

> It is a very hard task in accommodating all the voices at this table. We spoke before and I asked that you do not become emotionally attached to the work. But definitely you are standing for a cause and I would ask that you speak to the people for three minutes and then I would ask that you maturely excuse yourself. Because at the end of the day this is a democratic

> process that has been closed now ... We know that you are not going to let your self-serving interests make this event a failure, because you are wise, you are a leader and we look forward to seeing you in future candidate debates. But today is here for the top three people. (cited in Tecle, 2015)[15]

This encounter suggests that such rude acts, or "creative insubordinations," as Tecle (2015) terms it, are likely to foreclose any attempts to engage leaders of the Black communities – particularly those who take on the responsibility of being arbitrators, corrective agents, and role models. For as Clarke exemplifies, they take seriously their role to "keep the peace," maintain discipline, uphold democracy, expect white-normed social and cultural practices (capital), and not allow self-interest and "immature" behaviours of community members to thwart what they consider to be trustworthy and respectful behaviours. Furthermore, arbitrators operate in ways that safeguard their privileged positions and personal comfort. And in cases where arbitrators and corrective agents form alliances or coalitions for purposes of expediency, having to satisfy mainstream expectations is likely to result in loss of focus on the issues about which they advocate (see Howard in this volume).

Change Agents

Renée could be considered a leader who is a change agent – someone who in their exchanges advocates for action, and in the process is determined to change the tenor of the construction, representation, and expectations of members of the various Black communities – in other words, an activist. In the context of societal cultural norms and logic, change agents are more likely to be regarded as agitators, provocateurs, or extremists than as advocates working to change the social, economic, and educational situation of community members. In fact, in 1990, city officials referred to community leaders who voiced their anger about police shootings and the treatment of Black people as "radicals" and "cowards" (see note 10); and in 2014, as we saw, Antonius Clarke implied that Renée and her supporters who wanted space for their voices to be heard were immature, saying "This is not a circus." Further, in reporting on the Black Lives Matter (BLM) protest of 27 July 2015, Madeline Smith (2015) in the *Globe and Mail* used the term "activists" to refer to the young (twenty-something) "founders" who organized the protest. The leaders were quoted as saying: "It's really important to understand the collective rage that black folks in this city are experiencing" (Rodney Diverlus, twenty-five); and "Politicians who have been trying to ignore us couldn't ignore us after that" (Sandy Hudson, twenty-nine).

But change agents are up against not only the hegemonic establishment and its agents – such as civic leaders, social service agents, and education brokers – but also other Black community leaders who are looking for "their replacement" – people like them. Take the case, discussed above, of the leaders who were looking for "young leaders" to whom to pass the baton. In their response to the claim that they tend to be complacent, Annette Walker and two colleagues (2015), who describe themselves as "young black leaders committed to social change in the Jamaican community," write: "If the older generation of activists has not noticed our work or that of our cohorts it may [be] because ours is, for our community, a new kind of more democratic activism ... too many black youth feel isolated and marginalized from the activist community. That too many of these older activists seem to fail to understand the needs and realities of Black youth and in so doing actively stifle their voices." Along the same lines, in her letter to the *Toronto Star* Adaoma Patterson (2015) writes:

> Toronto does not need to search for the next generation of black leaders – they are here doing the work quietly, relentlessly and without much fanfare but in very different ways than 40 years ago. This article generated interest, criticism and commentary on social media; this is one of the ways we engage, discuss and debate. Engagement and learning is a two way street and elders have to be open to doing things differently, listening and not just speaking about their accomplishments and the past.

The tactics of change agents go a long way in their attempts to address the needs and aspirations of the various Black communities. Consider, for instance, the tactics of the young leaders of Black Lives Matter Toronto (BLM-T). Ostensibly compelled by the long history, just as in the United States, of police violence towards Black people that resulted in death, the young leaders saw themselves engaged in a "movement" described by Diverlus as "a call to action on an issue that's existed since I've lived, since I've been born, and generations and generations before" (Smith, 2015). In one protest march, BLM led demonstrators, as a journalist writes, "through the city's Little Jamaica neighbourhood[16] ... to the busy Allen Expressway" where for about two hours in the early evening they sat on the road blocking traffic. It was reported that as they sat, one of the leaders, Sandy Hudson, "started getting text messages saying that Mayor John Tory had committed in a TV interview to meeting with them" (Smith, 2015). This supposed "potential victory" for the group might be a reflection of their consistent actions, which escalated with each new occurrence, and the seemingly rising tide of a North American movement protesting police violence against young Black men and women.[17]

It is also worth considering an earlier action of BLM, a protest rally held in front of the US consulate on 25 November 2014. Writing in *Now Magazine* about that protest, which attracted about three thousand people, one of the leaders, Akio Maroon (2014), noted:

> The protest was organized by Black Lives Matter, a Toronto-based, informal coalition of concerned black community members, activists, students, youth and professionals. We are working in solidarity with the people of Ferguson[18] and racialized working class communities in Toronto to actively take on fighting against all forms of police violence and racial profiling.
>
> Organizers, mostly young women and trans folks, specifically asked for nonviolence, and we specifically asked allies to centre blackness in quantifiable ways in order to have black voices heard and black actions visible. Janaya Khan requested for black trans people, black folks with differing abilities, black sex workers – black folks usually left out of the conversation – to come out of the fringes and into the centre of the demonstration. Khan also asked white folks and other people of colour to decentralize themselves by stepping back.

Significant here is the attempt of BLM to name and centre the diverse identities and voices of members of the Black communities who are "usually left out of the conversation," and in doing so, to insist that their non-Black allies keep a low profile – for example, refrain from talking with the media. So, the coalitions that change agents establish tend to be largely predicated on their terms, or they seek to ensure that their advocacy goals are not appropriated or commandeered by others. And the group took pride in saying that they are "young organizers working with minimal resources. We have received some goods and services donated by progressive grassroots organizations, largely we've had to empty our own pockets and take time away from our studies, day jobs and families" (Maroon, 2014). The message here is that they are not mobilizing with funds from any particular political or economic establishment to whom they will be obligated, which they think positions them as trustworthy activist leaders who are committed to doing what they can to bring to the attention of societal leaders the fact that "Black people are sick and tired of unequal treatment," harassment, and dehumanization (Maroon, 2014).

Like the Black Lives Matter group today, the Black Action Defence Committee (BADC), which was founded in 1988, similarly mobilized action (including mass demonstrations and delegations to various governments and their agencies) in response to police shootings of Black men in Toronto. BADC is credited with calling for a stop to "police investigating police," which was seen as a practice that contributed to the acquittal of the police officers charged with the shootings. And it might be said that the so-called Yonge Street Riot in 1992[19] helped to crystalize community members' discontent with police acquittal. This action brought together the three levels of government (federal, provincial, and municipal) and community leaders to develop a response to community needs (see Lewis, 1992; Working Group, 1992). Other activists' activities included the Anti-Apartheid Movement in Toronto supported by the annual Black Liberation marches in the 1970s, and activism supporting the establishment of the various African-centred education programs in the 1970s and 1980s through organizations like Black Education Project, Harriet Tubman Community Organization (known then as Harriet Tubman Centre), and African Heritage Programs;[20] and there are the African-centred or Black-focused schools of the mid-1980s at D.B. Hood in the York School Board and in 2008 the Toronto District School Board's Africentric Alternative School. Writing about the resistance to the establishment of the Africentric School, Andrew Wallace (2009) reminds us that

> there has always been a strong, although mostly underground, push for a black-focused school in Toronto. Activists within the black community have been searching for ways to keep young, black students engaged in the public system for nearly as long as there's been a black population in the city. While the current debate over black-focused schools may appear to have dropped from the sky, there is actually a long history of grassroots advocacy behind it. In fact, the Africentric school that's supposed to open next September is not the first of its kind. It's actually the second.[21]

It would not be a stretch to say that the activisms of the 1970s and 1980s created a context on which today's change agents/activists continue to build. Certainly, it is not only now that Black leaders – and young activists in particular – have escalated their actions in their attempts to change the situation of Black people in Canada. Indeed, Black activists or change agents have long experimented with different mobilizing strategies that have contributed to whatever gains (however small) we see in the community today. But engaging in strategies that are contrary to the leadership norms of a society dominated by Euro-Christian capitalist norms and processes has a cost: these leaders are likely to be summarily dismissed, not taken seriously, and disparaged on the grounds that they are uninformed, immature, or are radicals – constructed as underachievers and foreigners (or non-citizens) who, as such, do not know better. And the cost of their "creative insubordinations" (Tecle, 2015) or unconventional ways of making their case to community members, civic and business authorities, and members of society generally is borne not only by the change agents themselves but by their communities as a whole. Nevertheless, there is clearly a need for activist/change agent leadership if Black communities are to resist marginalization, be heard, and obtain at least some level of the respect and opportunities they seek in the society.

Cultural Curators

A notable component of Black leadership, and one upon which some approaches to leadership are based, embedded, or foregrounded, is culture. Variously conceptualized, culture is instrumentally used to define, differentiate, and identify the community or communities and provide the structure for the political, social, and educational activities on which support, resistance, and advocacy are based. I refer to those leaders who centre the culture of the community in their performance of leadership as "cultural curators." This approach to leadership, like others, is not mutually exclusive, for as role models, corrective agents, and change agents, leaders will sometimes employ a cultural curation approach to their work. Notwithstanding that there is little agreement on what culture is,[22] or what constitutes the culture of the Black community or communities, the fact remains that culture serves to signify and organize the ways in which people make sense of their lives, their realities, and their social existence. Culture also functions to connect the various members of a community and helps to establish collective identification. As such, it is critical to the work of community leaders, especially in a society where the raced bodies of community members mark them as different (or foreign) and contribute to their marginalization and alienation – all of which is maintained by the white logic of Canadian multicultural ethos.

Essentially, the ideas, values, beliefs, attitudes, behaviours, traditions, practices, and aspirations of community members is representative of their culture, which is informed by country or region of origin as well as the structure of Canadian society and the socio-economic situation in which members find themselves. For some leaders, it is cuisine, music, clothing, entertainment (and their appreciation thereof), and language that constitute culture and differentiate the community. The various ways culture is conceptualized were made evident in a July 2015 discussion in which I participated with the leaders of a number of Black communities in Edmonton, Alberta. The predominant thinking among the leaders was that culture is the customs, food, traditions, music, artefacts – in short, the observable elements, or what Jackson and Meadows (1991) call "anthropological curiosities" – which leaders viewed as differentiating and giving meaning to their communities. But as Benhabib (2002) argues, culture is not "a unified, harmonious, seamless whole that speaks with one narrative voice," and which some community leaders and outsiders (e.g., politicians, educators, social service agents, policymakers) tend to use to comprehend, control, classify, and represent the community (p. 102). The singular or visible culture that some community leaders and members as well as outsiders tend to promote and maintain has to do with their search for truth and/or social control – sometimes in the form of nationalism. Unfortunately, this application of culture tends to silence dissenting views and contradictory perspectives, and in the process asserts a dominant narrative of what constitutes the culture of the community or communities, signalling who is in and who is out (Benhabib, 2002, p. 194; see also James, 2010).

One of the most significant community initiatives founded on the culture of African Canadians is the Toronto Caribbean Carnival – best known as Caribana (from 2011 to 2015, because of sponsorship, it was re-branded the Scotiabank Caribbean Carnival Toronto). The festival was established in 1967 as part of Caribbean people's contribution to Canada's centenary celebrations. (Similar initiatives existed or still exist in Montreal, Ottawa, Edmonton, and Vancouver.) It was initiated at a time of increasing immigration from the Caribbean, and leaders used the occasion to "showcase"[23] the observable forms of Caribbean culture (costumes, music, food, etc.), to bring members of the various island associations together (Caribana Board then was also made up of representatives of different island associations), and to garner recognition, respect, and acceptance of their presence in Canada (see also Gooden, 2008). While some might say that this ambitious enterprise generated some degree of success, insofar as the "festivals" continue today, we cannot overlook the fact that, at least in Toronto, the corporatization of the festival has meant that the community has little influence, and least of all control of the program and its proceeds. It seems that leaders did a good job of delivering a very economically viable midsummer program to the city and businesses. Indeed, as one television reporter claimed, the Caribbean Carnival is the third largest in the world behind Brazil's and Trinidad's. A concern with these cultural events is that they get used to brand Black communities, and in the process re-inscribe the Canadian multicultural ethos of their foreign, static, or "jump and wine"[24] (see letter below) culture, which functions to limit expectations and advancement of the communities. On this point, in Toronto, some community leaders have repeatedly appealed to civil leaders to do more to make the festival more helpful to the community. A letter of 18 August 2015 titled "URGENT: Call for economic justice for the African/

Caribbean Community" sent by Trevor Fortune to Toronto's mayor, John Tory, and copied to a number of other civic and community leaders is worth quoting at length:

> This letter is a follow up to the Scotiabank Toronto Caribbean Carnival 2015, and a promise that you made to Black and Caribbean people at the Mayoral Forum on Friday, August 29th, 2014 at the Novotel Hotel.
>
> You were asked the [following] question about the over $4 billion dollars that has been generated since the expropriation of the Caribana festival:
>
> "Would you commit to supporting a thorough CONSULTATIVE COMMUNITY DRIVEN REVIEW of the relationship between the City/ Metro Hall, and the Toronto Caribbean Carnival Festival, with the goal of Carnival becoming more economically self-sufficient to create employment and business opportunities in the community?" ...
>
> Mr. Tory, you stated in response to this question that the various interest groups are disunited, and you would like to have all of them around the table. You also spoke about going to the private sector to help build a fund for youths from the Black community for scholarships, and you spoke about negotiating with the Federal government for them to give back a larger part of the HST taxes ...
>
> The expropriators of the Caribana festival promised better financial accountability and management, but nine (9) years later only the government and corporate sponsors seem to be the financial beneficiaries. *The Black community still has nothing to show as a return on our investment of our volunteered time, talents/skills, and marketing by bringing our friends and families to celebrate our indigenous cultural heritage with the rest of Canada* [italics in original].
>
> It is very important to know, Mr. Tory, ... that Black people are not only interested in "Jumping up and Wining," we know that there are other business models that could be implemented to serve ... in a more satisfactory and equitable manner.
>
> On behalf of members of the African/Caribbean community, we believe that the time is right for a conversation with community, government, and private sector stakeholders ... of this event within a reasonable time.
>
> We believe that it is only just, that the benefits of Carnival ... come back to our community which has invested so generously in bringing it to life and keeping it alive for the last 48 years.[25]

While not all creative and cultural artists, educators, and journalists take on leadership roles in Black communities, some do; and others, because their work, standing, or activities speak to the concerns and issues within the community, have leadership thrust upon them. Whichever is the case, these cultural curators play a significant role in voicing, and placing into "mainstream" conversation, the concerns and perspectives of the Black communities, which invariably affect the social and cultural discourses of the communities and of society generally.[26] We cannot ignore the fact that since the seventeenth century, African peoples through their presence and activities in Canada have been resisting erasure and consistently inserting ourselves into the cultural and sociopolitical structures of society – Black History Month is one example. Canada today is a product of the contributions Blacks have made,[27] through the work not only of activists and role models but also of Black cultural curators. Cultural curators do not merely act as representatives of African Canadian communities, they exert meaningful influence on the society as a whole. And since there are no boundaries surrounding culture, it cannot be policed as some community members and leaders might wish to do. In this regard, we must accept that the practices, schoolings, and thinking of Black communities – just like food, music, and other cultural artefacts – do become incorporated or will drain or percolate into the "mainstream" culture of society. Relevant to this process is the work of today's young second-generation, especially millennial, African Canadian leaders, whose hybrid culture and identification – bred from their parents' and grandparents' socializations, their interactions with a diversity of Black people, and their alienating Canadian existence – have provided them with the knowledge to speak in innovative and dynamic ways across differences (e.g., the leaders of Black Lives Matter) within their communities. Using their intellectual and technological abilities, they have mobilized action that has generated optimism and possibilities, especially among younger members of the Black communities (see Campbell, 2012; Cole, 2015).

Education is a major area to which cultural curators have devoted their time and energies – from community-organized tutoring and youth programs (in such organizations as Black Education Project and the Harriet Tubman Centre in the 1970s and 1980s,[28] where I volunteered as well as worked) to Black-focused secondary (1980s) and elementary (2000s) schools, to the Transitional Year Program at the University of Toronto (Brathwaite, 2003). This investment in education is understandable, since the liberal promise of education continues to be a persuasive force. But as Wallace (2009) notes, Black community activists have long sought ways for Black students to productively and successfully engage in school. Yet despite the various efforts of community leaders, members, and parents, the rate of poor educational performance, academic attainment, and school disengagement, suspensions, and dropping/stopping out among Black students has remained the same over the years (see also Dei in this volume). To address this situation, and after community consultation, in fall 1986 Jackie Wilson as leader, supported by Veronica Sullivan and Afua Cooper, established the Afro-Caribbean Alternative Secondary School with a "curriculum[29] which offered advanced and general-level courses on black culture and the developing world" (Wallace, 2009). However, the school closed after three years, because of limited support and opposition from school board members as well as from members of the Black communities. According to one of the school's creators, "influential people in the community rallied against the project, claiming students were receiving substandard educations and that the teachers were under-qualified; meanwhile, those closest to the school said it was achieving positive results" (Wallace, 2009). We see here how differences within the communities can thwart the efforts of leaders. Will the same thing happen today with the current Africentric Alternative School? Will similar "segregationist rhetoric" that hijacked the debate over Black-focused schools in the past (Wallace, 2009) polarize the Black communities and immobilize the leadership that might be able to help establish schooling that is relevant and responsive to the needs, interests, and aspirations of Black students? In answering these questions, we need to take into account what the leaders who mobilized to establish today's Africentric School were up against. The *Globe and Mail* (2007) branded the school as "school by skin colour," and the then premier, Dalton McGuinty, told the *Toronto Star*, "I don't think that it is a good idea. I think our shared responsibility is to look for ways to bring people together. One of those most powerful agents of social cohesion is publically funded education" (James, 2009). He went on to encourage Torontonians, if "they really feel strongly about this ... [to] speak to their duly elected representatives and tell them how strongly they are opposed to this proposal." The opposition leader was not any more favourable, nor was the then minister of education, who said: "We don't want to see kids separated from each other. We don't think the board should be moving in this direction" (cited in James, 2009, p. 26). This multicultural neo-liberal ethos stands in the way of cultural curators, or the cultural approach.

Conclusion

> Only a mass protest movement dedicated to Black empowerment and human equity can produce the principled leadership necessary to "speak truth to power." (Marable, 2008, p. 4)

As pointed out earlier, the various styles or approaches to leadership I describe above are not mutually exclusive: they exist in relation to social, cultural, political, and economic issues, contexts, and networks, as well as experiences, affiliations, and personalities. Functioning at two levels, the typology is greater than the sum of its parts: at one level it is an analytical contribution that is useful from the vantage point of theory-seeking, to apprehend and describe specific norms in action; but at another level we are offered a way to represent the contradictions, complexity, shifts, and paradoxes of various types of leadership practice. The point is that social reality cannot be frozen by static representations such as typologies given that no individual can be identified as totally embodying one leadership type. It is true that based on any number of factors – such as age, ideology, experiences, and sociocultural networks – individuals might more often use one or a particular combination of these ideal approaches in their work: this in turn becomes the leadership approach or perspective with which they might be identified. What should be clear is that with a diversity of individuals and their experiences, there is going to be a diversity of approaches and perspectives, which means that the resulting differences will need to be negotiated. It cannot be otherwise, for we cannot expect that there will be a homogeneous approach to leadership in any community. The issue will be how we define the differences found in the diversity of African Canadians and work to forge some working relationship across these substantive differences. It will not do, therefore, to simply understand difference and diversity within and among African Canadians as a function of competing "interest groups." This latter discourse allows the differences among African Canadians to be politically mobilized by white power logics as evidence that, as Mayor John Tory claimed, African Canadians are a "disunited" community. Presumably, for the state to listen and respond to their real needs, African Canadians must show a higher level of solidarity than is found among, say, Progressive Conservatives, New Democrats, Liberals, or white people for that matter. Ironically, the richness provided by different perspectives from African Canadian leaders is treated as a deficit rather than an opportunity to be exposed to a wide range of narratives and voices.

I hasten to add that just as individual leaders have a right to enact their particular interpretation of the issues facing Black communities and to undertake a leadership approach that they determine is appropriate, so too community members reserve the right to criticize or disagree with the approach taken or related actions. Then again, the existence of divergent views, criticisms, and disagreements among community members is, in white essentialist logic, interpreted as a "divided" community: one that "does not know what it wants" or "what is good for it." This is where corrective agents or arbitrators might be summoned by civic leaders or other members of the dominant society to intervene and help to carry out their bidding, to the exclusion of more critical voices.

Whatever approach leaders employ, the reality is that accomplishing any goal is tied to the ways in which leaders engage with the community – for leadership depends on shared vision, communal goals, reciprocal support, and collective action. Leaders, as Wyper (2014) points out, "do not work in a vacuum but are a part of a larger community" and, as such, leadership is to be "shared and transferred between leaders and followers, each one only a temporary designation" (Foster, cited in Wyper, 2014, p. 5). Followership – the reciprocal role that individuals assume in the community or group, and by which they elect to actively follow the leader – is an integral component of the social process of leadership (see Kellerman, 2008; Wyper, 2014). This dialogic relationship between leaders and followers can be enhanced through education that offers opportunities for dialogue, insights, and knowledge. Through enriching the relationship of followership, we will be better able to apprise ourselves of twenty-first century realities – particularly "the anti-black 'post-racial' social reality animated and subtended by a black US president" (Sharpe, 2014, p. 61). We will be able to transcend Canada's multicultural deception, and the host of problems we encounter with police, social service agents, teachers, co-workers, and political leaders. Scholars have long argued that Black Studies is able to provide such education. Kitossa (2012) suggests that the knowledge and research produced by scholars through Black Studies can serve to elaborate the complex evolving engagement of African Canadians' diverse presence and experiences in Canada, their relationship to the nation state, and, as diasporas, their complicated engagement with their societies of origin (p. 259). There is, as Walcott (2014) maintains, a necessity and urgency to studying Black life in Canada given the demographic shifts in the Black population (p. 5).

As we move towards the end of the second decade of the twenty-first century, the Federation of Black Canadians,[30] under the leadership of Justice Don McLeod, promises to, as Brenda McCurdy anticipates, "give voice and power to our claim" for full participation in Canadian society. According to McCurdy, this was something her husband and former member of Parliament Howard McCurdy of Windsor, Ontario, hoped for.

> There has been but one goal for which Howard [McCurdy] has for a half century sought fruition. It has been to bring together the very best of leadership of African Canadian communities in a national organization. Such an organization would give voice and power to our claim for full social, political and economic participation in a fully multiethnic, multiracial and multicultural Canada. Too often that dream has been dashed upon the

> shelf of petty historic, political or geographical division of our own communities. As I look around me here to see new, more mature, more vibrant, more assertive voices from the diaspora there is new hope that together, at long last, we will fully share in shaping a new Canada in which our community's voice will at least be heard. (Dr Brenda McCurdy, speech delivered at Toronto Reference Library, 4 December 2017)

McCurdy was accepting her husband's award at the National Black Canadian Summit in Toronto, 4–6 December 2017, which was organized through a partnership between the Michaëlle Jean Foundation and Federation of Black Canadians to mark the International Decade for People of African Descent (see Gooch, 2017). At the closing of the summit, McLeod acknowledged that the Federation of Black Canadians was building on the work of earlier national Black organizations, like the National Black Coalition of Canada and the Congress of Black Women of Canada. Indeed, there are benefits to having a national structure/organization, but what might be realized through this "new hope?" What form of leadership can we expect? And how long will it be sustained?

In any case, we need leaders who will resist the essentialist and imposed singular construct of Black communities – no single leader can be expected to represent or serve as the sole spokesperson for our multiple communities – and in doing so value the complexity, variation, and ever-changing realities of our communities. The emerging leadership and potential of the growing second-generation-plus population of African Canadians or millennials cannot be underestimated. For in their multiple voices they demonstrate their entitlement (like their mainstream counterparts) to opportunities, recognition, and resources, and resist silencing and erasure while holding on to hope. In this dynamic context, leaders need to work to decentre white heteropatriarchy, challenge the myth of colour blindness, and help to mobilize actions that oppose the systems that produce and reproduce inequities. These are the leaders who deserve awards and recognition, not those whose approach to leadership is based on ensuring compliance with the existing social order and containment of community members. Ultimately, effective Black leadership will always be in opposition to the status quo (even where this occurs in Black communities); for the very system that is designed to recruit, influence, and control Black communities will never encourage, legitimize, and sustain Black leadership that enables our agency, enriches our lives, enhances our presence, and contributes to a broader project of social justice – this is the hope and promise of truly effective Black leadership.

NOTES

1 The program aired on 19 February, hosted by Marcia MacMillan and Marci Ien. The guests were then-senator Don Meredith, vice chair of the Toronto Argonauts Michael "Pinball" Clemons, executive director of the Council of African Canadian Education Delvina Bernard, and youth outreach worker Kwesi Johnson. The program is archived at https://www.mcintyre.ca/titles/CTV591.

2 Compton (2007) argues that "using American models in Canada is always tricky business, given the pseudo-colonial relationship we have with the Yankee leviathan" (p. 793). Yet, how could it be otherwise? In this volume, hampton and Rochat provide evidence of the historical reference that US Black organizations have provided Black Canada. As well, for many African Canadians the American-Canadian border is rather porous – not one dividing colonial power and "colony," as evidenced by the Black Lives Matter movement, which has spawned a pan-African consciousness. As Tamari Kitossa (personal communication, 4 August 2015) asks: "Is the question one of African American imperialism or that the narrative of multiculturalism so conceals the brutal realities of anti-Blackness in Canada that there is justifiable reach for discursive articulation of our presence in North America?"

3 This article has echoes of a *Globe and Mail* article by Sean Fine (1990) titled "Leadership in black community facing difficult internal problems," in which he reported on the challenges to the leadership within the community – "from a middle-class that appears to feel increasingly threatened, and from a more unpredictable and volatile group, the disaffected elements of Black youth." He mentions the failed meetings and retreats called by various leadership groups to set out "a community blueprint" and that "some older community leaders, frustrated by what they see as growing pressures of discrimination and intolerance, say it is time they step aside for younger people" (p. A11).

4 In a *Globe and Mail* article Fine (1990) wrote that Laws, Roach, Hall, and Farrell, as well as Akua Benjamin, were "dubbed by Toronto civic leaders as radicals." They were said to be "expressing an anger and frustration shared by those dubbed moderates, and by the greatest portion of the community" (p. A11; see also Black, Abdillahi, & Grandison, 2017).

5 In this volume, Kitossa asserts that "the discourse of 'crisis' in African Canadian leadership is a recursive articulation for the revitalization, rejuvenation, and creation of new organizations and strategies to meet the changing conditions of African Canadian life. The problem is that in the context of neo-liberal multiculturalism the internal self-criticism of 'crisis' is both a tactic of 'responsibilization' used to hold marginalized individuals and communities responsible for the social problems generated by racial capitalism" (pp. 71–2).

6 Edwards (2013) contends that while Christianity has historically been used for the purposes of colonization and imperialism, there is evidence that the Christian faith has also served in the decolonialization and liberatory process of racialized people. Paul Banahene Adjei, writing in this volume, would agree with Edwards that the Black church has historically served as a defender of the weak and liberator of the oppressed, though he notes the rise of the "prosperity gospel" undermines this historic mission (p. 328).

7 DiAngelo (2011) goes on to say: "Whites have not had to build tolerance for racial discomfort and thus when racial discomfort arises, whites typically respond as if something is 'wrong,' and blame the person or event that triggered the discomfort (usually a person of color)" – often going on to "confuse comfort with safety" (pp. 60–1).

8 I am not suggesting that Black Canadian leadership should only "be recognized if it is Canadian lived." Indeed, we have long referenced US scholarship, borrowed from US examples, and have modelled a number of our programs and practices on theirs. Since we live in a highly economically, politically, and culturally interconnected and interdependent world, with Black Canadians drawn from every corner of the world, I suggest it cannot and should not be otherwise. This means that Black leadership in Canada benefits as much from our southern neighbours as it does from experiences, views, perspectives, and strategies Blacks from elsewhere bring to the Black experience in Canada. As Kitossa notes in this volume, the claim of US Black leadership cultural imperialism is dubious when seen historically. He points out that the most weighty periods of US Black leadership in the nineteenth century were either influenced or undertaken by Caribbean expatriates such as Marcus Garvey, Claude McKay, and Kwame Toure (Stokely Carmichael). It ought not to be forgotten that not only were Malcolm X's parents Garveyites, but his mother was Trinidadian. We should also consider that African Vietnam draft resisters and radicals such as Norman Otis Richmond emigrated to Toronto, Montreal, and elsewhere in the 1960s to play a fundamental part in Black leadership in Canada. There are nevertheless important and significant differences between the two countries and the Black experience within them: this must be recognized and taken into account. It is precisely some of these differences and specificities that I seek to highlight in this discussion.

9 For instance, Viola Desmond acted against racial segregation nearly ten years before Rosa Parks (1946 compared to 1955), yet Canadians – even African Canadians, and Nova Scotians as well – are more familiar with Rosa Parks; so too with Martin Luther King Jr and Malcolm X and not Hugh Barnett. Lorne Foster (2011) refers to Barnett as "Canada's Martin Luther King Jr," and he continues to point out that Canadians familiarity with these Americans "is itself an indication that there is no place in Canadian

collective consciousness for Black leadership. It just does not compute ... Black leaders are always invariably American."

10 This would explain why governments and others in Canada would bring African Americans to Canada to consult on issues affecting the African Canadian community. The Rev. Eugene Rivers is a case in point. I will return to him later in the discussion.

11 It should be noted that Meredith's participation in the panel came before he had to resign from the Senate because of allegations of sexual misconduct (see Ballingall & Campion-Smith, 2017; see also Gosine in this volume).

12 Indeed, in his *Globe and Mail* article, Fine (1990) noted that "the Black community is actually multiple communities: rich, middle class or poor; Canadian-born or from Britain, the United States, Africa or the Caribbean." But we should not here ignore the seeming intent of the article: to let the community leaders know that Toronto civic leaders – namely, the metro chair and the police chief – were frustrated with them. The chair referred to Black leaders as "cowards who are leaving the centre stage to radicals for fear of being called Uncle Toms"; and on national television, the police chief declared that the community lacked the "leadership" of people who were willing to "express sanity" (p. A11).

13 It should be noted that the corporate media, governments, and others would also look to African Americans as "examples" whom Canadian leaders should emulate.

14 Rivers seemed to have played his role so well in representing the problems affecting Toronto's Black communities, and Black young men and boys in particular, that a year later the Progressive Conservative Party invited him to speak at their convention.

15 In her comment to the audience, Renée said: "I serve the interests of the public. I serve the interests of democracy. I serve the interests of inclusion, not exclusion or discrimination. Unfortunately what everybody has been observing in these debates is exclusion because you only seem to see three candidates ... I can tell you not one person on this platform has stood up for truth. And if you stand for truth, you stand boldly" (cited in Tecle, 2015, p. 8).

16 I remember participating in protests in the 1970s and 1980s that passed through this same area. Originally, it was an area of about one large block on Eglinton Avenue West, bounded by Marlee Avenue to the east and Oakwood Avenue to the west. The area mainly consists of businesses – such as eateries, beauty/hair salons (including barbershops where men would hang out), and clothing, hair product, and record stores – that are primarily located on the south side of Eglinton. Until about the early 2000s, the businesses were largely Caribbean (not just Jamaican), but today, with western expansion of the area to Dufferin Street, many of these businesses serving Black residents are now also owned by Africans and South Asians.

17 BLM is said to have "made its debut in Toronto in 2014 with a vigil" and thereafter "escalated its tactics to interrupting a Toronto Police Services Board meeting, sending specific demands for immediate action to Mr. Tory, and now, blocking a major road" (Smith, 2015). Mayor John Tory and the Black police chief, Mark Saunders (appointed in 2015), were also challenged by other Black activists to address racial profiling (see Cole, 2015). Since its formation, BLM has held various protests: they camped out at Toronto Police Headquarters for nearly two weeks in the dead of February, 2016; demonstrated in front of Premier Kathleen Wynne's house in April 2016; and, among other demands, called for an end to police in Toronto schools at a rally in the Jane and Finch community in May 2017.

18 Ferguson, Missouri, is a suburb of the Greater St Louis area, where an unarmed Black teenager, Michael Brown, was fatally shot by a white police officer, Darren Wilson, in August 2014. When in November the county's prosecutor announced that, as per the grand jury decision, the officer would not be indicted, the result was a wave of protests – as when Brown was first shot – in many US and Canadian cities.

19 The "Yonge Street Riot" – or to many in the Black community, "the Yonge Street Uprising" – of 4 May 1992 followed from a rally organized by the Black Action Defence Committee in solidarity with their American counterparts to protest the acquittal of four white police officers accused of beating Rodney King in Los Angeles. The rally was also to protest the brutality of police in the Greater Toronto Area, specifically the fatal shooting of Raymond Lawrence (twenty-two years old) two days before and Wade Lawrence (seventeen years old) two weeks earlier. The protesters marched to the US embassy and to city hall where they heard from Black leaders. Late in the evening the multiracial gathering, numbering about a thousand, "grew restless," as *Toronto Star* reporter Shree Paradkar (2017) writes, "and went from chanting 'No Justice No Peace' to smashing windows and pelting police." Members of the white supremacist Heritage Front also showed up to "denounce the racist murder of whites," as their posters stated. (See also Black, Abdillahi, & Grandison, 2017).

20 These programs, largely supported by the government of the far-sighted premier Bill Davis, were initiated, programmed, and staffed by Black community members. The Harriet Tubman Centre was housed in a YMCA building and received some financial and other supports from that organization. In addition to their educational, cultural, social, recreational, counselling, and summer camp programs, these organizations also played an advocacy role on issues pertaining to children, youth, and young adults.

21 Wallace also writes that "the first black-focused school opened in Toronto more than two decades ago. It wasn't just an Africentric program, a course on African history, or a tutorial service for black students, but an actual alternative school, a legitimate part of the York Board of Education. It had its own

students and staff. It had its own space, at D.B. Hood Community School in the northwest end of the city. And it had its own name: the Afro-Caribbean Alternative Secondary School."

22 In fact, Raymond Williams (1983) said that culture is one of the most misunderstood and "complicated words in the English language" (p. 87).

23 In his book *Toronto Caribbean Carnival: A Tribute*, David Ayres (2013) writes that to help celebrate Canada's "100th year as a country the government invited ethic groups to showcase their culture" (p. 8).

24 A particular style of dancing, typically to calypso music.

25 I was copied on the letter and quote from it here with the author's permission.

26 Consider here the activist cultural curators who advocated to stop the showing of *Out of the Heart of Africa* at the Royal Ontario Museum and *Show Boat* at a North York theatre.

27 I think here of African Canadians' participation in sports, which is also used to construct Black youth as "natural" athletes at the expense of their academic abilities and skills. In this regard, sports leaders have to work to ensure that Black athletes are not reduced to athletic prowess only.

28 These organizations provided educational supports to students and parents as well as opportunities for young people to cultivate an understanding of their issues and those confronting the community generally.

29 Developing and using a culturally relevant and responsive curriculum has long been a preoccupation of many educators and education activists. Today, the hip hop curriculum developed by Ramon San Vicente and others (2014) is one that is being used in schools in the Toronto District School Board.

30 We also heard calls on the Black-owned radio station FM 98.7 for community members to apply to become executive committee members of the "Congress of Black Canadians," seemingly a competing organization. At the time of writing, the difference between the organizations not only remains unclear, but is yet to be explained to African Canadian communities.

REFERENCES

Alcoba, N. (2006, January 10). Reclaiming lost sons: Crime-fighting Boston clergyman joins Toronto's battle. *National Post*, p. A7.

Austin, D. (2013). *Fear of a black nation: Race, sex, and security in sixties Montreal.* Toronto: Between the Lines.

Ayres, D. (2013). *Toronto Caribbean Carnival: A Tribute.* Mississuaga, ON: David Ayres.

Ballingall, A., & Campion-Smith, B. (2017, 9 May). Disgraced Sen. Don Meredith resigns over sex with teen. *Toronto Star.* Retrieved from https://www.thestar.com/news/canada/2017/05/09/disgraced-senator-don-meredith-is-resigning.html

Bannerji, H. (1996). On the dark side of the nation: Politics of multiculturalism and the state of "Canada." *Journal of Canadian Studies, 31*(3), 103–28. https://doi.org/10.3138/jcs.31.3.103

Benhabib, S. (2002). *The claims of culture: Equality and diversity in the global era.* Princeton: Princeton University Press.

Black, S. (2006, 17 April). Gangs, the media, and the myth of community. Retrieved from http://rabble.ca/news/gangs-media-and-myth-community

Black, S., Abdillahi, I., & Grandison, H. (2017). *It takes a riot.* Toronto: Akua Benjamin Legacy Project, Ryerson University.

Brathwaite, K. (Ed.). (2003). *Access and equity in the university.* Toronto: Canadian Scholars' Press.

Campbell, M.V. (2012). The Gwannings. In C.E. James & A. Davis (Eds.). *Jamaica in the Canadian experience: A multiculturalizing presence* (pp. 120–32). Halifax: Fernwood.

Cole, D. (2015, 21 April). The skin I'm in: I've been interrogated by police more than 50 times – all because I'm black. *Toronto Life.* Retrieved from https://torontolife.com/city/life/skin-im-ive-interrogated-police-50-times-im-black/

Compton, W. (2007). The diaspora's upper left-hand margin: Octopus and Callaloo. *Callaloo, 30*(3), 2007, 793–4. *Project MUSE.* http://doi.org/10.1353/cal.2008.0028

Day, D.V., & Antonakis, J. (Eds.). *The nature of leadership.* Los Angeles: Sage.

DiAngelo, R. (2011). White fragility. *International Journal of Critical Pedagogy, 3*(3), 54–70.

Edwards, K.T. (2013). Christianity as anti-colonial resistance? *Souls: A Critical Journal of Black Politics, Culture, and Society, 15*(1–2), 146–62. https://doi.org/10.1080/10999949.2013.803373

Fine, S. (1990, 2 June). Leadership of black community facing difficult internal problems. *Globe and Mail,* p. A11.

Foster, L. (2011). Black leaders relegated to fringe of society – Prof. Retrieved May 2015 from http://sharenews.com/archives/20110223black-leaders-relegated-fringe-society-prof/

Gillborn, D. (2015). Intersectionality, critical race theory, and the primacy of racism: Race, class, gender, and disability in education. *Qualitative Inquiry, 21*(3), 277–87. https://doi.org/10.1177/1077800414557827

Gilroy, P. (2013). "... We got to get over before we go under ...": Fragments for a history of black vernacular neoliberalism. *New Formations: A Journal of Culture/Theory/Politics, 80*–81 (Winter), 23–38. https://doi.org/10.3898/newf.80/81.01.2013

The Globe and Mail. (2007, 7 November). School by skin colour, p. A20.

Gooch, T. (2017, 10 December). An important moment for black political organization in Canada. *Toronto Star.* Retrieved from https://www.thestar.com/opinion/star-columnists/2017/12/10/an-important-moment-for-black-political-organization-in-canada.html

Gooden, A. (2008). Community organizing by African Caribbean people in Toronto, Ontario. *Journal of Black Studies, 38*(3), 413–26. https://doi.org/10.1177/0021934707309134

Haque, E. (2012). *Multiculturalism within a bilingual framework: Language, race, and belonging in Canada.* Toronto: University of Toronto Press.

Harris, C.I. (1993). Whiteness as property. *Harvard Law Review, 106*(8), 1707–91. https://doi.org/10.2307/1341787

Hewlett, S.A. (2013, 13 April). Mentors are good. Sponsors are better. *New York Times,* p. BU7. Retrieved from http://www.nytimes.com/2013/04/14/jobs/sponsors-seen-as-crucial-for-womens-career-advancement.html

Jackson, A.P., & Meadows, F.B. (1991). Getting to the bottom to understand the top. *Journal of Counseling and Development 70*(1), 72–6.

James, C.E. (2009). Multiculturalism in a colour-blind society and the education of black students. *Canada Watch,* Fall issue. Robarts Center for Canadian Studies, York University, Toronto, pp. 26–7. Retrieved from http://robarts.info.yorku.ca/files/2012/03/CW_2009_Multiculturalism.pdf

James, C.E. (2010). *Seeing ourselves: Exploring race, ethnicity and culture.* Toronto: Thompson.

James, C.E. (2012). Troubling role models: Seeing racialization in the discourse to "corrective agents" for black males. In K. Moffatt (Ed.), *Troubled masculinities: Reimagining urban men* (pp. 77–92). Toronto: University of Toronto Press.

Kellerman, B. (2008). *Followership: How followers are creating change and changing leaders.* Boston: Harvard Business Press.

Kitossa, T. (2012). Black Canadian Studies and the resurgence of the insurgent African Canadian intelligentsia. *Southern Journal of Canadian Studies, 5*(1–2), 255–84.

Leadership development: What is leadership? (n.d.). *Leadership Now.* Retrieved from https://www.leadershipnow.com/minute0005.html

Leonardo, Z., & Broderick, A. (2011). Smartness as property: A critical exploration of intersections between whiteness and disability studies. *Teachers College Record, 113*(10), 2206–32.

Lewis, S. (1992, 9 June). *Report of the advisor of race relations to the premier of Ontario, Bob Rae.* Retrieved from http://www.siu.on.ca/pdfs/report_of_the_advisor_on_race_relations_to_the_premier_of_ontario_bob_rae.pdf

Marable, M. (2008). The crisis of black leadership: Introduction to an international symposium. *Souls: A Critical Journal of Black Politics, Culture, and Society, 10*(1), 1–4. https://doi.org/10.1080/10999940801937318

Maroon, A. (2014, 29 November). Opinion: We protest in solidarity with Ferguson because we are the same. *Now Magazine.* Retrieved from https://nowtoronto.com/news/we-protest-in-solidarity-with-ferguson-because-we-a/

Paradkar, S. (2017, 5 May). The Yonge St. riot of 1992 ... or was it an uprising? *Toronto Star.* Retrieved from https://www.thestar.com/news/gta/2017/05/05/the-yonge-street-riot-of-1992-or-was-it-an-uprising-paradkar.html

Pastor preaches hope. (2006, 12 January). *Etobicoke Guardian.* Retrieved from http://www.insidetoronto.com/news-story/6368-pastor-preaches-hope/

Patterson, A. (2015, 23 March). Next black leaders are here [Letter to the editor]. *Toronto Star.* Retrieved from https://www.thestar.com/opinion/letters_to_the_editors/2015/03/23/next-black-leaders-are-here.html

San Vicente, R. (2014). *Rhymes to re-education: A hip hop curriculum: resource guide for educators with social justice activities.* Toronto: A Different Publisher.

Shannon, P. (1998). *Reading poverty.* Portsmouth: Heinemann.

Sharpe, C. (2014). Black studies: In the wake. *The Black Scholar: Journal of Black Studies and Research, 44*(2), 59–69. https://doi.org/10.1080/00064246.2014.11413688

Smith, M. (2015, 31 July). A call to action: Black Lives Matter Toronto continues the fight against racism. *Globe and Mail.* Retrieved from http://www.theglobeandmail.com/news/toronto/a-call-to-action-black-lives-matter-toronto-continues-the-fight-against-racism/article25809106/

Tecle, S. (2015). Rude acts: Creative insubordinations on lower registers. Unpublished paper. Department of Sociology, York University, Toronto.

Torkornoo, E. (2015, 7 April). What is leadership? Retrieved from http://www.alueducation.com/en/what-is-leadership/

Walcott, R. (1997). *Black like who? Writing black Canada.* Toronto: Insomniac Press.

Walcott, R. (2014). Shame: A polemic. *CLR James Journal, 20*(1), 275–9. https://doi.org/10.5840/clrjames201492318

Walker, A., Brady, J., & Hardware, S. (2015, 21 April). Time for a new kind of black activism in Toronto. *Toronto Star.* Retrieved from http://www.thestar.com/opinion/commentary/2015/04/21/time-for-a-new-kind-of-black-activism-in-toronto.html

Walker, B. (2010). *Race on trial: Black defendants in Ontario's criminal courts, 1858–1958.* Toronto: University of Toronto Press.

Wallace, A. (2009). The test: Africentric schools could be the key to success for a generation at risk. (Just don't call it segregation.). *This Magazine,* January-February. Retrieved from http://www.thismagazine.ca/issues/2009/01/black_schools.php

Wells, G. (2006). The answer within: The role of the church in the Black community: A community development response to the violence in Toronto. Paper presented at the First North American Conference on Spirituality and Social Work, May. Retrieved from http://www.spiritualityandsocialwork.ca/uploads/2/5/8/0/25806130/gillianwells.pdf

Williams, R. (1983). *Keywords: A vocabulary of culture and society.* London: Fontana.

Winsa, P. (2015, 21 March). Searching for Toronto's next generation of black leaders. *Toronto Star.* Retrieved from http://www.thestar.com/opinion

/commentary/2015/04/21/searching-for-Torontos-next-generation-of-black-leaders.html

Working Group. (1992). *"Towards a new beginning": The report and action plan of the Four Level Government/African Canadian Community Working Group.* Toronto: City of Toronto.

Wyper, L.E. (2014). Transformative leadership and diversity: The need for change agents, followership, and tipping points in our educational institutions. *Journal of Global Citizenship and Equity Education, 4*(1): 1–11.

2 War on Multiple Fronts: Black Leadership and Backlash Politics in the Context of Policing Controversies

CHRISTOPHER J. WILLIAMS

"Black leadership is dead," began an October 1994 *Toronto Star* op-ed piece; it was "assassinated by the relentless work of self-appointed culture cops who have taken upon themselves the role of purging our society of all opinions they themselves oppose," according to Ali Sharrif (1994), a freelance reporter. Continuing in a tone marked by bitterness and anger, he bemoaned the fate of "black leaders who have been consigned to the political graveyard for daring to speak their minds on issues of paramount importance to their community and, by extension, to all of society." The proximate catalyst for these remarks was the high-profile excoriation of Arnold Minors, a member of the Toronto Police Services Board, who was accused of comparing the Toronto Police Service to an occupying army in his explanatory response to a question about why black witnesses were (supposedly) silent following shooting incidents. But, more broadly, Sharrif was setting himself against the external imposition of race-specific speech standards capable of undermining the force of black contributions to critical public discourse. Analogically, then, the "culture cops," like their counterparts with badges and guns, aimed to sustain the dominant order via regular reminders, to racial others, of who wields predominant power and what effects can be produced by such power.

The standpoint of Sharrif was (and is) essentially sound and supportable, though a few qualifications and supplemental propositions are nonetheless in order. First, and most obviously, black leadership in Toronto was not *dead* in the mid-1990s – saying it was on the wane or in retreat would be more accurate – but, one supposes, Sharrif was legitimately exercising his commentative licence to be hyperbolic for the purpose of signalling urgency. Second, processes of white-on-black sociocultural discipline (carried out with the usual interrelated techniques of suppression, ostracism, and marginalization) are effected by primary orchestrators who are typically assisted by secondary players, some of whom are black and situated on the status quo–friendly side of the left-right political continuum. Third, black leadership per se is not objectionable, and is in fact desirable, from a hegemony-maintenance perspective, so long as such leadership is driven by neo-comprador consciousness. Indeed, if stifling stasis is the flipside of progressive societal transformation, then black leaders who forge trick coins that always land in favour of the former are bound to be in high hegemonic demand.

Much of this runs contrary to optimistic strands of thought anchored in visions of black leadership as situated atop antecedent shoulders, as committed to building upon traditions of cumulative struggle and developing ever more potent approaches to advancing the cause of social justice. Far from fanciful, this outlook enjoys firm historical grounding; examples are quite bountiful – particularly in studies of the black freedom struggle in the United States – and Simon Hall provides a representative snapshot in his examination of civil rights activism in Virginia:

> In the 1930s and 1940s, the NAACP had been at the forefront of the African American challenge to racism and segregation in the Old Dominion. But by the 1960s, in important respects the association found itself behind the times. In the direct-action era, the NAACP's commitment to litigation and lobbying, and its caution over civil disobedience, held limited appeal. Although the association sometimes still operated at the sharp end of the struggle, it increasingly found itself superseded by newer, more militant groups. (Hall, 2007, p. 255)

While it is true that black leadership succession usually equals progression, no tradition of collective struggle is immune to betrayal. Like boom-and-bust cycles in the domain of economics, the historical and current field of black sociopolitical contestation features cycles of progressive action *and* reactionary counteraction. Concrete reality and ideal (progressive) linearity are not constant bedfellows, however much one might wish otherwise.

The aim of this chapter, accordingly, is to chart and analyse shifts in black Canadian leadership in the context of struggles against oppressive policing: shootings, beatings, and daily harassment constitutive of petit apartheid. With a geographical focus on Ontario (along with some consideration of Quebec) and a temporal focus on a two-decade period beginning in the late 1980s, the case study that follows demonstrates how forces opposed to prominent black critics of the police embraced three key tactics – smear campaigns, strategic de-racialization, and issue displacement – to precipitate a partial transition from progressive to regressive black leadership.

Black Leadership as Resistive

Just as militaries are justified by reference to external enemies, the existence and supposed indispensability of police forces draws support from the spectre of internal enemies, construed almost exclusively as "dangerous criminals." But beyond the confines of state-centred justificatory ideology, critical analysts of policing recognize that the broad remit of police power allows for the systematic targeting of "police property," definable as

> low-status, powerless groups whom the dominant majority see as problematic or distasteful. The majority are prepared to let the police deal with their "property" and turn a blind eye to the manner in which this is done. Examples would be vagrants, skid-row alcoholics, the unemployed or casually employed residuum, youth adopting a deviant cultural style, ethnic minorities, gays, prostitutes and radical political organisations. The prime function of the police has always been to control and segregate such groups, and they are armed with a battery of permissive and discretionary laws for this purpose. (Reiner, 1992, p.118)

In Canada, indigenous peoples qualify as paradigmatic examples of police property, having been on the receiving end, since 1873, of oppressive pro-colonial policing as carried out by the North Western Mounted Police/Royal Canadian Mounted Police. And on a less grandiose scale, blacks – as quintessentially "problematic or distasteful" within the anti-black racist imagination – are reluctantly familiar with police aggression and violence, especially in urban centres such as Toronto, Montreal, and Halifax.

Police violence in the form of shootings resulting in serious injuries or deaths of civilians has long been a core concern of sizable black communities in Canada, with the late 1980s and early 1990s being particularly contentious times marked by seven police shootings of blacks in Toronto from August 1988 to May 1992 (Wong, 1992) and the shooting deaths of three young black males (Anthony Griffin, Presley Leslie, and Marcellus Francois) by the Montreal police over a roughly congruent timeframe (Contenta, 1991). For numerous community leaders, the involved officers were not anomalous "bad apple" agents but flesh-and-blood manifestations of Herrenvolk state power: "Canada is a racist state. If you have a racist state, then you have racist police," stated Dudley Laws of the Toronto-based Black Action Defence Committee (Hall, 1992). Denham Jolly, described by one journalist as a "businessman and activist," advanced a somewhat similar view when he cited a "white racial supremacy complex" as a notable aspect of police culture/ideology (Wilkes, 1992). Deep and uncompromising critiques of policing were also voiced beyond the borders of Ontario. In the summer of 1991, during calls by blacks for an enquiry into the criminal justice system of Quebec, the leader of the National Black Coalition of Quebec, Dan Philip, denounced police as "lawless" and "out of control" perpetrators of "brutality toward black people" (Contenta, 1991). Considered as compatible, interlocking claims, the words of Laws, Jolly, and Philip were suggestive of a racially selective Hobbesian state of affairs: not a war of all against all, but a war by police against blacks.

Although secular black leaders were at the forefront of mounting opposition to police violence, certain religious figures, unwedded to the dictates of haughty other-worldliness, decided to join the terrestrial fray. Recognizing that good character, conventionally conceived, offered no guarantee of protection from police bullets, Pastor Basil Miller, head of the Metro Black Clergy Association (an umbrella group of over one hundred churches), made this observation: "I can understand why people are scared. I'm concerned, too – because it could happen to me ... I could be pulled over by police and who knows what can happen. So many black people have been killed ... you have to wonder" (Wong, 1992, ellipses in original). The upshot was that a key class-linked division in the black community – between "rough" and "respectable" elements – became increasingly dubious, at least when considered vis-à-vis police violence; the pastor standing at the pulpit and the pusher standing on the street corner were equally likely, in some circumstances, to wind up staring down the barrel of a gun.

Five hundred kilometres away, in Montreal, a counterpart of Pastor Miller charged that "some police are having a field day harassing and shooting blacks." The speaker, Reverend Leicester Bigby, was delivering a November 1991 sermon at Union United Church, in which he argued that racist policing was anchored in, and normalized by, widely held white perceptions of blacks as manifestations of subhumanity. In his words, "the majority of white folk view blacks as animals or even less than animals" (Contenta, 1991). Absent a formal poll, one could argue that Bigby ought to have replaced the word "majority" with "many" or "some," but the basic thrust of his message was sound: discourses of dehumanization, of the blacks-as-bestial variety, occupy a central place in anti-black racist thought and should be taken into account when one seeks to understand the particular vulnerability of black bodies to official (state-sanctioned) violence.

Far from settling for voicing idle woe-unto-us lamentations, black leaders invested in the struggle against police violence made two types of appeals – community centred and state centred – driven by visions of (1) enhancing community cohesion and capacities for defensive mobilization and (2) diminishing the opportunities and abilities of the police to engage in lethal violence. Representative examples of community-centred appeals include a statement by Akua Benjamin of the Black Action Defence Committee who, at one point, advised that "we want all community groups to cease talking to police until they acknowledge racism is rampant in the police force" (Joseph & Armstrong, 1990). It was, on the surface, a simple entreaty, but its deeper significance is rooted in the connection between dialogue and legitimacy; specifically, dialogue presupposes legitimacy and legitimacy is partially inferred on the basis of dialogue – which is why the NAACP does not hold discussions with the Ku Klux Klan, to use a stark example. Less starkly, Benjamin called for a suspension of community/police dialogue because, it seems, she held that communities with legitimate grievances should not engage with institutional actors who espouse denialist positions (e.g., "policing in Toronto is not systemically racist") lest the former somehow lend legitimacy to the latter. In a similar community-centred spirit, though with different practical emphases, Leith Hamilton, director of the Black Community Council of Quebec, proposed a program of collective defence: "We need to have some strategies, from a community level, where we're able to protect our people from police" ("Man's death," 1991). A logical affinity exists between Hamilton's proposal and Laws's view of the state because if the police are a racist arm of a racist state then targeted communities are necessarily left to their own defensive devices.

From another standpoint, however, a certain brand of realpolitik dictated that some black leaders made state-centred appeals for counteracting oppressive policing. Their reasoning can be summed up straightforwardly: the grossly asymmetrical imbalance between black power and state power generates a need to petition the state for grievance alleviation. So, for instance, after an incident in which a police officer shot a black man in the head at close range following a foot chase, lawyer Charles Roach was apparently gripped by a sense of weary resignation when he admitted, "it seems clear the black community does not have the power to stop police shootings" (Duncanson, 1991). Accordingly, as one journalist noted, "Roach called for provincial intervention to prevent any more black people from being shot by the police" (Duncanson, 1991). Moving along a more racially generalized path, Wilson Head, a founding member of the Urban Alliance on Race Relations, sought to add breadth to the subject of police shootings by proclaiming, "it's not only black people who have been shot by police. There have been a lot of white people shot too" (Tyler & Girard, 1990). At the risk of propagating the bland rhetoric of all-inclusive victimization, Head aimed to emphasize police shootings in their entirety with the hope that the issue, thus universalized, could provide fuel for police disarmament; rather than speaking about the desirability of more restrained use of police guns, he wanted the guns eliminated altogether, a measure that, of course, could only be realized through state intervention.

State-centred appeals also came in the form of warnings about the possibility that ongoing police violence could lead to explosive urban unrest reminiscent of the dozens of uprisings that have occurred in the United States since the turbulent 1960s. Highlighting the limits of their leadership, black leaders – particularly in Toronto – informed white elites that official refusals to address police-related concerns of the black community carried the danger of impelling black youth to revolt in the streets, at which point black leaders would be powerless to rein in leaderless rebels. Invoking the familiar powder keg metaphor, Wilson Head stated, "kids are feeling tremendous bitterness and anger; all it needs is a spark to set that anger off," while Dudley Laws, speaking a few days after the onset of the 1992 Los Angeles uprising, predicted that "if something is not done very, very urgently, we will see the violence of Los Angeles come to Metro very, very soon" (Toughill, 1992). The power of such cautionary words stems, in part, from the fact that elites cherish trains-running-on-time stability; a figure like J. Edgar Hoover was merely being more candid than most when he declared "justice is incidental to law and order" (Quinney, 2001, p. 313). *In*justice is compatible with law and order, in other words, meaning appeals to justice/morality tend to be less compelling than warnings about mass subversions of law and order. Black leaders, crafting rhetoric based on these understandings, were simply addressing elites in a language they might respect rather than summarily reject.

Black Leadership as Sinister

Reactionary responses to the words and deeds of insurgent black leadership are an old story. The black leader with a microphone in her hand, like the black youth with a brick in his palm, is bound to be construed as a system-challenging threat. The counteractive imperatives of system maintenance, as actuated by institutional power brokers, contradict pluralist propositions about the alleged openness of the politico-cultural field. Perhaps this is why Kwame Ture and Charles V. Hamilton (1992) could confidently write the following with reference to the United States:

> Those who would assume the responsibility of representing black people in this country must be able to throw off the notion that they can effectively do so and still maintain a maximum amount of security ... It may well be – and we think it is – that leadership and security are basically incompatible. When one forcefully challenges the racist system, one cannot, at the same time, expect that system to reward him or even treat him comfortably. (p. 15)

From job terminations to death threats to frame-ups to outright assassinations, the United States has been a hotbed for the refinement of techniques designed to neutralize oppositional black leadership. Important differences exist between the United States and Canada in this respect – assassinating black leaders is not the Canadian way, one might say – but black leaders in Canada have not been exempt from attempts to undermine their critical agendas; on either side of the border, then, the standard burden of such leaders is a sense of perpetual jeopardy.

Equating blackness with incivility and violence is a well-established tactic employed by police officials in furtherance of various ends, including the aim of discrediting black leadership. Operating within this dubious tradition, Toronto police chief William McCormack claimed "some blacks incite unrest ... possibly for their own gain," during a period of heightened community frustration stemming from the police wounding of Marlon Neal, a black teen, who was shot in the back of the head in May 1990 while driving away from a radar trap (McLeod, 1990). "The greatest concern that I have is the advocacy of violence that is coming from some quarters of ... the black community," he elaborated, with Dudley Laws and kindred leaders in mind. "I feel that is reprehensible. Nothing can be solved by it" (Miller & Moloney, 1990). Here, one can identify how Manichean notions combine with symbolic inversions to construct an image of contestation along these lines: if the police have a monopoly on virtue then their opponents are vessels of vice, so much so that denunciations of (police) violence issued by the latter ("stop killer cops," "no justice, no peace," etc.) are taken as evidence of *their* taste for violence. And further still: unrest, if it occurs, cannot be a rational, organic communal response to police violence; instead, it arises due to the manipulative machinations of puppet masters, black leaders who purposely steer their flocks in destructive directions.

Not content to take specific aim at publicly identifiable black leaders, other commentators crafted broad indictments of the black professional class for not propagating McCormack-inspired scripts. In this vein, David

Lewis Stein (1992), a *Toronto Star* columnist, took the liberty of lecturing core segments of the black community in this manner:

> Where are the leaders from the black middle class, the lawyers and teachers and nurses and doctors and business people? Most have stayed inside their churches and their own communal organizations, working quietly away in the background while the foreground has been taken over by hallucinating demagogues. If a black middle-class father says to his children now, "Be afraid of the police because you are black," perhaps he should also say, "I have to share some of the responsibility for the extremism that is poisoning this city because I let others act as leaders in my name."

Dripping with racial paternalism and invested in wild caricatures of oppositional black leaders, Lewis's comments demonstrate the forcefulness of the burden of negation, that is, the apparent requirement, on the part of the black community, to wield swords against any black leader deemed odious from the perspective of white opinion leaders. In the spirit of colonial norms whereby Africans were often forced to beat or mutilate fellow Africans at the behest of sadistic European administrators, this burden of negation is dedicated to fostering black-on-black discursive violence, leading to the deflection of attention away from anti-black racism itself. It should be added that Lewis never bothers to consider a counterargument that, ironically, can be derived from his own words: if black parental advice can legitimately include instructions for black children to be on fearful guard when police are present, that itself would be indicative of extremist police racism, in which case the pronouncements of "hallucinating demagogues" would be commensurate with the anti-black threat posed by police.

The politics of policing discourse about policing extended, in tentacle-like fashion, to a range of local black leaders in ways that generated reputational repercussions and material losses. As mentioned in the opening paragraph of this chapter, Arnold Minors, the sole black member of the civilian Toronto Police Services Board, was famously attacked for calling the police an occupying army – or so his critics charged. Here is the key excerpt of his statement to a journalist regarding alleged black non-cooperation with police investigations:

> There is a long, long, thousand-year history of people not speaking to occupying armies. And this goes back to ... the divide between police officers and the community. And I'm damned if I have any clear understanding of what the solutions are. But I do know that when police officers talk about "These people won't speak to us," it is precisely the same thing

> that occupying armies talk about: These people won't speak to us. I take that as a measure of the quality of the relationship and the effectiveness of the relationship, and we need to do something about that, too. I see that as symptomatic of a larger problem. (Walkom, 1994)

Insofar as Minors was attempting to foster understanding via analogy, he was stating nothing outrageous, at least not by the standards of critical analysts of policing who, for example, sometimes explain, genealogically, twenty-first-century police techniques of racial/spatial control in terms of nineteenth-century slave patrols; or who invoke the apartheid South African pass law system in discussions of North American police emphases on stopping, questioning, and demanding identification from blacks who are thought to be "out of place." Nonetheless, Minors, speaking about a police force with officer sub-units called *platoons* led by individuals known as *sergeants,* was placed in the crosshairs of multiple parties. The police union demanded his firing, a fellow board member said he should quit, the solicitor-general of Ontario ordered an investigation, the *Toronto Sun* mounted a multi-week campaign against him, and on it went. Summing up the affair, one journalist described it as "a case of shooting the messenger without bothering to assess the validity of the message" (Walkom, 1994). In the immediate period, Minors, an anti-racism consultant, lost his training contracts with the provincial government, and later on, in 1996, he was denied reappointment to the board.

In some ways the ordeal of Arnold Minors was an exclamation mark preceded by the casting of much wider police-woven condemnatory nets. Police in Toronto, like their major urban counterparts throughout the United States, are organizationally and ideologically committed to monitoring and containing oppositional black leadership, lest the groups they spearhead become "unduly" influential. Exemplifying these suppressive aims, a 25 April 1989 intelligence report produced by the Toronto police detailed the results of surveillance concerning thirteen organizations and eighteen individuals. "The majority of persons mentioned in this report are self-appointed spoke persons [*sic*] or so called leaders within the Black Community," began the narrative portion of the report, followed by a summary of their collective aspirations: "The main objectives of these new groups are to stamp out racism within the Police Force, Mandatory Affirmative Action and the establishment of an Independent civilian police review board to restore confidence in the public" (Williams, 2005, pp. 104–5). The targeted groups included the Black Action Defence Committee, the National Black Coalition of Canada, and the National Council of Jamaicans among others, all of whom were cited as possible criminal and/or terrorist groups by police *after* the report went public (Tanovich, 2006, pp. 58–9). In absolute or proportional terms the police intelligence apparatus in Canada is modest compared to that of the United States, yet "police property," in either nation, is comparably susceptible to state surveillance for talking back and acting back vis-à-vis the police.

Considered in their totality, such assaults on insurgent black leadership can generate very disparate outcomes. It is possible, for instance, that black leadership can be strengthened to the extent that external attacks stiffen the resolve of leaders who refuse to be intimidated while providing validation for their original analyses of their adversaries (e.g., "We said the police are racist and, true to form, they came after us because we seek to 'stamp out racism'"). Additionally, new oppositional groups may form, or existing groups may coalesce, in these confrontational contexts: "Antagonism against a common enemy may be a binding element in two ways. It may either lead to the formation of new groups with distinct boundary lines, ideologies, loyalties and common values, or, stopping short of this, it may result ... in instrumental associations in the face of a common threat" (Coser, 1956, p. 140). On the other hand, black leadership can surely be weakened when under attack. The specific and general deterrent power of public demonization and secretive surveillance can compel established leaders to retreat from oppositional politics and discourage others on the cusp of leadership from reaching for mantles within their grasp. When these chilling effects are compounded by the wretched grip of fatalism – "the forces we are up against are unbendable and undefeatable" – then status quo defenders are well positioned to wave triumphalist flags. Beyond these polar possibilities, somewhat more complex outcomes may emerge, one of which entails partial leadership succession marked by the rise of black leaders who gain mainstream recognition and acceptance by setting themselves against oppositional leadership.

Black Leadership as Regressive

To understand the processes by which regressive black leadership rises (and perhaps flourishes), it is helpful to add nuance to the implicit conception of power – as overwhelmingly repressive – that has underpinned the analysis to this point. Contra this conception, Foucault (1980b), in a widely cited lecture, railed against the "automatic" tendency of social theorists "to define power as an organ of repression" (p. 90). In an interview published one year later he explained how power-as-repression, as a school of thought, was reductive and hence incapable of accounting for the broad-gauge effects, attractions, and products of power:

> If power were never anything but repressive, if it never did anything but to say no, do you really think one would be brought to obey it? What makes power hold good, what makes it accepted, is simply the fact that it doesn't only weigh on us as a force that says no, but that it traverses and produces things, it induces pleasure, forms knowledge, produces discourse. It needs to be considered as a productive network which runs through the whole social body, much more than as a negative instance whose function is repression. (1980a, p. 119)

Theorized in these terms, and applied to the subject of black leadership, the Janus face of power can marginalize *or* centralize, denigrate *or* elevate, stultify *or* amplify – depending on the nature of the leadership agenda as assessed by mainstream power brokers. Needless to say, regressive black leaders can exhibit impeccable understandings of these insights without having ever read Foucault.

Years after the Arnold Minors affair, in the early 2000s, by which time some degree of black leadership turnover was likely to occur, a *Toronto Star* op-ed by a former Toronto city councillor approvingly declared that "a new generation of black leaders is emerging." The writer, Gordon Chong, commented on the virtues of "introspection and self-criticism ... in any community," but the title of his piece – "Facing Up to Black Crime" – made it clear he was taking aim at one population segment (Chong, 2003). The effectuation of issue displacement (in this case, the displacement of police violence by "black crime") was a key enabling factor for the rise of black leaders who quickly endeared themselves to right-wing assemblages.

Enter Reverend Don Meredith, head of the Greater Toronto Area Faith Alliance, who asserted, "It's not white officers shooting black men. It's black men shooting each other" (Small, 2004). Meredith was speaking in April 2004, and from January 2000 to June 2006 twenty black people in Ontario were seriously injured or killed by police bullets (Wortley, 2006, p. 92), so, on the contrary, police were indeed shooting blacks. But regressive discourses are valued on the basis of ideological utility, not factual accuracy, a point not lost on Meredith, who at the same time said, "twenty-two young black men last year were killed by gun violence. This year the numbers are already up to about fourteen" (Small, 2004). Actually, the numbers were otherwise: thirteen males *in total* had been killed by that point (mid-April 2004), including seventy-eight-year-old Henry Durost, the first homicide victim of 2004, who was strangled in his apartment – not young, not black, not shot. Still, "facing up to black crime" was an endeavour energized by hyperbole and welcomed by police officials and politicians. In early 2004, for instance, Toronto police chief Julian Fantino met and conversed with black religious figures about crime in the black community, and two years later the premier of Ontario, Dalton McGuinty, praised their stance: "I'm very heartened that representatives of the faith community have decided that they're going to take on ... responsibility for the black community when it comes to addressing the issue of crime and guns" (Gillespie, 2006). Now take note of the issue displacement trajectory: in 1991 Charles Roach was appealing to the government of Ontario to stop police shootings of blacks; by 2006 the head of the government was enthused by the willingness of some blacks to deflect attention from such shootings.

Intensification of the issue displacement agenda was enabled by the tendency of regressive black leaders to link offences committed by a small percentage of blacks to overarching webs of cultural pathology. Striking moralistic poses while engaging in anti-sociological hectoring rooted in anti-black stereotypes, figures like Don Meredith used all available platforms to announce, "We have to stop blaming others and admit our community has a huge problem. There is a lack of core values in parenting. There is an absence of fathers. They're in jail or they're dead, or they're out there – and useless" (Hurst, 2005). Reflecting on his speech at the funeral of a young man in late December 2005 – driven by the injunction "I say to our parents, be parents" – Meredith told a reporter, "I could have talked about parents taking responsibility for their kids instead of buying them $300 running shoes. I could have been a lot more graphic about how you don't have to profile us, we profile ourselves. But it was a funeral" (Hurst, 2005).

The habit of issuing scattershot claims of a morally degenerate, materialistically obsessed black community was also taken up by Wendell Gibbs, an assistant pastor at Heron Park Baptist Church. In a set of pronouncements worthy of Ronald Reagan, Gibbs railed against "teenage girls with two, three children by different fathers who keep getting better public housing because welfare gives in to them, instead of working things out with the parents." But what about single mothers who work heavy hours to provide for their children, one might ask? Gibbs, being fully committed to the black pathology script, questioned their motives: "Sure, there are mums working two jobs, but you know sometimes it's for materialistic reasons, to get a 50-inch TV" (Hurst, 2005). What we have here, then, is a closed universe of discourse marked by claims that are impressionistic, not statistical, and conveniently non-falsifiable ("well, she works two jobs but ..."). The upshot is that issue displacement might be too mild a term to describe these developments; perhaps "issue obliteration" would be more suitable.

Unlike oppositional black leaders who were tagged as "hallucinating demagogues," Meredith, Gibbs, and similar figures enjoyed preferential exclusion from being labelled as, say, fulminating ideologues. And insofar as power "induces pleasure," to re-cite Foucault (1980a), regressive black leaders were free to pleasurably circulate the patriarchal notion that fatherless families are essentially worthless; the classist notion that access to social housing should be sharply curtailed, irrespective of the fact that such a measure would swell the ranks of homeless mothers and children; and the racist notion that blacks are culturally inferior to other groups in terms of "core values." Given the longstanding pedigree of these ideas in the United States, it was perhaps fitting that in early 2006 the Faith Alliance raised twenty thousand dollars to bring Reverend Eugene Rivers to Toronto for a three-day consulting stint. Rivers, who gained fame in connection with the "Boston Miracle" (a steep decline in homicides in the 1990s), apparently earned the money – enough to purchase sixty-six pairs of three-hundred-dollar running shoes – by providing Torontonians with a mono-causal account of street violence ("violence is a symptom of fatherless kids in the black community"); by disparaging black leaders and community members alike ("you have a black community and black political leadership in denial"); and by propagating the anti-black image of blacks as explicitly or implicitly pro-criminal: "I am saying that the extent to which the black community does not send a clear signal or message to black criminals that their behaviour will not be tolerated, they are a failure" (Welsh, 2006). Right-wing rhetoric logically appeals to right-wing institutions, so the police chief and his senior command met with Rivers to engage in the ideologically incestuous ritual of welcoming him to tell them precisely what they wanted to hear.

Gauging the overall success of these black leaders is a task best reserved for a lengthier study but, briefly, they did garner ample mainstream legitimacy and visibility by repudiating racial defiance and embracing racial deference. What, specifically, does this mean? An answer can be derived from the work of Charles W. Mills (1998), who in his discussion of "the politics of personhood within the framework of white supremacy" makes this argument:

> Not only must one's fellow persons respect one, but one must also be paid what could be termed *racial deference* from the subperson population. Failure to receive this deference then becomes a threat to one's sense of self-worth, since self-worth is defined hierarchically in relation to the class

> of inferior beings. So it is crucial to the maintenance of the system that the moral economy of deference is maintained, with a watchful eye for signs of insubordination in the subperson population. By posture, body language, manner, speech, and gaze, subpersons need constantly to demonstrate that they recognize and accept their subordinate position. (pp. 110–11)

This persons (white) / nonpersons (black) hierarchical arrangement was buttressed by Meredith, Gibbs and others in ways that found expression in the local press. Consider, for example, this excerpt from an August 2003 *Toronto Star* editorial: "Black leaders in Toronto have tried to work with police. They've attended summit meetings and made presentations to the police services board. They realize 'black-on-black' crime is a tragic problem, and that youth violence needs to be fought. They've spoken out – forcefully – about crime in their community" ("Runciman attack," 2003). Or this November 2005 editorial from the same paper: "No one can, with fairness, accuse Toronto's black leaders of ignoring the gangsters, guns and gore threatening to overwhelm their community. From church to community centre, they are demanding an end to the 'code of silence' that keeps witnesses from talking to police" ("Summit," 2005). Whether one examines historical racial deference (stepping off a sidewalk when a white person approaches) or contemporary racial deference (ranting about "black-on-black" crime when a white reporter approaches), the master narrative of black socio-cultural inferiority is sustained. And by contributing to this form of "success," regressive black leaders succeeded in profiting personally, most notably Don Meredith, who was appointed to the Canadian Senate in 2010.

Conclusion

On the basis of this case study two core propositions can be reasonably advanced. First, black leadership is not necessarily anathema from the standpoint of major institutional powers. While the polemicist may imagine that a monolithic white power structure aims to wholly eliminate black leaders and prevent the ascendance of new ones, the analyst – as a respecter of empirical evidence and the nuance it provides – is compelled to argue otherwise. The grand machinery of status quo maintenance is confronted or comforted by two very different types of black leaders: those who seek to throw wrenches into the machine and those committed to lubricating the machine. Such bifurcation means it would be illogical for the dominant society to exhibit undifferentiated hostility to black leadership; instead, a two-track approach exists, featuring the complementary goals of neutralizing black system-challengers and energizing black system-defenders. Naturally, no guarantees attach to either endeavour, but the motives, in and of themselves, establish the fact of (white) elite affinity for *some* strands of black leadership.

Second, full or partial black leadership succession – from oppositional to regressive and vice versa – is a cyclical and nearly inevitable feature of black community life. This is so, and will remain so for the foreseeable future, because both categories of black leadership have advantages that preclude any ultimate, final victory of one over the other. Oppositional black leadership has the advantages of close ideological alignment with communities in which oppositional consciousness is prevalent, namely, black communities; of exercising autonomous action as a result of not being tethered and beholden to powerful mainstream interests; and of having a historical track record of achieving progressive gains for blacks (and, almost invariably, other groups). Regressive black leadership enjoys the advantages of being able to secure funding from a variety of established, resource-rich entities; of making pronouncements and carrying out projects without the threat of state repression; and of garnering the support of segments of the black community afflicted by internalized racism. For these reasons and others, black leadership succession does not equal, in straightforward fashion, pure progression or regression. And at the risk of sliding into a pit of postmodernist platitudes, one can say that conditions of fluidity and non-finality do indeed prevail in this subject area.

REFERENCES

Chong, G. (2003, 21 February). Facing up to black crime. *Toronto Star.* Retrieved from ProQuest.

Contenta, S. (1991, 18 June). Bourassa nixes call by blacks for probe. *Toronto Star.* Retrieved from ProQuest.

Contenta, S. (1991, 18 November). Angry blacks in Montreal mourn victims of shootings. *Toronto Star.* Retrieved from ProQuest.

Coser, L.A. (1956). *The functions of social conflict.* New York: Free Press.

Duncanson, J. (1991, 12 November). Suspect was shot accidentally when officer stumbled, police say. *Toronto Star.* Retrieved from ProQuest.

Foucault, M. (1980a). Truth and power. In *Power/knowledge: Selected interviews and other writings, 1972–1977* (S. Gordon, Ed.) (pp. 109–33). New York: Pantheon.

Foucault, M. (1980b). Two lectures. In *Power/knowledge: Selected interviews and other writings, 1972–1977* (C. Gordon, Ed.) (pp. 78–108). New York: Pantheon.

Gillespie, K. (2006, 10 January). Premier asks pastors for plan. *Toronto Star.* Retrieved from ProQuest.

Hall, J. (1992, 8 May). Laws: The man behind the protests. *Toronto Star.* Retrieved from ProQuest.

Hall, S. 2007. "Civil rights activism in 1960s Virginia." *Journal of Black Studies, 38*(2): 251–67. https://doi.org/10.1177/0021934705285719

Hurst, L. (2005, 3 December). Black leaders say it takes a family. *Toronto Star.* Retrieved from ProQuest.

Joseph, A., & Armstrong, J. (1990, 2 June). Irate blacks vent anger at meeting. *Toronto Star.* Retrieved from ProQuest.

Man's death stirs fresh black anger at Montreal force. (1991, 19 July). *Toronto Star.* Retrieved from ProQuest.

McLeod, B. (1990, 22 May). The real voices of unrest. *Toronto Star.* Retrieved from ProQuest.

Miller, C., & Moloney, P. (1990, 18 May). Some blacks incite unrest chief says. *Toronto Star.* Retrieved from ProQuest.

Mills, C.W. (1998). *Blackness visible: Essays on philosophy and race.* Ithaca: Cornell University Press.

Quinney, R. (2001 [1970]). *The social reality of crime.* New Brunswick: Transaction.

Reiner, R. (1992). *The politics of the police.* 2nd ed. Toronto: University of Toronto Press.

Runciman attack inflames conflict. (2003, 8 August). *Toronto Star.* Retrieved from ProQuest.

Sharrif, Ali. (1994, 25 October). Culture cops ever eager to muzzle black leaders. *Toronto Star.* Retrieved from ProQuest.

Small, P. (2004, 18 April). "I may as well die, too, because my son died." *Toronto Star.* Retrieved from ProQuest.

Stein, D.L. (1992, 6 May). Riot put the long struggle for equality in jeopardy. *Toronto Star.* Retrieved from ProQuest.

Summit on gun crime. (2005, 22 November). *Toronto Star.* Retrieved from ProQuest.

Tanovich, D.M. (2006). *The colour of justice: Policing race in Canada.* Toronto: Irwin Law.

Toughill, K. (1992, 3 May). "This could not have come at a worse time." *Toronto Star.* Retrieved from ProQuest.

Ture, K., & Hamilton, C.V. (1992 [1967]). *Black power: The politics of liberation.* New York: Vintage.

Tyler, T., & Girard, G. (1990, 15 May). Police shoot, wound teen after Scarborough chase. *Toronto Star.* Retrieved from ProQuest.

Walkom, T. (1994, 27 October). Minors' words may have been impolitic but accurate. *Toronto Star.* Retrieved from ProQuest.

Welsh, M. (2006, 8 January). Pastor hopes to help city curb shootings. *Toronto Star.* Retrieved from ProQuest.

Wilkes, J. (1992, 4 May). Shooting by police "troubling" – Premier. *Toronto Star.* Retrieved from ProQuest.

Williams, C.J. (2005). To unnerve and detect: Policing black activists in Toronto. In L.A. Visano (Ed.), *Law and criminal justice: A critical inquiry* (pp. 95–113). Toronto: APF.

Wong, T. (1992, 17 May). Metro's blacks seeking solidarity. *Toronto Star.* Retrieved from ProQuest.

Wortley, S. (2006). *Police use of force in Ontario: An examination of data from the Special Investigations Unit, final report.* Toronto: African Canadian Legal Clinic.

3 African Canadian Leadership and the Metaphoricality of "Crisis": Towards Theorizing, Research, and Practice

TAMARI KITOSSA

Black politics can be viewed as the countermove by the dominated class/group in reaction to anti-black politics. Anti-black politics and the resulting policies and laws revolve around maintaining dominant structures and institutions of white privilege and hegemony.

Kevin Alexander Gray, *Waiting for Lightning to Strike* (2008, p. 5)

This essay offers a counter-intuitive perspective on the discourse of a "crisis" of African Canadian leadership as this affects civil society organizing. My examination of this discourse functions on two registers: manifest and latent. In a detailed and explicit way, it situates the presumption of Black leadership crisis as a metaphor for the challenges confronting African Canadian communities unable to leverage other sources of power beyond public protest. I suggest that, despite the implicit anti-Black pathologizing and almost boastful eulogies of a crisis of Black leadership by White journalists (Powell, 2012; Winsa, 2015), the facts are contrary. To be sure, African Canadians themselves also proclaim a crisis of leadership, but nowhere, as I will demonstrate, has this claim not in every instance been attended by some renewal initiative. I argue that leadership among African Canadians is constantly in regeneration and has always functioned on multiple registers, taking on forms of advocacy that bridge public articulations (e.g., Black United Front, Black Action Defence Committee) and private practice (e.g., as noted by Erica Lawson in this volume, Black mothers mobilizing grief as a site for leadership). I suggest, then, that aside from risks of appropriation by the "white power structure" (see James, this volume), the discourse of "crisis" in African Canadian leadership is a recursive articulation for the revitalization, rejuvenation, and creation of new organizations and strategies to meet the changing conditions of African Canadian life. The problem is that in the context of neo-liberal multiculturalism the internal self-criticism of "crisis" is a tactic of "responsibilization" used to hold marginalized individuals and communities responsible for the social problems generated by racial capitalism.

Scaffolding on previous chapters in this collection by Carl James and Christopher Williams, I assess three recent African Canadian leadership projects: the "Towards a Vision for the Black Community" project led by Hamlin Grange; the "Cipher project" sponsored by the Black Action Defence Committee and led by Christopher Harris; and a critical commentary of Black Lives Matter Toronto. My analysis is rooted in a *critical* Gramscian[1] Marxian analytic of civil-society organizing informed by a historiographic Africana sketch of some signal moments of leadership in the African diaspora.

I gesture towards a political sociology of African Canadian leadership that comes to terms with authority, bureaucracy, power, and state formation. To the extent there is no substantive field of sociological and political theory about African Canadian leadership, my attention to these issues is exploratory and largely speculative. Be that as it may, I believe that until and unless an ongoing body of theory and empirical research is developed to account for how voluntarist leadership can effectively cultivate and mobilize authority without coercive power, develop bureaucracy that does not ossify and become authoritarian, and avoid well-worn pitfalls such as heteropatriarchy and infiltration by *agents provocateur*, analysis and practice towards bettering the lives of African Canadians and in solidarity with other people will continue to be impoverished. This essay, therefore, quite apart from its critical engagement with Gramsci and Marx, enters further into a seemingly arid zone by drawing on the theoretical insights of "dead White men" such as Max Weber.

Given that this paper concerns itself with African Canadian leadership, I will certainly open myself to criticism for not drawing on Du Bois, as if Du Bois must be cited everywhere and dead White men not at all.[2] My strategic deployment of Marxism may also open me up to charges of "structural Marxism" unless it is realized that there are a variety of Marxisms and debates within and across schools of thought. As neo-liberalism's intellectual handmaid, post-structuralism, stands triumphant in the academy, the slightest scintilla of Marxist theory smacks of a musty nineteenth-century air. This view is mistaken, quite apart from its debilitating anti-intellectualism. As Hakim Adi (2014), Charles Mills (2003), and Cedric Robinson (2000) have shown, whatever may be the flaws of Marx's clairvoyance and the implicit Eurocentrism of Marxist theory (C. Moore, 1974), Marxism was and remains a potent epistemological and normative force informing the Black radical tradition as much as the Black radical tradition informs Marxism as a national and international force. From the African Blood Brotherhood, Harry Haywood, George Padmore, C.L.R. James, and Claude McKay straight through to the Black Panther Party, Stuart Hall, and the likes of Martin Luther King Jr and Malcolm X, who flirted with its analysis, something was inescapable:

> Notwithstanding its weaknesses, there was in Marxism a critical discourse to which no bourgeois ideology adequately responded. Capitalism's global regularities of war, expanding poverty and exploitation, the concentration of wealth, and the extension of repression persisted. Bourgeois thinkers displaced these endemic phenomena with the notion of termed resolvable dysfunctions. Marxists correctly declared they were no such things. (Robinson, 2000, p. 288)

Beyond this explicit debt to the Black radical tradition and Marxist theory, this essay hinges on a recognition of Weber's concern about the problematic of authority and power in human social organization. Here my engagement with a "bourgeois" theorist such as Weber will almost certainly run me afoul of some Marxists. But I stand on the solid ground paved by Ralph Miliband (1987), who recognized that issues of authority were beyond Marx's grasp in the early stages of capitalism to which he bore witness and gave eloquent testimony. I assert that theorizing the practice of authority without the power to compel is relevant for thinking about Black leadership wherever it may be found. To this end, this essay suggests that where there is substantively a "crisis" of Black leadership, it is symptomatic of a larger problem relevant to bureaucratic state-formation and contestations by oppressed groups within it.

In using theory in the way I propose, I suggest that since the state monopolizes offices of authority evident in (a) the power to command, (b) the right to demand obedience (by force if necessary), (c) the privilege of receiving "consent" from citizen-subjects by vote, and (d) the "hierarchy of credibility" (Becker 1967) to propagate ideology, all of which constitute a steep barrier to would-be oppositional leaders, we must confront the general problem of the relationship between charismatic leadership and the necessity of developing rational oppositional bureaucracy that can expose the contradictions of the state, as did, for example, Dudley Laws and the Black Action Defence Committee. If, as Mao Tsetung (1961) noted, the principal contradiction in political society is between the state and citizen-subjects, and conflict between citizens is secondary, then African Canadian leadership needs to be researched in ways other than the fractured political theory of postmodernism. To this end, analysis should centre on a critical Gramscian strategy for a long war of ideological contestation rather than a Leninist capturing of state bureaucracy by force: a basic reproduction of the extant bourgeois regime if it is not to be crushed by other capitalist states. Such a research question demands exploring whether Black liberation that conflates both contradictions rather than theorizing action in a dynamic and qualified programmatic way can, in fact, make the best of authority without coercive power, charismatic leadership, and the necessity for bureaucracy resistant to state infiltration when it also strategically decentralizes authority.

In this essay I offer an initial attempt at a sociology of African Canadian leadership vis-à-vis the discourse of a crisis of leadership, in five parts. First, I briefly address the genealogy of crisis theory. My aim is to show that, in one sense, African Canadian leadership is mimetic of the social and material conditions that compel it into being. Thus, the crisis of Black leadership is metaphorical, not actual: a narrative issued by and from the intelligentsia class itself as various persuasions within it compete to claim *authority* to speak on behalf of the masses and, in rare cases, to mobilize the masses to leverage the politics of protest. Second, I provide a crude historical snapshot of how the discourse of leadership crisis is belied by this very claim. Third, I offer a contemporary account of leadership by a select grouping of the African Canadian intelligentsia in Toronto who merge Du Boisian pastoral care with bourgeois liberalism. Fourth, I critically explore three leadership initiatives and practices that include reports and activism. By way of conclusion, I suggest possible future directions for sociological enquiry into African Canadian leadership.

Crisis Theory

Crisis theories fall within the domain of the sociology of knowledge and diagnoses of moral outrage and the making of social problems. There are essentially two variants on offer: the Weberian descriptive and pluralistic tradition pioneered by Herbert Blumer (1971), or a Marxian sociology based on a vibrant political-economic theory about the capitalist mode of production. Be it pluralist or Marxian, "crisis" is an epistemic assertion of baleful conditions, while "social problems" is the processes of political contention by which crises become objectively real. To some extent this is obvious since there are many damaging and harmful institutionalized behaviours that are not deemed "pathological" – capitalism, war, police brutality, and pollution – but viewed as tolerable consequences of business and "organized" existence. A crisis of whatever sort, therefore, is a metaphor for the political *process* by which a problem *successfully* comes to be recognized by the state, any state, and the constellation of forces with the capacity and credibility to influence the recognition and resolution of a problem. At some point, some constituency, usually an exploited one, conscientizes and mobilizes protest action rooted in the articulation of an issue ignored by the powerful. Once the "problem" emerges, however, it must be legitimated by the state and institutions that deliver the means of life or, in the case of the police and the military, its taking. If, at some point, there is recognition of the problem from within institutionalized centres of power, the problem is open to competing interpretations and knowledge claims by forces who reject the problem as such. Finally, if the state and powerful institutions either admit or are forced to officially admit "problem" into the realm of formal politics, it becomes the object of the official remediation (Blumer, 1971).

While Blumer (1971) admits coercive power is the determining factor in the "career" of a social problem, he notes that interests within the state bureaucracy, sometimes in collusion with outside forces of conservativism, will delay, divert, and undermine ameliorative plans of action. In the absence of a genuinely socialist party to represent the interests of the masses of people, this could hardly be otherwise, as noted by C. Wright Mills (1956) and Ralph Miliband (1987), given the shared ideologies and interlocking ties between economic, political, and military/police elites. Nowhere, however, does Blumer situate this process within a theory of capitalist social relations as it bears on the politics of moral outrage. This shortcoming is addressed by Frances Fox Piven (1976), who demonstrates that moral outrage, especially from below, leading to the discursive recognition of a social problem is both rare and heavily conditioned by alliances with powerful groups. As with the regime of Franklin Roosevelt, the capitalist state's conceding to a given social movement at a given time in defence of the overall integrity of capitalist social relations, but at the expense of the elite, is only provisional. In the absence of a vibrant and broad-based socialist party apparatus if not by and of the poor and dispossessed, then at least answerable to it, clawbacks and dissipation of progressive gains are assured by the logic of capitalist accumulation and social control (Piven, 1976). This account of social problems and social movements has primary and secondary points of relevance for the discourse of a crisis of Black leadership.

First, within the context of the bourgeois order, "successful" social problems are those that attract the attention and hence organizational leadership of concerned and sympathetic members of the elite and ruling class. Warren Buffet, Bill Gates, and other billionaires who condemn income inequality are an example (Hanauer, 2016; Sherman, 2015). This critical minority of the elites seeks to influence reforms that function as a "safety valve" that, it is hoped, will forestall a tipping point in the crisis of confidence in capitalism. In the present moment, the state has offloaded this responsibility to philanthro-capitalists. Second, and relatedly, leadership within the exploited race-caste reflects the existence of an elite cadre who experience blocked mobility and who understand extant social rules and the rhetoric of the oppressor group's ruling relations (Gouldner, 1979). Incidental to the foregoing is that in liberal democracies, when a social problem is mobilized from below – typically in the form of marches, strikes, and rebellions – it achieves formal recognition of the demand for amelioration when the state concedes, within definable limits, in defence of the status quo. In capitalist societies, however, the ability of the monied and elite classes to undermine restraints against "systemic"[3] exploitation always exceeds the organizational capacity of the dispossessed to institutionalize reforms in any long-term way (B. Moore, 1978; Piven, 1976). The elite and ruling classes do not, however, have it all their own way: social movements resist the machinations of the ruling elite even as the latter are aided by the logic of an exploitation in which consent-force acts in the long term to reverse gains won by the oppressed.

As Piven (1976) demonstrates, Blumer's Durkheimian approach to crisis theory admits conflict and describes its workings very well. The chief failing of this approach is that its reliance on pluralism constrains its description within the ideological limits prescribed by the liberal ideology of rationally competing interests (i.e., pluralism). Of consequence for the issue of a crisis of African Canadian leadership is that Black cultural politics are situated within an overall context of class division, ethnic and national differences, and capitalist exploitation within an overall context of anti-Blackness. The result is that African Canadian communities lack a coherent cultural socialist ideology and political process to establish internal authority and legitimacy that is not subject to "divide and conquer" by the liberal state.

Recent initiatives to establish national umbrella African Canadian organizations aim to bridge this gap, but they cohere around the identity of Blackness rather than *also* the identity of class and labour in relation to colonialism. The claim of a leadership crisis is, nevertheless, virtually always made by competing members of the intelligentsia class who are either "community-based" cultural and social service practitioners, Black business elites, or academicians. In this context, a crisis of leadership is a metaphor for the (in)capacity of the African Canadian intelligentsia class to place on the public agenda a perspective on issues germane to the failings of liberalism vis-à-vis Black citizenship and humanity. I argue, however, that whatever the merits of this metaphor, it is historical and rooted in the overall cultural, social, and political matrix of exploitation that African people in the diaspora experience generally.

In contrast to Blumer's approach, the Marxist account of crisis theory goes beyond the descriptive to articulate a normative judgement of social conditions and how they might be changed. With its emphasis on "social problems" arising from periodic economic, cultural, and political ruptures in capitalism, it functions as an analytical perspective that reveals the form and mechanics of social dynamics and the need for change (Hall, Critcher, Jefferson, Clarke, & Roberts, 1979; Harvey, 2005; Klein, 2007; Shaikh, 1978; Smith & Butovsky, 2012). In the social reality of African Canadians under capitalism, crisis has a multiplicity of functions and meanings that cannot be separated from the exploitation and exclusion of African Canadian communities. Crisis in this perspective is not merely about claims-making, it is organic to capitalism.

At one level, therefore, crisis is a statement of fact that signifies exploitation and the negation of Black existence. Qualitative and quantitative social indicators suggest that especially for working-class and poor African Canadians there is an objective crisis in the form of poverty and police brutality, *inter alia*. In this sense, "crisis" is an accurate description of the African Canadian social condition (Crichlow, 2014; Hum & Simpson, 2007; James et al., 2010; Lawson, 2012; Torczyner, 2010). At another and related level, however, *because* of the existential crisis arising from social injustice, the crisis of Black leadership is a metaphor that directs analysis to the social conditions that African Canadian leadership is expected to ameliorate. It is obvious that if African Canadian leadership is to be more than fiction, it must produce tangible results: police accountability (if not abolition), effective and high-quality education, guaranteed income, meaningful and well-paid employment, and the like. It is here that in the face of the incapacity of the Black intelligentsia and brick-and-mortar organizations to effect mass reforms beyond the narrow range of isolated and government-sponsored programs, often connected to "crime prevention," crisis emerges as a form of auto-criticism. The effect is to stimulate analyses of the material and social conditions confronting Black communities as a whole: this fact opens space to debate leadership practices and organizational forms that are required to meet the existential challenges confronting African Canadian communities.

What then are imagined as the limitations of the African Canadian intelligentsia to change the material and social condition of African Canadian communities dramatizes structural barriers to the ability of Black leadership to act autonomously of existing institutions and processes. Despite the incapacity of the African Canadian intelligentsia to substantively affect public policy, the discourse of a crisis of African Canadian leadership, rather than leading to a condition of malaise, is a stimulus for critical reflection and renewal of leadership. As Carl James and Christopher Williams note in this volume, the hegemonic White social order uses persistent and pervasive structural crises created by capitalism and White supremacy as a justification for warping the internally determined self-critique of crisis to its racist ends. We must, however, in contemporary and historical terms, treat White co-optation of the so-called crisis of Black leadership differently from its specificity in and to African Canadian communities. Deeply engrained in Black political culture post-slavery, from the time when African peoples became members of social classes rather than objects in property relations, the discourse has opened space for competing perspectives among the intelligentsia to articulate how, precisely, it will serve and meet the needs of the Black masses. Historically, these competing perspectives have run the gamut: capitalist separatism (e.g., Garveyism, Nation of Islam, Afrocentrism) versus integration (Du Bois), a Black workers' nation within a socialist state (Harry Haywood) versus Garvey's back-to-Africa (see Adi, 2013), accommodationism versus civil rights (Washington versus Du Bois), Democratic/Liberal versus Conservative/Republican, Black Panther Party versus SNCC, and a range of strategies in between. Nevertheless, the discourse of a crisis of Black leadership proves to be a metaphor for the personalities and organizations seeking to address the real needs of African peoples with respect to the capitalist state and Western liberal societies.

Crisis: A Recursive Leadership Stimulus

In 1910, the NAACP official news organ was named *The Crisis.* Its objective was to propagate the idea that the threat to "race relations" was "race prejudice," assuming the latter was an ever-present problem requiring strong civil rights protections. This claims-making, in part, drew on the anxieties of the light-skinned members of the Black intelligentsia class and petty bourgeoisie (à la Du Bois' "talented tenth"). *The Crisis* drew attention to conditions of exclusion that undermined the authority of the near-White bourgeois class to exercise leadership over and for the darkened masses. The theme of crisis would repeat itself in scholarly work that explored the political culture of African American leadership. E. Franklin Frazier's *Black Bourgeoisie* (1962), Harold Cruse's *Crisis of the Negro Intellectual* (1984), and Robert Allen's *Black Awakening in Capitalist America* (1969) are elaborations on the theme. The discourse of crisis in White supremacist societies, therefore, has served as both an analytic and a practical matter for the engagement of leadership in Black political culture. In the Americas, I suggest it should be understood as a metaphor of wider patterns and problems of Black life under capitalism and White supremacy and ways these articulate themselves in dynamics such as shadism, gender, and sexuality in Black political culture.

In its contemporary manifestation, the idea of crisis arises from the epochal transition of leaders minted in the fires of the 1960s revolutionary period to the present, where there is a sense that charismatic leaders are rare. Pushed too far, ironically, this internal critique becomes mimetic of the White supremacist ideology that Black people cannot lead and lack the constituent elements for the production of leaders. In Canada, the United Kingdom, and the United States, one is apparently challenged to name any person under fifty of the gravitas of a Jean Augustine, Dionne Brand, Rosemary Brown, Arnold Minors, Wilma Morrison, Rocky Jones, Dudley Laws, or Charles Roach, among others. At first glance, the supposed absence of such name-brand icons gives good reason to suspect Black leadership is in a state of disarray. This is clearly not the case, as demonstrated by the recognition of the contributions of Black women in Canada (http://www.100abcwomen.ca/). As also demonstrated brilliantly by the strategic acephalism and anarchism of Black Lives Matter, not only are hegemonic norms of gender and sexuality challenged by those at the forefront of the movement, there is studied avoidance of naming "leaders" who personify the movement, though this is changing.

Along with the apparent absence of high-profile charismatic personalities, though ironically the "leaders" of Black Lives Matter are fast becoming so, is that in recent years there have been notable national independence jubilees and commemorations of assassinated Black leaders: 2013 marked the fortieth anniversary of the assassination of Amilcar Cabral; 2015 marked anniversaries for the assassinations of Malcolm X (fiftieth), Patrice Lumumba (fifty-forth), and Walter Rodney (thirtieth); and 2018 marked the fiftieth anniversary of the assassination of Dr Martin Luther King. In addition to slain heroes, there are also significant organizational commemorations: 2014 marked the one hundredth anniversary of Marcus Garvey's founding of the Universal Negro Improvement Association and African Communities League (UNIA-ACL), and 2019 marks the 119th anniversary of the first Pan-African Conference in Paris. As well, the year 2019 marks the 114th anniversary of the W.E.B. Du Bois–led Talented Tenth meeting, the Niagara Movement Conference, that gave birth to the NAACP in 1909.

Be they of leaders cut down or the founding of organizations dedicated to transforming the consciousness and life conditions of African descendants in the diaspora, memoria are flashpoints that mark both the extent to which challenges have been met and whether leadership practices have risen to the occasion. With such commemorations behind us (and yet to come), we may be tempted to be nostalgic and so miss the dynamism in the present. But this might be beside the point as well as *the* point. That is to say, contemporary debates about Black leadership are not only recursive, they persist as a feature of Black political culture in the diaspora. Significantly, therefore, among the commemorations of 2015 was the 105th year of *The Crisis,* the official organ of the NAACP. It is not for nothing that the NAACP organ was so named, to encapsulate both the condition of African Americans and the state of its leadership. To this end, perception of a crisis or failure of leadership has been instrumental in providing the analytical insight that inspired Du Bois, Garvey, and Booker T. Washington. In fact, Du Bois was not only radicalized by the denial of civil and human rights to African Americans, but regarded the accommodationism, manual labour orientation, and strategic separatism of Booker T. Washington as a failure of leadership.

Garvey (1992), for his part, animated by the abuses and denial of African humanity, railed against the failure of the light-skinned middle classes of Jamaica and the United States, and he included Du Bois in this category, as self-serving, self-hating charlatans exploiting the misery of their darker-skinned brothers and sisters to the point of facilitating their genetic erasure, which he regarded as an inevitable outcome of White industrial capitalism. Garvey, who not only endorsed much of Washington's orientation, but also sought to imperialize it with a back-to-Africa movement, benefited heavily from Washington's Tuskegee machine in founding the UNIA. In fact, James Emmet Scott, former secretary to Washington, was essential to Garvey's organizational program in the United States (Cruse, 1984). Garvey (1992) contended that the "Sage of Tuskegee" passed on before developing a fully radicalized back-to-Africa movement (p. 56). Taken as a whole, this historical sketch illustrates how perceptions of crisis have ever been motivating forces for Black leadership and liberation.

A chronic problem of Black organizing is the basic fact that the structural conditions of capitalism that connect economic and political power severely constrain Black leadership's autonomy and ability to influence policy. As Sivanandan (1977) noted, Blackness on its own, independent of class consciousness among Black labourers and an allied intelligentsia who envision themselves *as* workers, inclusive of the differently abled, LGBTQ2S persons, and women, lacks sufficient gravity to change conditions for the masses of Black and other people: Blackness must always be twinned with class consciousness. Approvingly, Sivandan (1977) quotes Fanon's *Black Skin, White Masks*: "The Negro problem does not resolve into the problem of Negroes living among white men, but rather of Negroes exploited, enslaved, despised by a colonialist, capitalist society that is only accidentally white" (p. 341). The basic fact is that Black people who were once productive property do not own productive property in a meaningful sense, nor are they the hegemonically dominant force that controls the means of production. Their aspiration ought not to match or replace White people in this regard. The earth is full, especially with anger, hate, pollution, and above all nuclear weapons, so as Fanon (1968) warns: "We today can do everything, so long as we do not imitate Europe, so long as we are not obsessed by the desire to catch up with Europe" (p. 312). None of this precludes the necessity for maintaining radical opposition to anti-Blackness, even as cross-racial class solidarities are pursued (Deliovsky & Kitossa, 2013; Sexton, 2008).

These facts are of powerful consequence despite adepts of Black capitalism: Marcus Garvey, Elijah Mohammed, Louis Farrakhan, and Black Lives Matter (USA). The implication for political organizing is profound since the *capitalizing* of Black organizations, especially where their politics explicitly challenge capitalism, colonialism, and White supremacy, face serious financial constraints, not to mention attack and isolation by the state. Examples that fall into this category include the Black Panther Party (US), MOVE (US), the Black United Front (Canada), and the Black Action Defence Committee (Canada) (see Chris Williams, this volume). The problem, then, is as much theoretical as it is practical: how can African people in the diaspora create leadership strata and transformative organizations when they do not in themselves constitute a class in relation to the capitalist mode of production? As Gramsci (1971) argues:

> Every social group, coming into existence on the original terrain of an essential function in the world of economic production, creates together with itself, organically, one or more strata of intellectuals which give it homogeneity and awareness of its own function not only in the economic but also in the social and political fields. (p. 5)

As Willhelm (1979) argues, the closest any African intelligentsia of the diaspora came to representing this dynamic were precisely those leaders who enabled Black people to discover and recognize their class character *as* Black people: Martin Luther King Jr, Malcolm X, and the Black Panther Party – all of which were eliminated by the state because they represented ideological and political convergence in a way that embodied class awareness among Black people as dialogically working-class people: or least people who needed work and to control the means of production. Even Black Lives Matter in the United States, which started as a hashtag and slogan that sharply apprehends the concrete reality of the disposability of African-descended people – a fact that calls into doubt the Marxist normative moniker of "working class" I have used here (Allen, 1969; Willhelm, 1971) – has moved itself in the direction of converging the political reality of culture and identities with that of a dialectical materialism (see https://policy.m4bl.org/platform/) that transcends the particularism of Blackness without abandoning Blackness as a locus from which to articulate a demand for change to the human condition. There is evidence that BLM Toronto is undertaking a similar development, but in a more organic and practical way in its engagement with the Indigenous resistance Idle No More in particular and some anti-poverty African Canadian community organizations. It remains to be seen whether BLM Toronto will undertake a more radical shift to develop partnerships that struggle to develop a fully socialist agenda and substantive connection with African Canadian ghettoized communities. I nevertheless submit that BLM, as complicated and difficult as it is to make any generalizations about its origins, development, and present articulations, evidences some troubling modes and practices that belie its self-professed assertions as organically connected to Black communities and critical of neo-liberalism.

Recent historiographic work on African Canadian leadership has shown that debates over leadership styles and the methods that organizations (ought to) take in meeting the interests of African Canadians are filled with productive tension. Some organizations like the UNIA, as Marano (2010) shows, emerged in 1918 in response to the conflicting leadership objectives of Africadians versus a more politically strident, separatist, and skilled Caribbean immigrant community in Montreal and Toronto. Austin's *Fear of a Black Nation* (2013) shows that by the 1960s, the intra-racial conflict of the early twentieth century had given way to a generational divide. A young, radicalized, pan-African intelligentsia challenged both the state and traditional Black leadership. Austin shows, contrary to the full expression of radicalism, that gender conflicts, or more specifically patriarchalism, asserted itself in sixties Black radical leadership and organizational forms – a dimension that Marano (2010) shows was noticeably absent in organizations such as the early-twentieth-century UNIA.

The persistent cycle of the demise and rejuvenation of Black political culture in Canada is a theme picked up in Walker's (2014) assertion that leadership initiatives such as the National Black Coalition of Canada have waxed and waned over time. The nature of this ebb and flow is not simply due to the exhaustion and limitations of the African Canadian intelligentsia itself, though Walker certainly demonstrates that there were clear organizational missteps. These include too close an alignment with the state, formulating organizational objectives too directly consistent with liberalism, and building organizational coalitions that took intra-racial, cultural-national differences too seriously, to the exclusion of cross-racial solidarities. As a result, it is impossible to work out issues of authority and legitimacy that do not devolve into personal conflict. Missteps in political analysis, programs, and strategies of African Canadian leaders and organizations are not matters that can simply be overcome when confronted with the ideological machinery of capitalism and the in/security apparatus that thwarts African Canadian leadership when it raises concerns vital to the African Canadian community (see Williams, 2005).

Assessing African Canadian Leadership Projects: Toronto

The foregoing discussion of crisis as discursive and recursive in the critique, practice, renewal, and rejuvenation of Black leadership lays out the promise of a sociological enquiry into African Canadian leadership. To date, in Canada, the examination of African Canadian leadership is scattered throughout autobiographies, biographies, and historical scholarship. We lag behind sociological scholarship in the United States, though there it tends more towards polemic accounts of Black academics and the intelligentsia (Baker, 2008; West & Buschendorf, 2014) and descriptive laments of the African American elite (Benjamin, 2005; Cose, 1993). Measured against this body of work, our knowledge of the contemporary issue of Black Canadian leadership from sociological and other related social studies perspectives is lacking. That leadership ranges from the formally educated intelligentsia to clerical leaders and charismatic autodidacts to less obvious forms such as women's informal childcare organization.[4] Similar to the dearth of research that has been identified in the United Kingdom (Shepherd, 2011) and the United States (Spalter-Roth & Erskine, 2007), the near-total absence of such enquiry might be attributed to barriers that hinder the inclusion and movement of African Canadian graduate students in the "pipeline" to tenure-track positions (see Eisenkraft, 2010; Fleras, 2014; Henry & Tator, 2009).

Indeed, prominent African Canadian scholars such as Lorne Foster and Grace-Edward Galabuzi (cited in Fanfair, 2011) and Cecil Foster (2015) have remarked on the implications of the near-total absence of African Canadians in electoral politics and exclusion in the professional realm. Lorne Foster (2003a), moreover, without explicitly saying so, alerts us to alternative ways of looking at leadership when he comments that "the Black family is continuously undermined and pulverized by the hammer blows of a 'deindustrializing and downsizing' economy that quietly casts off Black men and excludes them from gainful employment." While he raises crucial issues such as the role of the state in attacking and undermining African Canadian leadership and the legitimacy of the community's claims (L. Foster, 2003b), and the fact that African Canadians are largely absent from the policy table (cited in Fanfair, 2011), this too narrowly construes what leadership looks like.

The Freedom Cipher Program

One study that examines leadership from the vantage point of its socialization among young African Canadians is Christopher Harris's (2011) doctoral thesis. Harris, a community organizer, union leader, and youth worker, explores the role of leftist "organic intellectuals" in trade unions, Black Canadian political culture, and the formation of the Black Action Defence Committee (BADC). His account is not merely a social history; it is also a political project complete with the Gramscian discourse of cultural "hegemony," "wars of movement and position," and Marxist-Leninist concepts such as "vanguard" and "zones of proximal development." This is a complicated and multifaceted work: it is part critical and self-corrective autoethnography and also candid assessment of the tensions in doing revolutionary conscientizing of youth in not-for-profit but government-funded programs. Along the way, it recognizes and elaborates the role that Black revolutionaries such as Norman Otis Richmond, Akua Benjamin, and Dudley Laws among others have played in the interests of Toronto's African Canadian community. Pertinent to the theme of crisis, Harris claims that in the wake of Black leaders' internecine conflicts and disorganization, these self-same Black revolutionaries "retreated from revolutionary politics to do reformist anti-racist organizing against police brutality" (p. 131). For Harris, the question is how to reinvigorate a moribund and emaciated radical leadership corps. Enter BADC's Freedom Cipher program that aimed to *create* an "organic intellectual vanguard" through "an anti-racism education initiative designed to lead the ideological development of a new generation of Black working-class organic intellectuals in the twenty-first century" (p. 132). The project was government funded to remediate "Black working-class and lumpen youth in gangs ... displaced by the new global economy" (p. 132). That the Freedom Cipher program would do so through job training and leadership development is a contradiction Harris identified as crucial to its mixed results. In short, whatever the objective of the funders, the explicit aim of the program was to produce a Black revolutionary vanguard.

Harris's rather severe criticism of anti-racism and disparagement of radical Black revolutionaries as "reformist" sets up stark categories that are more normative than analytical. With considerable irony, Harris chose to coordinate BADC's youth cultural and political education program because the organization was the lone extant "Black protest organization in Toronto with a rich tradition of mass struggle" (p. 132). With respect to the exacting intentions of the program and his efforts to "educate and train organic intellectuals" to become "communist organic intellectuals," Harris admits failing at his intended purpose. Instead, to his dissatisfaction, the program produced "social-democratic, anti-racist activists" (p. 132). Whether so invested a researcher as Harris, who was both participant and interpreter of the political results he sought to bring about – to create a Black revolutionary "vanguard" from among the lumpen proletariat – could adequately assess the effects of his efforts as a leader is a problem in its own terms. Harris fails to take the stance of the "informed stranger" (Shapin & Shaffer, 1985): an insider with the capacity to submit the aura of self-evidence surrounding his or her own worldview to scrutiny.

Harris's conception of leadership is, notably, unforgiving of diverse political styles. This makes perfect sense since pluralism is nothing but an endorsement of the status quo. To the extent revolutionary politics is only possible and practicable arising from revolutionary consciousness, Marx (1978) was explicit that radical consciousness must be wedded to a party, not simply an intellectual vanguard. To this extent, reforms as well as alliances with other socialists are strategic aims of a Communist Party: "The Communists fight for the attainment of immediate aims, for the enforcement of the momentary interests of the working class; but in the movement of the present, they also represent and take care of the future of that movement (p. 499). In the effort to create a revolutionary vanguard, the issue of a party that would prevent "deformation" and dilettantism is not considered. Harris, in addition, ignores that progressive possibilities towards Black radical leadership are possible even if not "revolutionary." The question, which I address below, is whether in taking up the crisis of Black leadership as real rather than metaphorical, Harris was in his practice led into making practical and theoretical errors. Practically, was it not naïve to assume that the capitalist state would fund a radical-left leadership program without the objective of containing and surveilling Harris and BADC and identifying young prospects who could be recruited into state service or decapitated? Given that "the reform of consciousness ... consists *only* in enabling the world to clarify its consciousness" (Marx & Engels, 1978, p. 15), is it possible to achieve a small qualitative change that would have major quantitative implications through a Pavlovian method?

As I see it, the problem with Harris's Leninist project to create a definite type of leader, who could only, according to Gramsci, arise from a class conscious of itself as a class in terms of its relation to capitalist production, is that it was based on mixed metaphors of past political projects. What I mean by this is simply that Gramscianism and Leninism are not entirely compatible political projects. In fact, if one reads Avineri's (1967) account, the mature Marx had little romanticism for his youthful exuberant self: a Marx who witnessed and participated in highly energetic but poorly thought through working-class actions against a strengthening bourgeois state. As Gramsci would be later, Marx was accused by some elements of the First International of savant gradualism (Avineri, 1967). For his part Marx astutely recognizes two related conditions for meaningful social transformation. The first is that the development of revolutionary class consciousness among workers will be as necessary as it will be painfully slow. And second, the development of workers' class consciousness will be tied to a committed socialist *party*, and an equally committed bourgeois intelligentsia who will defect to the side of workers (Marx & Engels, 1978). If one fails to distinguish the younger from the more mature Marx, one can certainly read him as having little patience for the slow conscientizing work inherent in Gramsci's statements about a "war of position." With hegemony in the centre of the frame, the effects of conscientizing versus vanguardism are expected to prove both certain and decisive – a working class aware of itself and that can act in its own self-interest: "We devote ourselves to a party which is precisely rather far from achieving power. Had the proletariat achieved power, it would have enacted not proletarian, but petty-bourgeois legislation" (Marx as quoted in Avineri, 1967, p. 271). In this regard Gramsci, though he admired Lenin, was a better Marxist than Lenin himself. Lenin's focus was the capturing of state power to bring about a socialist revolution. In a fluid context of multiple and competing social movements in a civil war, not to mention British, French, and US armed intervention, Lenin leapt over cultivating ideological transformation of the masses afterward. Gramsci, like Marx, resisted making a theoretical leap of faith that power outside of and imposed on the masses can constitute the making of revolutionary consciousness (Avineri, 1967; Karabel, 1976; Piccone, 1976). Weil (2010) asserts that in establishing a top-down revolutionary regime, Lenin, followed by Stalin, established a bureaucratic regime founded on charismatic authority and an absolutism that exceeded the control of even the tsars.

Loath in principle to extol the virtues of a revolutionary priest-class, Marx and Gramsci were suspicious of intellectuals who would lead and thus, in the process of solidifying their power, betray the masses (see Avineri, 1967). Lenin's "vanguard," a special category of priestly intellectuals of the workers' party, who instilled discipline and embodied the values of the "workers," manifested this betrayal (Gouldner, 1975/76). It is obvious that such a project and constitutive body – the vanguard – signify a disparagement and distrust of workers who Lenin believed were ignorant and had to be led for their own good by the party faithful (Gouldner, 1975/76, p. 16; Piccone, 1976, p. 500). Stalinism, then, rather than being a corruption of Lenin's political project, was its logical extension since the Leninist project centred on capturing state power rather than facilitating a society in which workers, through the elaboration of their organic intellectuals and the contribution of bourgeois intellectuals, developed their consciousness and capacities to the fullest in a way that enabled them to hold both intellectuals and governing representatives to account (Piconne, 1976).

The Gramscian project, as with that of the more mature Marx who realized the danger of counter-revolutionary tendency from within and against the vanguardist "workers'" state from without, eschewed "revolutionary practice without revolutionary theory" (Avineri, 1967). Thus, Gramsci's Marxism opposes the crass political project of creating a "vanguard" and, rather than having state power as its end goal, favours a careful and sensitive focus on developing the human person into a fully conscious being (Piccone, 1976). For Gramsci, the task for workers was to come to terms with their inherent intellectualism and discover their historic mission as a class – in partnership with intellectuals, not through their overlordship.

Vital to my critique of Harris's blueprint for the development of revolutionary lumpen and working Black youth vanguard in Canada is that we are presented with both an unremitting theoretical doctrine on what Black leadership ought to be and a leadership praxis that, though disciplined, is charismatic and zealous. Such work and praxis are open to the criticism Gouldner (1974, 1975/76, 1979, 1980) launched against the elitism, messianism, and totalitarianism implicit in the political theory of Marx and Engels. The irony Gouldner pointed out, applicable to Harris's endorsement of Lenin's statement that "the masses will never learn to conduct political struggle until we help to train leaders for this struggle, both from among the enlightened workers and from among the intellectuals" (as cited in Harris, 2011, p. 166), is that the anti-intellectualism, political arrogance, and bovine humanitarism of the

Marxist revolutionary is concealed by a theory that does not admit its author as an authoritarian political actor. The Cipher program is at best naïve, since revolution has never occurred from below in developed bourgeois states despite Marx's prediction, and at worst problematic in that in being state funded, it gives the capitalist state greater reach into the community by access to individuals it can readily turn into agents provocateur or can decapitate.

Whatever my criticisms of the practice and theory behind the Cipher project, Harris has offered probably the first sociological work on Black leadership in Canada, even if its scope is limited to the Black left and damns all other variants of leadership. Still, while Harris's work gestures towards a sociology of African Canadian leadership, the specific political orientation of his work takes for granted what needs to be explained. More general issues of authority, legitimacy, and power are sidelined, no doubt because in their sociological configuration they smack of pluralism and Weberianism, the stuff that most self-respecting Marxists will not permit into the hallowed precincts of their terms of reference.

"The Family Talk Meeting Group"

In 2009, the Jamaican Canadian Association in Toronto organized a celebration of Barack Obama's 2009 inauguration. That Black petite bourgeois triumphalism should take Obama's first (and second) term as evidence of its aspirations to reach the highest pinnacles in a capitalist society is, I suggest elsewhere, a critical self-delusion (Kitossa, 2011). A group of eight African Canadians of Caribbean heritage, four men and four women, comprised "The Family Talk Meeting Group" (hereafter The Group): Hamlin Grange, Gervan Fearon, Peter Sloly, Mitzie Hunter, Danielle Dowdy, Mark Beckles, Audrey Campbell, and Sharon Shelton met twice over 2012.

Reliant on a discourse of domesticity as its nomenclature indicates, this group is made up of the best among the African Canadian technocratic elite either serving or employed by various bureaucracies of the state and private sector. In a different age and time, these would be the "race uplift" men and women of the respectable classes who were the embodiment of civility and a sober, disciplined existence. Their vision is not one to be taken lightly. A mix of Garveyism, social democracy, and an understated small-*p* pan-Africanism, they managed to craft a policy document that could have had far-reaching effects, if only they had reached out to individuals/groups Carl James calls "change agents" and "cultural curators" and whom Christopher Williams describes as "radical" and "resistive" leaders. In short, the initiative failed on the ground where it succeeded: it neither appealed to nor collaborated with community-based mobilizers who could have stopped the trains running on time.

The Group produced a document whose grandiloquent title belies its rather restrictive geographical focus – *Towards a Vision for the Black Community* (Grange et al., 2012) – and which they hoped would confirm a "Renaissance" (p. 2) of Black leadership and community renewal. This is without question a daunting task. Usefully, the group compiled a broad range of contexualizing statistical and demographic data. With these the authors identified benchmarks for measuring *progress*: "definitive targets for progress, determine the underlying issues affecting these considerations, and develop strategies for closing the gap between the Black community's existing and desired situation" (p. 8). While I certainly recognize that the authors were well intentioned, and because my focus is not to critique the details of their initiative but to understand the political formation of the group more broadly, I will not critically comment in any substantive way on the various dimensions of the The Group's vision for the Black community. Yet to the extent that The Group is composed of upwardly mobile Black intelligentsia, well placed in the private and public sectors, the objectives of this initiative cannot but reflect (a) (pastoral) concern for those excluded by White supremacy in a liberal society and (b) a preoccupation with upward mobility as a sign of progress. More to the point, neo-liberalism is the dominant discursive framing through which "progress" is imagined.

The document is a sophisticated engagement with technical procedures for bureaucratic measurement of outcomes to reduce poverty and increase educational attainment, all without troubling capitalism. Since the document gives no hint of a critique of capitalism and neo-liberalism, it contains within itself considerable tolerance for contradiction. In a sense the report, as all are, is a compromise document that situates an agenda for the Black community within the parameters of liberal ideas of upward mobility. It balances, moreover, "over-policing" with the dictates of the capitalist in/security state, makes appeals to individual and family responsibility, and signals repeatedly to the neo-liberal code of "prosperity." In effect, reform is an end in itself, in part because the aspirations of the elites are conflated with a universal norm.

Despite my criticism, there are clear merits to this initiative. It is obvious that even at a most basic level, relief from want and mechanisms to create fairness to compete within the liberal frame have their merits. One hopes, thus, that the good intentions and innovation in establishing reformist "key performance indicators" for lifting African Canadians out of poverty, among other things, will succeed but would extend further to a general politics of working-class solidarity. There is a sense, however, that while The Group has taken gender parity seriously, the seeds of crisis are elsewhere evident. My principal concern here has to do with issues of authority and credibility regarding participatory democracy and pan-Africanism in which any African Canadian group takes on what Harold Garfinkel (1956) calls the "supra-tribal voice." While to its credit The Group recognizes that "'culture eats strategy all the time,' meaning that the underlying culture must be aligned to supporting the strategy being implemented" (Grange et al., 2012, p. 9), it failed to operationalize this observation. There is an absence of input from large African groups such as Ethiopians, Somalis, Nigerians, Ghanians, and francophone Africans whose interests and needs may not accord with those of the Afro-Caribbeans and Africadians represented by The Group.

In addition, the exclusion of various working-class and grass-roots leaders undermines the authority of leadership to call upon the masses to mobilize for the politics of protest. In fairness, one can hardly expect a group consisting of a police administrator (Sloly), a future provincial minister of education (Hunter), and Canada's first and still only Black university president (Fearon) to underwrite civil disobedience. The failure to take a pan-Africanist perspective that is both symbolic and real presents The Group with a problem of credibility and legitimacy. It is, therefore, deeply ironic that The Group should recognize Black diversity in its fullness and cultural complexity but fail to represent it. This non-representativeness goes a long way to account for the limited impact The Group has had, despite its good intentions and a policy document brimming with potential to, at the very least, remediate the worsening impact of neo-liberalism on African Canadian communities.

Black Lives Matter

When history is in the making it can only be assessed, however imperfectly, from hindsight interpretations, which are themselves always political in nature. There is nothing original here in claiming that BLM is but one of the most recent examples of just how rhetorical, though productive, is the discourse of a "crisis" of Black leadership. As with other African Canadian leadership initiatives in Canadian history, it mirrors the diasporic and transnational nature of African Canadian communities. Yet there are regional valences to BLM in Canada that are instructive of how various regions of the country engage Black radical organizing. Two things in this regard, I think, are notable. First, despite the obvious conditions of brutality, murderousness, and racial profiling of African Canadians by the police (Maynard, 2017), BLM is non-existent in Montreal and has had only marginal impact in Nova Scotia. What explains this? Montreal has its own very long tradition of pre-existing modes of Black radical confrontation and resistance that have a resonance all their own given the distinctiveness of Quebec in Canada's political life. As to Nova Scotia, and Halifax principally, it too has its own resolute, home-grown radical tradition with deep roots in the Black church, secular organizations such as the Black United Front, and a sort of Black nationalist culture that has no parallel elsewhere in Canada: in Nova Scotia's (understandable) parochialism, outsiders are looked upon askance.

Instructively, then, BLM's presence is most pronounced in Toronto, Canada's largest city with probably the deepest cultural connections to African American culture and the urban United States.[5] Think here of the Raptors surviving and thriving whereas the Vancouver Grizzlies did not; alongside athletes such as Jamal Magliore, Dwight Wiggins, and Cory Joseph, think of Drake, The Weekend, and other Greater Toronto–Hamilton area artists whose way was paved by earlier small-scale successes in the US urban music scene (e.g., Maestro Fresh Wes, Dream Warriors, Michie Me). Arguably also, Toronto is Canada's Black media "mecca," with the nation's only Black-owned radio station and the largest circulating community-based newspaper. Toronto and area also frequently host African American speakers, from Cornel West to, as noted by Carl James in his comments on "corrective agents," the reverend Eugene Rivers. And probably more than anywhere else in Canada, Toronto has the highest proportion of US expatriate African American academics, who are very much tapped into the city's Black intellectual network and political culture. Consider here that two of Canada's early and pre-eminent African Canadian historical sociologists were US expatriates: Wilson Head and Daniel Hill Sr.

Relevant to these cultural ties to the urban United States, Toronto has another dubious distinction that may well account for the emergence of BLM there: a very high rate of police brutality, racial profiling, and extrajudicial killings of African Canadians, men in particular. Even prior to BLM, Toronto was a high traffic zone of political interaction with radical groups in the United States such as the Black Panther Party. In this volume, Carl James draws attention to the fact that the 1992 BADC anti-police brutality protest march (and Yonge Street rebellion) – which ultimately led to the Stephen Lewis Report and the Commission on Systemic Racism, which in turn lead to the Special Investigations Unit and the Ontario Independent Review Directorate – was in solidarity with protests in the United States against police brutality. Vitally, the BADC not only marched to protest police brutality in Canada, it did so in solidarity with Rodney King and countless African men and women beaten and murdered by a racist police apparatus. Seen from this vantage point, BLM Toronto is less an outgrowth of US Black movement franchising than it is a new iteration of prior modes of radical activism and cross-border solidarities. It is, nonetheless, qualitatively different from its predecessors.

BLM is not easily summarized, marked as it is by contradictions that are implicit in its founding. It began its mercurial rise in the United States from the ashes of the Occupy Wall Street movement, which paid little attention to the interests of African Americans. But there is also a longstanding tradition of Black insurrection that informed the emergence of BLM. Beyond the germinating spark, it was an instance, as has *always* been the case in the past, of quotidian police violence that fanned the flames: George Zimmerman's murder of Trayvon Martin and Darren Wilson's murder of Mike Brown. The eruption of pent-up frustration at open and wanton murder by White supremacist civilians and police was summed up by the hashtag created by Alicia Garza, Patrisse Cullors, and Opal Tometi: #Blacklivesmatter. As Paul Street (2017)[6] notes, these are Black lesbian and professional women whose prior and current existence is as central figures in the non-profit Black industrial complex. While Street's critique is not itself without problems, bordering on the trite position that race is an epiphenomena of class, it opens up questions about the "radical" pedigree of BLM and the complex ways that it becomes the dominant framing for Black resistance movements. Whatever the case, the signal contribution of BLM in the United States has been to capture the narrative with an indicting phrase used to shame public officials and put the police on their back foot.

But does a hashtag make a movement? What constitutes a movement cannot seriously be addressed here, but certainly movements don't name themselves. Whereas prior to the emergence of BLM, localized grass-roots organizations challenged and protested without any media attention, this changed when BLM became the public face of the "new" civil rights movement. Its central distinction is that it explicitly centres queer politics mixed with an odd variant of Black capitalism and racial tribalism. The official BLM organization teamed up with OneUnited Bank to launch, in February 2017, a Black Lives Matter credit card (Edwards, 2017). Leaders of BLM insist there is no role for White people in the Black liberation struggle (Rigby & Ziyad, 2016), so cross-race working-class solidarity of the sort advocated by Fred Hampton is beyond consideration (Farber, 1996). Most recently, Garza and company have been showered with one hundred million dollars from the Ford Foundation to distribute to various approved community-based organizations, some of which are directed by BLM organization leaders. The "new" war on poverty is distinguished this time around by the fact that it is organized by philanthro-capitalists such as George Soros and the Ford Foundation, the very beneficiaries of the capitalism responsible for the crushing poverty of African Americans and so many others.[7] The Ford Foundation, with a dubious and deep history tied to the CIA and militarism (Black, 2016), in helping a consortium of fourteen organizations under the Movement for Black Lives (M4BL; https://policy.m4bl.org/platform/) umbrella distribute the hundred million dollars, offers charitably that

> as we continue to engage with and learn from the movement, we're eager to deepen and expand this community of social justice funders. We want to nurture bold experiments and help the movement build the solid infrastructure that will enable it to flourish. As we do so, we believe it's essential that our funding not dictate or distort the work underway. (Kelly-Green & Yasui, 2016)

Cutting through the subterfuge, however, Ford Foundation president Darren Walker, an African American, ex-banking executive at UBS, seeking "impact investing" (D. Walker, 2015) for foundation dollars, asks "What kind of Capitalism do we want to have in America?" (cited in Black, 2016). BLM would have to answer: the kind that, as in the 1960s and into the late 1970s, created a bureaucratic coterie of the Black universitariate to oversee and monitor the lives of the lumpen like those in Ferguson. Whether and how these realities will jibe with the aspirations of M4BL remains to be seen.

As mentioned above, in Canada Black Lives Matter is most prominent in Toronto, where it is principally a development of students and professors at the University of Toronto, Ryerson University, and York University. Its most familiar representatives include professors Rinaldo Walcott (University of Toronto) and Idil Abidi (Ryerson), and, at the time of founding, University of Toronto students Sandy Hudson, Pascale Diverlus, and Yusra Khogali. At this point BLM Toronto appears not to have gone the corporate route as has its US counterpart, yet there are parallels and substantive differences. The most fundamental difference is that BLM Toronto is far removed from corporate sponsorship. As well, whereas its US counterpart does not have a strong anticolonial foundation, BLM Toronto is strongly allied with an assortment of Indigenous Canadians. And while BLM in the United States has developed a coherent organizational structure, BLM Toronto is highly decentralized. This no doubt has benefits: it recognizes diversity and difference without sacrificing collective goals and objectives. The risk, of course, is that acephalous organizing relies on spontaneity and is highly susceptible to dissolution. According to BLM Toronto member Akio Maroon,

BLM Toronto works in coalitions with "concerned black community members, activists, students, youth and professionals. [BLM] is working in solidarity with the people of Ferguson and racialized working-class communities in Toronto to actively take on fighting against all forms of police violence and racial profiling" (Maroon, 2014).

The extent of BLM Toronto's engagement and reach into poor and working-class African Canadian communities, however, may not be as clear-cut as Maroon suggests. The group's preoccupation with lecturing poor and working-class communities (especially straight Black men), whose conception of gender is fairly traditional and who struggle with the normalization of homosexuality and trans identities as central to their reality of criminalization, mass incarceration, poverty, and substandard housing, casts doubt on Maroon's claim of BLM as a coalition partner with organizations that channel the needs of excluded neighbourhoods. While BLM Toronto claims to represent and be representative of African Canadians in Toronto, its 2018 award of funding from Groundswell Community Justice Fund suggests its connection with and immersion in the eponymous "Black community" is asymmetrical in terms of the focal point of identity (i.e., sexuality) and praxis. No doubt, at the heart of the asymmetry is that the vast majority of African Canadian organizations, both religious and secular, are staunch in their sexual conservativism. Yet that BLM Toronto's funding should not be grounded in the Black community, and that the "Freedom School"[8] centres not on the essentials of academic competence and self-esteem building, but is a project for the explicit politicization of children, is but the other extreme of the Cipher Project referred to above:

> BLM Freedom School is a three-week program for children aged four to ten years old, to respond to a lack of humanizing, self-affirming, queer-positive educational opportunities for Black children in the GTA. Freedom school provides an alternative setting for parents who do not feel that our children are being taught self-love, nor a passion for justice and liberation through formal education. The program is designed to teach children about Black Canadian and diasporic history, to engage children in political resistance to anti-Black racism and state violence through a trans-feminist lens, and to offer children an entry point into the #BlackLivesMatter movement. (Groundswell Community Justice Fund, 2018)

However well intentioned this grand vision, the initiative raises empirical and normative questions: Can its objectives be accomplished in three weeks? Is the curriculum based on best practices and research in child psychology for African Canadian children? Which Black parents in Toronto are likely to send their children to the initiative? Is this an effective way to politically educate prepubescent children? And would not a contemporary rendition of educational and social programs like the government-funded Black Education Project or the Harriet Tubman Centre of the 1970s and 1980s provide a more inclusive experience?[9] To be sure, the polemicist octane on which BLM Toronto appears to thrive, worn as a badge of honour in the culturo-politico trench warfare of the "call-out age," may certainly put White politicians on notice. This tendency may also be off-putting to most Black parents, whose major concern is for community-based programs that help their children develop the competencies and skills to navigate the neo-liberal regime and deep-seated anti-Blackness within social relations.

The group's penchant, moreover, for opening meetings with admonitions about who may speak, when, and how, constitutes a form of discursive policing rather than an invitation to civility. To the extent, however, that BLM Toronto is tapped into excluded Black communities, its high-stakes confrontational tactics – be they camping out at police headquarters in the freezing cold, demanding a meeting with the mayor, picketing the premier's residence, opposing carding and racial profiling or "school resource officers," shutting down the intersection at Dundas and Bloor to protest the prospective deportation of a post-partum Jamaican woman, or protesting the Toronto PRIDE organizers' decision to allow the police to march in the parade – pushed issues into public view that other groups have been challenging without media attention.

One challenge confronting BLM Toronto is the uneasy balance between acephalous resistance to state necropolitics and the need to develop a rational bureaucratic structure, as it must, to outline strategy and action plans guided by collectivistic, transgenerational principles and trans-sexualities and, above all, to deliver tangible change in people's lives. But this is a lot to ask of "young organizers working with minimal resources ... [who] receive ... some goods and services donated by progressive grassroots organizations ... [but] largely ... [have] had to empty ... [their] own pockets and take time away from [their] studies, day jobs and families" (Maroon, 2014).

We have seen this before: some of the protestors from the 1989 ROM protest were not only assaulted by police, but the lives of many were permanently shattered. Over the coming years it will be crucial that the established Black technical intelligentsia, whether forming the National Congress of Black Canadians (NCBC, http://ncbccanada.com/about-us/) or the Federation of Black Canadians (FBC, http://www.fbcfcn.ca/) (Government of Canada, 2019a), take serious stock of abilities and competencies of those involved in BLM Toronto. This, however, may be wishful thinking that a substantive dialogue between self-proclaimed radicals, centrists, and conservatives can ever occur. It is notable that the NCBC registered as a non-profit by Fitzroy Gordon (Government of Canada, 2019b), owner of G98.7FM, whose CRTC licence came about as the result of an intervention by then Progressive Conservative prime minister Stephen Harper. Clearly, with the federal Conservatives out of power, the NCBC initiative faces an uphill battle in terms of ruling party and corporate support. The smart money, apparently, is on the side of the FBC. Led by Justice Donald McLeod[10] with the aid of Michaëlle Jean and her foundation, this initiative appears to have tap roots in the Liberal Party[11] of Canada, from which it is lobbying for funds to support African Canadian communities. But more than this, in a move to develop Black capitalism Canadian-style, TD Bank and Deloitte, among others, are major backers of the FBC. Executives from both corporations spoke eloquently at the FBC's December 2017 Summit, which they funded, about diversity being good for the bottom line. As Deloitte general counsel Kenneth Fredeen noted, the profit motive is at the heart of corporate dalliance with diversity:

> Because what we saw in our report in the research we did was that businesses that are more inclusive make more money ... everybody benefits by it ... that's proven now ... We believe that it is critically important that if businesses in Canada are to be successful in the diverse communities we live in we must be inclusive, it's a business imperative. (Federation of Black Canadians, 2017)

Interestingly, on the second day of the three-day summit, a different sort of leadership that challenged "respectability politics" asserted itself. Desmond Cole and El Jones openly and roundly challenged the Liberal government's minister of immigration, Ahmed Hussen, for not making a public commitment to halt the deportation of a Somali youth refugee, Abdoul Abdi (Federation of Black Canadians, 2017). In effect, what was at play in this exchange were the different and opposing ways and styles in which African Canadian leadership productively articulates itself: direct confrontation of Black elites by younger leader versus an institutionalized form of Black leadership that moves within the orbit of corporate and state bureaucracy.

That the corporation or political party that "pays the piper calls the tune" is an unavoidable reality.[12] But quite aside from the trickle-downism of neo-liberalism and Black capitalism, it is worth mentioning that there is another, less well known pan-national organization called the National African Canadian Association, founded in 2007 by Michael A. Forrest (http://naca.ca/old-site/aboutnaca.php). The question of why there are multiple pan-national leadership initiatives, all vying to do the exact same thing, requires a rigorous analysis of interests, ties to government and industry, and level of concrete engagement with multiple African Canadian stakeholders with deep ties to grass-roots communities. That being said, given that race-based philanthro-capitalism in Canada is at best reformist, it is an open question to what degree these competing national leadership initiatives driven by the concerns of Black capitalism Canadian-style and a genuine commitment to electoral politics complemented by independent grass-roots socialist organizing are even taken into consideration. An important question is whether these initiatives are not also indissoluably linked to the opportunity for Black elites to undertake discipline and management of Black communities on behalf of a state sensitive to the optics of White control of Black people.[13]

To the extent that BLM Toronto is significantly populated by university students (who are also female, queer, and trans), there are questions about their class consciousness, class solidarity, and discipline. The challenge for would-be student revolutionary leaders has always been to develop a habitus that "organically" binds them to the working class and lumpen proletariat, who either lack the means to produce their own intellectuals or lose them to upward social mobility (Gramsci, 1992). Whatever the class background of the BLM membership, that it moves in the orbit of the bourgeois universitariate does not inevitably undermine its capacity to build effective solidarity with poor and working-class elements in the African Canadian community, but it is not at all clear that BLM Toronto has the sort of appeal in ghetto communities that it claims. Part of the issue here is its confrontational style, particularly around sexuality. There have been significant public disputes over the way that gender and sexuality are taken up by BLM.

Both in the United States and Canada, BLM has taken an approach to critiquing heterosexual Black men that has an undertone of competitiveness and misandry. More complex readings of heterosexual Black masculinity, such as that presented by Curry (2017) and Mutua (2006), are not considered. The call is for straight Black men to "decentre" themselves and stop "taking up space" – a curious demand, since much of BLM's mobilizing is built around the destruction of Black men by the necropolitical state. Yet at a public forum in 2015, BLM Toronto cofounder Pascale Diverlus issued this blunt claim:

> In considering that the first chapter of Black Lives Matter was created by three queer black women, that's what the organizing looks like in these spaces. It is the queer black folks, the black trans people, and the black women who are taking the lead in fighting for our rights. Because while we have the most to gain, we also have the most to lose. It is important that the

people more affected by the issues are the ones guiding towards a solution. (cited in Goldsbie, 2015)[14]

If a fundamental part of organizational leadership involves working to change consciousness, claims that "straight Black men are the White people of the Black community" (Anyabwele, 2017) are a strange platform for building awareness and solidarity across African Canadians of different genders and sexualities. And straight Black men are not the only targets for those at the forefront of BLM. Stances on Whiteness that are strictly racialist, of the sort by Frances Cress Welsing or any other, are irrational and hardly constitute a method for compassionate outreach to prospective cross-racial working-class solidarity (see, e.g., Di Fiore, 2017). By stating this point, I can hardly defend myself against the charge from BLM and its supporters that I am appeasing White fragility. This after all is the risk when critiquing the moral superiority of those whose octane is moral outrage.

Finally, one of the limits of BLM is also one of its greatest strengths: its decentralization. The problem is, who speaks in its name and under what terms? As a contributor to organizing the 2017 Black Canadian Studies Association in Brandon, Manitoba, I had the distinct displeasure of seeing how one BLM Toronto member engaged the "politics of confrontation." The member took to Twitter after the conference to voice frustration about the administration of the conference, most notably the high-profile role that some White administrators from Brandon University played; their feeling of being disrespected by a White university administrative assistant; and their experience of being racially profiled by Canadian customs officers at the Winnipeg airport. Conference organizers and Brandon University, led by Dr Gervan Fearon, Canada's first and only African Canadian university president (as of July 2017 at Brock University), were roundly castigated on Twitter in a lengthy and rambling diatribe. Judgment and discipline, the very traits Christopher Harris sought to inculcate in the youth who participated in the Cipher program, are attributes that seem sorely missing in BLM Toronto. That there appears little understanding of and engagement with the careful study of social movements and revolutionaries could well undermine much of BLM Toronto's ability to build lasting connections to a variety of elements within the African Canadian community. Fortunately, the future holds multiple possibilities for correction.

Conclusion

Given the impoverished state of sociological research on African Canadian leadership in Canada, this essay is only a sketch of its possibility. For sure, more researchers must undertake enquiry that is contemporary and is in full conversation with auto/biographical and historical scholarship. There is a vast domain of work that can provide perspectives on traditional and non-traditional forms of leadership. Some of this work can focus on organizations of all sorts and sizes to assist in their effectiveness and capacity to engage in a political community that elaborates prospects and praxis towards a socialist agenda. To my mind, neither Black radicalism nor pluralistic leadership can, in isolation and without a theoretical grasp of racial capitalism, achieve Black liberation outside of a broader dynamic of non-authoritarian socialism. Black liberation as an end in itself is a dead end, unless it is genuinely mobilized as one manifestation of collective human liberation from environmental degradation, war, want, and unkindness (Klein & Tometi, 2017). Research to this end might focus on faith leaders and what role they play in contemporary African Canadian political culture: are they forces of conservativism or liberation theology (see Paul Banahene Adjei in this volume)? What of the role of the in/security apparatus setting loose agents provocateur, spies, and disrupters within African Canadian organizations? Here, as shown by Austin (2013) and Williams (2005), hindsight provides the best evidence for the disruptive potentialities of the capitalist White supremacist state against which effective radical African Canadian leadership cannot be ignorant.

There is a whole domain of life where leadership articulates itself: in the effects on women and children of male leaders; in the practices of mothers; in the clear evidence of unsung adult heroes who lead heritage programs and run community centre programs; and in youth leaders in the ghettos, high schools, colleges, and universities who strive to play constructive roles (though in different and sometimes problematic ways). All of these elements of African Canadian political culture, and more, await exploration and reflection back to the community for it to engage in ongoing corrective assessments of practice and consciousness raising. In any event, the worst-case scenario for a crisis of African Canadian leadership is that the neo-liberal tendency to blame the victims will seize the day – ushering in a crisis that is not just metaphorical but will engulf the whole of society. Given that Africans of the diaspora have never ceased to be historical agents, revolutionary theory and revolutionary practice are the promises to be fulfilled in practice, theory, and research.

Acknowledgments

I thank the following persons for having read and commented on various iterations of this essay: Kevin Gosine, Anita Jack-Davies, Carl James, Tierney Kobryn-Dietrich, Christopher J. Williams, and the three anonymous

University of Toronto Press reviewers. This essay is inspired by the determination of my children, Adisa and Jelani, to make their own way, and by all African Canadian youth who, guided by history, struggle to make their way.

NOTES

1 My deployment of Gramsci and Marx is prefaced by the term "critical" given that my concern centres on the dual dynamic of transformation of self and society. One may ask why Gramsci (1891–1937), for all his insight about soviets and worker control being achieved by cultural transformation, had nothing of substance to say about colonialism and racism, despite 1896 and 1935 Italian invasions of Ethiopia. My response is that the fact that Gramsci's political intentions and practice were Eurocentric does not void the theoretical and analytical incisiveness of his political theory.

2 Du Bois, who spent two years in Germany on a study grant (1892–4), was a *cause célèbre* who brought back with him to the United States, but also adapted, the formal style of the German elite. To his dying day, he retained a deep and enduring affection for Willhemine Germany. While there and even after his return to the United States, Du Bois maintained an abiding, mutually informing, intellectual friendship with Max Weber (Barkin, 2005; Chandler, 2007). An erudite and internationalist scholarly such as Du Bois would shudder at the stultifying expression "dead White men."

3 While I cannot and do not undertake in this essay a disquisition on the obfuscatory ramifications of reified structuralist taxonomies, it is important, nevertheless, to flag this as a matter of concern. Following Marxian sociologists such as William Chambliss (1993) and Margaret Coulson and Carol Riddell (1980), I insist there are no such things as "structures," "systems," and the like. There are only particular patterns of relationships bound by authority (command and consent) and power. Only in this way can it be recognized that *people* are doing things in their interests and against others and, at all times, are ethically and morally responsible actors.

4 Interestingly, the claim I make about the poverty of research into African Canadian leadership was similarly voiced for African American politics in 1973 by Hanes Walton, Vernon Gray, and Leslie McLemore. They note that from the standpoint of political science, the books (anthologies and monographs) on African American leadership numbered no more than a dozen – since Reconstruction!

5 While White opinion-makers in Canada disparage the emergence of Black Lives Matter organizing in Toronto and in Alberta as but an unwarranted mimesis of African American politics, this only propagates the myth of

Canada as a haven of racial "tolerance." I take a different tack in my critique of BLM, which is less a "movement" than a franchise in every sense of the word, in terms of the hashtag founders granting their imprimatur to pop-ups in Canada, the United Kingdom, and the United States. BLM founders on numerous occasions have asserted proprietary claim over the BLM moniker, to the point of formally issuing a credit card through an African American bank (Edwards, 2017), and have been awarded one hundred million dollars from Ford, Soros, and others (Black, 2016). Given BLM's dalliance with the Democratic Party and with neo-liberal modes of capitalizing itself, the "revolution" will not be televised, but it is eminently fundable. The founders of the hashtag basically certify the use of the name "BLM" by exercising proprietary control, thus making it a franchise. There is a reaction in some parts of the United States against the corporatism of BLM, not least in Ferguson, but the instance of Cincinnati is instructive, where BLM has been called out for its champagne revolutionary oeuvre (Mass Action for Black Liberation, 2018).

6 I concur with the basic premise of Paul Street's (2017) and Gabriel Black's (2016) criticism that the creators of BLM USA operate from the vantage point of Black and philanthro-capitalism, and that, as a result, they are at odds with the organic resistance of many African American communities, such as Ferguson. I cannot agree, however, with their implicit Marxist determinism, which assumes race is an "identitarian" epiphenomenon to the objective reality of class. This is in fact a view inconsistent with Marx's contention that while class is objectively real within the context of capitalist social relations, class consciousness as an *identity* is a part of the "superstructure"that is socially constructed and must be both cultivated and negotiated (Marx & Engels, 1978; see also Hall et al., 1979; Mills, 2003; Robinson, 2000).

7 Black Lives Matter is not alone among African American social justice organizations in receiving funding from private donors and philanthro-capitalists. The NAACP, the National Urban League, the National Committee on Black Civic Participation, the National Council of LaRza, the National Conference of Black State Legislators, and the Congressional Black Caucus Foundation are regular recipients of funding from the Bill and Melinda Gates Foundation (Dixon, 2011). The Gates Foundation, Dixon notes, is a major shareholder in Monsanto, a rapacious organization responsible for forcing African (and Indian farmers) to use terminator seeds and toxic herbicides (Dixon, 2011). More recently, telecom giants who will profit from the Trump administration's killing of net neutrality have heavily financed both the NAACP and the National Urban League. So-called civil rights organizations are not alone: Transparency International, Sierra Club, American Diabetes Association, and American Heart Association, among others, are funded

by corporations and lobby groups that ought to be their natural enemies (Hedges, 2017).

8 This is an unacknowledged riff on the civil rights Freedom Schools of the 1960s, which had a comprehensive program for social transformation (see Zinn Education Project, n.d.).

9 I speak from experience. I was among the hundreds of Caribbean children who were expertly and holistically educated about Black art, culture, politics, and scholastics through the inclusive Black Education Project and the Harriet Tubman Centre in the 1970s and 1980s. My life's success is, in part, attributable to my community-based teachers and mentors who created an environment that was far more accepting and progressive in every way than what is currently proposed by BLM Toronto.

10 On 22 August 2018, the *Toronto Star* reported that Justice McLeod is formally under investigation by the Ontario Judicial Council for breach of ethics relating to his advocacy with the Federation of Black Canadians (Gallant, 2018). In a 27 February 2018 op-ed, Desmond Cole (2018) opined that Justice McLeod's advocacy may well be exposing him to censure:

> The FBC is led by chairperson Donald McLeod, a sitting judge in the Ontario Court of Justice. Whatever duty McLeod feels to our community, he also has a professional duty to the court. The Ontario Principles of Judicial Office state judges "must avoid any conflict of interest, or the appearance of any conflict of interest," in the performance of their duties; that a judge "must not participate in any partisan political activity"; that an Ontario judge "should not lend the prestige of their office to fundraising activities."

The day before Cole's op-ed, Sandy Hudson, co-founder of BLM Toronto, asserted that McLeod is not only in a compromising position but may be in violation of his judicial oath: "I have a hard time understanding how someone whose job it is to remain neutral can be the head of an advocacy organization" (Mussa, 2018). It bears noting that in October 2017 Hudson herself settled a fractious suit with the University of Toronto Student Union in which she was accused of defrauding the student union of $277,726.40, and she in turn accused the student union of anti-Black racism. The terms of the settlement are unknown, but "as part of the settlement, Hudson ... acknowledged that racism was not a motivation for the lawsuit" (*The Varsity* editorial board, 2017). Hudson's expedient retraction of the charge of anti-Black racism hardly stands as a ringing endorsement of her credibility, versus Justice McLeod's assertion that his advocacy work with the FBC was carefully articulated so as not to conflict with his role as a sitting judge.

Even prior to Hudson's and Cole's public musings, Associate Chief Justice Faith M. Finnestad challenged Justice McLeod to reconsider his public activism by and urged him to consult the Judicial Ethics Committee. The Ontario Judicial Council (2018) concluded "that Justice McLeod's conduct was incompatible with judicial office, but that it was not so seriously contrary to the impartiality, integrity and independence of the judiciary that it rose to the level of undermining the public's confidence in his ability to perform the duties of office or the public's confidence in the judiciary generally. Accordingly, we dismiss the complaint" (p. 41). Whatever else may be positive results of the qualified exoneration of Justice McLeod, it at the very least demonstrates that there are vibrant and vital contending forces of African Canadian leadership vying to advance the cause and interests of African Canadians.

11 Demonstrating the merits of growing influence and collaboration with the Liberal Party, on 30 January 2018, not much long after the FBC's December 2017 Summit in Toronto, Prime Minister Justin Trudeau not only invited FBC representatives, led by Judge Donald McLeod, to his office but also issued a statement endorsing the UN Decade of the African, fully four years after the Harper government ignored the UN declaration. What the future holds for the corporate and political collaboration with the FBC depends on whether the Liberals remain in power long enough for the concretization of a politically powerful Black middle class who take the lead role in representing the interests of African Canadians of modest means.

12 There is considerable writing and discussion about the implications of the African American community's Pavlovian response to the Democratic Party versus its incapacity to support non-corporatist and progressive third parties. Canada has neither scholarship nor substantive discussion on how African Canadians engage with political parties, short of the awareness of a general tendency to vote Liberal, if at all. Interestingly, Barrington Walker demonstrates that the National Black Coalition of Canada (NBCC) of the 1970s foundered on the rocks of ideological and personality conflicts in addition to its ties to Pierre Trudeau's fickle Liberal Party. It is revealing that in spite of the fanfare and high hopes being raised by these competing leadership initiatives, there is a wilful ahistoricism: a sort of brave new world of explorers blazing new trails unaware that they are in fact walking in well-worn grooves. Without careful study of Paula McClain's (1979) and Barrington Walker's (2014) work on the NBCC, and a recognition that the Coalition of African Canadian Community Organizations also held a similarly high-profile 2006 summit, we will learn nothing about corrective action and strategic realignment.

13 I am grateful to Afua Cooper for working out these particular ideas with me.

14 The unremitting criticism is that because, heretofore, most leaders recognized as charismatic have been Black men, the "balance" must need to be corrected with a pendulum swing the other way. While the depredations of such men must be criticized, what is being erased is that (a) they were not all of that ilk and (b) many of them were assassinated or, like Dudley Laws and Arnold Minors, were ruined financially for taking principled stances in pursuit of fundamental justice.

REFERENCES

Adi, H. (2013). *Pan-Africanism and communism: The Communist International, Africa and the diaspora, 1919–1939.* Trenton: Africa World Press.

Allen, R. (1969). *Black awakening in capitalist America: An analytic history.* Garden City: Doubleday.

Anyabwele, T.V. (2017). My response to "Straight black men are the white people of black people." *Huffington Post.* Retrieved from http://www.huffingtonpost.com/entry/black-girl-responds-to-straight-black-men-are-the_us_59c630ede4b0f2df5e83ae88

Austin, D. (2013). *Fear of a black nation: Race, sex, and security in sixties Montreal.* Toronto: Between the Lines.

Avineri, S. (1967). Marx and the intellectuals. *Journal of the History of Ideas, 28*(2), 269–78. https://doi.org/10.2307/2708422

Baker, H. (2008). *Betrayal: How black intellectuals have abandoned the ideals of the civil rights era.* New York: Columbia University Press.

Barkin, K. (2005). W.E.B. Du Bois' love affair with Imperial Germany. *German Studies Review, 28*(2): 285–302. http://www.jstor.org.proxy.library.brocku.ca/stable/30038150

Becker, H. 1967. Whose side are we on? *Social Problems, 14*(3): 239–47. https://doi.org/10.2307/799147

Benjamin, L. (2005). *The black elite: Still facing the color line in the twenty-first century.* New York: Rowman and Littlefield.

Black, G. (2016). Billionaires back Black Lives Matter. Retrieved from https://www.wsws.org/en/articles/2016/10/11/pers-o11.html

Blumer, H. (1971). Social problems as collective behavior. *Social Problems, 18*(3), 298–306. doi:10.2307/799797

Chambliss, W. (1993). On lawmaking. In W. Chambliss & M. Zatz (Eds.), *Making law: The state, the law, and structural contradictions* (pp. 3–35). Bloomington: Indiana University Press.

Chandler, N.D. (2007). The possible form of an interlocution: W.E.B. Du Bois and Max Weber in correspondence, 1904–1905. *New Centennial Review,* 7(1): 213–72. https://doi.org/10.1353/ncr.2007.0026

Cole, D. (2018, 28 February). Black advocates must put cause ahead of career. *Toronto Star*. Retrieved from https://www.thestar.com/opinion/contributors/2018/02/28/black-advocates-must-put-cause-ahead-of-career.html

Cose, E. (1993). *The rage of a privileged class: Why are middle-class blacks angry? Why should America care?* New York: HarperCollins.

Coulson, M., and Riddell, C. (1980). *Approaching sociology*. London: Routledge & Kegan Paul.

Crichlow, W. (2014). Carceral geography & the prisonization of Toronto black youth. *International Journal for Crime, Justice and Social Democracy, 3*(3), 113–31. https://doi.org/10.5204/ijcjsd.v3i3.120

Cruse, H. (1984). *Crisis of the Negro intellectual*. New York: Morrow.

Curry, T.J. (2017). *The man-not: Race, class, genre, and the dilemmas of black manhood*. Philadelphia: Temple University Press.

Deliovsky, K., & Kitossa, T. (2013). Beyond black and white: When going beyond may take us out of bounds. *Journal of Black Studies, 44*(2): 158–81. https://doi.org/10.1177/0021934712471533

Di Fiore, J. (2017). Black Lives Matter Toronto co-founder needs to resign. *Huffington Post*. Retrieved from http://www.huffingtonpost.ca/james-di-fiore/black-lives-matter-toronto-yusra-khogali_b_14635896.html

Dixon, B.A. 2011. Corporate funding of Urban League, NAACP & civil rights orgs has turned into corporate leadership. Retrieved from https://www.blackagendareport.com/corporate-funding-urban-league-naacp-civil-rights-orgs-has-turned-corporate-leadership

Edwards, B. (2017). OneUnited Bank, Black Lives Matter team up to organize Black America's spending power. *The Root*. Retrieved from https://www.theroot.com/oneunited-bank-black-lives-matter-team-up-to-organize-1792104750

Eisenkraft, H. (2010, 12 October). Racism in the academy. Retrieved from https://www.universityaffairs.ca/features/feature-article/racism-in-the-academy/

Fanfair, R. (2011, 23 February). Black leaders relegated to fringe of society – Prof. *Share*. Retrieved from http://archive.sharenews.com/local-news/2011/02/23/Black-leaders-relegated-fringe-society-prof

Fanon, F. (1968). *Wretched of the earth*. New York: Grove.

Federation of Black Canadians. (2017, 5 December). National Black Canadians Summit. Video 2. Retrieved from https://www.torontopubliclibrary.ca/programs-and-classes/featured/national-black-canadians-summit.jsp (See at 52:15–59:06)

Farber, S. (1996). Social decay and class in African-American struggle: The Black Panthers reconsidered. *against the current*, no. 64 (September-October). Retrieved from https://www.solidarity-us.org/site/node/2339

Fleras, A. (2014). *Racisms in a multicultural Canada: Paradox, politics, and resistance*. Waterloo: Laurier University Press.

Foster, C. (2015, 9 November). Canada's blacks: Still waiting for their moment of "real change." *Globe and Mail.* Retrieved from https://beta.theglobeandmail.com/globe-debate/canadas-blacks-still-waiting-for-their-moment-of-real-change/article27175310/

Foster, L. (2003a). Black leadership in the 21st century. *Share, 26*(61). Retrieved from https://www.yorku.ca/lfoster/documents/Foster%20Scanned%20Articles/Black%20Leadership%20in%20the%2021st%20Century_Foster_Share_26.06.03.pdf

Foster, L. (2003b). Social control of our black leaders. *Share, 26*(23).

Gallant, J. (2018, 22 August). Brampton judge faces discipline hearing over involvement in advocacy group. *Toronto Star.* Retrieved from https://www.thestar.com/news/gta/2018/08/22/brampton-judge-faces-discipline-hearing-over-involvement-in-advocacy-group.html

Garfinkel, Harold. (1956). Conditions of successful degradation ceremonies. *American Journal of Sociology, 61*(5), 420–4. Retrieved from https://gu.se/infoglueCalendar/digitalAssets/1776149608_BifogadFil_Conditions%20of%20a%20successful%20..%281%29.pdf

Garvey, M. (1992). *Philosophy and opinions of Marcus Garvey.* New York: Athenium.

Goldsbie, J. (2015). Police carding: Racist, anti-black, and useless. *Now Magazine.* Retrieved from https://nowtoronto.com/news/police-carding-racist-anti-black-and-useless/

Gouldner, A. (1974). Marxism and social theory. *Theory and Society, 1*(1), 17–35. https://doi.org/10.1007/BF00208221

Gouldner, A. (1975/76). Prologue to a theory of revolutionary intellectuals. *Telos, 26,* 3–36. https://doi.org/10.3817/1275026003

Gouldner, A. (1979). *The future of intellectuals and the rise of the new class.* New York: Continuum.

Gouldner, A. (1980). *The two Marxisms: Contradictions and anomalies in the development of theory.* New York: Seabury.

Government of Canada. (2019a). Federal corporation information – 1051454-3. Retrieved from https://www.ic.gc.ca/app/scr/cc/CorporationsCanada/fdrlCrpDtls.html?corpId=10514543&V_TOKEN=1548633604915&crpNm=Federation%20of%20Black%20Canadians&crpNmbr=&bsNmbr=

Government of Canada. (2019b). Federal Corporation Information – 786304-7. https://www.ic.gc.ca/app/scr/cc/CorporationsCanada/fdrlCrpDtls.html?corpId=7863047

Gramsci, A. (1992). *Selections from the prison notebooks of Antonio Gramsci.* (Q. Hoare & G. Nowell Smith, Ed. & Trans.). New York: International.

Grange, H., Gearon, G., Sloly, P., Hunter, M., Dowdy, D., Beckles, M., & Shelton, S. (2012). *Towards a vision for the black community.* Retrieved from http://jcaontario.org/wp-content/uploads/2010/05/TOWARDS-A-VISION-FOR-THE-BLACK-COMMUNITY-October-2013.pdf

Gray, K.A. (2008). *Waiting for lightning to strike: The fundamentals of Black politics.* Petrolia: CounterPunch/AK Press.

Groundswell Community Justice Fund. (2018). 2018 grant recipients. Retrieved from https://groundswellfund.ca/2018-grant-recipients/

Hall, S., Critcher, C., Jefferson, T., Clarke, J., & Roberts, B. (1979). *Policing the crisis: Mugging, the state, and law and order.* London: Macmillan.

Hanauer, N. (2016). Ultra-rich man's letter: "To my fellow filthy rich Americans: The pitchforks are coming." Retrieved from http://www.topinfopost.com/2014/06/30/ultra-rich-mans-letter-to-my-fellow-filthy-rich-americans-the-pitchforks-are-coming

Harris, C. (2011). *The development of working-class organic intellectuals in the Canadian black left tradition: Historical roots and contemporary expressions, future directions.* (Doctoral dissertation). Ontario Institute for Studies in Education, University of Toronto, Toronto.

Harvey, D. (2005). *A brief history of neoliberalism.* Oxford: Oxford University Press.

Hedges, C. (2017). On contact: Corporate crime with Russell Mokhiber [Interview with Chris Hedges]. Retrieved from https://www.youtube.com/watch?v=HJURmeW2M04

Henry, F., & Tator, C. (2009). *Racism in the Canadian university: Demanding social justice, inclusion, and equity.* Toronto: University of Toronto Press.

Hum, D., & Simpson, W. (2007). Revisiting equity and labour: Immigration, gender, minority status, and income differentials in Canada. In S.P. Heir & B. Singh Bolaria (Eds.), *Race and racism in 21st-century Canada: Continuity, complexity, and change* (pp. 89–109). Peterborough: Broadview.

James, C., Bernard, W.T., Este, D., Benjamin, A., Lloyd, B., & Turner, T. (2010). *Race & well-being: The lives, hopes, and activism of African Canadians.* Halifax: Fernwood.

Karabel, J. (1976). Revolutionary contradictions: Antonio Gramsci and the problem of intellectuals. *Politics & Society, 6*(2), 123–72. https://doi.org/10.1177/003232927600600201

Kelly-Green, B., & Yasui, L. (2016). Why black lives matter to philanthropy. Retrieved from http://www.fordfoundation.org/ideas/equals-change-blog/posts/why-black-lives-matter-to-philanthropy/

Kitossa, T. (2011). Obama deception?: Empire, "postracism" and white supremacy in the campaign and election of Barack Obama. *Critical Race Inquiry, 1*(2), 1–51. Retrieved from https://doi.org/10.24908/jcri.v1i2.3553

Klein, N. (2007). *The shock doctrine: The rise of disaster capitalism.* New York: Metropolitan Books/Henry Holt.

Klein, N., & Tometi, O. 2017. Forget Coates vs. West – We all have a duty to confront the full reach of U.S. empire. Retrieved from https://theintercept.com/2017/12/21/cornel-west-ta-nehisi-coates-feud/

Lawson, E. (2012). Single mothers, absentee fathers, and gun violence in Toronto: A contextual interpretation. *Women's Studies, 41*(7), 805–28. https://doi.org/10.1080/00497878.2012.707903

Mass Action for Black Liberation. (2018, 28 March). Why Black Lives Matter: Cincinnati is changing its name. Retrieved from http://blacklivescincy.com/home/2018/03/28/why-black-lives-matter-cincinnati-is-changing-its-name/

Marano, C. (2010). "Rising strongly and rapidly": The Universal Negro Improvement Association in Canada, 1919–1940. *Canadian Historical Review, 91*(2), 233–59. https://doi.org/10.1353/can.0.0309

Maroon, A. (2014). We protest in solidarity with Ferguson because we are the same. *Now Magazine.* Retrieved from https://nowtoronto.com/news/we-protest-in-solidarity-with-ferguson-because-we-a/

Marx, K., & Engels, F. (1978). *The Marx-Engels Reader* (2nd ed.) (R. Tucker, Ed.). New York: W.W. Norton.

Maynard, R. (2017). *Policing black lives: State violence in Canada from slavery to the present.* Halifax: Fernwood.

McClain, P. (1979). *Alienation and resistance: The political behavior of Afro-Canadians.* Palo Alto: R. & E. Research Associates.

Miliband, R. (1987). *The state in capitalist society: The analysis of the Western system of power.* New York: Quartet.

Mills, C.W. (1956). *The power elite.* New York: Oxford University Press.

Mills, C.W. (2003). *From class to race: Essays in white marxism and black radicalism.* New York: Rowman and Littlefield.

Moore, B. (1978). *Injustice: The social bases of obedience and revolt.* White Plains: Pantheon.

Moore, C. (1974). Were Marx and Engels white racists? The prolet-Aryan outlook of Marxism. *Berkeley Journal of Sociology, 19,* 125–56.

Mussa, I. (2018, 27 February). Activists question Federation of Black Canadians' leadership, ties to Liberals. CBC News. Retrieved from https://www.cbc.ca/news/politics/black-canadians-scrutiny-1.4549853

Mutua, A.P. (Ed.). (2006). *Progressive black masculinities.* New York: Routledge.

Ontario Judicial Council. (2018). Ontario Judicial Council in the matter of a complaint respecting The Honourable Justice Donald McLeod: A Judge of the Ontario Court of Justice in the Central West region. Retrieved from www.ontariocourts.ca/ocj/files/ojc/decisions/2018-mcleod-EN.docx

Piccone, P. (1976). Gramsci's Marxism: Beyond Lenin and Togliatti. *Theory and Society, 3*(4), 485–512. https://doi.org/10.1007/BF00161294

Piven, F.F. (1976). The social structuring of political protest. *Politics and Society, 6*(3): 297–326. https://doi.org/10.1177/003232927600600302

Powell, C. (2012, 9 September). The crisis of black leadership: As old hands like Al Sharpton show their age, who will take up the reins? Retrieved from http://www.mic.com/articles/13515/the-crisis-of-black-leadership-as-old-hands-like-al-sharpton-show-their-age-who-will-take-up-the-reins

Rigby, K., Jr, & Ziyad, H. (2016). White people have no place in black liberation. Retrieved from http://racebaitr.com/2016/03/31/white-people-no-place-Black-liberation/#

Robinson, C.J. (2000). *Black Marxism: The making of the black radical tradition.* Chapel Hill: University of North Carolina Press.

Sexton, J. (2008). *Anti-blackness and the critique of multiracialism.* Minneapolis: University of Minnesota Press.

Shaikh, A. (1978). An introduction to the history of crisis theories. In Crisis Reader Editorial Collective (Ed.), *US capitalism in crisis* (pp. 219–41). New York: URPE. Retrieved from https://communisme.nu/wp-content/uploads/2014/04/History-of-crisis-theories.pdf

Shapin, S., & Schaffer, S. (1985). *Leviathan and the air-pump: Hobbes, Boyle, and the experimental life.* Princeton: Princeton University Press.

Shepherd, J. (2011, 27 May). 14,000 British professors – but only 50 are black. *Guardian.* Retrieved from http://www.theguardian.com/education/2011/may/27/only-50-black-british-professors

Sherman, E. (2015). 7 billionaires worried about income inequality. *Fortune.* Retrieved from http://fortune.com/2015/11/28/billionaires-income-inequality/

Sivanandan, A. (1977). The liberation of the black intellectual. *Race Class, 18*(4), 329–43. https://doi.org/10.1177/030639687701800401

Smith, M., & Butovsky, J. (2012). Profitability and the roots of the global crisis: Marx's "law of the tendency of the rate of profit to fall" and the U.S. economy, 1950–2007. *Historical Materialism, 20*(4), pp. 39–74. https://doi.org/10.1163/1569206X-12341273

Spalter-Roth, R., & Erskine, W. (2007). Race and ethnicity in the sociology pipeline. Retrieved from http://www.asanet.org/images/research/docs/pdf/Race%20and%20Ethnicity%20in%20Soc%20Pipeline.pdf

Street, P. (2017, 29 October). What would the Black Panthers think of Black Lives Matter? *Truth Dig.* Retrieved from https://www.truthdig.com/articles/black-panthers-think-black-lives-matter/

Torczyner, J.L. (2010). Demographic challenges facing the black community of Montreal in the 21st century. Retrieved from http://www.mcgill.ca/mchrat/files/mchrat/ExecutiveSummaryBlackDemograhic2010.pdf

Tsetung, M. (1961). *Selected works of Mao Tsetung* (Vol. 1). Peking: Foreign Languages Press.

The Varsity editorial board. (2017, 22 October). A quarter-million-dollar thought experiment. *The Varsity.* Retrieved from https://thevarsity.ca/2017/10/22/a-quarter-million-dollar-thought-experiment/

Walker, B. (2014). The National Black Coalition of Canada, "race" and social equality in the age of multiculturalism. *CLR James Journal*, 20(1/2), pp. 159–77. https://doi.org/10.5840/clrjames201493020

Walker, D. (2015). *Darren Walker on the Ford Foundation's new strategy* [Video file]. *Bloomberg News.* Retrieved from https://www.bloomberg.com/news/videos/2015-11-09/darren-walker-on-the-ford-foundation-s-new-strategy

Walton, H., Gray, V., & McLemore, L. (1973). Black politics: The view from the readers. *American Politics Research, 1*(1), 139–44. https://doi.org/10.1177/1532673X7300100107

Weil, S. (2010). *Oppression and liberty* [electronic reproduction; e-book]. London: Taylor and Francis.

West, C., & Buschendorf, C. (2014). *Black prophetic fire.* Boston: Beacon.

Willhelm, S. (1971). *Who needs the Negro?* Garden City: Doubleday.

Willhelm, S. (1979). Martin Luther King, Jr and the black experience in America. *Journal of Black Studies, 10*(1): 3–19. https://doi.org/10.1177/002193477901000101

Williams, C.J. (2005). To unnerve and detect: Policing black activists in Toronto. In L.A. Visano (Ed.), *Law and criminal justice: A critical inquiry* (pp. 95–113). Toronto: Athenian Policy Forum.

Winsa, P. (2015, 21 March). Searching for Toronto's next generation of black leaders. *Toronto Star.* Retrieved from http://www.thestar.com/news/insight/2015/03/21/searching-for-torontos-next-generation-of-black-leaders.html

Zinn Education Project. (n.d.) Retrieved from https://www.zinnedproject.org/materials/freedom-summer-1964/

4 African Canadian Leadership: Pan-Africanism, Transnationality, and Community Organizing

AMOABA GOODEN

Black Canadian consciousness is shaped by a global understanding of the multiple systems of oppression that frame the lives of people of African descent.[1] It follows, then, that Canadian Black organizing and leadership is fostered by this global and political understanding. This consciousness is manifested in organizations such as the Canadian Negro Women's Association, the National Black Coalition of Canada, the Negro Citizenship Committee, Black Lives Matter Toronto, and the Black Liberation Collective. "Nurtured by dreams of liberation," the mere existence of these and other historic and contemporary organizations provides evidence that white supremacy, sexism, racism, displacement, heterosexism, colonialism, postcolonialism, and other forms of oppression provide a "common ground" for Black Canadian collective action that attempts to address "linguistic, cultural, class, and, to a lesser extent, gender divisions" (Walker, 2014, p. 163).

Evidence suggests that specific aspects of Black Canadian leadership that gave rise to the above organizations were/are built, shaped, and fostered by and in *community organizing and collective action.* Although the idea of collective struggle is contested, the value of this exploration is expressed in this volume by the work of scholars such as George Dei and Philip S.S. Howard. Dei, for example, posits that "in traditional Indigenous and African communities, leadership is less about individual attributes and skills than shared community expectations and roles" (p. 354), while Howard positions "Black/African Canadian leadership as the work done in directing initiatives that seek the ... collective African Canadian good" (p. 213). As Fairchild (cited in Rummel, 1970) indicated, it is the synergy that comes from social forces (collective action) that drives or motivates change. In this work, the value of collective leadership and action is not held at the expense of difference and an overvaluing of sameness, but instead recognizes that interlocking systems of imperialism, capitalism, and racialized patriarchy have created unique realities for people of African descent that make it possible for them to converge around a common struggle, primarily against anti-Black racism, through the process of "transversal politics" (Hill Collins, 2002, p. 245). According to Hill Collins:

> Within the assumptions of transversalism, participants bring with them a "rooting" in their own particular group histories, but at the same time realize that in order to engage in dialogue across multiple markers of difference, they must "shift" from their own centers. (2002, p. 245)

Struggles often assume differences and commonalities that are comparative in focus (Mohanty, 2003). Within Black Canadian organizing there were differences, tensions, and conflicts, some largely influenced by religious, gendered, and class ideology. As such, the organizations were not monolithic – they were full of contradictions that emerged as Black Canadians attempted to address specificities and commonalities in the Black struggle for social change. Yet these tensions were essential in helping some organizations identify, articulate, and act on the structural basis of oppression. These frictions facilitated new ways of thinking and organizing, and ultimately they either ended organizations or moved them forwards. In moving forwards, organizations such as the National Congress of Black Women and Black Lives Matter Toronto, as demonstrated below, rejected old ways of thinking and organizing. Influenced by the recursive relational process that undergirds the practice of African diaspora, pan-Africanism, and transnationality, these new organizations demanded a rethinking of Canadian organizing and leadership.

Utilizing examples from Black Canada's organizing and organizations, this chapter explores how diaspora, pan-Africanism, and transnationalism provide a lens by which to increase our understanding of African Canadian agency and political organizing and, therefore, leadership. The concepts are uniquely understood in this chapter as frameworks for analysis, as tools used by some Black Canadians to bear witness to their experiences and as a lens by which they view and articulate the larger global sociopolitical experiences of Blacks. Additionally, this chapter acknowledges conflict and cooperation as one value of Black Canadian leadership by highlighting aspects of that leadership that are a product of community organizing and organization.

Diaspora, Pan-Africanism, and Transnationalism

This chapter utilizes the concepts of diaspora, pan-Africanism, and transnationalism, because they give us a particular framework by which to view and analyse the histories, experiences, and actions of African

Canadians. These concepts complicate the varied experiences of Black Canada and write Black Canadian organizing and leadership onto the world stage in very nuanced ways. At their intersection, they offer up an understanding of the relationship that African Canadians have with each other, with the Canadian nation state, and with people of African descent in other places. In other words, traversed, the concepts (1) give us a frame by which to conceptualize how African Canadians "act or envision themselves as a group even though there are many indications that they are different" (Weinstein, n.d.); (2) complicate how African Canadians understand themselves in relation to the Canadian nation; (3) expand our understanding of the relationships that Blacks have with the global Black community/communities; and (4) provide insight into the ways history, material consequences. and beliefs bind people and their sense of identity together in very concrete ways. Finally, these intersected concepts disrupt the salience of the United States as a model of the universal subject of Black culture and offer the Black Canadian experience as a lesson that can be utilized by the African diaspora. Below, the concepts are elaborated on and the intersections between and among them are explained and briefly analysed.

Diaspora

The concept of "diaspora" is used in this chapter as both an analytical category and a term of self-description (Butler, 2001; Patterson & Kelly, 2000; Trotz, 2006). Diasporas are complex social and cultural communities, created out of geographies of unbelonging/belonging, dispersal, struggle, and exchange, at different moments and varying distances from a "homeland" (Butler, 2001; Harris, 1993; Patterson & Kelly, 2000; Zeleza, 2008). Therefore, much of the scholarship on the African diaspora focuses on the dispersal experiences of people of African descent and the (re)construction of communities across national boundaries (Patterson & Kelly, 2000). Yet scholars also "emphasize the development of a diasporic identity and its social, cultural, and poltical manifestations" (Patterson & Kelly, 2000, p. 13; see also Butler, 2001; Mann, 2010). Scholars such as Patterson and Kelly (2000) focus in particular on the "construction and reproduction of diasporic identities ... to the creation of a diasporan consciousness" (p. 14). Indeed, data from Black Canadian organizing suggests that such consciousness was evident in Ontario in the mid-1900s within organizations like the Canadian Negro Women's Association (CANEWA). CANEWA, which established the National Congress of Black Women in the early 1970s, linked Black Canadian and Caribbean Canadian women together – not to hide cultural and political differences, but to articulate the historical linkages between groups while acknowledging the complexities and contradictions of being Black and female in Canada.

Diasporas are also understood as both a process and a condition (Patterson & Kelly, 2000). As the above examples demonstrate, institutions and individuals within diasporas are forward looking in that they are continuously in the process of evolving. According to Harris (1993), the "African diaspora assumes the character of a dynamic, continuous, and complex phenomenon stretching across time, geography, class and gender" (pp. 3–4), thus disrupting the idea that the African diaspora is a unipolar link to Africa. As in Clarke and Thomas's (2006) work, this emphasizes diaspora as circular and influenced between and within spaces. At the centre of our understanding of diaspora is the concept of dispersal and historical change – it extends outwards, because in its process and conceptualization, it is not limited only to issues related to slavery and imperialism. It existed, in fact, prior to the transatlantic and Indian Ocean trade, and that relationship must be considered in its utilization. However, we must think about the African diaspora as relating not only to Africa, but as a recursive relational process that references multiple places in addition to Africa. For example, most African Canadians are, to use Hall's (1995) term, "twice diasporized" because they have lived in multiple places before settling in Canada. They are impacted by these lived social, cultural, economic, and political experiences.

Pan-Africanism

Pan-Africanism is a complex political movement that links people of Africa with people of African descent in the diaspora (Esedebe, 1994; Lemelle, 1992). With the larger goal of liberation for all people of African descent, on the continent and around the world, pan-Africanists understand the simultaneity of oppression and the fight for gender, economic, political, and human rights (Boyce Davies, 2014; Lemelle, 1992). Additionally, according to Drake (1993), pan-Africanists

> see their struggles as not only involving Black people everywhere, but also as being organically related to Third World struggles generally and to the worldwide struggle of proletariat and peasantry regardless of races. They visualize the struggle of Black people as organically related to, not subsumed under, the other struggles. (p. 454)

Like the concept of diaspora, pan-Africanism is a "product of the West" (Patterson & Kelly, 2000), referencing multiple places in addition to the African continent, and is recursive and relational. Both diaspora and pan-Africanism are tied to similar moments in time, and they constantly overlap and interweave; that is, they are framed by the same historical conjecture and are rooted in similar histories – the politics of patriarchy, slavery, capitalism, and colonialism. But while diaspora is a unit of analysis, a process (Butler, 2001; Patterson & Kelly, 2000), and is forward looking, pan-Africanism is a political position that looks forwards and backwards and assumes an interconnected past and future for African people in the diaspora and on the African continent (Butler, 2001; Boyce Davies, 2014). Moreover, pan-Africanism, unlike diaspora, is very much the product of the "internatal developments in Africa" (Patterson & Kelly, 2000, p. 13). Although the 1900 Pan-African Congress is often referred to as the first organized pan-African meeting, an earlier meeting of the movement can be traced back to Chicago in 1893 with the Chicago Congress on Africa. At that gathering, attendees included delegates from Africa, the Caribbean, and North America (Esedebe, 1994).

Pan-African articulation is evident in early and contemporary Black Canadian organizations. Such organizations often include members who have lived in various places in the African world (Austin, 2013; Harris, 2014; Onstad, 2017). Early organizations such as the Universal Negro Improvement Association (1920) and the Black Liberation Front of Canada (1969) believed that the liberation of Black Canadians was directly tied to remedying their socio-economic marginalization. Both organizations worked to bring attention to the political economy of racism and to the role Canada played in oppressing Blacks in the Caribbean or South Africa, for example (Harris, 2014). Contemporary organizations such as Black Lives Matter Toronto (BLM-TO), whose direct political action will be explored in more detail below, are deeply reflective of an intersectional approach to contemporary organizing that centres the multiplicity of oppressions that Black Canadians face. Formed as a direct response to the killing of Black bodies in Canada and the United States (Flare Staff, 2017), BLM-TO, like its counterpart in the United States, is guided by principles such as collective value, diversity, transgender affirmation, and intergenerational networking.

Such organizations often work with First Nations organizers and other marginalized groups to demand justice for the crisis Black and Brown populations are facing and to discuss and find solutions. In 2016, for example, BLM-TO joined with some First Nations organizations to occupy offices of Indigenous and Northern Affairs Canada in Toronto (*Democracy Now*, 2016). The 2006 Common Ground Gathering of Nova Scotia's Black and First Nations communities is another example of the widening of the pan-African concentric circle. Two days were spent exploring the challenges both communities face with respect to education, poverty, and high incarceration rates, to name a few (Public Safety Canada, 2009). The articulation of pan-African thought by the above organizations demonstrates that the idea of wide concentric circles supports alliances with non-African partners and allows for connection between the struggles of African Canadians, First Nations peoples, and other identities and centres of struggle not limited to women, labour, and sexualities.

Transnationalism

Transnationalism is understood here as a phenomenon whereby people develop or maintain relationships that link together multiple geographical places, not limited to their ancestral home (place of birth) and/or an adopted home (Basch, Glick Schiller, & Szanton Blanc, 2008; Trotz, 2006). With transnationalism, social life, social movement, economies, associations, and culture "cross ..., transcend ... and sometimes transform ... borders and boundaries in many different ways" (Khagram & Levitt, 2008, p. 1). Cross-border relationships and actions are created and sustained by historical, political, socio-economic, cultural, and other factors (Basch, Glick Schiller, & Szanton Blanc, 2008; Bayes & Gonzalez, 2011; Khagram & Levitt, 2008; Trotz, 2006). Ontologically then, transnationalism evokes diaspora and pan-Africanism, because as a framework it holds at its centre "persons displaced via global economic processes, who must constantly reconcile themselves to existing emotionally and physically in different spaces ... even as it identifies longing, homelands and a myth of origin" (Boyce Davies, 2014, p. 90).

One of the easiest ways to understand transnationalism is to think of the contemporary exchange of capital to support families, friends, or communities in the country of origin. Between 2015 and 2016, for example, remittance to the Caribbean increased by 7.8 per cent (Orozco, 2017). Monetary remittance, however, is only one of many ways in which Blacks who migrate to Canada are able to establish and maintain ties that transcend the Canadian border (Burman, 2002; Crawford, 2004; Plaza, 2007; Simmons, Plaza, & Piché, 2005). There are also multidirectional flows of information that speak to the fluid ways in which Black Canadians challenge notions of geographic space and social identity; there are regular visits back home and to Black family and friends in other parts of the world, and there is continued contact through the telephone, internet, and letters (Burman, 2002; Chamberlain, 1998; Plaza, 2007; Simmons, Plaza, & Piché, 2005; Burman, 2002; Vetoes, 2001). Constructs regarding political approach, gender roles, societal expectations, family ties, and cultural retentions are "traded" in these interactions (Basch, Glick Schiller, & Szanton Blanc, 2008; Gastaldo, Gooden & Massiquoi,

2004; Crawford, 2004; Chamberlain, 1998; Crawford, 2004; Gastaldo, Gooden, & Massiquoi, 2004; Trotz, 2006). In the act of financially, physically, or electronically crossing and recrossing the Canadian border, exchanging ideas with those "at home" or elsewhere, Black immigrants from Africa and the Caribbean are increasingly producing a cultural, political, economic, and social world that extends the borders of the Canadian nation state outward, in essence transforming it (Basch, Glick Schiller, & Szanton Blanc, 2008; Burman, 2002).

For instance, Toronto's Caribana, which stands as a transnational and diasporic space, has economically and culturally transformed Ontario – culturally, the festival links Canada to Africa and the Caribbean in particular and provides multiple educational and social opportunities for cultural exchange. In addition, the Canadian government, along with businesses such as hotels, restaurants, bus companies, and other modes of public transport, benefit from the revenue generated by the millions of individuals who descend on Toronto every summer to participate in the weekend festivities (Mihevc, 2017; "Scotiabank Caribana," 2010; Trotman, 2005). Unfortunately, very little of this revenue directly benefits the Black community.

In addition to Caribana, as stated above, the trading of social and political remittances impacts the Canadian nation, as immigrants bring with them a particular cultural, democratic, and networking knowledge. Here we should think of cultural, social, and political remittances as capital that flows in both directions. The forming of albeit small Black enclaves with grocery stores in various provinces offering food, music, and news from back "home" then reproduces various cultures in Canada (Trotman, 2005; Vertovec, 1999); the advocacy for fair practice laws and anti-discrimination policies fought for by early and contemporary Black Canadian leaders such as the Reverend Jennie Johnson (discussed below), Rosemary Brown, and Bromley Armstrong was influenced to some degree by their place of birth but also by Black civil rights activism from around the globe (see note 5); the activism of Black women, which insisted that a gender legacy of extended family networks providing support to women in the Caribbean and Africa be revitalized in Toronto, was influenced by the oppressive nature of the Canadian nation, but also by political and cultural ideas from their place of birth and by other civil rights advocacy from around the globe. This extended family network stood in stark contrast to a nation state where the traditional family was nuclear and where the African cultural tradition of an extended family network is not accepted. Community organizations such as Black Coalition for AIDS Prevention (Black Cap), Tropicana Community Services, and Women's Health in Women's Hands were called upon to play the role of the extended family in providing support, especially where single-parent families were headed by women (Fanfair, 1995b). Formed in high-density Black areas during the 1980s, these organizations offered a range of services that broadened to include employment counselling, job training, and health concerns.[2] Funded by all levels of government, these organizations had the notable feature, in contrast to mainstream service organizations, that both clients and workers were Black or persons of colour. In this way, Blacks established themselves in the sociocultural, economic, and political fabric of Toronto, thus contributing to reshaping the nation state.

These historical and contemporary actions speak to the dynamics of sociocultural, economic, and political processes of local and cross-border participation, connection, membership, identification, and belonging (Amelina, Nergiz, & Faist, 2012; Bayes & Gonzalez, 2011). They also reveal how organizing and leadership are performed and conceptualized within (and outside of) cross-border connections and how community organizing and leadership are, of course, simultaneously impacted by the political climate of the Canadian nation state.

Intersecting Diaspora, Pan-Africanism, and Transnationalism

Given the above, there is much to learn by intersecting diaspora, pan-Africanism, and transnationalism. At the point of their juncture, they provide a lens by which to grasp the discursive and material ways in which African Canadians, who feel (un)belonging to the nation, organize and connect with other Blacks both nationally and internationally. That is, Black Canadians develop and foster relationships with Blacks in other places and use the entire Black Atlantic network as a knowledge base for defining themselves and understanding the world (Hall, 1993; Stephen, 2015). In addition, they make political connections with Indigenous peoples and other people of colour. The contemporary and historical relationships that Black Canadians have with Blacks beyond the Canadian border are important in understanding Black Canadian leadership. Here diaspora, pan-Africanism, and transnationalism are emphasized as relational mechanisms and tools by which to view and think about Blackness and, therefore, Black Canadian leadership. How Black Canadians have used their understanding of diaspora, pan-Africanism, and transnationalism is an excellent illustration of how different geographical spaces can further practices and an understanding of diasporic identity. That is, in these places where they struggle to belong, Black Canadians are able to stress multiple identities simultaneously – for example as Canadian, Caribbean, African, gay, straight, and so on.

In addition to contributing to this sense of triple vision held by African Canadians, which allows for a connection to the African continent and to people of African descent across Canada and in other parts of the global Black world, the intersected concepts open up possibilities of understanding leadership and organizing in very complex ways. All three concepts are attentive to hegemony, capitalism, and the interweaving histories and collective "experiences of oppression, exploitation and the struggle and resistance" of people of African descent (Mohanty, 2003, p. 522). In addition, these concepts recognize that the current geographical spaces that Black bodies occupy are the product of multiple historical processes, many of which they had no control over (Boyce Davies, 2014). The development of a pan-African movement and a diasporic consciousness, then, comes out of repressions, while transnationalism, grounded in the experiences of people, makes relevant the systemic elements of their experiences (Wilson, 1997). Diaspora, pan-Africanism, and transnationalism allow us to understand, as Walcott (2014) posits, "that Black Canadian life takes its formations, its politics and its intellectual traditions, its cultural expressions, its contributions and consciousness in concert with other forms of global Blackness" (p. 275).

Certainly as analytical and political strategies respectively, diaspora and pan-Africanism make significant contributions to understanding the unique ways that systems of oppression, such as capitalism, imperialism, and patriarchy, come into being, rely on each other, and interlock in very complex ways to impact the lives of African people (Mohanty, 2003). What is emphasized in and common to both are the unifying experiences of people of African descent dispersed by the slave trade and the common interests and/or social connections of people of African descent (Amelina, Nergiz, & Faist, 2012; Drake, 1993; Kelly, 2000; Mohanty, 2003; Shepperson, 1993). In essence, pan-Africanism anchors the idea of solidarity among people of African descent, while diaspora focuses on the dispersal of Africans as one unifying factor in the lives of people outside of Africa. While pan-Africanism is a strategy and diaspora a process, at their intersection both assume differences and shared commonalities; this is in addition to privileging an analysis that includes "directionality of power" (Mohanty, 2003, p. 521). Both ask new questions: How is oppression visible across borders? And what are the global and oppressive structures that impact Black lives across the world?

Collective action, linked by history and experience to these three discursive domains, inherently challenges the social edges and political core of the Canadian nation state, which are nineteenth- and twentieth-century phenomena. At the place of their crossing, diaspora, pan-Africanism, and transnationalism force one to think in unorthodox ways about how Black

Canada (1) understands and acts on who we are in the world, across space and time; (2) produces and reproduces Blackness within time and space; and (3) fosters an awareness of larger sociopolitical and cultural forces and the multiple ways that Black lives are situated within those forces (Stephens, 2015, p. 90). Thus, the intersection of these concepts highlights the Black Canadian perspective on the geopolitical structure of the world and simultaneously gives attention to the ambivalence that Blacks feel towards the Canadian nationstate. This work also suggests that at their intersection, the concepts of diaspora, pan-Africanism, and transnationalism engender a social force. That is, they complicate our understanding of African Canadian leadership, because the concepts move away from focusing only on individual action by locating leadership at the place where individual action and collective social force converge.

The ability of people of African descent to use collective organizing is what sustains them in the face of hostile social-economic conditions. For centuries, Black Canadians have used collective action and organizing to intervene in the social workings of Canada and create avenues for democratic participation. Blacks have fundamentally organized around (1) freedom and identity, (2) regional concerns, for example, geographical stratification in rural regions and cultured convergence in urban regions, and (3) oppression that affects the conditions under which Blacks live (Gordon, 2000). Ontologically, questions around identity (who, what, how) emerged symbiotically with collective protest in hopes of changing the nation. As Lewis Gordon (2000) suggested, identity questions cannot be divorced from the liberation question.

So how have Blacks used collective action to organize? Given their common goal of eliminating anti-Black racism, why have they at times had problems in organizing? And conversely, given their differences, what has made collective organizing possible? To understand this, we must be sensitive to Rinaldo Walcott's (2007) appreciation of organizing as a "refiguring of and elaboration" of the Canadian landscape and thus influencing an emerging Black Canadian culture and identity. The colonial and postcolonial conditions of Black lives globally place Black Canada in a larger international sociohistorical pattern that ideologically ruptures the boundedness in which Black Canadian thought and action had been situated, that is, Black Canadian experience and action extend far beyond the boundaries of Canada. Diaspora, pan-Africanism, and transnationalism allow us to talk about and with Black communities across national boundaries, because they uniquely complicate and disrupt the various categories such as home and away and/or alterity and continuity, in which Black lives are often placed even as they mark Black Canada's ambivalence about the Canadian nation.

In addition, as triple visions, diaspora, pan-Africanism, and transnationalism have allowed African Canadians to organize, create communities, cross borders, connect with Blacks in other places, and be intentional citizens. They unsettle and simultaneously form notions of homogeneity, because they enable us to recognize oppression while allowing for diversity and difference. The notion of triple vision is offered here to emphasize the flow of overlapping non-restrictive history, ideas, and experiences across borders that take particular directions and connect Blacks to each other. This has important methodological implications, because it impacts the kinds of questions that African Canadians ask, such as: what is Black Canada's relationship to itself, to the Canadian nation state, and to people of African descent in other places? So, instead of exploring only what diasporic, pan-African, and transnational practices consist of, we must, to borrow Alissa Trotz's (2006) point, "follow the subject" to understand the relationships and connections Black Canadians have with each other and with Blacks in other places, and the connections between their personal experiences and their quest for liberation (p. 42).

Organizing, as a demonstrative interaction, creates spaces for diasporic, pan-African, and transnational cultural, political, and socio-economic development and preservation (Walker, 2007). For example, in Ontario, we see the development of pan-African and transnational institutions as early as the 1600s with marronage, and in the 1700s and beyond with the extension of the Underground Railroad into Canada. Marronage, the act of running away from enslavement, even across borders, gave rise to institutions with "autonomous leadership, social structures, institutions and cultural practices" (Diouf, 2014, p. 2).[3] The Underground Railroad, for example, arose out of the act of marronage. According to Hill (1981), organizations such as the Ladies Coloured Fugitive Association were formed "to help refugees who flooded into Canada West in the 1840's and 1850's" (p. 179). Another organization, the Provincial Union Association, formed in 1854, placed approximately thirty-five Blacks in leadership positions. Translocal in orientation, Black officers were from communities in Dresden, London, Amherstburg, Toronto, Chatham, and Hamilton (p. 180).

The development of the Black church in the mid-to-late 1800s facilitated further advancement of transnational and diasporic "communities of resistance" that extended across borders and into the United States in particular. Historian Karolyn Smardz Frost (2007) suggested that one should think of the United States/Canada border as a conduit for slavery and freedom. After the American Civil War, the border sustained shared kinship and social, religious, and economic interests.

Thus, it is not surprising that at times, even as early as the eighteenth century, African Canadians have operated as if the borders between the United States and Canada were malleable. This is evident in the life of the Reverend Jennie Johnson, a notable figure from the late 1800s to mid-1900s, and that of the Reverend Madison Lightfoot, who was a minister in Windsor in the mid-1800s. Both individuals lived "cross border" lives serving both African American and African Canadian communities. Their lives offer us a glimpse of the collective action that signifies a diasporic, pan-African, and transnational consciousness (Frost, 2013; Reid-Maroney, 2013). Both lived and worked in Canada and the United States and fought against the global anti-Black racism that people of African descent faced. During the Civil War, Lightfoot encouraged a pan-African philosophy among African Canadians and African Americans. For example, he urged his congregation to support Blacks in other geographical spaces, to join the armed forces in their home countries, and to honour the uprising in Haiti. A case in point was a decision at a meeting of the Detroit Second Baptist Church, which he chaired, when Lightfoot's congregation "resolved, that the colored citizens of Detroit shall hold the first of August as a day of celebration, in honor of the enfranchisement of their brethren in the West Indies" (Frost, 2013, p. 7). Nina Reid Maroney (2013), in her book on Reverend Johnson, showed that she continuously fought against the anti-Black racism that people of African descent faced in both Canada and the United States, and examined the ways in which she was actively involved in advocating for justice in the face of this oppression.

The political implications of the above actions – organizing and building communities – for the ideals of citizenship and belonging are profound. Homi K. Bhabha's (1994) idea of "culture's in between" is helpful in articulating the sense of action, understood here as an insurgent act, that people of African descent felt/feel as they encounter/ed, re-encounter/ed, and re-figure/d the Canadian nation. This insurgency, as seen in the lives of Johnson and Lightfoot, is most profoundly demonstrated through the act of organizing and community building that was continuously reinventing Black Canadian identity.

In Toronto, the first Black institution on record was the First Baptist Church. Founded in 1826, it was fundamental to the survival of Black Canadians, as it provided a place of respite and solace in times of spiritual and social need (Shad Shreve, 1983). In 1832, Nova Scotia saw the establishment of the African Baptist Church, now called the Cornwallis Street Baptist Church, which functioned as both a school and a church. In addition to churches, Toronto saw the establishment of a chapter of the Universal Negro Improvement Association (1919), followed by other Black organizations such as the Canadian League for the Advancement of Coloured People (1924), the Coloured Literary Association of Toronto (1920s), the West Indian Progressive Association (1920s), the Toronto United Negro Association (n.d.), the National Unity Association (1948), the Negro Citizenship Association (1951), and the Canadian Negro Women's Association (1951).[4] The establishment of these institutions allowed Blacks to participate in knowledge sharing and collaboration across borders and within multiple spaces, which assisted them in circumnavigating the socio-economic and cultural structure of the Canadian nation. They shared information about where to find employment and to rent, and survived in Canada by challenging racism and other forms of social oppression. By doing so, they cultivated a Canadian variant of diasporic, pan-African, and transnational sensibility enhanced by the common cause of "freedom."

Diasporic, pan-African, and transnational in nature, these organizations were integral to the success of major historical and contemporary Black leaders and thinkers, such as Fleurette Osborne, Reverend Richard Preston, Bromley Armstrong, Donald Moore, and Rosemary Brown, to name a few.[5] They initiated organizations that disrupted the historical and contemporary classic North American origin narrative of white settlers being the owners of North American nations. In addition, they made connections to Canada's Black abolitionist past, to its intellectual and activist traditions, and to other organizations and movements in the Caribbean, South America, Europe, Africa, and the United States (Reid-Maroney, 2013).

David Austin (2013) and Christopher Harris (2014) spoke of a powerful link between Canadian and US Black Power movements demonstrated, for example, with the establishment of the Montreal Congress of Black Writers in the 1970s and the Afro-American Progressive Association, founded in Toronto in 1968. This bond was further evident in the Toronto uprising after the 1992 Rodney King verdict, when Black and white Canadians connected the killing of Raymond Lawrence, an African Canadian man who was slain by a white undercover officer, to the acquittal of Los Angeles police officers for the beating of King. The current transnational movement Black Lives Matter (http://blacklivesmatter.com), with its tagline "Get Active, Get Organized, Fight Back," has also influenced young Black Canadians, who have started their own chapters of BLM as well as other groups, such as the Black Liberation Collective (BLC; http://www.blackliberationcollective.org), that reflect a radical pan-African and diasporic sensibility connectomg Black Canadian struggles with the struggles of Blacks across the globe. Incidentally, while BLM Toronto is comparable to some degree to the Black Action

Defense Committee (BADC), an organization in Toronto that fights police brutality and calls for police officers to be accountable to the community, BLM Toronto and the BLC modified and revitalized collective action in ways that BADC did not (Gooden, 2005; Maynard, 2017). For example, in addition to opposing police brutality, BLM Toronto and the BLC aim to transcend differences by reconceptualizing race, class, and gender in order to take up the issues of sexism, transgender and queer oppression, and the poverty of women in ways that BADC never has. In a September 2015 rally, BLM Toronto partnered with the Toronto Rape Crisis Center and Multicultural Women Against Rape and dedicated the rally to Black identities, as well as to missing Indigenous women in Canada (Donato, 2015). Additionally, their bold move of stalling the 2016 Pride parade to protest the erasure and silencing of Black bodies and voices at Pride and the lack of Black representation in the Pride organization, and to request that police floats/booths be removed from community spaces during the parade, challenged Pride's historic anti-Blackness and forced the organizers to confront its legacy of participating in the erasure of Black bodies from Canadian spaces (Craven, 2016).[6]

Black Canadian Leadership as Collective Centres

The idea of Black Canadian leadership in this work is broadly conceived; it extends beyond conventional definitions, which often limit leadership to process and sphere of influence. When one conceives of leadership, what frequently comes to mind are power, charisma, authority, vision, and goals of individuals. Such concepts assume contested ideas of individual trailblazers and collective followers engaging in a relationship in order to bring about change. While this may be true to some extent, it cannot be the only conception of leadership, as it offers a limited vision that dismisses or silences the social forces or synergy that arise from the consciousness of Black ontology. Similar to the proverbial saying "We stand on the shoulders of those who have gone before," we also stand on the shoulders of those who stand with us. Leadership cannot be conceptualized without situating it in collective action.

While there are numerous individuals whom we recognize as leaders (and who should be noted), there are many unnamed and understudied individuals who have organized tirelessly and have significantly impacted the social and political landscape of Canada. Their actions are a significant part of the Black collective approach that shapes the nation. My intention is not to diminish the work of high-profile and notable individuals, but merely to disrupt a Eurocentric "possessive individualism" or individual-exceptionalism lens by which some of us understand the efforts of Black Canadians (Hudson & Kamugisha, 2014).

Those we have named or claimed as leaders – think Anne Cools, Rosemary Brown, Rocky Jones, or Dudley Laws – do not stand alone, but are complex individuals tied together and yet sometimes divided from and within their own communities. They have clear connections to cultural capital and to traditional centres of Black political and social power, which exist collectively in Black communities (Gordon Nembhard, 2014). Anne Cools, for example, became the first Black senator in Canada and participated in the Sir George Williams University student uprising in Montreal in 1969; Rosemary Brown was an active member of the British Columbia Association for the Advancement of Coloured People before she joined the Canadian parliament; and Burnley "Rocky" Jones was intimately connected to US-bsed Black nationalism organizations, such as the Black Panther Party, and used these connections to influence Black politics in Halifax.[7] These connections to collective centres are invaluable, because individual leaders have to be situated in them to gather first-hand knowledge and experience of the conditions of Blacks.

Such participation is needed if one is to become influential, because these collective centres support an "intellectual and activist climate which allow[s] individuals and groups to thrive" (Gordon Nembhard, 2014). This use of the collective centre as the cradle of individual Black leadership captures David Austin's suggestion that leadership must have a common exchange and relationship with people, resulting in mutual learning, understanding and action (Hudson, 2014).

Transnational and Pan-African Alliances

The organizations founded by African Canadians are deeply influenced by the struggles of Indigenous communities against white supremacy, colonialism, and oppression and are buttressed by the cosmopolitan ideals of a multi-ethnic Canadian nation. Membership has varied in ethnicity and has included individuals from the Caribbean, Canada, the United States, and other parts of the Black world. With their varied makeup, these organizations re-envision the economic, political, cultural, and social structure of Canada, which was and is marked by exclusion and racial, ethnic, gender, and cultural inequalities; they are pronounced examples of the ways in which African people give substance to Canada as they carry out citizenship in and for the Canadian nation – that is, by organizing and establishing organizations, African Canadians have supported the social welfare of the Canadian nation and thus are continually and profoundly reframing Blackness and belonging in Canada.

Transnational alliances, along with national mobilization efforts by African Canadians, influence organizing and create associations to serve a social-agency function with occasional small economic components. These transnational and translocal relationships have given Blacks (new immigrants as well as other Black Canadians) access to an African Canadian approach facilitating the creation of institutions, which have been critical, especially in the early years when there were so few Blacks. Operating under the politics of respectability, organizations such as the above-mentioned Coloured Literary Association of Toronto facilitated the adjustment of new immigrants, while the investment company West Indian Trading (with an inception date of either 1917 or 1920) was designed to import West Indian produce to southwestern Ontario and create avenues for economic participation and achievement (Gairey, 1981). The credit union of the Toronto United Negro Association also created avenues for economic support, while in Dresden, the Canadian League for the Advancement of Coloured People, modelling its formation on the National Association for the Advancement of Colored People in the United States, functioned as an advocacy group to fight Canadian anti-Black sentiments and unify institutions that supported Blacks (Armstrong & Taylor, 2000; Gooden, 2005).

Black Canadian men and women turned to trade unions as a vehicle to express their collective concerns in the early to mid-1900s (Mathieu, 2010). Recognizing the benefits of unionizing, Black porters in Canada established the Brotherhood of Sleeping Car Porters, the first trade union in Canada organized by and for African Canadians, to lobby on their behalf. The Canadian Brotherhood had strong transnational ties to the US Brotherhood of Sleeping Car Porters movement, which was organized by African Americans and led by A. Philip Randolph and Milton P. Webster. African Canadians effectively lobbied for higher wages, shorter workdays, and seniority and were eventually successful in gaining for Black porters benefits previously denied. In addition, they pressured the federal government to create policies prohibiting discrimination in employment and housing (Soulliere, 2005). In an interview for the documentary *Journey to Justice* (McTair, 2000), Stanley Grizzle, who founded the Railway Porter's Trade Union Council in Toronto and served as the president of the Toronto division of the Brotherhood of Sleeping Car Porters, argued that the Canadian Brotherhood changed the Black community in Toronto.

As noted earlier, transnational African Canadian organizations had appeared in Canada as early as the 1600s, beginning with marronage, the Underground Railroad, and then the development of various Black churches. However, it was the establishment of the Universal Negro

Improvement Association (UNIA) that demonstrates how African Canadians conceptualized and organized themselves both culturally and politically. According to Dionne Brand (1991), Carla Marano (2010), and Keith Henry (1981), the UNIA was one of the first organized movements to offer a radically different political option and behaviour pattern in Black leadership; organizations that existed prior to the UNIA, such as the Home Service Association, established by African Canadians during the First World War, were viewed by some as conservative and cautious (Henry, 1981). While UNIA membership included second-generation African Canadians, the overwhelming majority were African Caribbean. Vincent Franklin (1993) pointed out that "Caribbeans confronted [Canadian] Blacks with the international dimension of their understanding of the Black world and their struggle, raising the level of consciousness among Blacks about the larger pan-African context, and suggest[ed] ways that Blacks could assist one another" (p. 188). Later, organizations such as the Canadian League for the Advancement of Coloured People and Reverend Stewart's Afro-Community Church (1936–7) also provided alternative political positioning. This positioning contrasted with the established Black conservative philosophy, which was based on class, historical, cultural, and generational differences (Henry, 1981; L. Johnston, interview with Huguette A. Casi Multicultural Society of Ontario, 3 August 1978).

The different historical realities of individual Blacks nuanced how each conceptualized his or her own political and organizing realities. Small in number and living in a nation divided along linguistic lines, long-established African Canadians tended to be older, financially established, and more conservative than African Caribbean people who came from nations where Blacks were the majority (B.L. Armstrong, interview with Lance Talbot Multicultural Society of Ontario, 2 February 1990; Henry, 1981). Henry (1981) suggested that the large number of Black Caribbean people who formed the UNIA in Toronto and Montreal had remigrated from Nova Scotia, where they had experienced a wide-ranging and disparaging form of anti-Black discrimination that had radicalized their approach to fighting racism. The gradual and small influx of Blacks to Toronto beginning in the 1850s had forestalled the large-scale systematic discrimination that Blacks in other parts of the country had faced (Silverman, 1985). As their numbers in southwestern Ontario increased and anti-Black resistance became more virulent, there was a complex interplay between the long-established African Canadian communities and a new Caribbean collective of recent immigrants (Henry, 1981; Silverman, 1985). But both the Home Service Association and the UNIA were transgressive organizations for their time. They strategized and established concrete institutionalized structures from which African people could carve out space in a hostile environment. The organizing projects of each group provide the frame by which to understand how, in its complexity and multiplicity, Blackness was engaged in Canada. The creation of both the Home Service Association and the UNIA, fashioned from the cultural centres of African Canadians and Caribbean Canadians, illustrates organizing as a culturally specific political action that is non-monolithic.

It was the far-reaching UNIA, using a transnational and pan-African social and political philosophy, that articulated the boundlessness of the African diaspora. It gave people of African descent "incentive[s] and taught [them to] love [their] Black skin" (Gairey,1981, p. 12). Daniel Hill (1960) reported that members of the UNIA thought that Marcus Garvey brought a new "aggressiveness to the British Negro. He represented the first real leadership the Negro had seen, and he gave Negroes a social and economic consciousness they had never known ... Garvey showed ... that all Negroes should unite to fight [oppression]" (p. 347). This quote captures the fundamental pan-African underpinnings of the UNIA. Although it was known for its radical vision of a "Back to Africa Movement," it was Garvey's pan-African philosophy on the connectedness and unity of African people that long-resident African Canadian communities and new Black Canadians took up and transformed into Black pride, self-determination, and the building of a Black economic community. Employing these principles, Black Canadians organized, advocated, and fundraised in order to secure enough capital to purchase a building under the UNIA banner as early as 1927, twenty years before the establishment of the oldest African Canadian social service agency, the Home Service Association (Henry, 1981).

The UNIA was a diasporic secular space. Many recalled that "ever Thursday night at the Hall there'd be a dance, every Thursday night – that was the night that the domestics got off. It was wonderful" (Brand, 1991, p. 179). Bromley Armstrong (Armstrong & Taylor, 2000), a Canadian civil rights activist, also recalls the importance of the UNIA not only as a pan-African and transnational but as a diasporic space:

The UNIA was not just a place for its members to hold their meetings; it was a community centre where Black adults and children went to socialize, attend debates, dance, and play music. In its edifice, leaders and members representing many different organizations gathered to plan the future direction of

> their community. When new arrivals and visitors to the city needed a place to go, they were referred to the UNIA. Jam sessions were regularly featured

> there, and musicians ... encouraged youth to develop an interest in music. All roads in the community led to the Saturday night dance of the UNIA. (p. 41)

Attendance at socials events included both Caribbean-born and long-established African Canadians. Gwen Johnston, wife of Lenny Johnston and co-owner of Third World Books, recalled her own experience; she remembered that as a youth "growing up, the UNIA was a wonderful place, sort of a second home for us" (Brand, 1991, p. 179). Violet Blackman, a woman born in the Caribbean and working in domestic service, recalled how the UNIA had a favourable impact on her social and political identity:

> I remember a friend came to where I was working in service – after I was here a year – and invited me this Sunday to go down to the UNIA, and when I went I liked it very much and I joined. From then I became an active member – I never missed a Sunday – and I worked with it. I was in everything. At that time I had a voice; I was in the choir – I was in everything in the UNIA cause I liked it all my life once I got in there and saw how interesting it was. (Brand, 1991, p. 40)

Such narratives suggest that community organizing played a major role in constructing Black women's and men's identities. In addition, established home-of-origin cultural values and practices, combined with the structure of the new "host" country and other forces, determined Caribbean migrants' trajectory in terms of how they (re)conceptualized, constructed, and negotiated space for themselves in Canada. These values and practices also shaped how they maintained and/or re-created identity in relation to their place of origin. African Caribbean people could be both African Canadian and Caribbean simultaneously. For example, Caribbean associations with their added transnational component keep migrants connected to their place of origin and also provide the added function and benefit of keeping the African Caribbean population connected to other Black people in Canada. Yet organizations like the UNIA were also sites of resistance and community, a place where individuals could learn resistance and a place where they valued and acted upon a Black Canadian diasporic sensibility.

Diasporic Sensibilities and Ambiguities

In more recent times, organizing has also introduced incommensurable cultural and political temporalities, such as Caribana, into the invention of Black Canadian spaces. Caribana's beginning is tied to the history of the Canadian Negro Women's Association (CANEWA), which was founded in 1951 (Hill, 1996). As hampton and Rochat point out in this volume, organizations such as CANEWA reconceptualized strategies of organizing and leadership by rejecting patriarchal constructions of activism and leadership, prevented fixed notions of Canadian identity, and infused and opened up possibilities of cultural hybridity. They entertained differences in ways that were new to the Canadian nation, even as the members infused notions of international, transnational, and translational sensibilities in a demand for a different Canada.

Similar to yet different from the US-based National Association of Coloured Women, the CANEWA emerged from a pre-existing group called the Dilettantes, a social club made up primarily of Black middle-class, Canadian-born (first-generation African Caribbean and long-established African Canadian) women. As we will see below, with its reformation the CANEWA articulated a robust African diasporic sensibility that would re-emerge among later generations and various organizations, particularly as the number of Black citizens increased. Concerned with racial uplift and the anti-Black racism that African Canadians were experiencing, its members wanted "to become aware of, appreciate, and further the merits of the Canadian Negro" (CANEWA, 1951; Hill, 1996). As such, they organized themselves in a pan-African and diasporic fashion, established scholarships and bursaries for needy students, and organized the first Canadian Negro History Week in 1967. They also worked to establish an inclusive organization once members recognized that tension existed between Caribbean-born and Canadian-born Blacks (Hill, 1996).

Working with a lens attuned to diasporic sensibility, the CANEWA organized a Calypso Carnival in 1952 to bring various African Caribbeans and African Canadians together to recognize and celebrate Africa and the Caribbean. There had been little contact between long-established African Canadians and African Caribbean migrants, especially women, since the latter worked mainly as domestics or in other service positions and had little time to join social clubs or self-help organizations frequented by the middle class. The Calypso Carnival, which ran until 1964, offered Black Canadians the opportunity to celebrate and honour their cultural differences and similarities, and was the forerunner of the now world-famous Caribana (Hill, 1996). The organizing of the Calypso Carnival flies in the face of the historical association between collective action and male "founders," and instead supports research that shows Black women have made strong organizing contributions.

To fight anti-Black racism on a national scale and to encourage the diasporic and pan-African unity espoused in the Calypso Carnival and by

CANEWA, the National Black Coalition of Canada (NBCC) was founded in 1969 in the aftermath of the Sir George Williams uprising (Walker, 2014).[8] From its inauguration, however, tensions surfaced about its sustainability and viability. In 1969, *Contrast*, the principal community-based Black newspaper, reported that

> while the manner of its inception leaves much to be desired in the minds of thinking people it is still a beginning. The possibilities of its usefulness and fidelity to our interests cannot be discredited ... there has been enough of suspicion and warring among ourselves as to each other's motives for doing our own thing, in our way for the Black brotherhood ... let us support each other's effort. (p. 2)

John Harewood (1982) suggested that the impetus to form the diasporic and translocal organization on a national scale "sprang from the refusal of Black moderates ... to succumb to the tactics of a vocal minority ostensibly committed to the Carmichael notion of Black power or the Black Panther philosophy of confrontation and self-defense" (p. 273). Stanley Grizzle, however, intimated that it was the lack of Black leadership in Canada, the division between West Indians and African Canadians, and the inability of Black people to mobilize and shape the welfare of Blacks throughout Canada that were the incentives for the founding of NBCC (Harewood, 1982; McCurdy, 1969). Regardless of the reasons behind its founding, the NBCC recognized that the small Black Canadian population made it difficult for Black activists to voice effective pleas against discriminatory acts, which were occurring in non-systematic ways. Jean Augustine (n.d.) pointed out that the NBCC desired to mirror the goals and objectives of the NAACP. According to Augustine, the vision of the NBCC

> was to have Blacks all across the country, that there'd be a national organization through which we would filter social programs, we would do different things. We would advocate on behalf of the concerns of Black people right across Canada ... We face racism, we have difficulties in empowerment, we have difficulties with our young people; we have challenges. Whether you're in Halifax, ... Calgary, ... Vancouver or Toronto; we found that our situations were the same and we felt that a national organization will give us an opportunity to bring our voices together.

Focusing on four major areas (human and civil rights, legal aid and defence, education, and immigration), the NBCC's three major aims and objectives were to (1) create an environment in which Black people of

Canada could achieve their fullest potential as human beings; (2) ensure Black people were able to fully participate socially, politically, and economically in the shaping of their society and that they benefited fully from it; and (3) eradicate all forms of racism and discrimination (McClain, 1979, p. 55). Twenty-seven organizations joined in 1969, including the Jamaican Canadian Association. By the early 1970s, over eighty organizations were members, with the largest numbers coming from Ontario (*Contrast*, editorial, October 1969).

The NBCC failed. Yet this failure holds tremendous lessons for contemporary Black Canadian organizing. It collapsed because, fundamentally, it could not articulate a unifying diasporic position that clarified its stance on classism, anti-Black racism, and sexism (Bobb-Smith, 2003). For example, the organization's failure to take a clear position on the Sir George Williams University affair forced many Black students to view it as a co-opted organization (*Contrast*, October 1969). Many Black Canadians understood that "any viable organization of Blacks in Canada must be prepared to confront the government in a consistent manner," and that people "cannot form an organization and say [they] are non-political" (McClain, 1979, p. 55). Further, others felt that the organization was not centred in the Black community; they argued that "the Black community needs [an] organization that will push people forward and will be based in the Black community" (McClain, 1979, p. 55).

While internal tension and conflict fuelled its collapse, the NBCC was also short lived because it relied heavily on government grants; it received over $173,000 between 1978 and 1982 (*Contrast*, 5 August 1983). In the end, the Canadian nation state "encouraged dissention within the organization's ranks" (Taylor, 2001, p. 11). NBCC became weak and ineffective, and funding was eventually withdrawn and allotted to the Harambee Centres of Canada, another government-supported Black organization, which, according to Sheldon Taylor (2001), was encouraged as a replacement.[9] The impossibility of the NBCC indicates that at times the political structure of the Canadian state co-opts the collective action of Blacks by promoting and perpetuating individuality with the nation state. As a national organization, the NBCC folded in the late 1980s, as it was not self-sustaining without government funding. Chapters are, however, still active today in a few places such as Calgary and Vancouver.

Building Alliances

Fighting the gendered leadership of the NBCC and embodying the same diasporic sensibility that produced the Calypso Carnival, the CANEWA organized the first national Black women's conference, which was instrumental in the creation of the National Congress of Black Women of Canada (NCBW) (Hill, 1996; NCBW, 1973). Members of CANEWA felt that Black women needed a national voice. They wanted both racism and sexism addressed and believed that male-dominated organizations such as the NBCC were not addressing Black women's concerns. Adding a national and united voice in defence of the entire Black community, the NCBW emerged out of CANEWA and brought issues to the national stage that had been largely ignored. For example, it wrote letters of protest on behalf of the Black population, and the first NCBW report discusses immigration as institutionalized racism (*Contrast*, October 1969; Hill, 1996). A resolution passed at the first conference stated:

> Considering the fact that the present immigration policies have produced a marked imbalance in the male/female ratio of immigrants in the Black community
> BE IT THEREFORE RESOLVED:
> That pressure be brought to bear on the Canadian policy makers by both West Indian and African governments and Canadian Black organizations to effect a reformation of these policies. (NCBW, 1973)

In addition to the above, the Congress passed resolutions to address the education of Black students and the needed anti-racist training of teachers within the institutionally racist school system (NCBW, 1973). By 1980, NCBW had become a coalition of twenty-three chapters across Canada and consisted of members from the working and middle classes. Diasporic and pan-African unity was a strong motto, evident in its 1990 assertion that Black collective action must include concerns of Black lesbians. Ron Fanfair (1995a) reported that the Congress urged unity within Black Canadian collective action because, for example, lack of support was forcing "Black lesbians ... to turn to White women's agencies for help."

In contemporary times, community activists such as Angela Robertson and Debbie Douglas organize and assist men and women in pooling resources (emotional and social capital) to build alliances and meet personal, family, social, political, and economic challenges. They interface with the social structure of Canada and try to buffer the social trauma that Black Canadians face. They fight for systemic change by addressing matters of immigration, gender, sexuality, health, childcare, violence against women, education, employment, and citizenship rights. Robertson, for example, is one of the co-founders of Blockorama/Blackness Yes!, a celebration of Black pride for the queer community from the African diaspora, while Douglas, the executive director of the Ontario

Council of Agencies Serving Immigrants, lobbies the Canadian government on behalf of racialized individuals from all over the world (Goldsbie & Cole, 2016; Douglas, 2014).

Movements such as BLM-TO also exhibit the diasporic sensibility of Douglas and Robertson and are continuities of African diasporic, pan-Africanism, and transnational leadership under capitalism. The killing of Michael Brown in Ferguson, Missouri, was the catalyst for the BLM movement in the United States. The Black women who started the movement and created the hashtag #BlackLivesMatter – Patrise Cullors, Opal Tometi, and Alicia Garza – state that an understanding of state-sanctioned violence was central to the movement (Taylor, 2016). Young Black Canadians connected the killing of Brown to Jermaine Garby and many other Black and Brown Canadians. The connection that African Canadians have with each other and with Blacks in other places speaks to the complexity of Black lives. The tagline of BLM-TO in the fall of 2014 – "From Toronto to Ferguson: Black Lives Matter" (Facebook, BlackLivesMatter-TO) – was fuelled by a diasporic and pan-African understanding of global violence and by deep historical grievances. Black Canadians are assaulted by anti-Black racism and state-sanctioned violence in a never-ending cycle of stop-and-frisk, arrests, harassments, and death (Adjetey, 2014; Maynard, 2017). BLM-TO organizes for the Black and Brown victims of carding and state-sanctioned violence, for Black trans bodies, and for all those who have lost their lives to white supremacy. It is from this presence (of simultaneously belonging and unbelonging) that Blacks have expanded upon and are ultimately transforming notions of Canadian-ness. As demonstrated by their demands, BLM-TO is able to express multiple intersecting identities (gay, straight, African Canadian), stand with Indigenous people and people of colour, and articulate a broader critique that places state violence within the interlocking systems of imperialism, capitalism, and patriarchy (Craven, 2016).

With clear diasporic, transnational, and pan-African strategies, BLM has utilized social media to gain momentum for its movement. Drawing strength from a cross-border connection with Ferguson, Baltimore, New York, and other places across the globe, it has shut down Allen Road in Toronto, stood with Indigenous populations to protest the Dakota Pipeline at Standing Rock in the United States, halted the 2016 Toronto Pride parade, and continues to participate in numerous campaigns aimed at ending anti-Black oppression (BLM-TO, n.d.; Craven, 2016; Jegroo, 2016; Khan, 2016; Onstad, 2017). Most recently, Blacks in the United States have utilized BLM-TO's strategy and have asked their local

Pride parade organizers to discontinue police booths/floats and to increase Black queer and trans participation (Nasser, 2017). Specifically, they said:

> Let us start off by saying that we stand in full solidarity with our siblings of the Toronto Chapter of #BlackLivesMatter. We have been inspired by the strategic moves made by the TO team, including the chapter's decision to not attend PRIDE this year in order to spotlight the reality of anti-Blackness in all areas of society. PRIDE is shared on the same day in both Toronto and New York City. We, like our Toronto comrades, write this public statement to PRIDE NYC organizers, the Gay Officers Action League-NY (GOAL-NY) and the NYPD. (BLM-NYC, 2017)

The social force that emerges out of BLM-TO's connection with Blacks in other places conveys how Black communities and identities are negotiated and conceptualized within transnational and pan-African spaces (Otero, 2000).

Conclusion

As social strategies, diaspora, pan-Africanism, and transnationalism are locations for social action. The synergy between their interactions and the creation of spaces by people of African descent in Canada is a phenomenon that began in the 1600s when, as described earlier, African Canadians utilized collective action in the form of marronage. Current movements such as BLM-TO are patterns of continuities between the past and the present – such movements are the result of the afterlife of slavery and a simultaneous recognition that the legacy of colonialism impacts Black lives in vicious ways. Black Canadians use collective action as a social force in the demand for socio-economic and political rights and in their articulation of ways that the Canadian nation can move forwards with transformational change.

In conjoining the analytical frameworks of diaspora, pan-Africanism, and transnationalism, this chapter reinforces the idea that some historic and contemporary leadership, borne out of collective action, is negotiated in social spaces through local and translocal networks, flows, and social movements in history. Using diasporic connections, pan-African structures, and transnational affiliations – religious, geographical, political, social – African Canadians have developed and promoted new ideas and visions and used the social force of collective action to form organizations and accomplish their goals. Some organizations, such as the

Home Service Association, the UNIA, and the Toronto United Negro Association, provided African Canadians with a sense of trust, solidarity, and sometimes nostalgia that helped solidify collective effort, while history, racial solidarity, and place of birth provided a resource for these organizations to thrive. Yet others, such as the CANEWA, the Congress of Black Women, and BLM-TO, have rejected old methods and introduced new ways of organizing. They have demonstrated the perseverance of Black Canadians in crafting alternative strategies that attempt to promote social and political stability in the face of anti-Black racism. While Black Canadian organizing was not seamless and coherent, African Canadians have transposed and utilized global political strategies, melding them into an organic whole, despite contradictions and tensions. They have negotiated, discarded, and combined strategies and approaches so that their communities remain works in progress. In doing so, they have emphasized that creating home is as much a fracture as it is about consistency and collective negotiation (Otero, 2000). In the process, they reconfigure the possibility of the Canadian nation for Black people.

NOTES

1 I use an uppercase *B* in “Black” when referring to people of African descent. This recognizes the practice of capitalization when referring to people of a particular ethnicity or group. White people, for the most part, are able to make connections to a past that many Blacks are unable to, due in large part to enslavement, colonialism, and forced migration. Using an uppercase *B* acknowledges this dispersal, the global marginalization of people of African descent, and also the creation of new cultures.

2 Black Coalition for AIDS Prevention and Women’s Health in Women’s Hands were initiatives by primarily Black women activists in Toronto in the late 1980s. Recognizing the need for advocacy and accessibility to primary health care, Black women pushed for government funding to establish these agencies to serve the Black community.

3 For a more expansive discussion of new definitions of marronage, see Diouf (2014). Diouf expands old definitions of marronage and offers new concepts and themes that allow us to understand marrongage as both individual and collective.

4 Lack of historical records prevent an accurate dating of some of these organizations. For example, for the only, and limited, documentary evidence on the Toronto United Negro Association (TUNA), see Armstrong and Taylor (2000, p. 38). Since evidence is limited, there is no record of inception or

end date for TUNA. What is known can be gleamed from the memoirs of Armstrong, written with Sheldon Taylor. TUNA worked towards a broader-based membership by attempting to incorporate Caribbean and Canadian members in its organization. Armstrong joined the organization in 1948 and recalls that it was established and headed primarily by middle-class African Caribbean people, although membership was inclusive of the general Black Toronto community. Armstrong reports that many of the members had migrated to Toronto in the pre-war years and, "through organizational development and a spirit of voluntarism," had taken proactive roles in helping to build their community. The organization created a Credit Union in the 1940s, and although Armstrong did not join the organization until after inception, by 1955 he was elected president. The Canadian League for the Advancement of Colored People (CLACP – mirroring the NAACP) was established by 1924 with branches in Toronto, London, Niagara Falls, and Dresden. National in focus, the league's mandate was to fight Canadian anti-Black sentiments and unify institutions that supported Blacks. This organization, however, did not gain the momentum or take the legislative initiative that its counterpart did in the United States, mainly due to the smaller Black population. For further discussion of these and other organizations, see Gooden (2005).

5 Fleurette Osborn was the first president of the National Congress of Black Women and advocated on behalf of women nationally and internationally. She migrated to Montreal from Barbados in 1960 and, as a student at Sir George Williams University, became an activist and worked with domestic Caribbean workers. For more on Osborn, see Shadd (2010) and Wharton-Zaretsky (1999). In 1816 Richard Preston escaped slavery in Virginia and travelled to Nova Scotia looking for his family. Reunited with his mother, he quickly became a leader of Black Nova Scotians, advocating for Black churches and other Black institutions. He was insistent that Africa remain central in Black Canadian institutions. For more on Preston, see http://www.cbc.ca/news/canada/nova-scotia/programs/informationmorningns/the-legend-of-richard-preston-1.3495288 and http://Blackhalifax.com/portfolio/richard-preston/. Bromley Armstrong, who holds both the Order of Canada and the Order of Ontario, is a civil rights activist who migrated to Toronto in 1947. In his early twenties, Armstrong quickly became active in the Black community in Ontario. He was an member of organizations such as the Universal Negro Improvement Association and joined forces with other Black Canadian activists nationally, for example, participating in sit-ins in Dresden with the National Unity Association. His tireless work led to Ontario's first anti-discriminatory policy. Armstrong was among ten individuals who in 1973 established the *Islander*, a newspaper geared to Caribbean

immigrants. Initially, the newspaper was intended to be a cooperative venture, but the other individuals abandoned the effort; Armstrong continued to publish the paper until 1977, when it joined forces with *Contrast*, another newspaper serving the Black community. For more on Armstrong, see Armstrong and Taylor (2000) and http://www.thecanadianencyclopedia.ca/en/article/bromley-armstrong/. Donald Moore, also an immigrant from Barbados, was chair of the Negro Citizenship Association (NCA). Moore migrated to Montreal and then Toronto via New York in the early 1900s. Over a three-year period, he, the NCA, and various other community activists organized and lobbied the local, provincial, and federal governments for changes to the Immigration Act. A thirty-five-member delegation, including members of the Brotherhood of Sleeping Car Porters, travelled to Ottawa in 1954 to press for changes to the racist immigration policy. They urged immigration officials to use the NCA as an intermediary between immigration authorities and persons held for deportation and immigration, and they advocated on behalf of individuals who faced difficulties or were being held awaiting deportation. In addition, the NCA recognized the vulnerable position Black women were placed in and lobbied for female guards. In response to the Canadian labour shortage of nurses, the organization acted as an advocate, securing jobs prior to the nurses' arrival, obtaining job letters for immigration officials, and even transporting Caribbean nurses to areas outside of Toronto once they arrived in the city. For more on Donald Moore, see Moore and Selvon (1985). Rosemary Brown was a feminist British Columbian activist who arrived via Montreal. Born in Jamaica, she was the first Black woman in Canada to be elected to a provincial legislature. She was also the first Black woman to run for leadership of a Canadian federal political party. She held the Order of Canada and the Order of British Columbia. Brown established the Vancouver Status of Women in 1972 and was an active member of the British Columbia Association for the Advancement of Coloured People.

6 See Julia Craven for the list of demands at https://www.huffingtonpost.com/entry/Black-lives-matter-toronto-pride_us_577c15aee4b0a629c1ab0ab4.

7 See the 2015 National Film Board of Canada documentary *Ninth Floor*, written and directed by Mina Shum; see also Brown (1989) and Jones & Walker (2016).

8 Between 29 January and 12 February 1969 approximately two hundred students (African Caribbean, African Canadian, and white supporters) occupied the computer centre at Sir George Williams University (now Concordia University) in Montreal, Quebec, levelling charges of anti-Black racism against a university professor, Percy Anderson. Anderson had failed the majority of African Caribbean students in his class the previous year. The students filed a formal complaint with the iniversity, who then set up a board

of enquiry that included two white faculty members and the only two Black faculty members. The two Black members resigned over "conflict of interest." Changes were then made to the board without the students' knowledge, and students were denied the opportunity to attend an open meeting to discuss the issue. Additionally, a student from the Caribbean, Errol Thomas, was charged with forcible detention when he attempted to get the acting vice principal of the university to sign a statement that the university was guilty of racism. The students occupied the computer centre to inconvenience businesses in downtown Montreal, hoping that doing so would pressure the university into listening. However, the police were called and given permission to remove the students by whatever means necessary. A riot squad with tear gas, clubs, and shields entered the centre. With over two million dollars worth of damage to buildings and equipment, ninety-six students (forty-five of whom were Black) were arrested, jailed, and charged. One of the students arrested was Ann Cools, later the first Black Canadian senator. Black students were singled out as leaders and expelled from the university. Three African Caribbean students were deported after serving time in prison. See Hamilton (1969); see also Austin (2007), Forsythe (1971).

9 The Harambee Centres Canada was a national organization funded by the federal government and launched in Ottawa. Established to provide an integrated range of support services in a culturally appropriate manner, Harambee had regional representatives in nine areas of Canada. The defining principle of Harambee, which means "pulling together," was the ideas of racial uplift and self-help. Although defunct in Toronto, the centres still function in other parts of Canada. The Toronto centre closed in the early 1990s due to "what one academic assessed as Harambee suffering from the cult of leadership" (see Taylor, 2001; see also *Contrast,* 13, 20 December 1985).

REFERENCES

Adjetey, W. (2014). *Policing race: Rethinking the myth of national exceptionalism in a Canadian context.* New York: Humanity in Action.

Amelina, A., Faist, T., Nergiz, D., & Glick Schiller, N. (2012). *Beyond methodological nationalism: Research methodologies for cross-border studies.* New York: Routledge.

Armstrong, B.L., & Taylor, S.E.A. (2000). *Bromley, tireless champion for just causes: Memoirs of Bromley L. Armstrong.* Toronto: Vitabu.

Augustine, J. (n.d.). National black coalition of Canada. Retrieved from http://archives.library.yorku.ca/exhibits/show/pushingbuttons/Black--caribbean-community/national-black-coalition-of-ca

Austin, D. (2007). All roads led to Montreal: Black power, the Caribbean, and the black radical tradition in Canada. *Journal of African American History, 92*(4), 516–39. https://doi.org/10.1086/JAAHv92n4p516

Austin, D. (2013). *Fear of a black nation: Race, sex, and security in sixties Montreal.* Toronto: Between the Lines.

Basch, L., Glick Schiller, N., & Szanton Blanc, C. (2008). Transnational projects: A new perspective and theoretical premises. In S. Khagram & P. Levitt. (Eds.), *The transnational studies reader: Intersections and innovations* (pp. 261–72). New York: Routledge.

Bayes, J.H., & Gonzalez, L. (2011). Globalization, transnationalism, and intersecting geographies of power: The case of the Consejo Consultivo del Instituto de los Mexicanos en el Exterior (CC-IME): A study in progress. *Politics and Policy, 39*(1), 11–44. https://doi.org/10.1111/j.1747-1346.2010.00281.x

Bhabha, H.K. (1994). *The location of culture.* New York: Routledge.

Black Lives Matter NYC. (2017, 25 June). Not like this-#NoPrideHere. Retrieved from https://medium.com/@blmnyc/not-like-this-notopride-8b3f414a3d5a

Black Lives Matter Toronto. (n.d). Demands. Retrieved from https://Blacklivesmatter.ca/demands/

Bobb-Smith, Y. (2003). *I know who I am: An African Caribbean women's identity in Canada.* Toronto: Women's Press.

Boyce Davies, C. (2014). Pan-Africanism, transnational black feminism and the limits of culturalist analyses in African gender discourses. *Feminist Africa, 19,* pp. 78–93.

Brand, D. (1991). *No burden to carry: Narratives of black working women in Ontario 1920s–1950s* (with the assistance of L. De Shield and the Immigrant Women's Job Placement Centre). Toronto: Women's Press.

Brown, R. (1989). *Being Brown: A very public life.* Toronto: Random House.

Burman, J. (2002). Remittance; or, diasporic economies of yearning. *Small Axe: A Caribbean Journal of Criticism, 12,* 49–71. https://doi.org/10.1215/-6-2-49

Butler, K. (2001). Defining diaspora, refining a discourse. *Diaspora: A Journal of Transnational Studies, 10*(2), 189–219.

Canadian Negro Women's Association. (1951). Constitution. Papers of the Ontario Black History Society.

Chamberlain, M. (Ed.). (1998). *Caribbean migration: Globalized identities.* Routledge: London.

Clarke, K.M., & Thomas, D.A. (Eds.). (2006). *Globalization and race: Transformations in the cultural production of blackness.* Durham: Duke University Press.

Craven, J. (2016, 6 July). Black Lives Matter stand by pride parade shut down. *Huffington Post.* Retrieved from https://www.huffingtonpost.com/entry/black-lives-matter-toronto-pride_us_577c15aee4b0a629c1ab0ab4

Crawford, C. (2004). Sending love in a barrel: The making of transnational Caribbean families in Canada. *Canadian Woman Studies, 22*(3/4), 104. Retrieved from https://cws.journals.yorku.ca/index.php/cws/article/view/6420

Democracy Now. (2016, 20 May). Occupied Canada: Indigenous & black lives matter activists unite to protest violence & neglect. Retrieved from https://www.democracynow.org/2016/5/20/occupied_canada_indigenous_black_lives_matter

Diouf, S.A. (2014). *Slavery's exiles: The story of the American maroons.* New York: NYU Press.

Donato, A. (2015, 28 September). Black Lives Matter takes back the night and shuts down downtown Toronto, *Huffington Post Canada.* Retrieved from http://www.huffingtonpost.ca/2015/09/28/Black-lives-matter-toronto_n_8209932.html

Douglas, D. (2014). *Proceedings from Ms. Debbie Douglas, executive director, Ontario Council of Agencies Serving Immigrants (OCASI) at the Citizenship and Immigration Committee.* Retrieved from https://openparliament.ca/committees/immigration/41-2/23/debbie-douglas-1/only/

Drake, S.C. (1993). Diaspora studies and pan-Africanism. In J.E. Harris (Ed.), *Global dimensions of the African diaspora* (2nd ed., pp. 451–514). Washington, DC: Howard University Press.

Esedebe, P.O. (1994). *Pan-Africanism: The idea and movement, 1776–1991.* Washington, DC: Howard University Press.

Fanfair, R. (1995a, March 16). Racism no excuse. *Share,* 4.

Fanfair, R. (1995b). Unity urged. *Share,* 2.

Flare Staff. (2017, 17 September). #HowIMadeit: Janaya Khan, Activist. Retrieved from https://www.flare.com/how-i-made-it/janaya-khan/

Forsythe, D. (1971). *Let the niggers burn: The Sir George Williams University affair and its Caribbean aftermath.* Montreal: Black Rose.

Franklin, V.P. (1993). Caribbean intellectual influences on Afro-Americans in the United States. In A. Hennessy (Ed.), *Caribbean intellectuals in the twentieth-century Caribbean,* vol. 1 (pp. 179–90). London: Macmillan.

Frost, K.S. (2007). Communities of resistance: African Americans and African Canadians in antebellum Toronto. *Ontario History, 99*(1), 44–63.

Frost, K.S. (2013). African American and African Canadian transnationalism along the Detroit River borderland: The example of Madison J. Lightfoot. *Journal of American Ethnic History, 32*(2), 78–88. Retrieved from https://doi.org/10.5406/jamerethnhist.32.2.0078

Gairey, H. (1981). *A black man's Toronto, 1914–1918: The reminiscences of Harry Gairey.* Toronto: Multicultural History Society of Ontario.

Gastaldo, D., Gooden, A., & Massaquoi, N. (2004). Transnational health promotion: Social well-being across borders and immigrant women's subjectivities. *Wagadu: A Journal of Transnational Women's and Gender Studies, 2,* 1–16. Retrieved from http://colfax.cortland.edu/wagadu/Volume%202/Printable/gastaldo.pdf

Gooden, A.Y. (2005). *Betta must come: African Caribbean migrants in Canada: Migration, community building and cultural legacies* (Doctoral dissertation). Temple University, Philadelphia.

Goldsbie, J., & Cole, S. (2016, 29 June). 6 Toronto LGBTQ heroes worth celebrating this Pride weekend. Retrieved from https://nowtoronto.com/news/6-local-heroes/

Gordon, L.R. (2000). Africana thought and African diasporic studies. *The Black Scholar, 30*(3–4), 25–30. https://doi.org/10.1080/00064246.2000.11431105

Gordon Nembhard, J. (2014). *Collective courage: A history of African American cooperative economic thought and practice.* University Park: Penn State Press.

Hall, S. (1993). What is this "black" in black popular culture? *Social Justice, 20*(1/2), 104–14. Retrieved from http://www.jstor.org/stable/29766735

Hall, S. (1995). Negotiating Caribbean identities, *New Left Review, 209,* 3–14. Retrieved from https://newleftreview.org/I/209/stuart-hall-negotiating-caribbean-identities

Hamilton, A.W. (1969, February). "Sir George explodes: Alleged racism charges lead to vandalism." *Contrast.*

Harewood, J. (1982) The impact of the national black organization and the sphere of influence it transmits on black life in Canada. In V. D'Oyley (Ed.), *Black presence in multi-ethnic Canada* (pp. 273–87). Vancouver: Center for Curriculum, University of British Columbia.

Harris, C. (2014). Canadian black power, organic intellectuals, and the war of position in Toronto, 1967–1975. *CLR James Journal, 20*(1/2). https//doi.org/10.5840/clrjames20149159

Harris, J E. (1993). *Global dimensions of the African diaspora.* Washington, DC: Howard University Press.

Henry, K.S. (1981). *Black politics in Toronto since WWI.* Toronto: Multicultural History Society of Ontario.

Hill, D.G. (1960). *Negroes in Toronto: A sociological study of a minority group* (Doctoral dissertation). University of Toronto, Toronto.

Hill, D.G. (1981). *The freedom-seekers: Blacks in early Canada.* Agincourt: Book Society of Canada.

Hill, L. (1996). *Women of vision: The story of the Canadian Negro Women's Association, 1951–1976.* Toronto: Umbrella.

Hill Collins, P. (2002). *Black feminist thought: Knowledge, consciousness and the politics of empowerment* [E-edition]. New York: Routledge. Retrieved from https://uniteyouthdublin.files.wordpress.com/2015/01/black-feminist-though-by-patricia-hill-collins.pdf

Hudson, P. (2014). Research, repression, and revolution – On Montreal and the black radical tradition: An interview with David Austin. *CLR James Journal, 20*(1/2), 197–232. https://doi: 10.5840/clrjames201492319

Hudson, P.J., & Kumugisha, A. (2014). On black Canadian thought. *CLR James Journal, 20*(1/2), 3–30. https://doi.org/10.5840/clrjames201492216

Jegroo, A. (2016, 13 September). Why Black Lives Matter is fighting alongside Dakota access pipeline protesters. *Splinter.* Retrieved from https://splinternews.com/why-black-lives-matter-is-fighting-alongside-dakota-acc-1793861838

Jones, B.R., & Walker, J.W.St.G. (2016). *Burnley "Rocky" Jones: Revolutionary.* Halifax: Fernwood.

Kelly, R.D. (2000). How the west was one: On the uses and limitations of diaspora. *The Black Scholar, 30*(3–4), 31–5. https://doi.org/10.1080/00064246.2000.11431106

Khagram, S., & Levitt, P. (Eds.). (2008). *Constructing transnational studies: The transnational studies reader: Sections and innovations.* New York: Routledge.

Khan, J. (2016). Standing Rock resistance. Retrieved from http://janayakhan.com/2016/08/30/standing-rock/

Lemelle, S. (1992). *Pan-Africanism for beginners.* London: Writers and Readers.

Mann, K. (2010) Shifting paradigms in the study of the African diaspora and of Atlantic history and culture. *Slavery and Abolition, 22*(1/2), 3–21. https://doi.org/10.1080/714005181

Marano, C. (2010). Rising strongly and rapidly: The Universal Negro Improvement Association in Canada, 1919–1940. *Canadian Historical Review, 91*(2), 233–59. https://doi.org/10.1353/can.0.0309

Mathieu, S.J. (2010). *North of the color line: Migration and black resistance in Canada, 1870–1955.* Chapel Hill: University of North Carolina Press.

Maynard, R. (2017). *Policing black lives: State violence in Canada from slavery to the present.* Halifax: Fernwood.

McClain, P.D. (1979). *Alienation and resistance: The political behavior of Afro-Canadians.* Palo Alto: R & E Research.

McCurdy, H. (1969, October 2). Letter to the editor. *Contrast.*

McTair, R. (Director). (2000). *Journey to justice* [Documentary]. Toronto: National Film Board of Canada.

Mihevc, J. (2017, 2 August 2). Toronto Caribbean carnival deserves funding from Canada, Ontario. *Toronto Star.* Retrieved from https://www.thestar.com/opinion/commentary/2017/08/02/toronto-caribbean-carnival-deserves-funding-from-canada-ontario-mihevic.html

Mohanty, C.T. (2003). Under western eyes revisited: Feminist solidarity through anticapitalist struggles. *Signs: Journal of Women in Culture and Society, 28*(2), 499–535. https://doi.org/10.1086/342914

Moore, D., & Selvon, S. (1985). *Don Moore: An autobiography.* Toronto: Williams-Wallace.

Nasser, S. (2017, 25 June). Black Lives Matter NYC "inspired" by Toronto chapter's call for removal of uniformed police. CBC News. Retrieved from http://www.cbc.ca/news/canada/toronto/Black-lives-matter-toronto-pride-2017-1.4177554

NCBW (National Congress of Black Women). (1973, 6–8 April). *Report of the First Congress.* In Papers of the Ontario Black History Society.

Onstad, K. (2017, 27 February). Rebel rebel. *Toronto Life.* Retrieved from https://torontolife.com/city/toronto-politics/rebel-rebel/

Orozco, M. (2017, 10 February). Remittances to Latin American and the Caribbean in 2016. *The Dialogue: Leadership for the Americas.* Retrieved from http://www.thedialogue.org/wp-content/uploads/2017/02/Remittances-2016-FINAL-DRAFT-1.pdf

Otero, S. (2000). Rethinking the diaspora: African, Brazilian, and Cuban communities in Africa and the Americas. *The Black Scholar, 30*(3–4), 54–5. https://doi.org/10.1080/00064246.2000.11431110

Patterson, T.R., & Kelly, R.D. (2000). Unfinished migrations: Reflections on the African diaspora and the making of the modern world. *African Studies Review, 43*(1), 11–45. https://doi.org/10.2307/524719

Plaza, D. (2007). An examination of transnational remittance practices of Jamaican Canadian families. *Global Development Studies, 4*(3–4), 217–50.

Public Safety Canada. (2009). *Common ground: An examination of similarities between Black and Aboriginal communities.* Retrieved from https://www.publicsafety.gc.ca/cnt/rsrcs/pblctns/cmmn-grnd/index-en.aspx#moving

Reid-Maroney, N. (2013). *The Reverend Jennie Johnson and African Canadian history, 1868–1967.* Rochester: University of Rochester Press.

Rummel, R.J. (1970). The field of social forces. Chapter 14 in *Understanding conflict and war: The conflict helix.* Beverly Hills: Sage. Retrieved from https://www.hawaii.edu/powerkills/TCH.CHAP14.HTM

Scotiabank Caribana 2010 and Ipsos Reid release economic impact study results. (2010). Retrieved from http://www.newswire.ca/news-releases/scotiabank-caribana-2010-and-ipsos-reid-release-economic-impact-study-results-539728982.html

Shadd, A. (2010). *The journey from Tollgate to Parkway: African Canadians in Hamilton.* Toronto: Dundurn.

Shadd Shreve, D. (1983). *The Africanadian church: A stabilizer.* Jordan Station: Paideia Press.

Shepperson, G. (1993). African diaspora: Concept and context. In J.E. Harris (Ed.), *Global dimensions of the African diaspora* (2nd ed.) (pp. 41–9). Washington, DC: Howard University Press.

Shum, M. (Director). (2014). *Ninth floor* [Documentary]. Toronto: National Film Board of Canada.

Silverman, J.H. (1985). *Unwelcome guests: Canada West's response to American fugitive slaves, 1800–1865*. Millwood: Associated Faculty.

Simmons, A., Plaza, D., & Piché, V. (2005). *The remittance sending practices of Haitians and Jamaicans in Canada*. Toronto: Centre for Research on Latin America and the Caribbean (CERLAC), York University.

Soulliere, H.M. (2005). Brotherhood of sleeping car porters. Retrieved from http://www.windsor-communities.com/african-labour-brotherhood.php

Stephens, M. (2015). New points of recognition: Stuart Hall's gift to the study of blackness. *Small Axe: A Caribbean Journal of Criticism, 19*(1), 88–99. https://doi.org/10.1215/07990537-2873242

Taylor, K.Y. (2016). *From #blacklivesmatter to black liberation*. Chicago: Haymarket.

Taylor, S. (2001). *Keeping them adrift: Canadian state-sponsored under-development of African Canadians*. Proceedings from Conference on the Rights of Minorities of African Descent in the Americas. Montreal: Concordia University.

Trotman, D.V. (2005). Transforming Caribbean and Canadian identity: Contesting claims for Toronto's Caribana. *Atlantic Studies, 2*(2), 177–98. https://doi.org/10.1080/10494820500224392

Trotz, A. (2006). Rethinking Caribbean transnational connections: Conceptual itineraries. *Global Networks, 6*(1), 41–59. https://doi.org/10.1111/j.1471-0374.2006.00132.x

Vertovec, S. (1999). Conceiving and researching transnationalism. *Ethnic and Racial Studies, 22*(2), 447–62. https://doi.org/10.1080/014198799329558

Vertovec, S. (2001). Transnationalism and identity. *Journal of Ethnic and Migration Studies, 27*(4), 573–82. https://doi.org/10.1080/13691830120090386

Walcott, R. (2007). Towards a methodology of reading hip-hop in Canada. In D. Divine (Ed.), *Multiple lenses: Voices from the diaspora located in Canada* (pp. 48–61). Newcastle: Cambridge Scholars.

Walcott, R. (2014). Shame: A polemic. *CLR James Journal, 20*(1–2), 275–9. https://doi.org/10.5840/clrjames201492318

Walker, B. (2014). The National Black Coalition of Canada, "race," and social equality in the age of multiculturalism. *CLR James Journal, 20*(1/2), 159–77. https://doi.org/10.5840/clrjames201493020

Walker, J. (2007). Approaching African-Canadian history. In D. Divine (Ed.), *Multiple lenses: Voices from the diaspora located in Canada* (pp. 2–10). Newcastle: Cambridge Scholars.

Weinstein, W. (n.d). Articulation theory for beginners. Retrieved from http://www.personal.kent.edu/~mweinste/CI67095/Articulation.PDF

Wharton-Zaretsky, M. (1999). Fleurette Osborne: A black woman activist. *Macomere: The Journal of the Association of Caribbean Women Writers and Scholars, 2*, 148–63.

Wilson, C. (1997). Conceptualizing the African diaspora. *Comparative Studies of South Asia, Africa and the Middle East, 17*(2), 118–22. https://doi.org/10.1215/1089201X-17-2-118

Zeleza, P.T. (2008). The challenges of studying the African diasporas. *African Sociological Review/Revue Africaine de Sociologie, 12*(2), 4–21. https://doi.org/10.4314/asr.v12i2.49831

PART TWO

Women and Leadership

5 To Commit and to Lead: Black Women Organizing across Communities in Montreal

ROSALIND HAMPTON AND DÉSIRÉE ROCHAT

Black community organizing in Montreal has always depended on the commitment and leadership of Black women. The Coloured Women's Club of Montreal, established in 1902, was the first Black community organization and laid the foundation for a nexus of Black institutions sustained by a network of dedicated community workers. The work of Black women has ensured the survival and ongoing development of Montreal's Black communities within the broader context of persistent structural inequity and racialized colonial hierarchy.

In this chapter we examine Black women's community work in Montreal during the twentieth century while considering the impact of migration and labour policies and of neo-liberalism on the social, economic, and political conditions under which these women organized. We identify leadership and community-building strategies that emerge from this analysis, mainly around two areas of organizing: mutual aid and education, and women's advocacy and mobilization. Drawing on Black feminist theories, we assert an anti-vanguardist form of leadership informed by our reading of a century of community-building efforts by Black women in shifting local, national, and diasporic contexts. We argue against the construction of high-profile individual leaders in favour of building community capacity and coalitional movements that embrace the heterogeneity of Black communities. Finally, we examine the creative historical and archival work of women organizers as a way to share leadership and build intergenerational learning spaces.

In building an understanding of Black women's organizing as leadership, we engage in a Black feminist analysis that focuses on coalition building across differences. This approach is particularly salient in the context of Montreal, historically a city largely divided by language, both socially and geographically. Through examining the experiences of women working in French- and English-speaking communities, as well as through drawing on literature published in both languages, we reveal Black women's rejection of this cultural-linguistic dichotomy and the myth of Canada's two founding nations that it supports.

A Black Feminist Methodology

Black feminisms emerge from the social locations, lived experiences, and intellectual, cultural, and political work of Black women as they navigate interlocking relations of race, class, gender, and sexuality in local and diasporic contexts (Collins, 2009; Lorde, 1984; Massaquoi, 2007; Wane, 2002). We refer to feminisms in the plural, recognizing the multiplicity and fluidity of Black feminist theories and practices. To share a common location within power relations does not mean that any given group is a homogeneous one; "Black women" represents a diverse yet partial and fluid perspective, reflecting the experiences of women who also identify with various social-economic classes, trans/nationalisms, cultural traditions, and political positions. Black feminisms include liberal, radical, and revolutionary ideologies and politics (James, 2013), and engaging critically with these variations in Black women's organizing is part of what interests us as we advocate an approach to leadership that prioritizes building political solidarity across differences (James, 2013; Lorde, 1984) and emphasizes "cooperation and collectivism over competition and individualism" (Ransby, 2003, p. 365).

We hasten to note that the dominant location of feminist theory remains within the academy, and this limits its accessibility and resonance outside of academe, particularly among racialized poor and working class women (Ferguson & King, 2011; James, 2013; Reece, 2007; Yee, 2011). Consequently, we hesitate to name as "feminist" women who did not know or identify with the term, or who may have rejected it. As Barbara Ransby (2003) critically observes, it is important that feminist scholars and activists remain "ever cautious of the danger inherent in our work: imposing our contemporary dilemmas and expectations on a generation of women who spoke a different language, moved at a different rhythm, and juggled a different set of issues and concerns" (p. 2; see also Affan, 2013).

Narrow definitions of activism, leadership, and politics tend to overlook the everyday social and political organizing of women and delimit the assumed political sphere. Black feminists have challenged patriarchal constructions of activism and leadership, such as those that privilege direct confrontation with authorities, charismatic and high-profile male spokespeople, and political involvement through institutions that are recognized and validated by the state (Collins, 2009; hooks, 2000;

Reece, 2007). We work from a holistic definition of leadership as "the desire, ability and efforts to influence the world around us, based upon an ethic of care for self and other and fuelled by a vision that one sustains over time" (Ferguson & King, 2011, p. 11). The community organizing and cultural and educational work of Black women in our communities thus emerges as an important "lens through which to understand [their] sense of citizenship and 'the political'" (Fisher, 2012, p. 125).

Our positions as Black women of mixed-race ancestry who live and work in Montreal also shape the content of this work; we draw on our own experiences as community workers, educators, and researchers in Black communities. Hence as well as the scholars whose work and influence will be acknowledged in references throughout this chapter, we recognize the long-term community work of Black women in Montreal whose knowledge we also draw on here. We are especially grateful to Suzie Boisrond, Adeline Chancy, Monique Dauphin, Brenda Paris, Maguy Métellus, Mireille Métellus, Dolores Sandoval, Marjorie Villefranche, and Dorothy Williams for their longstanding leadership in our communities and the knowledge and stories they have generously shared with us.

In addition to long-term community participation and observation, informal conversations and formal interviews, this chapter draws on a review of academic publications, theses, and unpublished community documents. The history we discuss, like all history, is neither comprehensive nor fixed. While LGBTQ Black women have certainly been involved in community work in Montreal, for example, the literature regarding Montreal Black history is generally heteronormative and silent about experiences specific to queer Black people, while the literature about Montreal queer communities is generally silent on issues of race (this issue is not specific to Montreal; for the Canadian context, see Lee, 2009).

Community Building across the Twentieth Century

Historical and ongoing processes of colonization and racialization are key "determinants of socio-political and economic outcomes that determine access to resources and life chances for Indigenous and racialized groups in Canada" (Wallis, Sunseri, & Galabuzi, 2010, p. 2). As neoliberal policies and practices advance, in Québec as elsewhere, political and economic inequity is exacerbated and social hierarchies are further entrenched. During periods of economic crises Black communities have had to cope with fewer resources, worsening labour conditions, and increased racism at institutional and interpersonal levels. We can identify cycles of responsive community organizing during these periods, with a notable shift in the 1970s towards a proliferation of government-funded non-profit organizations. In this section we reflect on Black women's community work within these socio-economic contexts, rejecting a binary opposition between "community work" and "activism" and asserting instead that all organizing is work (see D.E. Smith, 2005) and all Black community work within a racialized settler colonial nation is activism.

Mutual Aid and Education

Well into the twentieth century, Montreal was a city with remarkably poor living conditions for all but the wealthy elite, and very few social aid and service agencies. The white population often excluded and refused services to Black people in Montreal, even where there was no official policy of segregation (Small & Thornhill, 2008; Williams, 1997). The Black community, within which women formed a majority, had to organize its own social aid: the Coloured Women's Club (CWC) offered a variety of services, including a clothing depot, services for war veterans, a community soup kitchen, a bed in a local hospital, and a cemetery plot.

Several women were involved in building community infrastructure beyond the CWC and played instrumental roles in establishing a number of other groups and organizations. In 1907, CWC members and their husbands established the multidenominational Union Congregational Church (later Union United) "to serve its Community in whatever ways became necessary to foster its development" (J. Bertley, 1982, p. 15). The next major organization established was the Montreal division of Marcus Garvey's pan-African/Black nationalist United Negro Improvement Association (UNIA), inaugurated in 1919. This was followed by the creation of the Negro Community Centre (NCC) in 1927. These organizations, all located in the St Antoine (now Little Burgundy) neighbourhood, together formed the bedrock of the emerging community, and many folks were active in all four. Black women were involved in all levels of organizing, and the UNIA constitution explicitly called for shared power among men and women in the form of a joint presidency (Williams, 1997).

Educational organizing was a particularly salient area of Black women's leadership. The Union Church's first Sunday school superintendent, Ethel Gaspard, for example, "possessed a great deal of autonomy and responsibility" as an officer of the church (J. Bertley, 1982, p. 32) and coordinated classes on spiritual and religious teachings, community values, performing arts, and public speaking for community members of all ages. Women also organized, managed, and taught in education programs at the NCC and UNIA (J. Bertley, 1982; Williams, 1997). Classes were offered in literary arts, maths, public speaking, practical skills and trades, and arts education (particularly music and theatre performance). Several organizations, clubs, and women's auxiliaries offered scholarships for Black students and, given its international status and pan-Africanist philosophy, the UNIA made a particular effort to provide financial support to university students coming from the African continent (L.W. Bertley, 1980). Women such as lifelong community worker Ann De Shields and Miss L. De Shields, who was most likely "the first black librarian in the city," played prominent roles in the Literary Club (est. 1920) (L. Bertley, 1980, p. 282). One of the most successful auxiliary programs of the UNIA, the club provided access to a library and encouraged members to read Black history (L. Bertley, 1980). When the club was discontinued during the Depression, the women of the Sunday school established a Library and Literary Forum to fill the gap (J. Bertley, 1982).

Domestic Worker Policies and Programs

Racialized and gendered immigration policies geared towards attracting Black women's labour set the demographic patterns in Montreal's Black community, as in the rest of Canada (Calliste, 1993). Moreover, these policies would set up the racist and sexist discourses that shaped the experiences of Black women migrating from the Caribbean for decades to come. The first Domestic Workers Scheme, in 1911, recruited women from Guadeloupe to work for wealthy French Canadian families (Calliste, 1993; Williams, 1997). The program was abruptly terminated, however, for two principal reasons: anxiety that unmarried women might become pregnant, and a downturn in the pre-Second World War economy that saw an increase in white women willing to work as domestics. Consequently entry into Canada was blocked, and many Black women from Guadeloupe and other Caribbean nations were deported between 1913 and 1915 (Williams, 1997).

In 1955, the Canadian government passed its second Domestic Workers Scheme to recruit women from the Caribbean – including those educated to be teachers, nurses, and clerks – to act as servants, cleaners, and caregivers in Canadian homes (Handleman, 1964; Williams, 1997). The development of the Pioneer Girls program at the NCC in 1957 in response to the new influx of domestic workers suggests the persistence of the above noted anxiety regarding Black – particularly female – morality and sexuality. Funded by the federal government, the program can be understood as a formal attempt to shape and control the newly arrived domestic workers' behaviour, reflecting the dominant society's desire to control Black bodies as well as an arguably necessary Black community internal policing and politics of respectability. Fraternal organizations and affiliated women's branches had always offered their members gendered guidance, support, monitoring and, when they deemed it necessary, pressure regarding "clean living and an upright, moral life" (Israel, 1928, p. 171). The increase in domestic workers from the Caribbean in the 1950s escalated such concerns at the intersections of race, class, gender, and sexuality in a city well known for its sex industry (Mortimier, 2009) and interracial socializing (Austin, 2013; Israel, 1928). Some of the middle-class Caribbean immigrants in the city were angered by the prospect of the dominant white society judging them based on the behaviour of domestic workers who were, by definition and regardless of previous status in the Caribbean, considered "lower class" (Handleman, 1964).

The Pioneer Girls program was intended to help the women "adjust" to Canada through teaching them national geography and history, what clothing to wear in the winter, where they might secure jobs following their work as domestics, and about "sex, morals and personal sanitation" (Handleman, 1964, p. 75). The group worker took a "very authoritarian stance" towards the women: "'A well-adjusted domestic,' in the words of the group worker, 'is a girl who does her job as a domestic well, and who has good relations with her employer and doesn't get into trouble'" (p. 75). Some women refused this "adjustment" and disengaged from the group, which was discontinued in 1960 due to a lack of participation. The significance of this refusal should not be underestimated. As Erica Lawson (2002) reminds us, discourses informed by denigrating stereotypes of Black women are used to justify the exploitation of their labour and sexuality. Domestic workers in Montreal as elsewhere were "at the mercy of their employers when sexual harassment and physical intimidation were part of the job" (Williams, 1997, p. 48); what did doing one's job "well" while maintaining "good relations" with one's employer and "not getting in trouble" suggest in such contexts? Black women domestics were thus imagined as "Mammies" and "Jezebels" who lacked the intelligence to so much as dress themselves for Montreal's colder climate. This paternalism echoed racist immigration policies that from 1910 to 1953 limited the eligibility of newcomers from southern countries based on "climate unsuitability."[1]

While the 1955 Domestic Scheme allowed some Caribbean Black women to immigrate to Canada to fill labour demands, their presence remained a perceived threat to the constructed whiteness and Eurocentric values of Canadian nationhood (Lawson, 2002).

Community Organizations in the Second Half of the Twentieth Century

Community education was a critical political practice geared towards building individual and collective empowerment, whether its primary aims represented liberal or more radical political positions. This was particularly the case during the second half of the century as the Black population grew and established a significant presence in neighbourhoods other than Little Burgundy. Systemic racism in Montreal at all levels of schooling was increasingly exposed and challenged in a global climate of anti-colonial and Black uprising. This volatile context reached a climax in Montreal in 1969 when Black student mobilization against institutional racism and a thirteen-day sit-in at Sir George Williams University ended in a confrontation with police and multiple arrests (Affan, 2013; Austin, 2013).

It was within this context that the Quebec Board of Black Educators (QBBE, est. 1969) and the Black Studies Center (est. 1971) were formed. Building on the success of a remedial school program for Black youth at the UNIA from 1965–7 (L. Bertley, 1980), the QBBE established the DaCosta Hall program in 1970 to provide Black learners with academic support and mentorship. This marked the beginning of an era of non-profit organizations, government lobbying, and emphasis on promoting Black economic and "social entrepreneurship" (Bayne, n.d.). In 1972 alone, three new anglophone Black community associations were established in neighbourhoods with significant Black populations, the Black Theatre Workshop was incorporated, and the Black Community Central Administration of Quebec (which became the Black Community Council of Quebec) was created to pursue community development initiatives and coordinate the neighbourhood associations (Williams, 1997). While women were involved in the founding and operation of these newer organizations, they now were a minority, and for the next several decades the dominant organizations of the English-speaking community were strongly associated with the public personas of the men who served as founders, presidents, and board members (see Bayne, n.d.; Community Forum, 1992).

The Maison d'Haïti and the Bureau de la communauté chrétienne des Haïtiens de Montréal (now the called Bureau de la communauté haïtienne de Montréal, BCHM) were also founded in 1972 and remain key Haitian community organizations. Since the early 1960s there had been a sustained Haitian migration to Québec, made up at first of a mostly urban, French-speaking, middle and upper class fleeing escalating repression by François Duvalier's dictatorial regime. Haitian migration intensified in the late 1960s and early 1970s, and by then included technical professionals from the urban working class and an increasing majority of Creole-speaking rural and agricultural workers, also fleeing unprecedented levels of violence and economic hardship. As had been the case within other Caribbean communities, class-based tensions within the Haitian community erupted as increased numbers of migrants arrived in the city. Recognizing and pushing back against these tensions, the emerging organizations opened up spaces for inter-class expatriate organizing and mobilization, both against the Duvalier regime and for the rights of the newly arrived (S. Mills, 2016).

As in the anglophone organizations of the era, high-profile and charismatic men were the face of the BCHM during its first decades. Nevertheless, some of the women who actively participated in the organizations' activities during these years also formed groups of their own, and continue their work with BCHM and these groups to this day. Maison d'Haïti's leadership from its origins relied on coalitional approaches to organizing, and many women played strong roles in leading the organization and arranging mutual aid, education, cultural programs, advocacy, and mobilization for all members of the Haitian community (Sanders, 2013). Many of the women from Maison d'Haïti and BCHM were also involved with other community groups and networks, such as feminist and labour groups and popular literacy programs.

"You Don't Abandon Your Own People": Women's Advocacy and Mobilization

While the mandates of most Black community organizations were framed around mutual aid and education, this aid has always necessarily included various forms of advocacy, particularly in relation to immigration matters and confronting systemic racism. Groups banded together at times to respond to specific incidents of racial discrimination; however, at other times class tensions, nationalism, and individualism impeded community building. The British socialization and middle-class aspirations of Anglo-Caribbean immigrants are noted in a number of studies, contrasted against a "Canadian Negro" population that is described by researchers as compliant (Handleman, 1964; Israel, 1928; Potter, 1949). Stereotypes contrasting Canadian- and Caribbean-born Black people persisted throughout the political mobilizations of the 1960s and 1970s. Indeed, some older members of Black communities shared the perception of the Canadian state authorities that Caribbean exchange students were radical agitators manipulating and corrupting an acquiescent African Canadian population (Affan, 2013; Austin, 2013). At the same time, some of the leaders of established anglophone Black community organizations were seen by new arrivals as old-fashioned gatekeepers who were too conservative, self-interested, and/or complacent to fight for meaningful social change (Affan, 2013; Handleman, 1964; Williams, 1997). The younger activists did not always recognize the value and experience of the older generation of organizers. In return, established community leaders employed various strategies to preserve the status quo within "their" organizations, including blocking proposals and establishing restrictive membership policies aimed at denying the new arrivals access to positions of power (Handleman, 1964).

Political differences between perceived "assimilationists" and "radicals" were much intensified as Caribbean and other Black university students exerted pressure on the community. The Black Action Party (BAP), composed of six men and women who were studying at McGill, began volunteering at the NCC in 1970. They offered Black history lectures and provided high school students with political mentoring, but from the onset the politics and approach of BAP members were in constant tension with the NCC's official multicultural approach that made the centre eligible for new government funding (Williams, 1997). The NCC had always been a racially integrated organization, and 35 per cent of the NCC membership was white (Handleman, 1964), including two board members. Under pressure from the students, it was agreed that white people be removed from the board. The NCC, however, would not budge on the students' demand for "Negro" to be removed from the centre's name. Consequently, the BAP "turned their backs on the Negro Community Center in disgust" (Williams, 1997, p. 129).

Although charismatic young men from the Caribbean were the most prominent figures of student activism around the universities in the late 1960s and into the 1970s, Black young women remained very much involved. Despite the intra-community tensions, in the events at Sir George Williams University and their aftermath Black women rose above political differences and mobilized to meet the varied needs of high-profile activists. Once again, Black women organized to provide food, moral support, and legal representation. One of the women who was actively involved in this organizing highlights the communal orientation that anchored this work in remarks to historian Samah Affan (2013):

> It was nonsense. You don't abandon your own people because somebody tells you they're a Marxist and they're lining up with you ... The division was ideology. Because they [student activists] thought they had an ideology and they thought we didn't. But our ideology was what we referred to as African Socialism. Because in the village, if one person eats, everybody eats ... And yet! That same [activist] who was so Marxist, when he was in prison, I used

> to go to see him every week and bring him clothes and food. And when he needed anything he would write to me for it. I don't know why he didn't ask his white-uh Marxist brothers and sisters. (p. 79)

This woman's comments directly confront gendered, racialized, and class-based assumptions about whose ways of knowing and whose knowledge is valuable. Her activism is grounded in a social-political analysis that pushes back against the assumed authority of what she understands as Marxist ideology and asserts a personal and collective connection to Africa and to African knowledge systems.

The consequences for student activists of this time were severe and included prison sentences and deportations (Forsythe, 1971). As is characteristic of the neo-liberal state, the last decades of the century saw increasing forms of domestic and international surveillance, violence, and intimidation to repress resistance and dissent. By the mid-1970s several major Black community organizations were involved in popular education, lobbying, negotiations with governments, and mobilizing protest against racism and police violence (Community Forum, 1992; Ruggles & Rovinescu, 1996).

Black Nurses Organize

In the late 1970s, Black nurses organized labour associations to challenge institutional racism and discrimination in their workplaces. Racist practices and discourse were not new to the nursing sector. Black women and community organizations had been advocating on behalf of Black nurses and nursing students since the 1930s (J. Bertley, 1982; Calliste, 1996). Haitian nurses faced even more explicit racism than Black women from the Anglo-Caribbean (Flynn, 2003). Starting in the late 1950s, immigration officers and hospitals circulated stereotyped information about Haitian nursing students and nurses aimed at excluding them from the sector. These representations drew on stereotypes that linked "colonial religious discourses that associated 'blackness' with sin, dirt and filth" with speculation the women were just using the profession to gain entry into Canada (Flynn, 2003). Haitian nurses also faced intensive surveillance by immigration authorities and hospitals, as well as by other nurses and nursing associations (Flynn, 2003). Black nurses formed The Ralliement des infirmières et infirmières auxiliaires Haïtiennes de Montréal in 1977 and the Black Nurses Association of Quebec (BNAQ) in the early 1980s. While promotion of worker solidarity was among the goals of the former, the extent to which the two groups directly collaborated is uncertain. In the 1980s the BNAQ, supported by several Black community organizations, filed a number of individual and collective complaints to employers and the Québec Human Rights Commission, ultimately challenging the practices of the commission itself (BNAQ & NCC, 1987; Calliste, 1996, 2000). There is no indication, however, that this lobbying included Haitian organizations or extended support to Haitian women (Flynn, 2003).

Haitian Feminists

At the beginning of the 1970s, women involved at the BCHM and the Maison d'Haïti also formed their own advocacy and mobilization platforms. The Point de Ralliement des Femmes d'Origine Haïtienne was formed in 1971, included women involved at the BCHM, and had consciousness raising for Haitian women as one of its aims (Charles, 1995). Based on their anti-Duvalier activism, these women had become critical of the sexism within anti-Duvalier and nationalistic groups. Hence, they started to discuss and theorize women's subordination in the Haitian community as well as in the broader Québec society (Charles, 1995; Rateau, 2009; Sanders, 2013). They organized reading circles, took part in feminist mobilizations, and later started a Creole radio show, Pawòl Fanm – still airing every week – on community station Radio Centre Ville (Rateau, 2009).

Women organizers from Maison d'Haïti were also involved in Rasanbleman Fanm Ayisyèn (RAFA), formed in 1973 and transformed into Nègès Vanyan in 1979 (Charles, 1995). Some of the core women of RAFA/Nègès Vanyan had also been involved in the communist party in Haiti, the Parti Unifié des Communistes Haïtiens, and were in close contact with international women's movements. They had ties to various communist parties around the world and participated in women's conferences in East Berlin, Panama, Moscow, and Cuba (Charles, 1995). Nègès Vanyan organized educational and cultural activities, produced community newsletters, and collaborated with other groups within and outside the Haitian community (S. Mills, 2016; Monique, Myriam, Rosemary & Viviane, 1982; Sanders, 2013).

The Congress of Black Women

Through their participation in various groups, women across communities came into contact with one another and developed a network of Black women organizers in Montreal that went on to form an active contingent of the Congress of Black Women of Canada. In 1973, the Ontario-based Canadian Negro Women's Association organized a congress in Toronto that was attended by more than five hundred Black women from across Canada (Small & Thornhill, 2008). Black women from the Montreal network, including members of the CWC and Nègès Vanyan, formed the Montreal Regional Committee of the Congress of Black Women (Kouka-Ganga, 1982) and organized the next Congress of Black Women in Montreal in 1974 (Small & Thornhill, 2008). This second conference was titled "The Black Woman and Her Family," and workshop themes reflected an understanding that concerns "of the Black woman and her family" spanned social, political, and economic spheres: "Health and Welfare, Youth and Education, Immigration, Economics and the Black Family, and the Triple Repression of Black Women" (J. Mills, 2015, p. 9).

While the membership of the regional committee was predominantly English speaking, efforts were made to involve Black francophone women, and Haitian community anti-racist struggles received unconditional support (Kouka-Ganga, 1982). As Haitian activist Adeline Chancy (n.d.) noted, the congress's efforts were part of a larger struggle against racism that demanded Black women organize together for popular and critical education and protest and to denounce acts of aggression and unite with other Black women in Africa, the Caribbean, and the United States. Over the next several years women from the CWC, Nègès Vanyan, Point de Ralliement, and the Montreal Regional Committee participated in the development of the national organization. The Congress of Black Women of Canada (CBWC) was formally established in 1980 and from the onset took public positions on local struggles affecting the Haitian community, opposing the deportations of Haitians (S. Mills, 2013) and supporting Black, mostly Haitian, taxi drivers who mobilized against racism in the industry and demanded an enquiry from the Québec Human Rights Commission in the mid-1980s (J. Mills, 2015; S. Mills, 2016). The CBWC delivered a presentation before the enquiry (J. Mills, 2015).

The CBWC was, and continues to be, a space for Black women to explore and theorize their experiences, create alliances, build solidarities, and articulate their Black feminist visions and practice (J. Mills, 2015). Their Black feminist praxis aims to empower Black women and their nuclear and extended families, as Shirley Small and Esmerelda Thornhill (2008) explain:

> Congress has always tried to adopt a discourse that is not only critically grounded in the historical trajectory of Black women but, more significantly, a discourse that also is accessible to our men folk – boy-children, sons, fathers, brothers, male partners, spouses, and grandfathers. (p. 434)

This inclusive, issue-based approach to organizing across linguistic, national, and cultural differences represents a community-oriented feminist politics gleaned through decades of experience.

Black Feminist Community Building as Leadership

Drawing from this feminist politics and Black community knowledge base, we discuss three critical strategies for feminist organizing in the context of neo-liberalism: first, the explicit rejection of vanguardist forms of leadership in favour of non-hierarchical approaches that promote community capacity-building and the active involvement of a wide range of community members; second, working across intra- and inter-community differences; and third, the importance of historical and archival retrieval as an organizing practice for community building and sharing leadership. These strategies demand multiple forms of political, social, and cultural action guided by an abiding, deep-rooted commitment to and membership within the community.

Rejecting Vanguardism

Throughout the twentieth century there was competition and conflict between Black community leaders (particularly men) and the organizations they represented (Bayne, n.d.; Handleman, 1964; Israel, 1928; Williams, 1997). We contend that such rivalry is exacerbated by attempts at race-based organizing that erase rather than embrace intra-community differences, and such debility is worsened by hierarchical leadership and organizing. Consequently, we assert the need to reject vanguardist approaches to community organizing and activism that posit individuals as "experts" and "leaders" who set the agenda and speak for the rest of the community. Such approaches attempt to steer movements according to particular ideologies and to dictate one-official-model-fits-all solutions that disregard the social, political, and cultural histories of specific communities and movements in particular locations.

The long-term commitments to community organizing and community building of the Black women whose work we have highlighted positioned them to take initiative and to be present to "answer the call." Our perspective is that Black feminist leadership ought to eschew the use of community work as a vehicle for self-promotion or personal social-economic mobility: a leader's interests are always tethered to those of the community for and within which she works. Moreover, rather than leaders asserting power as *power-over,* we argue for building community through exercising *power-with* and developing groups with structures and practices that do not promote or permit the use of power to dominate others (Guinier & Torres, 2003). Reflecting on collective lessons from the past, we should be wary of superficial forms of solidarity that assume common goals based on essentialized identity politics. We must engage in the difficult work of understanding how we are both oppressed and implicated in the oppression of others (Lorde, 1984) and focus on "building strategic alliances based on where each of us is situated in the political economy." (A. Smith, 2011, n.p.)

Working across Differences

In addition to accepting intra-community differences, an important aspect of the future of Black women's organizing will be how we collaborate with Indigenous women on common goals, while recognizing and respecting the important differences within and between our communities. This is not a new concern. In the 1970s the CBWC was in contact with the Quebec Native Women's Council and had a position of solidarity with Indigenous peoples (J. Mills, 2015). In recent years Indigenous and Black feminist scholars and activists have returned to the importance and urgency of this coalitional work. As Eve Tuck (2015) recently asserted, Black and Indigenous peoples must engage in a co-theorizing project that reveals and challenges how we "have been made Other to each other" through the mechanisms of settler colonialism. We join Tuck in urging that we shift our primary focus from how we matter to the white settler state to how we matter to one another, understanding that "the opposite of dispossession is not possession, it's *mattering*" (Tuck, 2015).

We also note the potential for intersectional class-based analyses and coalitional labour organizing in Quebec, understanding that elevated levels of inequity also produce greater chances for instability and popular resistance. Quebec has strong histories of working-class organizing and Québécois identification with the anti-colonial struggles of Indigenous and Black peoples. Such identifications are complicated; they are problematic because of cultural appropriation and fetishism, and have often relied on the denial of histories of French settler colonialism and the experiences of Indigenous and Black people in Québec (âpihtawikosisân, 2015; Austin, 2013). This underscores the need for Indigenous- and Black feminist-led movements committed to deconstructing and dislodging colonial, racist, and patriarchal ideologies and creating alternatives to capitalist exploitation as seen in recent Idle No More and Black Lives Matter movements (see Garza 2014; Moe 2013). As Leanne Betasamosake Simpson (2011) has written:

> Our Elders and Knowledge Holders have always put great emphasis into *how* things are done. This reinforces the idea that it is our own tools, strategies, values, processes and intellect that are going to build our new house. While theoretically we have debated whether Audre Lorde's "the master's tools can dismantle the master's house," I am interested in a different

question. I am not so concerned with how we dismantle the master's house, that is, which sets of theories we use to critique colonialism; but I am very concerned with how we (re)build our own house, and now I want most of my energy to go into visioning and building our new house. (p. 32)

Our insistence on Black-Indigenous solidarity and building power-with is grounded in an understanding of how race plays a hyper-visible, public role in neo-liberalism. Neo-liberalism is not only something happening *to* Black and Indigenous communities, it is also increasing inequality *within* our communities. Under neo-liberalism, broadly speaking, political and institutional leaders are increasingly encouraged to "think of themselves as entrepreneurs" (Spence, 2012, p. 144) whose role is to get individuals to self-govern through entrepreneurial solutions rather than critical political organization and radical mobilization. Challenging neo-liberalism and creating alternatives to it requires the kinds of leadership that creates, shares, and expands spaces without seeking to dominate and own them.

Archaeologists of Memory: Black Women as Family and Community Archivists

Effective community organizing and resistance also requires a constant vigilance against what Gary Kinsman and Patricia Gentile (2010) so aptly describe as "the social organization of forgetting" (p. 21). One of the mechanisms through which "capitalism and oppression rule," they explain, is through "the annihilation of our social and historical memories" (p. 21). This highlights the importance of retrieving and documenting historical and organizational knowledge for its philosophical and pragmatic value to our communities and future organizing.

Myriam Chancy (2012) explores how Caribbean women artists become "the new archaeologists of a historical site we would do well to call 'amnesia'" as they work to un-silence hidden moments of history and collective memory (p. xxii). The work of many Black women in Canada parallels that of Chancy's "archaeologists of amnesia." We could, however, call them our "archaeologists of memory" since, as Afua Cooper (2000) notes, "Black women have been in the forefront of keeping, retrieving, and recording Black history" (p. 47). Cooper knows well of what she speaks, having engaged in the painstaking and painful retrieval and telling of the revolutionary life story of eighteenth-century Montreal slave Marie Joseph Angelique (Cooper, 2006). In retrieving and documenting community histories, Black women scholars and organizers can create invaluable works that become archives in their own right. We offer several examples below, beginning with two academic studies that stand out in this regard.

First, community worker and educator June Bertley's (1982) master's thesis, *The Role of the Black Community in Educating Blacks in Montreal*, draws on extensive primary source material, including interviews, as well as souvenirs and community documents from early-twentieth-century Black community institutions and events. Information gleaned from her interviews provides access to people's memories of that period, and Bertley identifies interviewees by name with biographical notes. Another example is provided by the doctoral dissertation of historian, community organizer, and educator Dorothy Williams (2006), *Sankofa: Recovering Montreal's Heterogeneous Black Print Serials*. Williams grounds her study in the Ghanaian notion of *Sankofa*, meaning "it is not taboo to go back and fetch what you forgot," emphasizing that Black diaspora histories assumed lost can be retrieved and restored. Through interviews and extensive research in a range of archives, Williams identifies 196 (French and English) Montreal Black serials between 1934 and 2005, an impressive scholarly contribution and indispensable community archive.

Representing another format for this sort of work, in 1982 the Hostesses of Union United Church published a genealogical book entitled *Memories*, which retraces the history of the church through "life stories, family genealogy, the history of protest, and watershed events of the community" (Williams, 1999, p. 16). In 1999, the CWC published a cookbook of their favourite recipes edited by Shirley Gyles, president of the club since 1997, to raise funds for a Black student scholarship.

Black women have also used creative approaches to document and pass on valuable community histories. The documentary film *Mami Wata* by Haitian activist Monique Dauphin (1991) presents interviews in French and English with Black women who discuss their identities, community work, entrepreneurship, employment, racism, and more. *Mami Wata* remains one of the only audiovisual documents representing such a wide array of Black women's voices in Québec. The play *Coloured Pictures in Family Frames* by scholar, political activist, and artist Dolores Sandoval (2002) provides a final example. The play is based on Sandoval's extensive genealogical research and flair for storytelling, and offers a rich narrative of her family's mixed-race ancestry and movement across the Canada-US border before settling in Montreal in 1880. In the final months of her life, Sandoval curated an exhibition of her artwork and mentored and directed a cast of local Black university students in performing the play in French and English. These examples highlight the un-silencing of history that Black women have pursued through storytelling and other creative forms of archival work. The creation of living archives through arts is a way not only to share these pieces of history, but also to build and share power through popular community education.

Concluding Thoughts

Black women continue to take up both formal and informal positions of leadership in a range of community organizations throughout the city. Montreal's Black community represents 10.3 per cent of the city's population and its largest visible minority group, and 6.8 per cent of the Census Montreal Area population (Statistics Canada, 2017). Just over half of this community are immigrants, predominantly from Caribbean and (especially since 2001) African countries, many of whom have witnessed decades of uninterrupted struggle against European colonialism, US imperialism, globalization, and the early imposition of neo-liberalism on the former colonies (Campbell, 2012). They bring with them valuable knowledge and experiences of resistance. As we move forwards in Black community organizing and building in Quebec, it is crucial to constantly retrieve local historical knowledge in dialogue with newcomers' histories of organizing and resistance. This involves defying oppositions set up by settler colonialism and capitalism that (re)produce hierarchical and oppressive social relations.

In the face of a neo-liberal emphasis on measurable outcomes and products, community leadership must be about *process*: interpersonal relationships, and intercommunity connections built over time; intergenerational and diasporic knowledge transmission; creatively expanding power-with. Our communities will not be well served by the rapid construction of high-profile individual "leaders" whose success is measured by the terms of neo-liberal capitalism and who reify its values. As we have shown, the critical remembering of Black women's organizing in our communities offers important alternatives to this style of leadership. Black feminist leadership praxis in Montreal must be a collective, ongoing, multilingual, intergenerational project that carries the lessons of the past into the present and engages an anti-colonial Black diasporic imaginary as a political resource that increases our collective power-with through sharing and working across differences.

NOTE

1 The Immigration Act: An Act Respecting Immigration, S.C. 1910, Chapter 27, article 38c. Prohibited classes of immigrants identified in chapter 3 of this act included persons who were deemed "mentally defective" (3a), "diseased" (3b), "dumb, blind or otherwise physically defective" (3c), and "prostitutes and women and girls coming to Canada for immoral purposes" (3e). See http://www.pier21.ca/research/immigration-history/immigration-act-1910.

REFERENCES

Affan, S. (2013). *Ethical gestures: Articulations of black life in Montreal's 1960s* (Master's thesis). Concordia University, Montreal. Retrieved from https://spectrum.library.concordia.ca/977124/

âpihtawikosisân (Chelsea Vowel). (2015, 11 March). The mythology of Métissage: Settler moves to innocence [blog post]. Retrieved from http://apihtawikosisan.com/2015/03/the-mythology-of-metissage-settler-moves-to-innocence/

Austin, D. (2013). *Fear of a black nation: Race, sex and security in sixties Montreal.* Toronto: Between the Lines.

Bayne, C.S. (n.d.) Black Community Resource Center. Retrieved from https://bscportal.wordpress.com/black-community-resource-center/

Bertley, J. (1982). *The role of the black community in educating blacks in Montreal, from 1910 to 1940, with special reference to Reverend Charles Humphrey Este* (Master's thesis). McGill University, Montreal. Retrieved from http://digitool.library.mcgill.ca/R/?func=dbin-jump-full&object_id=62385&local_base=GEN01-MCG02

Bertley, L.W. (1980). *The United Negro Improvement Association of Montreal: 1917–1979* (Doctoral dissertation). Concordia University, Montreal. Retrieved from https://spectrum.library.concordia.ca/6/1/NK53488.pdf

Black Nurses Association of Quebec and Negro Community Centre. (1987, 21 November). *Reply to the Commission des Institutions.* Retrieved from http://www.bibliotheque.assnat.qc.ca/DepotNumerique_v2/AffichageNotice.aspx?idn=43702

Calliste, A. (1993). Race, gender and Canadian immigration policy: Blacks from the Caribbean, 1900–1932. *Journal of Canadian Studies, 28*(4), 131–48. https://doi.org/10.3138/jcs.28.4.131

Calliste, A. (1996). Antiracism organizing and resistance in nursing: African Canadian women. *Canadian Review of Sociology/Revue canadienne de sociologie, 33*(3), 361–90. https://doi.org/10.1111/j.1755-618X.1996.tb02457.x

Calliste, A. (2000). Nurses and porters: Racism, sexism and resistance in segmented labour markets. In A. Calliste & G. Sefa Dei (Eds.), *Anti-racist feminism: Critical race and gender studies* (pp. 143–64). Winnipeg: Fernwood.

Campbell, H. (2012). A response to austerity measures requires audacity not timidity. *Souls: A Critical Journal of Black Politics, Culture and Society, 14*(3–4), 240–64. https://doi.org/10.1080/10999949.2012.768080

Chancy, A. (n.d.). La triple oppression de la femme noire. Unpublished manuscript.

Chancy, M.J. (2012). *From sugar to revolution: Women's visions of Haiti, Cuba, and the Dominican Republic.* Waterloo: Wilfrid Laurier University Press.

Charles, C. (1995). Gender and politics in contemporary Haiti: The Duvalierist state, transnationalism, and the emergence of a new feminism (1980–1990). *Feminist Studies, 21*(1), 135–64. https://doi.org/10.2307/3178323

Collins, P.H. (2009). *Black feminist thought.* New York: Routledge.

Community Forum. (1992, 3–5 July). Proceedings from Montreal Black Community Forum, Val Morin, Quebec. Retrieved from https://bscportal.files.wordpress.com/2016/08/revised_summry-of-val_mor-forum-for-bcrc-jun_16_16_june-14_16.pdf

Cooper, A. (2000). Constructing black women's historical knowledge. *Atlantis: Critical Studies in Gender, Culture & Social Justice, 25*(1), 39–50. Retrieved from http://journals.msvu.ca/index.php?journal=atlantis&page=article&op=view&path%5B%5D=1544

Cooper, A. (2006). *The hanging of Angélique: The untold story of Canadian slavery and the burning of old Montréal.* Toronto: HarperCollins.

Dauphin, M. (1991). *Mami Wata* [documentary film]. Distributed by Le Groupe Intervention Vidéo. Montreal, Québec.

Ferguson, S.A., & King, T.C. (2011). *Black womanist leadership: Tracing the motherline.* Albany: State University of New York Press.

Fisher, T. (2012). *What's left of blackness? Feminisms, transracial solidarities, and the politics of belonging in Britain.* New York: Palgrave Macmillan.

Flynn, K. (2003). Race, the state and Caribbean immigrant nurses, 1950–1965. In G. Feldberg, M. Ladd-Taylor, A. Li, & K. McPherson (Eds.), *Women, health, and nation: Canada and the United States since 1945* (pp. 247–63). Montreal/Kingston: McGill-Queen's University Press.

Forsythe, D. (1971). *Let the niggers burn: The Sir George Williams University affair and its Caribbean aftermath.* Montreal: Black Rose.

Garza, A. (2014, 7 October). A herstory of the #BlackLivesMatter movement. Retrieved from http://www.thefeministwire.com/2014/10/blacklivesmatter-2/

Guinier, L., & Torres, G. (2003). *The miner's canary: Enlisting race, resisting power, transforming democracy.* Cambridge, MA: Harvard University Press.

Handleman, D. (1964). *West Indian associations in Montreal* (Master's thesis). McGill University, Montreal.

hooks, b. (2000). *Feminism is for everybody.* Cambridge: South End.

Israel, W.E. (1928). *The Montreal Negro community* (Master's thesis). McGill University, Montreal.

James, J. (2013). *Seeking the beloved community: A feminist race reader.* Albany: State University of New York Press.

Kinsman, G.W., & Gentile, P. (2010). *The Canadian war on queers: National security as sexual regulation.* Vancouver: UBC Press.

Kouka-Ganga, J. (1982). Femmes noires au Canada. *Canadian Woman Studies, 4*(2), 29–30. Retrieved from https://cws.journals.yorku.ca/index.php/cws/article/view/13884/12937

Lawson, E. (2002). Images in black: Black women, media and the mythology of an orderly society. In N. Wane, K. Deliovsky, & E. Lawson (Eds.), *Back to the drawing board: African Canadian feminisms* (pp. 199–223). Toronto: Sumach.

Lee, W.J.E. (2009). Visualizing the margins: The experiences of queer people of colour (Master's thesis). McGill University, Montreal. Retrieved from https://www.researchgate.net/profile/Edward_Lee26/publication/38437903_Visualizing_the_margins_the_experiences_of_queer_people_of_colour/links/582157ad08ae12715afc2a29/Visualizing-the-margins-the-experiences-of-queer-people-of-colour.pdf

Lorde, A. (1984). *Sister outsider: Essays and speeches by Audre Lorde.* Trumansburg: Crossing Press.

Massaquoi, N. (2007). Introduction: Future imaginings of black feminist thought. In N. Massaquoi & N. Wane (Eds.), *Theorizing empowerment: Canadian perspectives on black feminist thought* (pp. 5–24). Toronto: Inanna.

Mills, J. (2015). Conferencing as a site for the mobilization of black feminist identities in the Congress of Black Women of Canada, 1973–1983. *Journal of Black Studies, 46*(4), 415–41. https://doi.org/10.1177/0021934714568456

Mills, S. (2013). Quebec, Haiti, and the deportation crisis of 1974. *Canadian Historical Review, 94*(3), 405–35. https://doi.org/10.3138/chr.1476

Mills, S. (2016). *A place in the sun: Haiti, Haitians, and the remaking of Quebec.* Montreal/Kingston: McGill-Queen's University Press.

Moe, K. (2013, 18 January). Indigenous women take the lead in Idle No More. Retrieved from http://www.yesmagazine.org/peace-justice/indigenous-women-take-lead-idle-no-more

Monique, Myriam, Rosemary, & Viviane (1982). Femmes Haïtiennes (noires, immigrantes, réfugiées). *Canadian Woman Studies/Les Cahiers de la femme, 4*(2), 48–51. Retrieved from https://cws.journals.yorku.ca/index.php/cws/article/view/13889/12942

Mortimier, S. (2009, 9 November). Shedding a red light on history. *McGill Daily.* Retrieved from http://www.mcgilldaily.com/2009/11/shedding_a_red_light_on_history/

Potter, H.H. (1949). *The occupational adjustments of Montreal negroes, 1941–48* (Master's thesis). McGill University, Montreal.

Ransby, B. (2003). *Ella Baker and the black freedom movement: A radical democratic vision.* Chapel Hill: University of North Carolina Press.

Rateau, M. (2009). Pawol Fanm: Des femmes haïtiennes de Montréal au micro de Radio Centre Ville. In J. Brun (Ed.), *Interrelations femmes-médias dans l'Amérique française* (pp. 177–86). Québec: Presses de l'Université Laval.

Reece, R. (2007). Canadian black feminist thought and scholar-activist praxis. In N. Massaquoi & N.N. Wane (Eds.), *Theorizing empowerment: Canadian perspectives on black feminist thought* (pp. 266–84). Toronto: Inanna.

Ruggles, C., & Rovinescu, O. (1996). *Outsider blues: A voice from the shadows.* Halifax: Fernwood.

Sanders, G.L. (2013). *La voix des femmes: Haitian women's rights, national politics and black activism in Port-Au-Prince and Montreal, 1934–1986* (Doctoral dissertation). University of Michigan, Ann Arbor. Retrieved from https://deepblue.lib.umich.edu/handle/2027.42/99799

Simpson, L. (2011). *Dancing on our turtle's back: Stories of Nishnaabeg re-creation, resurgence and a new emergence.* Winnipeg: Arbeiter Ring.

Small, S., & Thornhill, E.M.A. (2008). HARAMBEC! Quebec black women pulling together. *Journal of Black Studies, 38*(3), 427–42. https://doi.org/10.1177/0021934707306584

Smith, A. (2011). Building unlikely alliances: An interview with Andrea Smith. *Upping the Anti,* No. 10. Retrieved from http://uppingtheanti.org/journal/article/10-building-unlikely-alliances-an-interview-with-andrea-smith

Smith, D.E. (2005). *Institutional ethnography: A sociology for people.* Lanham: AltaMira.

Spence, L.K. (2012). The neoliberal turn in black politics. *Souls: A Critical Journal of Black Politics, Culture and Society, 14*(3–4), 139–59. https://doi.org/10.1080/10999949.2012.763682

Statistics Canada. (2017). *Focus on geography series, 2016 census.* Statistics Canada catalogue no. 98-404-X2016001. Ottawa: Statistics Canada.

Tuck, E. (2015, May). *The meaning and matter of materialist (anti)racisms in educational research* [panel]. Paper presented at the Critical Ethnic Studies Association conference Sovereignties and Colonialism: Resisting Racism, Extraction and Dispossession, York University, Toronto.

Wallis, M.A., Sunseri, L., & Galabuzi, G.-E. (2010). *Colonialism and racism in Canada: historical traces and contemporary issues.* Toronto: Nelson.

Wane, N.N. (2002). Black-Canadian feminist thought: Drawing on the experiences of my sisters. In N.N. Wane, K. Deliovsky, & E. Lawson (Eds.), *Back to the drawing board: African Canadian feminisms* (pp. 29–53). Toronto: Sumach.

Williams, D.W. (1997). *The road to now: A history of blacks in Montreal.* Montreal: Véhicule.

Williams, D.W. (1999). *The Jackie Robinson myth: Social mobility and race in Montreal, 1920–1960* (Master's thesis). Concordia University, Montreal.

Williams, D.W. (2006). *Sankofa: Recovering Montreal's heterogenous Black print serials.* (Doctoral dissertation). McGill University, Montreal. Retrieved from http://digitool.library.mcgill.ca/webclient/StreamGate?folder_id=0&dvs=1546897368553~521

Yee, J. (Ed.) (2011). *Feminism for real: Deconstructing the academic industrial complex of feminism.* Ottawa: Our Schools/Our Selves.

6 Standing Firm on Uneven Ground: A Letter to Black Women on Academic Leadership

ANNETTE HENRY

My dear sisters:

I am encouraged by the activism/leadership in which you are engaged at your various institution despite resistances and obstacles, whether you are working for change within or outside the formal mechanisms of administration and leadership. I would hope that more of you would consider moving through the official ranks to positions of greater academic responsibility in order to literally change the face of university leadership. I have had many conversations with Black women in Canada and the United States who have contemplated academic administration as a possible career path. I have found most choose to remain in the professorial track. Indeed, most of us entered our fields so that we could contribute to intellectual production in our disciplines and/or for a love of teaching at the tertiary level.

As I share my thoughts, I draw from my own experiences as well as research literature. I offer thoughts on Black women and the possibilities of academic leadership and some strategies for working in our institutions with an open heart and with an oppositional consciousness. My choice to write a letter reflects my desire to reach a particular audience – Black women – more intimately. Paradoxically, unlike in everyday life, I am writing in a scholarly volume, referring briefly to academic and corporate literature on leadership and adhering to academic conventions. In some ways, then, this is a meditation on Black women's agency in academic leadership in which I invite Black women to join. You see, I am troubled by the ubiquitous discourses of equity and diversity in higher education and the glaring absence of racial and ethnic diversity in Canadian universities, especially at the senior levels (Smith, 2018; Smith, Gamarro, & Toor, 2017). I want to explore the possibilities and limitations of such academic leadership for Black women. We shall take a look at societal perspectives on leadership, as well as what researchers have written on leadership. I am most interested in how we carry out our activism-leadership in the university as Black women. I shall conclude with some thoughts about ways to re/frame our thinking and remain joyful and purposeful in our university work. I hope these thoughts will be useful to you.

I begin with two stories from my own life experience.

I was a middle-school French and music teacher in Waterloo County, Ontario. I shared home-room responsibilities with a physical education teacher, "Reg." We both were scheduled for a thirty-minute annual evaluation in the principal's office on the same afternoon. I found my session uneventful: the principal engaged in unsubstantial chatter. Disappointed, I asked Reg what he had discussed with the principal. He replied, "Not much. He just told me what steps to take to become a principal." Although I showed no emotion, I was taken aback, but not unfamiliar with this kind of racism. Clearly, I had just experienced differential treatment in the workplace based upon race and gender. Such experiences are corroborated in a recent study of gender and school leadership by Kerry Robinson and colleagues (2017).

These interactions with the principal and my colleague Reg reminded me of an Eddie Murphy (1984) skit that aired on *Saturday Night Live* at about the same time. With the help of professional make-up artists, Murphy was disguised as a White man and went "undercover" only to discover how different life is for White people. For example, while riding the bus disguised as a White man, he witnesses what happens when the one other Black man disembarks at the 45th street bus stop: the White people start partying, dancing, and playing music and a cocktail waitress serves them drinks! Early on in the skit when Murphy tries to buy a newspaper, the White owner gives him back his money and says, "Take it!" Murphy says, "Slowly I began to realize that when White people are alone, they give things to each other" (http://criticalmediaproject.org/cml/media/eddie-murphy-White-like-me/).

The encounter with the principal was a reminder to a young Black woman starting a career that, in professional settings, things are not always as they seem, and that White privilege and patriarchy are at work in the smallest interactions. Conversations differ when Black people are or are not in the room. I carried this memory with me as I moved from teaching children to graduate school and into academic positions.

Years later as a professor, I worked with a dean who occasionally tried to pressure me into performing tasks that other colleagues were reluctant to do. The dean would say to me, "Annette, why don't you take the *leadership* and ..." The statement reflects how "leadership" has become a buzzword, popularized in everyday speech. This comment is also related to the idea that Black women are supposed to take on the work that no one else wants to do. What I found out later was that a White female faculty member was paid summer salary to do what I was asked to do as "service." Black women in the professions are, in essence, domestic help.

These exchanges exemplify where Black women are in the racial logic, and how we are often treated in the workplace. In the first example with the school principal, I was overlooked and not given an equal opportunity to explore professional development towards school leadership. I was positioned as unworthy of a discussion about acquiring the knowledge and skills to become a school principal. The dean's choice to only offer my White colleague a summer salary invalidates or at least takes for granted my worth to the institution. A White woman's labour was worth more than mine, yet I was expected to "take the leadership." Both examples revealed that gendered racism is a normal part of the institutional practices wherein we are often the ones to do the less prestigious work that supports our faculties for little or no reward or acknowledgment. In both examples, I might have remained unaware of this racialized and gendered treatment had my colleagues not shared their interactions with our superiors.

Perspectives on Gender, Race, and Leadership

What is leadership? What does leadership look like for women? For Black women? Leadership scholar Peter Northouse (2004) writes, "After decades of dissonance, leadership scholars agree on one thing. They can't come up with a common definition of leadership" (p. 5). Northouse offers a traditional view of leadership: "an interactive and transactional process, a process by which one individual influences a group of individuals to achieve a common goal" (p. 5). One has only to go to a bookstore and peruse the abundance of popular literature on management and leadership to glean the societal image of leadership and leaders. The corporate literature, indeed, reflects a fascination with wealth and power as well as the association of leadership with men. Its authors are mostly successful White male executives.

Alice Eagly and Linda Carli (2007) note that our mental associations about leadership "not only shape stereotypes about leaders but also influence organizational norms and practices" (p. 137). Depending on the organization, a women's attire might even change to a more "corporate" or "masculine" look when promoted to a position of leadership, reflecting this norm. Historically, leadership has been the domain of men. Ruth Simmons, former president of Brown University and the first African American woman to head an Ivy League university, recalled in an interview that when she was graduating, only men were described by the term "brilliant" (Hartman, 1999, p. 245). In their insightful chapter in *The Equity Myth,* Malinda Smith, Kimberly Gamarro, and Mansharn Toor (2017) draw on Phelan, Moss-Racusin, and Rudman's (2008) research and note that

> the research on letters of reference, evaluations, and peer reviews all highlight the ways in which White men are socially reproduced as brilliant, excellent, and competent, and, in turn, as natural-born leaders. In contrast, women, particularly racialized minority women, who comport themselves in similar ways to their male colleagues are subjected to double standards and even face a backlash. (p. 293)

These are the subtle ways in which men are groomed for success and great achievements. Racialized women are disregarded.

So, how do Black scholar-activists define leadership? How have they addressed the leadership of Black women? Black women throughout history have been leaders in a range of activist contexts, as highlighted in this volume (see chapters by Gooden, Lawson, and hampton and Rochat). However, they have often been overlooked as leaders. It is interesting that in his formidable book *Black Leadership,* Manning Marable (1998) does not highlight a single Black woman. Economic anthropologist Willie Baber wrote, "Black leadership combines the elements of 'choice and action' regardless of situational constraints" (quoted in King, 2015, p. 22). This definition recognizes that we often work in prohibitive contexts, that issues of power, gender, race, and class make up some of these "situational constraints." African American educational leadership scholar Linda Tillman (2013) addresses the paucity of literature on African American female leadership in higher education and school leadership: "The consistent leadership of Black women has received minimal attention in both historical and contemporary literature" (p. vii). Tillman also notes, "Despite the many accomplishments of Black women in leadership roles, media portrayals continue to cast us as dressed-up versions of Prissy in *Gone with the Wind*" (p. vii).

In Canadian public and political life Black women are rarely conceived of as "leaders" unless they assume a title – Glenda Simms, Jean Augustine, Zanana Akande, Michaëlle Jean – or unless they have been a "first," such as Rosemary Brown, the first Black woman to run for the leadership of the federal New Democratic Party and, in fact, the first Black woman to run at the federal level of any political party in Canada. Rosemary Brown (1989) reminded us in her autobiography that "for feminists, the whole point of moving into power arenas is to revolutionize them, rather than to use them as a stepping stone to personal and private advancement" (p. 231).

Black Feminist Praxis: Possibilities for Change

I am using a broad definition of Black feminism regarding academic leadership to be inclusive of the range of ways that Black women engage in and view their praxis. We are not homogeneous. We embody a range of ethnicities, cultures, nationalities, ideological perspectives, and life experiences, to name only a few dimensions that shape our identities and activism. Inspired by the UK group Black Feminists Manchester (https://Blackfeministsmanchester.wordpress.com/about/), I am envisioning as feminist all Black women who are actively organizing, strategizing, and mobilizing around Black women's concerns, and/or feminist/womanist practices in everyday life. Of course, all Black women do not adopt the term. All definitions are problematic at some level (see Collins, 2009; Henry, 2005, 2011; hooks, 1992). However, this broad definition serves the purpose of inclusivity regarding Black women in academic settings across politics and across the country. What is the use of definitions and theories that exclude the majority of women you wish to address and who are doing the very work that is considered "feminist"?

As Black women, we are doing all kinds of political, cultural, and spiritual work as well as struggling to work against anti-Black sexism and racism in the university, in our communities, churches, mosques, women's organizations, and community programs (see Gooden, and hampton & Rochat, this volume). In *Feminism without Borders*, Chandra Mohanty (2003) discusses feminist practice at a number of levels:

> At the level of daily life through the everyday acts that constitute our identities and relational communities; at the level of collective action in groups, networks, and movements constituted around feminist visions of social transformation; and at the levels of theory, pedagogy, and textual creativity in the scholarly and writing practices of feminists engaged in the production of knowledge. (p. 5)

The kinds of work that most Black women are doing in their families and communities represent the first two categories. The kinds of work that Black women carry out in academic settings can represent all of these, but most often represent the third. In my opinion, administrative leadership holds the potential to be another form of "theory, pedagogy and textual creativity." That is, at best, under favourable conditions and circumstances, it can be an intellectual, relational, and pedagogical process of production and exchange similar to that conceptualized by David Lusted (1986): a relationship that allows us to produce knowledge together with our colleagues that can potentially change consciousness.

An administrator is not necessarily a leader. A university leader is not hired to disrupt the status quo. An activist-leader approaching her responsibilities with a critical stance and oppositional consciousness *might*, despite structural constraints, succeed in making her institutional environment more meaningful and intelligible to the diverse community it purports to serve. In my view, a Black feminist vision of administration would involve a productive negotiation and exchange of ideas and strategies, in democratic collaborations with colleagues working towards transformative action. Menah Pratt-Clarke (2013), associate vice chancellor at the University of Illinois, conceptualizes the important synchrony between activism and leadership: "Transformative change in higher education requires scholars to be activists and activists to be scholars ... unafraid to speak and to give voice to justice and equality in all settings and circumstances" (p. 158).

Canadian Black Feminist Scholarship on Leadership: Where Is the Research?

There has been a proliferation of literature on women and leadership in higher education over the past thirty years (e.g., De la Cancela, Chin, & Jenkins, 2016; Stead & Elliott, 2009). Although some of the literature on "women" definitely is applicable to Black women, these texts, written by mostly White women, often fail to consider how Black women construct their praxis within the multiple interlocking lived dimensions of race, gender, sexuality, class, and their geo-political, transnational, and postcolonial realities (see Collins, 2009; Douglas, 2012; Gutiérrez, Muhs, Nieman, González, & Harris, 2012; Henry, 2015; Smith, Gamarro, & Toor, 2017; Razack, Thobani, & Smith, 2010). The literature on Black women and leadership in higher education is still not robust. This is an area in dire need of Canadian Black feminist scholarship.

Can Black Women Break Through the Concrete Ceiling?

Much research points to a "glass ceiling" – a barrier that prevents women and people of colour from moving into higher levels in their institutions. The metaphor of "concrete ceiling" is used to describe the barriers encountered by Black and other racialized workers. Concrete is more difficult to shatter than glass and, unlike glass, one cannot see through it. At least with glass one can see what others are doing on the other side, even if one cannot easily break through it.

Malinda Smith and colleagues (2017) remind us of the pervasive structural discrimination in Canadian institutions. For the most part, "racialized women remain locked out of most university leadership positions" (p. 292). They found that "racialized minorities, rarely women, have cracked the concrete ceiling and currently serve in top leadership positions in only 7 percent of Canadian universities" (p. 292). In her role as president of the Academic Women's Association at the University of Alberta, Dr Smith, an exemplary Black feminist leader, has been conducting an ongoing diversity gap campaign with her team, providing much-needed national data from U15 (research-intensive) universities and documenting several areas of diversity deficits in leadership as well as in other areas (e.g., Canada Research Chairs, faculty representation, awards and recognition). You might want to take a look at these findings; they are accessibly presented as infographics online: https://uofaawa.wordpress.com/awa-diversity-gap-campaign/the-diversity-gap-in-university-leadership-2018/.

Studies in the corporate world are helpful in understanding the dimensions of the concrete ceiling. Yap and Konrad (2009) examined race and gender effects on promotion in a Canadian company. They studied twenty-two thousand workers at three distinct levels in the corporation. Their findings indicated that "promotion disadvantages were experienced by visible minority men, visible minority women, and White women compared to White men. Of these groups, visible minority women experienced the largest promotion disadvantage compared to White men" (p. 609). (The specificity of Black women remains hidden when we are conflated into the category of visible minority.)

An American corporate study conducted by Sylvia Ann Hewlett and Tai Green of The Centre for Talent Innovation offers some insights regarding opportunities. They found that "while Black female professionals are more likely [than White women] to seek top leadership roles, they are treated as virtually invisible" (Purdie-Vaughns, 2015). There have also been several recent studies on Black women's lack of "sponsorship" (e.g., Gonzalez & Sponsel, 2012; Hewlett, Leader-Chivée, & Sumberg, 2012). These findings support the claim that highly qualified women do not have the powerful (White male) backing to propel them through the concrete ceiling or the "marzipan layer" (that is, the layer just before the executive level, where women "get stuck" as middle and senior managers (e.g., department heads, deans). Black women are 26 per cent less likely than straight White men to have their ideas endorsed. Seventy-two per cent of Black women believe that executive presence at their company is defined as conforming to traditionally White male standards. Additionally, 34 per cent of Black women say they need to compromise their authenticity in order to conform to the executive presence standards at their company (Hewlett & Green, 2015). In this White male environment, it is no wonder that a corporate study of one thousand men and women in the United States found that women's career aspirations to leadership and confidence in leadership opportunities eroded after two years (Gadiesh & Coffman, 2015).

Similar to the corporate research by Hewlett and Green, Canadian research on academic leadership suggests that, of the 7 per cent of racialized leaders in Canadian universities, none would have reached their positions without having been "'tapped,' coached, sponsored or mentored by senior men, and to some extent, senior women" (Smith, Gamarro, & Toor, 2017, p. 292). It would seem quite simple to put in place programs and strategies to address what has been referred to by many names, such as the concrete ceiling, the marzipan layer, the "bottleneck" (referring to being stuck in mid-career and middle-management positions), or the "sticky floor" (referring to the differential promotion rates and pay scales of men and women) (see Booth, Francesconi, & Frank, 2003; Yap & Konrad, 2009). Is there the political will to work towards this promotional equity?

Whether one belongs to the small group of racialized faculty in a formal position of university leadership (department chair, director, dean, or senior executive positions) or in another position of leadership in an academic or professional organization, Black women are carrying out the work they feel compelled to do – organizing, disrupting, and disturbing the status quo wherever we find ourselves, because the work is wherever we are. Sometimes we are thrust into situations in which the best position to take in the name of changing the status quo is to remain strategically silent, or listen, or wait, or even not participate at all, in protest. Other times, we have to speak up or step up for our own survival, for that of our community, our colleagues, or our students. We may be hired with the expectation that we will magically solve institutional problems. Hiring and promotion of Black women may be interpreted institutionally as "evidence of commitment, of change, of progress" (Ahmed, 2009, p. 41) as long as we promote a happy narrative and do not raise too many issues of inequity, especially racism. Much depends on the institution, and where or how one can effectuate change within its infrastructure, or whether one is given the latitude or even the opportunities for leadership. Importantly, "each of us must find our work and do it" (Lorde, 1984, p. 141).

It is understandable that some Black women prefer to work for social change outside of formal university leadership structures, working "below the radar" or in alternative associations, unconstrained by the predefined university roles and expectations of "leadership." These spaces can be powerful places to contest and disrupt existing discursive practices. One example is Researchers and Academics of Colour for Equality (RACE), whose founders (Sunera Thobani, Sherene Razack, and Jasmin Jawani) defined their own agenda by themselves, for themselves (see Razack, Thobani, & Smith, 2010). RACE is a national network of Indigenous and racialized critical race and anti-colonial academics, activists, researchers, and practitioners who have been meeting at national and regional conferences since 2001, exploring pressing social issues of the day (e.g., post-911 racisms, racial violence, anti-colonialist struggles).

So, my sisters, as Black women, how then do we proceed day to day "moving into power arenas" (Brown, 1989) and living as "activist/scholars" (Pratt-Clarke, 2013)? How do we better the state of our universities? In what follows, I offer a few thoughts about ways to think about our activist-leadership efforts in the university.

Redefine Leadership

Let's define "leadership" differently by asking critical questions such as: What does leadership mean for each of us personally? For one's community? What are its parameters? In "A Black Woman Speaks on Leadership," Joyce King (2015) redefines the role of a Black academic and the nature of scholarship, "so that scholarship, community/public service, and parenting, another aspect of the Black liberation struggle, are compatible and interdependent" (p. 24). Each of these arenas, she continues, is a potential "catalyst for social change" (p. 24). King also names what is often hidden in assuming an activist or leadership stance:

> Even decisions about where to live, in a Black community or suburbs, or where to send our children to school – private or public – are seemingly personal dilemmas which are shaped by the politics of domination and have implications for our leadership responsibilities. (p. 23)

Rosemary Brown would concur with this often unnamed area of Black women's leadership: decisions that affect the well-being of one's own family and loved ones. She raised her children in Vancouver, a city with a different racial history from Oakland, California, where King raised her children. Brown (1989) discusses how she and her husband desperately wanted to bring up their children in a Black environment, fearing the deleterious effects of racism in Canadian schools. For many reasons, however, the Browns decided to remain in Vancouver. She writes, "With the birth of our children, we became mobilized into wanting to change the community and world in which we lived" (p. 56). Indeed, Black women's leadership is not relegated to one area of life. It involves a commitment to Black people "and to mak[ing] the society more just" (King, 2015, p. 23).

Change the Conversation

By our very presence, we change the conversation. Everything we do and say matters. I am reminded of an experience in graduate school. A White feminist professor was teaching a doctoral seminar entitled "The History of Canadian Women in Education." Of the five students, three of us were Black women – Afua Cooper and Dionne Brand were the other two Black women. Our presence completely changed the conversation and curriculum and revealed the limitations of the professor's course planning. She realized that her course, by exclusion, was not representative of women in Canada.

Although it can be tiring, as Black women we often find ourselves in a position of teaching others; sometimes we have to embrace it as an opportunity to engage and bring about the possibility of new understandings. This is not easy. As Audre Lorde reminds us, "It means doing the unromantic and tedious work of forging coalitions ... It means fighting despair" (p. 142).

In everyday conversation, there are opportunities to raise questions about equity, no matter how simple. A search committee chair once asked in a meeting, "Are we a predominantly White faculty? Hmmm. I don't know." (Out of twenty-six faculty members, two were Latinas, one was Asian, and one was Black.) Of course, I called the chair on his pretence. It was flagrantly obvious that we were a predominantly White faculty! Often there is a deafening silence after we raise a question about inequity or race. Our colleagues do hear us. Some may publically act as if nothing was said. For the most part, they will not speak up or tell you publicly that your voice is important. A few might. After I left my position as department head a colleague emailed, "I think it's the whole Faculty's loss that you won't be Head ... your energy, challenge, and general willingness to ask, 'What are we doing here? Who's forgotten?' Your voice is still sorely needed, and I sincerely hope you'll keep raising that voice." I greatly appreciated this acknowledgement. Still, I wondered how many other colleagues were listening. Even when they seem to not listen, let's continue raising questions that challenge and change the conversation with the belief that change is possible.

In Canadian institutions, it is rare for us to have other Black colleagues in our departments or faculty to help us change the conversations. Indeed, the lack of a critical mass of Black faculty or of workplace confidantes can sometimes put us in isolating situations. But the presence of other Black faculty by no means guarantees solidarity or a safe environment. For example, the sexism that I encountered from a potential Black male colleague while considering a faculty position at a Canadian university was one of many factors in my decision to accept a position in the United States. As Erna Brodber (1990) has written, "The enemy can be a ghost who talks through Black faces" (p. 165).

Our very presence and the work we do challenge the status quo and change the conversation. I once had a dean who could not understand my work in the conventional ways and asked, rather confused, "Is this research or outreach"? I replied, "it's outsearch," as a way of undoing and even deriding the research/outreach, scholarship/activism binaries. In these situations, we necessarily take on a kind of leadership in our curriculum choices, our pedagogical practices, our service and outreach activities, in our interactions with colleagues, and in our research. As we speak up or write up our ideas from our own frames of reference we bring much-needed lenses to issues and challenge the views that exclude our perspectives. (We also have to be strategically aware that there are often consequences for taking a critical stance that may affect our tenure, promotion, and ability to work with and amongst our colleagues.)

Be Prepared

Let's be prepared for leadership writ large in all its various forms. Let's be prepared to move forwards in the name of justice, equity, in the name of Black people and for the university community, again not necessarily in a formal position. Despite the research that shows that we are overlooked, we never know when we might be able to slip through, or drill through a little crevice in the concrete ceiling and do some anti-racist work. A colleague took on a position as interim dean in 1998 for two years at a time when deans were mostly men at her institution. She thought that her position would be temporary and thus capitalized on the hiring power of her role to change the institution. She hired as many racialized faculty as possible during those two years. She ended up being dean for fifteen years and continued this anti-racist practice.

You might consider acquiring formal leadership training. It might seem strange to be encouraging you to acquire formal leadership preparation whenever possible, especially since I believe that Black women are already carrying out potentially transformative leadership activities outside of formal leadership positions, from which we are often "locked out" (Smith, Gamarro, & Toor, 2017, p. 292). Moreover, you may be wondering, why bother when "racialized women professors experience a rate of unemployment that is almost twice as high as for their non-racialized women colleagues" and "a worsening earnings gap" in relation to white faculty (Canadian Association of University Teachers, 2018, pp. 7–8) Why exacerbate the stress that already exists in the workplace with additional leadership responsibilities of strategic planning, faculty development, fundraising, budgeting, dealing with conflicts, extra events outside of work, increased business trips, and longer hours at the office (to name only a few requirements of these positions)? Why bother when the research mentioned earlier reveals demoralizing findings?

Many of us entered academia with a disdain for "corporate America"; we soon found out, however, that we were embroiled in institutions with corporate, individualistic, neo-liberal values, or as a former graduate student used to say, "It's corporate America without the money!" Why would anyone take on leadership in this competitive, hierarchical structure? Can the presence of Black women make a difference? I think so.

Our leadership experiences depend on our settings, our colleagues, their values and politics, and the general culture of the institution. I had a friend who was a chair in an African American studies program in the United States. She believed that it was the *only* setting in which she could see herself taking on such a position; the program was small and the faculty members shared similar values and a similar vision. Units specifically established as alternative spaces of possibility have more intellectual flexibility for transformative thinking, even though they still must adhere to the institutional guidelines of their universities and the pressures of this neo-liberal environment. One such example is the Social Justice Institute at UBC, directed by Dr Denise Ferreira da Silva. Much depends also on where and how we want to effectuate change and, importantly, whether our institution is open to the prospect of transformative innovation. Some institutions are not ready to envision Black women in positions of authority (Hewlett & Green, 2015). Here is a personal example of this reality: at the end of a doctoral seminar in which a White female student spoke to me inappropriately, a Black woman in the class leaned over to me and whispered, "She wants to be where you are!" In other words, she was uneasy that I was the one in the position of authority.

I must emphasize that even when we assume a position of leadership, we are not guaranteed respect or inclusion. As a faculty member as well as former department head, I have had occasions on which colleagues have undermined my efforts, or disregarded my suggestions, or acted as if I were not in the room. Moreover, as a Black woman administrator, I was not always allowed the moral authority to make decisions that would change the way things had always been done (Henry, 2015).

St. Jean and Feagin (1998) assert that being ignored is one of the racialized forms of exclusion that Black women endure in the workplace, along with "facing stereotypes, not being mentored, being excluded from work cliques and being harassed" (p. 41). In a study comparing the negative effects of harassment and ostracism in the workplace, O'Reilly and colleagues (2015) found that ostracism was associated with more health problems, lower job satisfaction, higher psychological withdrawal, and even a greater likelihood of leaving the organization.

Since we are often perceived as unqualified, intellectually inferior, or incompetent or are simply overlooked for interesting positions at our universities, and given that we work in a competitive environment, extra credentials can be a way for us as Black women to position ourselves to be ready to make changes at another level in the university, changes that may lead to a more just and equitable campus. Returning to the idea of leadership preparation, research shows that leadership institutes are helpful for emerging women leaders (Madsen, 2010). I suggest that such professional development might better prepare us to be more effective leaders, develop supportive networks, participate in communities of practice, and even withstand some of the gendered racism encountered in performance evaluations. Let's be honest, in the competitive and inequitable environment of academia, credentials count.

I attended a number of leadership institutes. I found them to be helpful in understanding the inner workings of higher education institutions. They provided the opportunity to meet people in a range of academic administrative positions, at senior levels across a range of public and private institutions. I was also able to develop personal and professional skills: I was selected for a year-long fellowship in the CIC-Academic Leadership Program, a program among "the big ten" universities in the United States. We visited three universities: University of Illinois-Chicago, University of Pennsylvania, and University of Iowa. Importantly, I participated in the HERS leadership institute at the University of Denver campus. The institute is also held at two other elite private colleges: Wellesley (Massachusetts) and Bryn Mawr (Pennsylvania). As the acronym HERS implies, it allowed for a safe woman-centred environment as it prepared women for senior and executive university positions. The HERS institute that I attended (2008–9) focused heavily on finance and budgeting as a consequence of the 2008 economic downturn, as well as leadership development. When I came to UBC as department head, I attended the academic leadership program for new heads and directors. These three programs were strikingly similar in that they focused mostly on understanding the operations of higher education organizations and acquiring the necessary knowledges. Disappointingly, none of these courses (at least for my cohort) provided adequate discussion of the intersectional dynamics pertinent to the lives of Black women, nor a critical racial analysis of these institutions.

Vincent Harding (1974) wrote that the vocation of the Black scholar, among other things, is to "speak the truth." How can we speak these truths without a full understanding of the system? If we have chosen to work towards the betterment of the university, some of us need to be at the table where decisions are made or else we perpetuate the current system, one in which, for the most part, White males and a few White females continue to occupy the upper echelons of the university and make decisions that affect our lives. As I discussed elsewhere (Henry, 2015), I was struck by the comment of a colleague at an emergency meeting for all tenured Black faculty at an American university where I previously worked. Disappointed with the lack of institutional commitment to Black faculty and African American studies, he said that until someone in central administration looked like him, he could not take them seriously! How does this translate in Canadian universities with so few racialized or Black faculty at the executive level?

At present, there are no Black women in central administration in Canadian universities (at least at the time of writing). Recently retired Black women who have been deans or directors in Canada tend to have held these positions in applied professions (e.g., law, nursing, social work, and education). In the field of education, at the time of writing to you, there was only one Black woman dean in the country, Dr Marie-Josée Berger at Bishop's University. Canadian universities are racially stratified; many competent racialized Canadians remain at the bottom of the hierarchy as part-time or underemployed lecturers.

Stay Connected to Your Community

At a community breakfast in Boston in 1990, I heard Barbara Smith emphasize that "to be a Black feminist means being connected to your community." I was a graduate student at the time. This statement, along with reading Joyce King's "A Black Woman Speaks on Leadership" and Vincent Harding's "Vocation of the Black Scholar," framed my thinking in the early stages of my academic career. Harding (1974) believed that it is the "community-in-struggle ... through which vocation, purpose, direction and life itself are most fully known and lived" (p. 7). This is very important. We are often courted and paraded about as evidence of "diversity" in our departments and faculties. We need to keep focused and determined about our goals, purposes, and directions. We in the university have the luxury of being as connected or as distant from the larger Black community as we choose. It is easy to live solely at a level of theory and textual production. Scholars carry out a diversity of writing and artistic productions; some remain unconcerned about, or leave to others, the practical applications and political implications of their research.

Whether we recognize it or not, we are linked to a community-in-struggle at our universities. Etymologically, a university is a "whole," a "community." Rather than thinking in "us and them" ways, I believe that our leadership as Black feminists should involve our lives and work in relation to others' lives – including those of our colleagues and students. Rosemary Brown's alignment with the Voice of Women to protest nuclear testing points to the need to work across boundaries and in community. Reflecting on the need for solidarity and how it fully reflected her praxis as a Black woman, she wrote, "I realized my sisterhood with those women was greater than whatever divided us" (1989, p. 81). Chandra Mohanty (2003) defines solidarity in terms of "mutuality, accountability, and the recognition of common interests as the basis for relationships among diverse communities" (p. 7). This relationality is always fraught. For we know that in our workplace we are embroiled in a competitive, hierarchical, predominantly White middle-class institution that still has difficulty with our presence. As Cassandra Chaney (2013) writes, "Black women are more likely to experience, racism, sexism, classism, loneliness, microaggressions, marginality syndrome and the status of outsider within" (p. 120). Our challenge is to retain the very wholeness that may become eroded by political work.

Keep Race/Gender on the Agenda

It is often a challenge to engage faculty (and students) in discussions on race. Some colleagues feel offended or fall silent when a Black person suggests socially just practices even in small tangible ways (e.g., tweaking an all-White course outline or suggesting Black external reviewers outside of the usual networks). It is our responsibility as Black women activist/leaders to keep race and gender from a Black perspective on the table in our teaching, research, service, and leadership, even in the smallest ways. Here is an example from my teaching: in a recent teacher education class, I announced that all my PowerPoint images that day were of Black people. A student at the back of the room shouted, "It's about time!" (I had previously shown the slides to teachers in a workshop in Jamaica.) Indeed, it's about time that we boldly interrupt the hegemony of Whiteness! Just a small adjustment in the visual presentation of material allowed me to refocus the traditional curriculum and afforded the opportunity for new conversations. (Of course, we will encounter occasions where students are not open to curricular change. For example, in another class, when students realized that the first four readings for the course were written by Black women, one student asked, "Is this course going to be just about Black people?") Even though we will encounter questions and resistances, we must continue to take steps – however small – towards a larger goal. "In the end," explains

Ruth Simmons, leadership "is something on a tiny scale, because what you are looking at, immediately, is something that will probably make a difference in only a small arena" (p. 253).

While universities are places of exciting political and intellectual ideas, the specificities around Blackness and Black women are rarely broached. As mentioned earlier, it is important to participate in meaningful coalitions and support our colleagues in their various struggles. It means, as Audre Lorde (1984) points out, "knowing which coalitions are possible and which are not" (p. 142). Our Black female identities many intersect with other identities, such as class, disability, or sexuality. That said, we also have to be vigilant that our own struggles do not get co-opted or erased. While many oppressed groups draw on the language of "the Black experience" and Black civil rights struggles of the 1960s as reference points, our own issues and struggles can get subsumed by theirs, especially when we are interacting with more powerful groups. On many campuses, it seems easier to have discussions about gender (meaning White women) and sexuality than race or class. Yet these dimensions (sexuality, race, class, disability, etc.) are all interconnected; they play out differently across different social locations and life experiences.

Take Good Care of Yourself

The relationship between race, gender, and stress in the workplace for Black women has been understudied (Hall, Everett, & Hamilton-Mason, 2012; Lewis, Williams, Peppers, & Gadson, 2017; White, 2009). We know that the body does not lie. It expresses what we suppress. Emergent research in epigenetics makes me wonder about the far-reaching effects of stress and trauma in Black lives. Rachel Yehuda (2015), professor of psychiatry and neuroscience and director of the Stress and Trauma Division at Mount Sinai School of Medicine, has found that stress and trauma can not only change DNA but also be transmitted biologically to the next generation! Rosemary Brown was painfully frank about the chronic stress and physical costs of political leadership and public life: loneliness and depression, the beginnings of a brain tumour, angina, and bladder, gallbladder, eye, skin, and teeth problems. Hall, Everett, and Hamilton-Mason (2012) also write, "Discrimination in the workplace on the basis of race and gender is a chronic stressor for Black women" (p. 210).

Working for institutional change can wear on the body and the soul. Universities tend to "eat their own" and can make us lose sight of our brilliance. While easier said than practised, it is important *not* to postpone doing or acquiring what your body and soul need – a spiritual community, a yoga class, time with a confidante, a nap or a holiday. In this age of unending emails, overscheduled calendars, and beeping notifications, we need to give ourselves permission to nurture the spirit, to get adequate nutrition and sleep, to take time for ourselves, to say no ... or just do nothing. We Black women often find ourselves caring for others more than for ourselves. We need to put our jobs in perspective. Let's cultivate the ability not to accept every request. Our careers are only one of many important aspects of our lives.

***

I would hope that despite the unsettling institutional realities that I have raised, we continue to find joy, meaning, and purpose in the work that we do. The university is a base from which to carry out our activism as scholars, teachers, and leaders. There is much work to be done. We have to continue to believe in working towards change and shifting consciousness towards equity and justice. In whatever arena we find ourselves, our activism/leadership as Black women – whether in the classroom or in the boardroom – matters.

In faith and hope,

Annette

REFERENCES

Ahmed, S. (2009). Embodying diversity: Problems and paradoxes for black feminists. *Race Ethnicity and Education, 12*(1), 41–52. https://doi.org/10.1080/13613320802650931

Booth, A.L., Francesconi, M., & Frank, J. (2003). A sticky floors model of promotion, pay, and gender. *European Economic Review, 47*(2), 295–322. https://doi.org/10.1016/S0014-2921(01)00197-0

Brodber, E. (1990). Fiction in the scientific procedure. In S. Cudjoe (Ed.), *Caribbean women writers: Essays from the First International Conference* (pp. 164–8). Boston: University of Massachusetts Press.

Brown, R. (1989). *Being Brown: A very public life.* Toronto: Random House.

Canadian Association of University Teachers. (2018). Underrepresented and underpaid: Diversity and equity among Canada's post-secondary education teachers. Retrieved from. https://www.caut.ca/sites/default/files/caut_equity_report_2018-04final_0.pdf

Chaney, C. (2013). The leadership of First Lady Michelle Obama: Perceptions of black female college students. In D.J. Davis & C. Chaney (Eds.), *Black women in leadership: Their historical and contemporary contributions* (pp. 99–123). New York: Peter Lang.

Collins, P. (2009). *Black feminist thought.* New York: Routledge.

De La Cancela, V., Chin, J.L., & Jenkins, Y. (2016). *Community health psychology: Empowerment for diverse communities.* New York: Routledge.

Douglas, D. (2012). Black/out: The white face of multiculturalism and the violence of the Canadian imperial academic project. In G. Gutiérrez, Y. Muhs, F. Nieman, C. González, & A.P. Harris (Eds.), *Presumed incompetent: The intersections of race and class for women in academia* (pp. 50–65). Boulder: University Press of Colorado.

Eagly, A.H., & Carli, L.L. (2007). *Through the labyrinth: The truth about how women become leaders.* Boston, MA: Harvard Business School Press.

Gadiesh, O., & Coffman, J. (2015, 18 May). Companies drain women's ambition after only two years. *Harvard Business Review.* Retrieved from https://hbr.org/2015/05/companies-drain-womens-ambition-after-only-2-years

Gonzalez, R., & Sponsel, V. (2012). Sponsorship in academia: Observations from the faculty perspective. *NCURA Magazine,* pp. 2–5. Retrieved from http://www.utsa.edu/today/2012/10/ncuramagsepoct12.pdf

Gutiérrez, Y., Muhs, G., Nieman, Y.F., González, C.G., & Harris, A.P. (2012). *Presumed incompetent: The intersections of race and class for women in academia.* Boulder: University Press of Colorado.

Hall, J.C., Everett, J.E., & Hamilton-Mason, J. (2012). Black women talk about workplace stress and how they cope. *Journal of Black Studies, 43*(2), 207–26. https://doi.org/10.1177/0021934711413272

Harding, V. (1974). The vocation of the black scholar and the struggles of the black community. In Editorial Committee, Institute of the Black World (Ed.), *Education and black struggle: Notes from the colonized world* (pp. 3–29). Cambridge, MA: Harvard Educational Review.

Hartman, M.S. (1999). Ruth J. Simmons in conversation with Alice Kessler-Harris Cora Kaplan. In M.S. Hartman (Ed.), *Talking leadership: Conversations with powerful women* (pp. 242–55). New Brunswick: Rutgers University Press.

Henry, A. (2005). Black feminist pedagogy: Critiques and contributions. In W. Watkins (Ed.), *Black protest thought* (pp. 89–106). New York: Peter Lang.

Henry, A. (2011). Feminist theory in education. In S. Tozer, B. Gallegos, & A. Henry (Eds.), *Handbook of research in the social foundations of education* (pp. 261–82). New York: Routledge.

Henry, A. (2015). "We especially welcome applications from visible minorities": Reflections on race, gender and life at three universities. *Race, Ethnicity and Education, 18*(5), 589–610. https://doi.org/10.1080/13613324.2015.1023787

Hewlett, S., & Green, T. (2015). Black women: Ready to lead [Executive summary]. Center for Talent Innovation. Retrieved from http://www.talentinnovation.org/press-media/

Hewlett, S., Leader-Chivée, V., & Sumberg. (2012). Sponsor Effect, UK [Abstract]. Center for Talent Innovation. Retrieved from https://www.talentinnovation.org/publication.cfm?publication=1320

hooks, b. (1992). *Black looks: Race and representation.* Boston: South End.

King, J.E. (2015). A black woman speaks on leadership. In *Dysconscious racism, Afrocentric praxis and education for human freedom: Through the years I keep on toiling: The selected works of Joyce E. King* (pp. 22–30). London: Routledge.

Lewis, J.A., Williams, M.G., Peppers, E.J., & Gadson, C.A. (2017). Applying intersectionality to explore the relations between gendered racism and health among black women. *Journal of Counseling Psychology, 64*(5), 475–86. https://doi.org/10.1037/cou0000231

Lorde, A. (1984). *Sister outsider.* New York: Crossing Press.

Lusted, David. (1986). Why pedagogy? *Screen, 27*(5), 2–14.

Madsen, S. (2010). Women's leadership in education: University presidents. In K. O'Connor (Ed.), *Gender and women's leadership: A reference handbook* (pp. 574–83). Thousand Oaks: Sage.

Marable, M. (1998). *Black leadership.* New York: Columbia University Press.

Mohanty, C.T. (2003). *Feminism without borders: Decolonizing theory, practicing solidarity.* Durham: Duke University Press.

Murphy, E. (1984, 15 December). *White like me* [Video file]. Retrieved from http://criticalmediaproject.org/cml/media/eddie-murphy-White-like-me/

Northouse, P.G. (2004). *Leadership: Theory and practice.* Thousand Oaks: Sage.

O'Reilly, J., Robinson, S., Berdahl, J., & Banki, S. (2015). Is negative attention better than no attention? The comparative effects of ostracism and harassment. *Organization Science, 26*(3), 774–93. https://doi.org/10.1287/orsc.2014.0900

Phelan, J.E., Moss-Racusin, C.A., & Rudman, L.A. (2008). Competent yet out in the cold: Shifting criteria for hiring reflect backlash toward agentic women. *Psychology of Women Quarterly, 32*(4), 406–13. https://doi.org/10.1111/j.1471-6402.2008.00454.x

Pratt-Clarke, M. (2013). Higher education leadership: One black woman's story. In D.J. Davis & C. Chaney (Eds.), *Black women in leadership: Their historical and contemporary contributions* (pp. 144–62). New York: Peter Lang.

Purdie-Vaughns, V. (2015, 22 April). Why so few senior managers are black women in 2015. *Fortune Magazine.* Retrieved from http://fortune.com/2015/04/22/Black-women-leadership-study/

Razack, S., Thobani, S., & Smith, M. (Eds.). (2010). *States of race: Critical race feminism for the 21st century.* Toronto: Between the Lines.

Robinson, K.K., Shakesha, C., Newcomb, W.S., & Grogan, M. (2017). Necessary but not sufficient: The continuing inequality between men and women in educational leadership: Findings from the AASA Mid-Decade Survey. *Frontiers in Education, 2*(12): 1–12. https://doi.org/10.3389/feduc.2017.00012

Smith, M. (2018, 16 February). The diversity gap in university leadership. Retrieved from https://uofaawa.wordpress.com/awa-diversity-gap-campaign/the-diversity-gap-in-university-leadership-2018/

Smith, M., Gamarro, K., & Toor, M. (2017). A dirty dozen: Unconscious race and gender bias in the academy. In F. Henry, E. Dua, C. James, A. Kobayshi, P. Li, H. Ramos, & M. Smith (Eds.), *The equity myth: Racialization and indigeneity at Canadian universities.* Vancouver: UBC Press.

Stead, V., and Elliott, C. (2009). *Women's leadership.* New York: Palgrave McMillan.

St Jean, Y., & Feagin, J. (1998). *Double burden: Black women and everyday racism.* Armonk: M.E. Sharpe.

Tillman, L.C. (2013). Foreword. In D.J. Davis & C. Chaney (Eds.), *Black women in leadership: Their historical and contemporary contributions* (pp. vii–viii). New York: Peter Lang.

White, D.G. (Ed.). (2009). *Telling histories: Black women historians in the ivory tower.* Chapel Hill: University of North Carolina Press.

Yap, M., & Konrad, A.M. (2009). Gender and racial differentials in promotions: Is there a sticky floor, a mid-level bottleneck, or a glass ceiling? *Relations Industrielles/Industrial Relations, 64*(4), 593–619.

Yehuda, R. (2015). How trauma and resilience cross generations [Interview]. Retrieved from http://www.onbeing.org/program/rachel-yehuda-how-trauma-and-resilience-cross-generations/transcript/7791

7 Mercy for Their Children: A Feminist Reading of Black Women's Maternal Activism and Leadership Practices

ERICA S. LAWSON

On my first day of junior high school in Toronto, my mother went to see the school's guidance counsellor. I had recently arrived from Jamaica and she wanted to put the counsellor on notice that I was not to be streamed into vocational courses, nor was he allowed to provide guidance on courses I should take without consulting with her. A working single parent, my mother was unable to attend all of the parent-teacher meetings, but she let my teachers know that I was university bound. Slightly embarrassed by her assertiveness, I did not realize the politics of my mother's proactive behaviour in the context of an educational system that steered Black students – especially those from the Caribbean and Africa – towards the lower end of the academic scale (Brathwaite & James, 1996; Dei, Mazzuca, McIsaac, & Zine, 1997). And it would be much later still, pre-anti-racist feminist consciousness, before I would appreciate her intervention as a form of maternal activism as resistance to institutional racism within the education system. What my mother did is not unique. Many Black mothers and fathers quietly or publicly advocate for their children to address the social injustice that they encounter in the everyday world (see, for example, Smith, 1998), and this, I argue, is a form of activist leadership in its own right. By this I mean exercising agency in their self-interest and that of their children and families by giving direction to, or working collaboratively with, institutional actors to achieve equitable and just outcomes.

This chapter addresses how maternal activism, as it is engaged in by both biological and social mothers, is one important but overlooked form of Black women's leadership in Canada. It examines how maternal activism is theorized; responds to structural racism, which is a form of violence; and reflects the principles of feminist standpoint theory and Black feminist thought. It provides and discusses examples of women's activism at the sites of education, economics, women's labour, and women's critical analysis of violence, as well as examples of the decisions that women make to steer their children out of circumstances that have the potential to limit their life chances. In so doing, this chapter locates women's activism, agency, and leadership in the practices of the "everyday," highlighting embodiment, difference, and inequality in the lived experience of differently located subjects (Bee, Rice, & Trauger, 2015, p. 6).

My arguments in this chapter are shaped by women's narratives, scholarly literature, and the politics of lived experience to illuminate an overlooked practice. To this end, the chapter discusses the epistemologies and practicalities of maternal activism, as well as the social and structural problems it seeks to address. Furthermore, my arguments are informed by unequal social relations as these are produced through racial projects and within which the lives of Black mothers are embedded. I share the view that "race is situated where meaning meets social structure, where identity frames inequality" (Winant, 2000, p. 171). Moreover, I take the position that a full discussion of Black women's realities must be grounded in the specific materiality of their lives in a way that interrogates the "racialized and gendered discourse of the Canadian nation" (Massaquoi, 2007, p. 7).

A grounded reading of women's lives illuminates the actual politicized practices of their maternal activism, that is, the critically informed analysis that they engage in to make sense of the challenges they face, the decisions and actions that they take as a result, and how these actions or decisions demonstrate forms of leadership, activism, or agency. In this way, I think of leadership, activism, and agency as phenomena that are collective, individual, and interpenetrating. Arguably, activism and agency can be viewed as stepping stones towards leadership (of self and others), but I do not necessarily view them as mutually exclusive, especially with respect to the marginalizing practices that place Black women at the periphery of Canada's (neo)liberal-racial project.

Although this chapter focuses on maternal politics among African Canadian mothers, in a transnational context, maternal leadership responds to gendered racism – explained as the ways in which racism is organized in and expressed through gender inequalities (Essed, 1991). This view dialogues with the reality that racism continues to emerge in tandem with changing practices and ideologies within a racial global framework (Arat-Koc, 2010; Winant, 2000) and in an environment of increasingly unequal relations of power that are felt in women's households. In this way, maternal activism bridges the gap between socio-economic and political inequalities at the micro and macro levels to the extent that women's lives are located in both.

Given the complexity of immigration and settlement patterns in Canadian colonialism and nation building, maternal politics also reflects diasporic identities and concerns that complicate the ideologies and practices of national or local forms of activism and leadership in a changing racial context. Accordingly, I will briefly spotlight some examples of these and how I view maternal activism as responding to social challenges and problems, not just in the actions that women take, but also in the epistemologies or situated knowledges that frame these actions within a transnational purview.

To be sure, women of African descent do not share a single definition or a unified sense of Blackness, class, sexuality, or gender; nor do they navigate the world with the same levels of physical and intellectual abilities. Rather, I contend that many Black women are harmed at the intersection of gender and race despite appeals to "post-feminist" and "post-racial" discourses. They are, therefore, subjected to a shared set of oppressive experiences to which they respond, where appropriate, on the basis of politicized approaches to caring and advocating for children. The arguments presented here, furthermore, presume that many Black women choose to participate in an affiliative political network on the basis of a collective anti-racist struggle, while striving to achieve a more "pluralistic community of belonging" (Anim-Addo, 2014, p. 50). Such an affiliation, however, in both symbolic and practical terms regarding belonging, identity, and practice, also engenders its own tensions – increasingly so in neo-liberal societies that shape and shift the meanings of communities and the terms of belonging to them (Hamilton, 2017). In this context, some Black women work collectivity or individually to challenge social injustice, thus exercising what we can think of as personal agency or group-focused advocacy. By addressing these frameworks of possibilities and utilizing appropriate feminist theories, this chapter both discusses and demonstrates how Black maternal activism draws on community-cultural wealth (Yosso, 2005) to express resilience through leadership within a disadvantageous racial-political economy (Gabriel, 1999). Finally, any discussion of maternally informed activism runs the risk of representing women's lives in essentialist terms. Thus, the chapter does not seek to make fixed claims about Black women's complex and contradictory lives, but instead aims to examine maternal subjectivity as an epistemological platform that engenders expressions of leadership and agency for some Black women.

The Social Dimensions of Maternal Activism

Black women's maternal activism responds to racial domination, economic exploitation, and political oppression. The pressures from these oppressions are evident in increasingly neo-liberal economic policies that burden women and concentrate them in low-paid work where they lack job protection, and in government's abdication of its social responsibilities, most evident in neo-liberal policies that tie citizenship to responsibilization (Brown, 2016). Because motherhood is framed within the complexities of women's sexual, cultural, and social realities, the activities that women engage in are reflective of the uniqueness of their circumstances. Given both the generalities of racism and the specificity of anti-Blackness, Black women have a history of mobilizing their maternal identity for political and social change. Among others, the objective of this activism is to bring relief from both immediate and long-standing brutalities and injustices: to save their children from the horrors of slavery through infanticide (Reinhardt, 2002); to confront the violence of white racists who kill their children (Feldstein, 1994); in more recent years, to utilize extended kinship networks to ameliorate the worst consequences of structural adjustment policies (Harrison, 1997) so that their children (and extended families) can eat, go to school, have a place to live; and to challenge detention and incarceration systems that target them and their children in the age of "terrorism" (Tyler, 2013). Because the social production of Black motherhood is integral to laws and policies in the racial state (Kandaswamy, 2012; Roberts, 1997), indeed, to how the nation is imagined, a critical reading of Black women's maternal resistance undermines accusations of essentialism.

Scholars have argued that contemporary forms of unequal social relations facing Black women in the diaspora are manifestations of slavery's afterlife (Dillon, 2012; Hartman, 1997). While not all Black women in the diaspora trace their heritage to the plantation economies of the transatlantic slave trade, they share felt impacts of the racial-gendered organization of economic structures and social practices that underpin European domination. I will address how shared oppressions are manifested among Black women by drawing on the language of structural violence as this chapter unfolds. While structural and gendered racism are not the same as they would have been in enslavement, or within different points of political-economic processes that shape the particularities of contemporary racism, variations of these discriminatory practices continue to impact Black women's life chances (Kandaswamy, 2012), and these, in part, frame the motivations for maternal activism.

Black women's maternally informed activism occurs in everyday decisions and actions, although it is not readily identified as such. When a Black mother identifies and questions the connection between her child's inability to function in school and the hidden or overlooked forms of racial exclusion in that school, she expresses a form of activism that has the potential to improve her child's educational chances as well as to change educational policy. This is an example of how some women's mothering activities are politicized. Yet these decisions and activities are largely ignored as constituting examples of "leadership," for four reasons.

First, the bodies in question are racialized and rendered invisible in the Canadian political landscape. Second, "valid" expressions of leadership are widely associated with elite groups within institutional, political, and corporate spheres, and not also within the daily, less visible but crucial mothering work done by women. Third, within some Black communities and liberation movements, public leadership is largely viewed as the legitimate domain of men, with women working behind the scenes to support them. For example, it is not accidental that accomplished women like Amy Jacques Garvey are footnoted in the archives of Black nationalist movements. Depicted as Marcus Garvey's "surrogate" or "helpmate" in scholarship about him, Amy Jacques Garvey, Garvey's second wife, is rarely recognized for the true value of her contribution to the Garvey movement and as an advocate for social justice over the course of her life (Adler, 1992, p. 346). Fourth, because political participation is typically viewed as self-interested in neo-conservative/liberal states (see, for example, Brown, 2006), actions that are grounded in a collective good are overlooked in contemporary political analyses (Naples, 1991, p. 478). Yet through their daily actions and choices, Black women contest the core ideas and practices that permeate how social relations are organized to reinforce inequality through what has been described as relations of ruling (Smith, 1996). These include ruling through law, education, economics; employment, and in the criminal justice system, to name a few of the textual/political processes in Canadian society through which structural discrimination is manifested.

Simultaneously, I think of maternal activism as not necessarily resulting in collective action but also as pertaining to individual decisions that women make to challenge systemic oppression to meet anti-racist goals, alleviate immediate hardship, and act in the personal-political interest of children. This type of decision making on which individual action is predicated can be thought of as agency rather than "leadership" per se; yet, it cannot be dislocated from a broader culture of racist aggression to which women and their children are subjected. It is from this perspective that I use "individual" in reference to a maternal subject who, through critical decision making, challenges institutionalized racism. As such, I draw on Black feminist literature that names ordinary Black women as intellectuals in their own right, as they assess the scope of the challenges they face and the actions they take as a result, in ways that negotiate the multidimensionality of their experience.

The Social Situated-ness of Maternal Thinking

In referencing maternal activism I mean to signal the ways in which Black mothers undertake leadership activities to challenge what Paul Farmer (2004) describes as the "social machinery of oppression" within the framework of structural violence (p. 307). By confronting iterations of this social machinery, Black maternal activism animates how personal troubles are politically constituted such that, for Black women, "practice informs our theory" (Massaquoi, 2007, p. 5). In Canada, these structurally organized troubles are often rooted in intersectional and interlocking oppressions and manifested in high rates of unemployment or low-paid precarious employment; removal of Black children from their families by children's aid societies; incarceration of African Canadians in jails, prisons, and immigration detention centres; and high levels of school drop-out and push-out rates among Black Canadian students. Subject to class locations and other intersectional factors, these troubles constitute a form of structural violence that Black women must traverse in what Collins (1998) describes as their "search for justice."

The aforementioned social problems are not new challenges for African Canadians as a group. As demonstrated by hampton and Rochat and Gooden in this volume, a number of organizations have a history of working to address inequalities facing African Canadians through varied leadership initiatives. Because of structural racism, Black women, indeed Black communities, cannot take for granted the well-being of their children within institutions such as schools. Many African Canadian women simultaneously advocate for educational transformation aimed at advancing community interests while seeking to fulfil their personal aspirations for their children. Furthermore, political advocacy emanating from Black women's maternal activism is at once collaborative, self-interested, and contradictory, thus presenting women as heterogeneous actors with contested epistemological standpoints and desires.

These factors, I argue, were most evident in the heated debates of 2008 about establishing a Black-focused school within the Toronto District School Board (Wallace, 2009). On the one hand, among the many advocates for this initiative[1] were Angela Wilson and Donna Harrow: both are community activists who pushed hard for such a school. On the other hand, Lorraine Small, whose fifteen-year old son, Jordan Manners, was shot and killed at his school in 2008, registered her disagreement with this approach. She stated that "Martin Luther King and so many of our fathers fought to come together so that blacks and whites could be together ... This black school thing, no it ain't right" (Alcoba, 2008). Small was not alone in her dissent; other African Canadians echoed her concern that such a school could not advance the interests of community members already struggling to find a place in Canadian society.[2] That she made her views known at a public meeting with trustees of the Toronto District School Board before a vote on whether to establish such a school illuminates her advocacy, though from a dissenting position.

I do not know if Donna Harrow and Angela Wilson are biological mothers, but their willingness to struggle for a school that they passionately felt would benefit the African Canadian community intimates a commitment to social mothering and a wider interest in advancing a progressive educational agenda for African Canadian students. Their position, in my view, is a critique of the limits of an education system located in a liberal-multicultural framework, and desired by some community members. I locate Harrow and Wilson's actions in what bell hooks (1992) describes as a struggle to construct a self and an identity that is at once oppositional and liberatory (p. 29). I argue, furthermore, that this type of opposition is shaped, in part, by the material conditions of Black lives in Canada and an embodied knowledge, consistent with a politicized awareness that these conditions produce.

Knowledge that propels (social) mothers to act collectively, individually, or both, is entrenched in the "social situated-ness" of women as knowers (Grasswick & Webb, 2002, p. 190; Stoetzler & Yuval-Davis, 2002). Arguably, then, we can think of Harrow and Wilson as situated-knowers located within a larger community of African Canadians who hold shared, historical, and contemporary knowledge about the struggle for equity in education, even as there are disagreements about what form this should take. In other words, the two women's advocacy for educational advancement is shaped by an epistemic standpoint with historical roots, and one that is informed by an awareness of the material consequences for Black students who are pushed out and subsequently drop out of the mainstream school system (Dei et al., 1997).

Viewed as a method of enquiry, a standpoint perspective, or situated knowing, calls for a mapping of how people's lives are shaped by and embedded in systems of power (Smith, 1998), particularly within the framework of historical materialism (Hawkesworth, 2008). That is to say, the economic mode of production within which women participate informs their social position in a given society and, therefore, the interpretive tools they employ to understand their realities, make decisions, and take action. Not merely reducible to the economic dictates of a given society, however, a feminist reading of historical materialism encompasses an analytical approach that is attentive to historical specificity and adept at engaging complex differences among women and men within and across boundaries of race, class, sexuality, and nation (Hawkeworth, 2008, p. 319).

Indeed, at least with respect to Black women, a standpoint that is shaped by the racial-sexual dimensions of historical materialism "posits a distinctive relationship among a group's position in hierarchical power relations ... and the standpoint that a group constructs in interpreting [their] experiences" (Collins, 1998, p. 194).

By putting Collins's (1998) perspective in dialogue with that of Gaile Pohlaus (2002), we see that a "standpoint" is not a fixed social position, "but rather is an engagement with the kinds of questions [substantively produced by that location]" (Pohlaus, 2002, p. 287). In signalling a social position informed by historical materialism in a racial project, I mean to point out that the particular questions of concern to Black maternal leaders and activists, indeed to the politicized practices of mothering, are shaped by women's location in the Canadian political economy; women's non/citizenship status; the shifting and intersectional articulations of gendered racism; women's care-giving responsibilities; and the questions that these invite about the power relations among state, economy, and labour as women's lives are located within them.

At the risk of stating the obvious, therefore, questions about racial inequalities in Ontario/Canadian schools, centred in an embodied standpoint, inform Harrow and Wilson's leadership activities as these pertained to a Black-focused school and access to resources (e.g., employment facilitated by educational accomplishments). As mentioned earlier, these questions focused on how to address high drop-out rates among African Canadians students, how to push the boundaries of what constitutes "academic success," and how to advocate for a curriculum and educational outcomes more reflective of the realities of African Canadian children and youth.

Motherwork against Structural Violence

A critically informed understanding of structural racism situates social problems facing Black communities in racial histories whose legacies are evident in contemporary inequities. It also highlights how inequities are implemented through iterations of white supremacy and, finally, challenges the seductive notion, increasingly common in minimalist welfare states like Canada, that individuals are solely responsible for "failing" to take advantage of opportunities that facilitate upward mobility. In this section I will discuss how maternal activism, through what is described as women's motherwork, responds to structural racism.

Structural racism apprehends the reality that maternal activism struggles against matters of life and death, or, more succinctly, what Achilles Mbembe (2003) describes as necropolitics – that is, the normalization of death-making public policy and profiteering in capitalist societies – which emanates from the plantation as a mode of economic production. The material ramifications of the plantation economy are politically, culturally, and economically salient today such that we can speak of slavery as "haunting" the present (Dillon, 2012; Hartman, 1997; James, 2005; Sexton, 2010), although this discourse is erased in liberal racism (see, for example, Singh, 2012). Slavery's afterlife and its impacts on Black communities are starkly evident in what Naomi Klein (2007) describes as disaster capitalism, framed by the principles of the Chicago School of Economics under the direction of Milton Friedman. Increasingly, disaster capitalism has no uses for Black life, save as a commodity for the politics of fear and the criminal industrial complex. The lack of value placed on Black lives is further reflected in Mbembe's argument that the neo-liberal state establishes full sovereignty by exercising its power over life and death. Mbembe explains how this exercise in power blurs the boundaries between life and death both in the plantation economy and in the contemporary sovereign-racial state wherein Black lives are disposable (Gibson, 2006; Giroux, 2012) and to which, I argue, maternal activism responds.

Although obviously not direct, there is a variable connection between the two: the past and the present. The disciplinary practices that governed Black motherhood during slavery and in the aftermath of emancipation, including laws that managed their re/productive capacities, are similar to those found in contemporary welfare policies that seek to manage Black women. (Kandaswamy, 2012; Roberts, 1997). Mbembe argues that, within the plantation, "the slave condition results from a triple loss: loss of a 'home,' loss of rights over his or her body, and loss of political status" (p. 21). These losses exemplified "the state of exception in the very structure of the plantation system and its aftermath" (Sexton, 2010, p. 32).

From these perspectives, I contend that we can think of Black women's praxis of motherwork as resistance to the vestiges of slavery and colonialism (Collins, 1994; see also Udel, 2001). Collins describes motherwork as resistance to the external factors that pressure and erode Black family life in newer, neo-liberal articulations of oppressive practices. Therefore, as praxis, motherwork engenders the cultural, social, and economic epistemologies that politicize mothering activities. Moreover, its epistemic foundations are constituted by "the cognitive capacities, metaphysical attitudes[,] criteria of truth and conceptions of virtues" (Ruddick & O'Reilly, 2009, p. 17) that shape mothering practice. Politicized Black mothers operate within an epistemic framework that utilizes maternal thinking to address racism. And in doing so, they attempt to mitigate or recover from the past-present loss of embodied rights and personhood through both a communitarian and individual reading of what these mean.

If we think of the social production of the "Black mother" in a Eurocentric, capitalist, heterosexist society as a constellated discursive being rather than solely as a biological entity, we can begin to identify the epistemic dimensions of "motherwork" that are involved in Black women's activism. And we can more clearly apprehend how such work articulates a different set of maternal-leadership practices oriented by a shared worldview arising from a consciousness of the forces that produce the social being of Black mothers who exist in ruling relations. Typically, the socially and externally constructed "Black mother/woman" engenders problematic assumptions about who these women are and, simultaneously, invites a counter-reading of how their lives are actually organized within frameworks of exploitative laws and policies. That is, as they are politicized by circumstances, Black mothers become adept at reconfiguring externally imposed tropes to express oppositional and activist identities to advance the fullest range of their personal, familial, and communal interests to the extent this is possible in a racial state (Goldberg, 2002).

To take one example, elsewhere I have written about the plight of seven Jamaican women who in the late 1970s were targeted for deportation from Canada for "lying" about their family status: that is, by declaring that they had no children in order to gain entry into the country (Lawson, 2013).[3] I place quotation marks around "lying" because the women were participants in an iteration of the erstwhile West Indian Domestic Scheme that had once aggressively recruited Caribbean women to work as domestics in Canada. The scheme required women to be childless, single, and available to work, unencumbered, in Canadian homes – at best, a questionable set of requirements for women of childbearing age, thus setting up women to "lie."

Among the number of reasons why the women fought the deportation orders was the fact that their children and extended family members in Jamaica had come to rely on their remittances. Limited access to economic opportunities resulting from the imposition of austerity measures in a global market remain central to the reasons why most mothers continue to cross borders in search of jobs, thus prompting scholarly investigations into the practice of transnational mothering (Hewett, 2009; Hondagneu-Sotelo & Avila, 1997; Horton, 2009). Then, as now, a loss of remittances resulting from deportation would have been catastrophic, especially in the midst of austerity measures imposed on Jamaica by the International Monetary Fund (IMF) at the time that the deportation orders were issued. The collective protest undertaken by the women and their allies to stay in Canada and to change punitive immigration laws was rooted in motherwork and maternal thinking as I have described it here. This incident (dubbed "Save the Seven") is an example of maternal activism and political leadership[4] as well as being indicative of women's leadership activities located within an anti-racist movement.

We can trace the plight of these Jamaican women and many others like them – the fact of crossing borders to work as domestics with limited rights – to the ramifications of slavery and colonialism in relation to Farmer's description of the "social machinery of oppression" discussed above, and as an example of slavery's afterlife; that is, how the theft of labour and other ravages of the plantation economy continue to haunt the present and frame politicized mothers' responses to social injustice. Although beyond the scope of this chapter to fully address, it is crucial to acknowledge the dialectical nature of Black women's positionality in Canada's racial project, and its emergence in and through immigration and labour policies that staked out an imagined [white] community (Anderson, 2006).

Material Conditions and Maternal Decision Making

The examples of Black maternal activism discussed so far (i.e., Harrow and Wilson and the seven Jamaican women) have focused on women's collaborative engagement to address racism as a form of structural violence. Yet, I mentioned earlier that women's activism and leadership on a smaller but similarly important scale in the day-to-day critically informs decisions they make respecting their children's well-being and future opportunities. Maternal activism responds to, for example, the injustices within racialized spaces and the hidden or obvious ways in which they limit access to educational, employment, and other opportunities for Black youths and their families while increasing the likelihood of encounters with the police. In other words, the spatial-racial organization of urban and city neighbourhoods and their segregative implications are of interest to maternal activism.

The high-profile activism and leadership initiatives undertaken by African American mothers in recent years – for example, Sybryna Fulton (Trayvon Martin) and Lucia McBath (Jordan Davis), resulting from the murders of their sons – is in part the result of the perpetrators' perception that these young men did not belong in particular spaces: that they threatened the right of the white citizen to move safely in urban neighbourhoods and cities. Although these are American-based experiences, they can be read as encapsulating a wider North American phenomenon rooted in anti-Blackness and culturally produced white fears. In addition to how space facilitates citizenship rights for some and restrictions for others, my analysis of these murders animates how the racialization of space (Razack, 2002) is organized to limit opportunities for Black youth and their families who aspire to upward mobility. Indeed, containment in urban-racial spaces re-articulates segregative practices that are no longer legally or socially acceptable. A critical counter-reading of such confinement reveals the language of personal responsibility and failure to take advantage of equal opportunities, including the "right" to live in a place of one's choosing. Certainly, this a prevalent view in a Canada that prides itself on working to establish diverse communities and cities.

That these segregative realities in urban/city spaces shape mothers' understanding of and responses to the barriers facing their children is evident in Hubert Davis's 2009 documentary *Invisible City*. For three years, Davis chronicled the lives of two teenaged boys, Kendell and Mikey, living in Regent Park, a public housing community in Toronto. The film is set against the backdrop of an extensive "revitalization" project to create a mixed-income community, and the negotiated meanings of Black masculinities in an urban space. Both fifteen years old when the filming began, the boys lived in single-mother households with only fleeting interactions with their respective fathers. Anderson (2010) summarizes the struggles they faced:

> They've both had tangles with the police already and are aware of the direction they may be headed. Kendell says he's determined to "keep level headed and not get negative on myself." Mikey knows what can happen if "you keep going on the wrong path and hang with the wrong crowd," but he seems all too aware of the lack of guidance. Their overworked mothers express their own feelings of helplessness. (Anderson, 2010)

Davis's interviews with the boys' Caribbean Canadian mothers, Sharon (Mikey) and Sandy (Kendell), are relevant to thinking about Black women's paid labour, mothering work, how they make sense of the problems facing their sons, and the limited intervention strategies that they are able to employ to steer their children away from the criminal justice system. Simultaneously, both women work to survive in, and express a desire to leave, public housing. Sharon is shown at her low-wage job in a school cafeteria. She and her children dream about leaving Regent Park but have few real options of acquiring the money to do so. The pressing need to make ends meet takes her away from home early in the mornings, and she expresses frustration at her inability to monitor her son.

> I go to work early in the morning, I get up at 5 o clock. I work two jobs just to make ends meet. It doesn't meet but I'm trying. I have no time to get

> up and stay up late at night and go walk the street look for Michael on my own. I said Michael, "what do you want from me?" He said he wants me to be home. I said, tell me, how can I be home? Who's gonna pay the bills? I sure don't want to be on welfare, I've been there and seen how people talk to people and I never want to go back there. I want to give Michael some of the things that he wants; it's not all the time I can give it to him because I'm the only one he can look to for anything. I can't say, "go call your father" and ask him for something because he's never there for them. (Davis, 2009)

The economic realities of mothering for poor Black women like Sharon reflect Dorothy Smith's (1998) observation that women often parent in the context of a system that "take[s] no account of the actual material and social conditions of mothering work" (p. 168). The material and social conditions of Black women's mothering work, as in these two cases, can be charted in the journeys of Black Caribbean, other diasporic, and continental African women, descendants from the plantation, and/or victims of colonialization, who make their way to Canada. As well, those conditions are rooted in questions of the theft of re/productive labour, and women's low-wage positions within a capitalist system. Indeed, in Canada, it is still the case that poverty is deeply feminized and racialized. Andrea Smith argues that women still face gendered occupational segregation in the workplace, a gendered wage gap, "glass ceilings," over-representation among part-time and low-wage workers, the double burden of unpaid care work and wage earning, and inadequate supports such as childcare and paid parental leave (Smith, 2008).

Not only is it difficult for them to make ends meet, it is almost impossible for Sharon and Sandy to implement idealized "good mothering practices," which "presuppose time and effort" (Smith, 1998, p. 168) that they do not have. Yet, they continue to devise strategies informed by critical thinking, rooted in an embodied standpoint, to exercise a type of agency to ensure the well-being of their children.

The broader context in which I assess Sharon and Sandy's mothering practices as spotlighting maternal activism or agency is shaped by my reading of Tara Yosso's scholarship on cultural resiliency and wealth. Yosso (2005) argues that we hardly think of racialized communities as having their own form of cultural wealth to make sense of and respond to institutionalized oppression. "Community cultural wealth," she argues, "is an array of knowledge, skills, abilities and contacts possessed and utilized by Communities of Colour to survive and resist macro and micro-forms of oppression" (p. 77). To my mind, these mothers draw on "aspirational, navigational, social, linguistic, familial, and resistant capital" (p. 76) in their expression of maternal agency. Viewed as such, maternal activism takes place at the level of consciousness in ways that allow women to read and act against the hegemonic grain because of their self-identified aspirations for, and commitment to, their children.

Because of the systemic limits placed on Black women, I do not speak exclusively of them as exercising public leadership that influences large groups of people, but in addition to recognizing that, for Black women, agentic expression partly emanates from a critique of tropes that seek to limit the value of their lives. This act of redefinition evinces an expression of self-valuation and self-definitions that appears "in patterns of economic and political activity" (Collins, 1986, p. S22) within a shared culture and community. Therefore, in thinking about Black women's agency and leadership we must be willing to look in non-traditional places and to assess the ways in which their engagement in socially reproductive work is political (see, for example, Harrison, 1997).

As knowing subjects, Black mothers like Sandy and Sharon advocate on behalf of their children with a defined standpoint and with the realization that a great deal is at stake. For example, Sandy states that

> The main thing that's on my mind now is that I just don't want Kendell to have a police record, because I think when they go through the court system or the justice system or they get arrested it just become like a norm and they think it's okay for it to happen again. I don't want this to stick anywhere in his mind. (Davis, 2009)

Her decision to help her son work through a difficult stage in his life, while not connected to a social movement, is nonetheless framed by the epistemology of her social location and sense of connection to a shared community of knowers. In other words, Sandy is speaking about the ways in which young Black people, once entangled in the justice system, are less likely than their white peers to get second chances. She is keenly aware of what this entanglement might mean for her son without her intervention – although she does not specify what form this intervention may take.

Sandy's motivation to mitigate the possibility of long-term consequences for her son emerges from an epistemology at the meeting point of lived experience and her social location in both a materially and ideologically designed white supremacist structure. Her fears for her son, and the questions with which she grapples, are shaped by an awareness that his encounter with the criminal justice system is not distinct from those in the larger Black community. In fact, young Black people are disproportionately racially profiled (Cole, 2015; Wortley & Owusu-Bempah, 2011) and more likely to be charged with and spend more time in jail for minor offences. These are some of the realities, framed by the limitations of poverty and racial-spatial arrangements that shape Black women's interventions on behalf of their children.

A Maternal Perspective on Violence

A knowing type of subjectivity is further evident in Black women's critical insights about the injuries and killings of their children by state agents or by other Black people. This is evident in the critical consciousness they express and the actions they take to prevent further violence. The perspective of Julia Farqurhason, a bereaved Caribbean Canadian mother, provides an example of what I mean. Ms Farquharson's twenty-one-year-old son, Segun Farquharson, was shot and killed in Toronto in 2001, and the killers have yet to be caught. She channelled her grief into co-founding United Mothers against Violence Everywhere (UMOVE) with other mothers of murdered children, including Audette Sheppard, whose nineteen-year-old son Justin was also killed in 2001 (Morales, 2008). As a social movement, one of UMOVE's objectives was to advocate for legislation banning hand guns. In expressing her "thoughts on what ... government[s] and communities could be doing better [to prevent violence]," Farquharson stated:

> There are a lot of people who can't find a good job. If they try, they do get a job but it's a mediocre job. It's not sufficient for them to live off. To take the TTC, it's $120.00 [a month] for an adult fare to go to and fro. If you're in a job that is only paying you a certain amount, how can you afford it? Your rent is expensive. You're going to the supermarket and food is expensive ... Education is also a problem. There are lots of dropouts, problems in school and they get kicked out. But where did they go? It's just like when you arrest someone and send them to jail for whatever crime they commit, they spend time in there and then they come out. All they have to do is report to a probation officer and that's it. What do they do? Where is the follow up? You have a criminal record, you can't get a job. So how do you expect those people to live in society and be productive in society? You can't. (Rankin, 2012)

As a maternal activist, Farquharson's responses illuminate a critical standpoint that comments on the barriers facing young Black people involved in crimes, as well as the conditions that could lead to criminal activities. She talks about personal responsibility while expressing an awareness of its limits in the face of barriers to education and employment. As such, her insights are applicable to the idea that the knowledge that propels motherwork "is not a product of mere observation or a disinterested perspective of the world, but is achieved by struggling to understand one's experience through a critical stance on the social order within which knowledge is produced" (Pohlaus, 2002, p. 285, summarizing Harding).

In addition, as a standpoint position that articulates a critical stance, Black Canadian feminist scholarship takes Pohlaus's argument further by addressing the specificities of how the social order within the Canadian nation state organizes discrimination (Massaquoi, 2007); the epistemic perspectives that women must devise to identify its operationalization (Massaquoi, 2004); and the multi-pronged strategies that they must engage for transformation (Bobb-Smith, 2007). This emerging feminist scholarship, which addresses the multidimensionality of Black women's lives, remains to be expanded to more fully examine their leadership and activism in Canada.

Conclusion

I have argued that Black women's maternal politics is informed by a standpoint that is struggled for; that maternal activism and leadership are evident in collective action as well as individual decisions informed by a broader historical-community context; and that women engage in activism as social and biological mothers to address structural violence and gendered-racial discrimination. Maternal activism reflects the experiences of "situated" and embodied knowers, and it implicates the body at the nexus of the physical and the emotional. It also works to transform a judicial-political system based on what Charles Mills (1997) describes as the racial contract to demand full citizenship rights for Black and other racialized groups.

Although this chapter is narrowly focused on specific examples of maternal activism, it is important to note that Black women occupy leadership positions across almost all spectrums in Canadian society, although at the highest levels within institutions and corporations their presence is extremely rare. To be sure, these varied locations engender their own possibilities for a different analysis of Black women's leadership and activism. Therefore, I view this work as a contribution to an anti-racist feminist-informed conversation about the multiplicities of Black women's leadership practices in the shifting and contested meanings of an emerging Canadian liberal democratic project.

NOTES

1 This recent debate about Black-focused schools has a longer history. For example, in 1985, Jackie Wilson, Afua Cooper, and Veronica Sullivan began talking about and advocating for a school to meet the needs of Black students. This grew into the Afro-Caribbean Alternative Secondary School,

which was housed at D.B. Hood Community School in northwest Toronto. However, its tenure was short lived due to accusations of segregationist practices, much like the accusation levelled at more recent discussions of a Black-focused school (see http://www.thismagazine.ca/issues/2009/01/black_schools.php).

2 The Africentric Alternative School, part of the Toronto District School Board, opened its doors in 2009.

3 The seven women were among a group of fifty women facing deportation for similar reasons. Their challenge to the state became popularized under the slogan "Save the Seven," and they became the public faces of the movement to stop the deportations.

4 In the end, the seven women were forced to leave the country in January 1979, but were informed by the immigration minister that they would receive a sympathetic hearing if they tried to return. Six months later, the seven were allowed to re-enter Canada on permits from the minister of employment and immigration (Bayefsky, 1979–80, p. 467).

REFERENCES

Adler, K.S. (1992). "Always leading our men in service and sacrifice": Amy Jacques Garvey, feminist, black nationalist. *Gender & Society, 6*(3), 346–75. https://doi.org/10.1177/089124392006003002

Alcoba, N. (2008, 30 January). Toronto trustees vote in favour of Afrocentric school. *National Post.* Retrieved from http://www.nationalpost.com/news/story.html?id=272389

Anderson, B. (2006). I*magined communities: Reflections on the origins and spread of nationalism.* London: Verso.

Anderson, J. (2010, 5 February). Invisible city: Growing up fast in Regent Park. *Toronto Star.* Retrieved from http://www.thestar.com/entertainment/movies/2010/02/05/invisible_city_growing_up_fast_in_regent_park.html

Anim-Addo, J. (2014). Activist-mothers maybe, sisters surely? Black British feminism, absence, and transformation. *Feminist Review, 108*(1), 44–60. https://doi.org/10.1057/fr.2014.35

Arat-Koc, S. (2010). New whiteness(es), beyond the colour line?: Assessing the contradictions and complexities of "whiteness" in the (geo)political economy of capitalist globalization. In S. Razack, M. Smith, & S. Thobani (Eds.), *States of race: Critical race feminism for the 21st century* (pp. 147–68). Toronto: Between the Lines.

Bayefsky, A. (1979–80). The Jamaican Women case and the Canadian Human Rights Act: Is government subject to the principle of equal opportunity? 18 *U.W. Ontario L. Rev.* 461. Retrieved from http://heinonline.org/HOL/Page?handle=hein.journals/uwolr18&div=25&g_sent=1&collection=journals

Bee, A., Rice, J., & Trauger, A. (2015). A feminist approach to climate change governance: Everyday and intimate politics. *Geography Compass, 9*(6), 339–50. https://doi.org/10.1111/gec3.12218

Bobb-Smith, Y. (2007). "We get troo ...": Caribbean Canadian women's spirituality as strategy of resistance. In N. Massaquoi & N.N. Wane (Eds.), *Theorizing empowerment: Canadian perspectives on Black feminist thought* (pp. 55–71). Toronto: Inanna.

Brathwaite, K.E., & James, C.E. (1996). *Educating African Canadians*, Toronto: James Lorimer.

Brown, W. (2006) American nightmare: Neoliberalism, neoconservatism, and de-democratization. *Political Theory, 34*(6), 690–714. https://doi.org/10.1177/0090591706293016

Brown, W. (2016). Sacrificial citizenship: Neoliberalism, human capital, and austerity politics. *Constellations, 23*(1), 3–14. https://doi.org/10.1111/1467-8675.12166

Cole, D. (2015, 21 April). The skin I'm in: I've been interrogated by police more than 50 times – all because I'm black. *Toronto Life.* Retrieved from http://www.torontolife.com/informer/features/2015/04/21/skin-im-ive-interrogated-police-50-times-im-black/

Collins, P.H. (1986). Learning from the outsider within: The sociological significance of black feminist thought. *Social Problems, 33*(6), S14–S32. https://doi.org/10.1525/sp.1986.33.6.03a00020

Collins, P.H. (1994). Shifting the center: Race, class, and feminist theorizing about motherhood. In D. Bassin, M. Honey, & M. Mahrer Kaplan (Eds.), *Representations of motherhood* (pp. 56–74). New Haven: Yale University Press.

Collins, P.H. (1998). *Fighting words: Black women and the search for justice.* Minneapolis: University of Minnesota Press.

Davis, H. (Director). (2009). *Invisible city* [film]. Toronto: National Film Board of Canada.

Dei, G.J.S., Mazzuca, J., McIsaac, E., & Zine, J. (1997). *Reconstructing "drop-out": A critical ethnography of black students' disengagement from school.* Toronto: University of Toronto Press.

Dillon, S. (2012). Possessed by death: The neo-liberal carceral state, black feminism, and the afterlife of slavery. *Radical History Review, 112*, 113–25. https://doi.org/10.1215/01636545-1416196

Essed, P. (1991). *Understanding everyday racism: An interdisciplinary theory.* Newberry Park: Sage.

Farmer, P. (2004). An anthropology of structural violence. *Current Anthropology, 45*(3), 305–25. https://doi.org/10.1086/382250

Feldstein, R. (1994). "I wanted the whole world to see": Race, gender, and the constructions of motherhood in the death of Emmett Till. In J. Meyerowitz (Ed.), *Not June Cleaver: Women and gender in postwar America, 1945–1960* (pp. 263–303). Philadelphia: Temple University Press.

Gabriel, C. (1999). Restructuring at the margins: Women of colour and the changing economy. In E. Dua & A. Robertson (Eds.), *Scratching the surface: Canadian anti-racist feminist thought* (pp. 127–64). Toronto: Women's Press.

Gibson, J.R. 2006. *Have they decided to kill us yet? Global black labor obsolescence and manufactured black genocide: Sidney M. Willhelm's* Who needs the Negro? *and Samuel F. Yette's* The choice revisited. Southfield: Kitabu.

Giroux, H.A. (2012). *Disposable youth: Racialized memories and the culture of cruelty.* New York: Routledge.

Goldberg, D.T. (2002). *The racial state.* Oxford: Blackwell.

Grasswick, H.E., & Webb, M.O. (2002). Feminist epistemology as social epistemology. *Social Epistemology, 16*(3), 185–96. Retrieved from https://philpapers.org/rec/GRAFEA

Hamilton, P. (2017). *"We do this too": Black mothers' engagements with attachment parenting in Britain and Canada* (Doctoral dissertation). University of Western Ontario, London, ON.

Harrison, F.V. (1997). The gendered politics and violence of structural adjustment: A view from Jamaica. In L. Lamphere, H. Ragone, & P. Zavella (Eds.), *Situated lives: Gender and culture in everyday life* (pp. 451–68). New York: Routledge.

Hartman, S. (1997). *Scenes of subjection: Terror, slavery, and self-making in nineteenth-century America.* New York: Oxford.

Hawkesworth, M. (2008). The pragmatics of Marion Young's historical materialism. *Politics & Gender, 4*(2), 318–26. https://doi.org/10.1017/S1743923X08000226

Hewett, H. (2009). Mothering across borders: Narratives of immigrant women in the United States. *WSQ: Women's Studies Quarterly, 37*(3–4), 121–39.

Hondagneu-Sotelo, P., & Avila, E. (1997). "I'm here, but I'm there": The meanings of Latina transnational motherhood. *Gender & Society, 11*(5), 548–71. https://doi.org/10.1177/089124397011005003

hooks, b. (1992). *Postmodern blackness.* Baltimore: Johns Hopkins University Press.

Horton, S. (2009). "A mother's heart is weighed down with stones": A phenomenological approach to the experience of transnational motherhood. *Culture, Medicine, and Psychiatry, 33*(1), 21–40. https://doi.org/10.1007/s11013-008-9117-z

James, J. (2005). Introduction: Democracy and captivity. In Joy James (Ed.), *The new abolitionists: (Neo)slave narratives and contemporary prison writings* (pp. xxi–xlii). Albany: State University of New York Press.

Kandaswamy, P. (2012). Gendering racial formation. In D.M. HoSang, O. LaBennett, & L. Pulido (Eds.), *Racial formation in the twenty-first century* (pp. 23–41). Berkley: University of California Press.

Klein, N. (2007). *The shock doctrine: The rise of disaster capitalism.* Toronto: Knopf.

Lawson, E. (2013). The gendered working lives of seven Jamaican women in Canada: A story about "here" and "there" in a transnational context. *Feminist Formations, 25*(1), 138–56. https://doi.org/10.1353/ff.2013.0002

Massaquoi, N. (2004). An African child becomes a black Canadian feminist: Oscillating identities in the black diaspora. *Canadian Women's Studies, 23*(2): 140–4.

Massaquoi, N. (2007). An unsettled feminist discourse. In N. Massaquoi & N.N. Wane (Eds.), *Theorizing empowerment: Canadian perspectives on black feminist thought* (pp. 75–94). Toronto: Inanna.

Mbembe, A. (2003). Necropolitics. *Public Culture, 15*(1), 11–40.

Mills, C.W. (1997). *The racial contract.* Ithaca: Cornell University Press.

Morales, D. (2008, 25 April). Tragedy turns mother into activist. *Toronto Observer.* Retrieved from http://torontoobserver.ca/2008/04/25/tragedy-turns-mother-into-activist/

Naples, N.A. (1991). "Just what needed to be done": The political practice of women community workers in low income neighborhoods. *Gender and Society, 5*(4), 478–94. https://doi.org/10.1177/089124391005004003

Pohlaus, G. (2002). Knowing communities: An investigation of Harding's standpoint epistemology. *Social Epistemology, 16*(3), 183–93. https://doi.org/10.1080/0269172022000025633

Rankin, J. (2012, 30 July). Gun violence: Three Toronto mothers of murdered sons share their stories. *Toronto Star.* Retrieved from http://www.thestar.com/news/gta/2012/07/30/gun_violence_three_toronto_mothers_of_murdered_sons_share_their_ideas_for_change.html

Razack, S. (2002). Introduction. In S. Razack (Ed.), *Race, space, and the law: Unmapping a white settler society* (pp. 1–20). Toronto: Between the Lines.

Reinhardt, M. (2002). Who speaks for Margaret Garner? Slavery, silence, and the politics of ventriloquism. *Critical Inquiry, 29*(1), 81–119. https://doi.org/10.1086/367999

Roberts, D. (1997). *Killing the black body: Race, reproduction, and the meaning of liberty,* New York: Pantheon.

Ruddick, S., & O'Reilly, A. (2009). A conversation about maternal thinking. In Andrea O'Reilly (Ed.), *Maternal thinking: Philosophy, politics, practice* (pp. 14–38). Toronto: Demeter.

Sexton, J. (2010). People-of-color blindness: Notes on the afterlife of slavery. *Social Text, 28*(2), 31–56.

Singh, N. (2012). Racial formation in an age of permanent war. In D.M. HoSang, O. LaBennett, & L. Pulido (Eds.), *Racial formation in the twenty-first century* (pp. 276–301). Berkley: University of California Press.

Smith, A.M. (2008). Neoliberalism, welfare policy, and feminist theories of social justice. *Feminist Theory, 9*(2), 131–44. https://doi.org/10.1177/1464700108090407

Smith, D.E. (1996). The relations of ruling: A feminist inquiry. *Studies in Cultures, Organizations, and Societies,* 2, 171–90. https://www.tandfonline.com/doi/abs/10.1080/10245289608523475?journalCode=gsco19

Smith, D.E. (1998). *The everyday world as problematic: A feminist sociology.* Toronto: University of Toronto Press.

Stoetzler, M., & Yuval-Davis, N. (2002). Standpoint theory, situated knowledge and the situated imagination. *Feminist Theory, 3*(3), 315–33. https://doi.org/10.1177/146470002762492024

Tyler, I. (2013). Naked protest: The maternal politics of citizenship and revolt. *Citizenship Studies, 17*(2), 211–26. https://doi.org/10.1080/13621025.2013.780742

Udel, L.J. (2001). Revision and resistance: The politics of Native women's motherwork. *Frontiers: A Journal of Women's Studies, 22*(2), 43–62. https://doi.org/10.2307/3347054

Wallace, A. (2009, 8 July). The case for all-Black schools. *This: Progressive Politic, Ideas & Culture.* Retrieved from https://this.org/2009/07/08/case-for-afrocentric-black-schools/

Winant, H. (2000). Race and race theory. *Annual Review of Sociology, 26*(1), 169–85. https://doi.org/10.1146/annurev.soc.26.1.169

Wortley, S., & Owusu-Bempah, K. (2011). The usual suspects: Police stop and search practices in Canada. *Policing & Society, 21*(4), 395–407. https://doi.org/10.1080/10439463.2011.610198

Yosso, T.J (2005). Whose culture has capital? A critical race theory discussion of community cultural wealth. *Race, Ethnicity, and Education, 8*(1), 69–91. https://doi.org/10.1080/1361332052000341006

PART THREE

Organizing and Mobilizing

8 Forging Fortuity, Asserting Humanity: The Emotional Labour and Resistance of Black Racial Equity Leaders in Predominantly White Institutions

PHILIP S.S. HOWARD

Rooted in critical race theory and a critical race Africology framework I have elaborated elsewhere (Howard, 2008), this chapter considers the experience of Black persons with the responsibility of leading racial equity work. My specific focus here is on the ways that African Canadian[1] leadership takes shape when it is done in collaboration with white colleagues in institutional settings. Here, I define racial equity work[2] as any institutional equity venture undertaken where race is named as a salient (though not necessarily exclusive) consideration.[3] Racial equity leaders thus include corporate and social service managers, supervisors, and coordinators and, in educational institutions, equity/anti-racism officers, school superintendents, principals, university chairs, and deans involved in developing policy and implementing programs motivated by an awareness of racial inequity.

I define Black/African Canadian leadership as the work done in directing initiatives that seek the (admittedly contested) collective African Canadian good. Black individuals who lead racial equity work in institutional settings might be considered African Canadian leaders in one sense simply by virtue of their institutional roles. However, I wish to consider their African Canadian leadership in another sense. It is a popular sentiment within Black communities that an important anti-racist strategy is to promote racial justice "from the inside" of predominantly white institutions (James, 2012, p. 148). In a climate where racial exclusion and disparity have monumental impacts upon employment patterns, Black employees are often a very small minority in organizational settings (Alexander & Moore, 2008, p. 5) – particularly at the middle- and upper-management levels occupied by those who perform racial equity work (Wingfield & Alston, 2014, p. 281). Thus, Black communities often have high expectations of those who attain leadership positions (E.L. Bell, 1990, p. 460) – and particularly racial equity positions – within predominantly white institutions. On the basis of anecdotal evidence, it is also safe to say that, for better or worse, there is a community expectation that Black persons "represent" (to use a colloquial term) on the job. As, often, Black "firsts" or "one of few," Black community members see these persons as having the potential to open doors and secure equity in their institutions' dealings with Black folk. Those who ignore this implicit vocational challenge risk being dismissed as out of touch with their Blackness and their stake in Black struggle, while those who aim to rise to it in their institutional roles are positioned as leaders. One need only consider the extraordinary (and perhaps unrealistic) expectations of Barack Obama by Black communities worldwide upon his election as US president, on the one hand, and the widespread Black community disappointment with persons such as Police Chief Mark Saunders and Deputy Police Chief Peter Sloly of the Toronto Police Services, on the other, to appreciate the dynamic I am articulating here. This chapter focuses on the work of Black workers who take up the call to "represent."

However, leading racial equity work in predominantly white institutional settings is, as I shall argue, a contradictory form of work that Black racial equity leaders must navigate carefully to achieve any measure of success while remaining in good graces at work. Read from within white institutional culture, these positions, which are considered sites of power and potentiality by Black people outside the institutional setting, are sites characterized by tokenism and isolation (Alexander & Moore, 2008, p. 5; Essien, 2003) and the pressure to embrace individualism (Payne & Suddler, 2014, p. 399). The opportunity to collaborate with other Black people within the institution is rare if not impossible; thus where collaboration does happen, it usually takes place across lines of racial dominance with white people. Collectively, then, these factors mediate the kind of leadership that is possible for Black people in such settings.

This chapter is an analysis of the narratives of seven Black racial equity leaders in Canada, whom I interviewed in 2008, and who work in collaboration with white colleagues. It offers an overview of some ways that Black racial equity leaders navigate inter-racial collaborations under these less than ideal, yet typical, institutional circumstances. It establishes these collaborations as contradictory and the Black leaders' work as emotionally laborious, given the machinations of institutional whiteness in neo-liberal times. Yet, I argue that in the context of racial equity work, emotional labour should not be understood solely as a burden that racial equity leaders must endure at work, but also as a resource they deploy to further their work. Nevertheless, this labour, like all racialized emotional labour, requires self-subjugation, and thus racial equity leaders engage in it at risk to their full humanity and equality. They must make choices about whether, how, and to what extent they will engage in racialized emotional labour to achieve racial equity objectives. I argue that these choices are inherent to leadership in these anti-Black contexts, where Black racial equity leaders must balance commitment, the benefits in the short and long term for the Black collective, and the personal/emotional costs inherent in this fraught line of work. I further consider the ways that Black racial equity leaders might make choices in the context of the gendered organization of work and gendered anti-Black narratives. I thus seek to highlight the ways that the agency of Black racial equity leaders takes shape in and through the institutional and broader discursive and relational contexts of gendered anti-Blackness such that Manichean notions of good/progressive versus bad/regressive Black leaders prove inadequate to capture the complex negotiations they undertake in these settings. Rather, Black leaders exhibit multiple and variously textured strategies in their shows of leadership, agency, and resistance. I end with some thoughts, drawn from the narratives, about how Black leaders in these constrained circumstances might expand their agency so that they are not entirely limited to the terms of institutional whiteness.

Analysing Agency

Of particular import to this study is the notion of African/Black agency drawn from African-centred thought. In this context, agency is understood at the level of the group, referring to Africans'/Black people's prerogative to evaluate matters in terms of their liberation (Kershaw, 1992, p. 163), and to choose their own terms for collaborating with other groups (Asante, 1999, p. 108).

Within African-centred literature, this framework is normally used to distinguish between cultural and intellectual efforts superficially associated with Africans and those undertaken with a resolute view towards African liberation (Asante, 2003, p. 38). In an approach I call a "critical race Africology" (Howard, 2008, 2009), I apply this African-centred perspective on agency to a broader context than the contemplation of African culture, to consider racial equity projects. As I have argued elsewhere (Howard, 2008), racial equity endeavours ought, by definition, to seek the liberation of the racially oppressed, and therefore must promote their agency and interests. These endeavours cannot uphold that which is anchored in the logic of white supremacy. The hegemonic reach of whiteness and the technologies through which it is normalized, as well as contemporary post-racialist arguments, make such a framework indispensable for evaluating racial equity collaborations within predominantly white institutions and the broader climate of neo-liberalism.

It offers an analytical lens to assess the ways such collaborations promote or thwart Black agency.

Methods

This study sought the perspectives of racial equity leaders who self-identify as Black and who collaborate with white colleagues. All participants self-identified as Black or African, and no participant asked me what I meant by "white." It is important to note that none of the participants found the racial designations "Black" and "white" problematic, though one indicated that he preferred the phrase "of African descent/ancestry" to refer to Black people. This does not suggest that participants reified race as biologically real, but does indicate that they understand the ways in which these labels structure social life and create racialized social relations.

This research also respects diversity among those who identify as Black. Consequently, participants were sought from a broad range of Black identities. This was not an attempt to achieve a "representative sample," but simply to give the study access to a rich variety of Black perspectives. Table 8.1 gives an overview of the participants.

As per Maxwell and Miller (2008), both categorizing and connecting analysis strategies were used in order to gain fuller understandings of the data. Coding, the categorization strategy, was complemented with a connecting strategy – a variation of Mauthner and Doucet's (1998) narrative analysis method, which uses multiple close readings of each interview transcript. I did three different readings:

Reading 1: to identify recurring terms, concepts and metaphors participants used to describe their racial equity work
Reading 2: to pay attention to "I-statements" in order to understand the participant's sense of personal agency and leadership
Reading 3: to attend to statements of obligation in order to understand the ways the participant's leadership might be constrained by social structures, and the matters they felt were imperatives in racial equity work

While I take the position that Black people are authorities on their own lives, I also avoid romanticizing Black racial equity leaders as voices of *pure* resistance unaffected by hegemonic ideology (Okolie, 2005, p. 257). Therefore, to assess the relationships among a participant's perspective, critical race understandings, and hegemonic racial ideas, I identified "sentinel statements" – "*those statements that signal a text's*

Table 8.1. Variety among Black Participants

Gender	Men (3)	Women (4)	
Place of birth	Canada (2)	Ghana (1)	Guyana (1)
	Haiti (1)	Jamaica (1)	Somalia (1)
Length of time in Canada (if not born in Canada)	12–35 years		
Age range	40–49 yrs (3)	50–59 yrs (3)	60–69 yrs (1)
Province of residence	Ontario (6)	Nova Scotia (1)	
Occupation*	Education (youth sector) (1)		
	Education (tertiary) (3)		
	Corporate sector (executive) (1)		
	Corporate sector (skilled work) (1)		
	Public sector (non-education) (3)		
Length of time doing equity work	10–40 years		
Site of racial equity work*	Community-based volunteer organization (1)		
	Government (2)		
	Race-based organization, paid position (1)		
	Corporation (2)		
	Schools/school boards (2)		
	Union (1)		
	University (2)		

* Many participants fit more than one category.

location ... used as standards by which [to view the] entire text" (Asante, 2002, p. 98). These statements were triangulated by comparing them with the overall themes of the interviews from reading 1.

Black Racial Equity Work in Predominantly White Institutions: Engaging the Literature

To understand the work of Black racial equity leaders, I pursue two areas in the relevant literature: (1) the experiences of Black employees in predominantly white institutions and (2) the experiences of racial equity workers (of whatever racial location), in order to consider their overlap as they relate to Black racial equity leaders. My purpose is to highlight the contradictory nature of Black racial equity leaders' work, and the salience of emotional labour and interest convergence where these leaders collaborate with white people.

Black Employees in Predominantly White Institutions

We have already seen that Black experience in predominantly white institutions is marked by isolation and alienation. It is also marked by racialized expectations or the responsibility for "racial tasks" – defined as "the work minorities [*sic*] do that is associated with their position in the organizational hierarchy and [that] reinforces Whites' position of power within the workplace" (Wingfield & Alston, 2014, p. 276). Black employees, particularly Black women, must carefully manage their own behaviour and the impressions others may have of them (Durr & Wingfield, 2011), obeying implicit "feeling rules" (Wingfield, 2010) in order to "become more palatable to the White majority" (Wingfield & Alston, 2014, p. 285) and to be considered professional, competent, and worthy of promotion (Froyum, 2013; Wingfield, 2010). For them, this emotional labour – the ways that employees must "summon ... legitimized feelings [in themselves and/or others] in exchange for wages" – is racialized labour that involves negotiating both the racial dynamics of the workplace *and* the tacit feeling rules uniquely applied to racialized employees (Wingfield, 2010, p. 266). In particular, so as not to rock the boat or ruffle the feathers of white colleagues, Black employees are pressured to avoid identifying or addressing racial injustice in the workplace (Durr & Wingfield, 2011). Further, Black employees – particularly those in middle and upper management, and thus the leaders I am concerned with in this chapter – are tasked with policing the racial order within their institutions (Wingfield & Alston, 2014), and are expected to manage white people's feelings of racial discomfort at work (Froyum, 2013, p. 1085). The onus is placed on them to improve conversational dynamics when inter-racial communication breaks down (Martin, Hecht, & Larkin, 1994, p. 248). Overall, Black employees in predominantly white institutions must navigate between "fitting" into the organization (which implies adapting and acquiescing to its whiteness) and addressing racial matters that affect their work environment (which implies transforming it).

Institutional Diversity Work

Also relevant are the contradictions inherent in the diversity work of those (of whatever racial location) who do this institutional work in institutional settings. In Ahmed's (2012) phenomenology of equity work (which she terms "diversity work"), one of her central arguments is that institutional equity roles and policy commitments to equity are "non-performative"; they do not accomplish what they say, and may serve to mask the inequity or lack of diversity that gives rise to them (p. 117).

For example, she explains how gathering the few non-white persons in an institution for publicity photographs only becomes necessary because of the whiteness of the institution that it attempts to conceal. Thus, "whiteness recedes when diversity becomes a solution to the problem" (p. 185).

Equity work is, then, the work of "attending to what recedes from view" (p. 14) – that is, the implicit and taken-for-granted whiteness of the institution, which, through its institutionalization, has become so integral to the institution's functioning that it is generally not apparent to those whom it best serves. Yet it is simultaneously that which equity workers and other non-white persons who uncomfortably occupy the institution continuously confront and negotiate in institutional life. Ahmed describes this institutionalized whiteness and its inertia as a brick wall, and defines the equity worker's job as "banging your head against [it]" (p. 32), and making the wall visible in the face of post-racialist claims that it no longer exists (pp. 180–2). Equity work is also institutional plumbing – learning where equity objectives get blocked (p. 186) and devising strategies for clearing these blockages (p. 32). Yet according to Ahmed, the work of making evident that which recedes is itself seen as obstructive by those who do not perceive the wall. As such, equity workers are themselves mistaken for a wall – in this case, that which blocks the free flow of institutional whiteness – and therefore as the problem (p. 186).

Black Racial Equity Leaders in Predominantly White Institutions

I consider the foregoing categories together to understand the circumstances of Black racial equity leaders in predominantly white institutions. It is implicit in Ahmed's analysis that the categories "diversity worker" and "diverse Other" overlap significantly, and we know the familiar ways that racial equity work falls to people of Colour in institutions (James, 2012, p. 136; Westerman & Huey, 2012, p. 229; Wingfield & Alston, 2014, p. 278). Thus, in most cases, equity workers are racialized persons, and racial equity work is considered most suitable for the racialized. This racialization of equity work gives rise to disturbing double binds for Black racial equity leaders in predominantly white institutions: as equity workers, they are expected to implement racial equity, but as Black employees they are simultaneously expected to uphold a white supremacist status quo in order to "fit in" – which includes performing the emotional labour of suppressing responses to racial injustice at work. They are caught between doing the contentious work of pointing out the wall of whiteness while obeying the feeling rules of appearing agreeable to (white) colleagues and bosses. Compounding these contradictions is the anti-Blackness that attends Black labour in Canada whereby Black labour is desired but Black people are perpetually seen as "out of place" and are always at risk of being ousted (Bashi, 2004; Henry, 2015). These factors taken together allow us to appreciate the high stakes associated with Black racial equity leadership.

At the same time, these conditions should disabuse us of any essentialist conceptions of the motivations, ideological positions, or leadership strategies of Black racial equity leaders. Rather, these conditions lay bare the multiple, competing factors informing the decisions they make in their leadership work. Further, this dynamic speaks to the contested understandings of institutional racial equity work itself, perhaps perceived by some Black leaders as promoting racial equity within the institution and its operations, while the institution may largely be interested in managing race-based claims against the institution and defending a presumed non-racist reputation (Wingfield & Alston, 2014, p. 278). This institutional climate is a microcosm of the broader climate of racial neo-liberalism in which anti-racism is conflated with anti-racialism (Goldberg, 2009). Here, challenges to systemic racial inequity are interpreted as "demands for 'special treatment' by 'interest groups'" that must be "depoliticized" (or neutralized) *by racial equity leaders* – particularly those of Colour – to make them legible within these post-racialist institutions (Westerman & Huey, 2012, p. 228). Clearly, racial equity work in predominantly white institutions is highly contradictory, and Black racial equity leaders' professional agency and autonomy are tightly constrained.

Fraught Collaborations

One strategy that Black racial equity leaders employ to overcome these constraints is to seek out white people with whom to collaborate as a means to further the work, lend it credibility, and garner greater institutional support (Ahmed, 2012, p. 131; Howard, 2009). Yet it is also crucial to understand that while, on the one hand, the wall of whiteness is more than individual bigotry, it cannot, on the other hand, be conceived as being of the ether. It materializes through the real human encounters Black racial equity leaders have within the institution – most often with their white colleagues who outnumber them. White workers play a role in creating a contradictory atmosphere through their implicit assumptions and expectations (Henry, 2015; Wingfield & Alston, 2014, p. 284).

Furthermore, given that equity leaders who see "the wall" and who are racialized are understood as a problem, institutions will often look for solutions to those who do *not* see the wall – that is, to those who appear to least obstruct institutional flows precisely because they comfortably inhabit its whiteness (Ahmed, 2012, pp. 185–7). To identify those who "do not see" as solution is to involve white people in racial equity work *because* they inhabit whiteness! In these circumstances, Black people are seen as less competent leaders, and white people as more savvy, less confrontational leaders (Henry, 2015; Westerman & Huey, 2015, p. 226). Thus, whether Black racial equity leaders choose to work alongside white people or are forced to do so because of decisions made for them, they often do their work in collaboration with white people.

The extant literature on white people involved in racial equity work agrees that their subjectivities are particularly complex (see, e.g., Patton & Bondi, 2015; Thompson, 2003). Moreover, in the contemporary moment, whiteness often manifests itself and establishes its superiority through a desire to be identified as "good" (see, e.g., Mahrouse, 2010) or exceptional – different than the imagined unaware white person against whom it measures itself. White racial equity work, which might be interpreted in this dominant imaginary as selflessly advancing the causes of racialized Others, thus becomes a productive site for constructing these exceptional or "good" white identities. This is perhaps especially salient in the Canadian context, where Canadianness, as a racial construct, is dependent on rosy narrations of Canada's relationships with racialized persons within and beyond the borders of the nation (Razack, 2004, p. 9; Thobani, 2007, p. 144). In particular, Canada's national relationship to Blackness is mythologically referenced in relation to the Underground Railroad, painting (implicitly white) Canadianness as benevolent and progressive (Cooper, 2006, p. 69).

The potential for white subjectivities to be both resisted and constructed through racial equity work therefore raises the possibility of an interest convergence. Interest convergence refers to the critical race theory tenet positing that ostensible racial equity gains are seldom significantly influenced by white concern about racial injustice (D.A. Bell, 2004, p. 69), but rather are made where there is an apparent convergence with the interests of white people (D.A. Bell, 1980, 2004). Interest convergence is therefore important to consider as a factor mediating the nature and extent of white involvement in racial equity work. Patton and Bondi (2015) observe that to the extent that white people seek to construct a "good" white identity, they will most often be involved in superficial forms of racial equity work where they "either get their needs met (rewards, accolades, immediate results) or do not have to do much work (no risk-taking, little complexity)" (p. 507). As D.A. Bell (1980) points out, racial progress achieved on these terms is both contradictory and given to reversal when Black and white interests no longer converge or when white supremacy is threatened (p. 526).

Overall, then, romanticized understandings of white racial equity leaders as those with selfless, uniformly critical subjectivities are untenable. Instead we must appreciate that, as with the Black racial equity worker, there are multifarious, often racially defined processes that bring the white racial equity worker to this type of work. Thus, given Bell's interest convergence principle, and the laws of probability, Black racial equity leaders seeking to work with white colleagues may find themselves in quests to "forge fortuity" (D.A. Bell, 2004, p. 189) – that is, to find and exploit potential for the alignment of Black and white interests. White desire to construct "good" white subjectivities provides one such opportunity.

This context where racial equity work is deeply connected to psychic investments and white subjectivities – personal, institutional, and national – yet where collaboration with white people may seem strategically wise, only increases the emotional burden on Black racial equity leaders. Forging fortuity where racial equity objectives and "good" white subjectivities converge clearly implies emotional labour that will facilitate and sustain the convergence, for where white people engaged on this basis cease feeling good or feeling "good," their motivation for the work dissipates (Froyum, 2013, p. 1085).

Results: Stories of Navigating the Contradictions

Given the above review, several questions arise: How do Black racial equity leaders navigate the contradictions inherent in this institutional racial equity work? In what ways does the wall of whiteness manifest itself most problematically for them in their collaborative work? What form does emotional labour take for them? What agency and resistance strategies do they employ throughout? What factors govern their choices of strategy?

This section responds to these questions from interviews with seven racial equity leaders in Canada. The categorizing analysis methods I used established that, in keeping with the literature, the participants in the study find their collaborative racial equity work necessary and strategic, yet fraught and contradictory (Howard, 2009). The narrative summaries that appear below are a result of the narrative analysis methods. They give information about the specific types of work that these leaders do, but more importantly, offer a glimpse into the variety of ways that these leaders navigate the contradictions of their collaborative work with white people.

Sharon: The Right Not to Engage

Sharon has led racial equity work in academic settings and social service organizations, where she offers anti-racism workshops and does advocacy work on behalf of Black persons. Sharon has worked hard to acquire a critical understanding of the ways race works, paying careful attention to how she is both oppressed and complicit in the oppression of others. Sharon sees value in collaboration with white people to do racial equity work, especially where they are invited to do that work in all-white spaces into which she is not invited, and where they will respond when, as often, white individuals express their racial sentiments with a candour that is rare in mixed company (Picca & Feagin, 2007). Sharon expects her white colleagues to examine their personal and social location with the critical rigour that she applies to her own positionality. Consequently, she finds it problematic when her white colleagues have "not done their homework," which becomes evident to her where their conceptions of racial equity work reinforce rather than challenge asymmetric power relations. Teaching is a large component of Sharon's work, and she expects to teach the attendees in her workshops. However, she is unwilling to "teach" her colleagues, upon whom she feels the onus rests to "do their homework." She says:

> I'm not saying that when you work with people you shouldn't learn something from them ... but I'm not here to hold your hand. I'm not here to say, "Oh, you know, this is how racism works, and I'm gonna tell you stories that have happened to me to enlighten you."

Sharon is likely in these moments to challenge what she sees as her colleagues' presumption that they can do racial equity work without these critical understandings of the structures they purport to be undoing. Their presumption and her indignation are compounded where she is expected to do the emotional labour of a "caregiver" upon challenging them:

> When I try to challenge white people on their foolishness, especially white women, they bawl ... as a person of Colour, you either walk away and say, "I'm not dealing with this," or you fall into the role of caregiver. It's really sick! ... I've learned, "Uh, uh! If you wanna cry, you go ahead and you cry. I'm gonna sit here until those tears dry up, and then we'll continue, but I'm *not* your therapist ... I'm *very* resistant to that. I'm not your mammy."

Sharon is committed to doing racial equity work, but feels it cannot be achieved under these troubling circumstances. She therefore speaks about "finding the spaces to do the work," which also entails leaving spaces that are not conducive to the work. She says often that she "won't go down that road."

> You know, I'm quite facety [i.e., cheekily outspoken] and I don't take anything from anybody – which is why I haven't had like a string of steady jobs for a long period of time because I generally get pissed off and say, "f*** off!"

Here, Sharon demonstrates her agency in refusing to engage, seeing this as a form of self-preservation. In a climate of risk, where fear of being fired serves as a racial disciplinary mechanism, Sharon inverts the power dynamic in order to assert her freedom.

James: Institutional Power in the Black Body

James holds a designated racial equity position in government. In his executive role leading an equity program, he sees himself as a part of the institutional power structure. James resists the subordinating aspects of racial equity collaborations by insisting on being in charge. His white colleagues in racial equity work are actually those who report to him. When asked if he would do racial equity work in a context where he was taking direction from white colleagues he says he would not.

James believes that his white colleagues, and institutional structures in general, allow equity projects to stall indefinitely, never producing actual equity outcomes – largely because of a lack of political will and institutional commitment. This stalling is what concerns him most about working with white colleagues. Backed by policy, he aims to use his institutional authority to move such projects forwards. He talks tough at work about his intentions to take radical moves to advance the work:

> You guys have been taking five years to complete one evaluation, which is *nonsense*. So I'm saying you're going to finish that evaluation in eight months and if that group doesn't meet the requirements, we're gonna *prosecute* them!

Given his rank, as well as the ways he deploys his embodied connection to the work, he avoids emotional labour. He is not obliged to be as diplomatic as he might have to be were he not in charge because, as he says:

> I tell them off when I want to ... I realize here I have a little bit of power ... I can actually effect change without listening too much to who the power is up there, because I have to advise them. They don't tell me what to do.

Interestingly, though, an analysis of James's I-statements suggests that he may have a somewhat exaggerated sense of his own agency at work. James *speaks* boldly about his *intentions* to make radical moves in the racial diversity projects he leads, and to take a more aggressive approach to achieving equity outcomes than his white predecessors. However, he does not relate specific instances of having made substantive change. This is not to suggest that the effectiveness of racial equity work can be measured solely in terms of major shifts, but it does indicate that despite James's perception of power, he continues to be constrained by structures that are larger than his sense of agency.

James's awareness of this contradiction emerges when he considers the broader context. In these moments, he paints a more modest assessment of his power to effect change – even for his family.

> I'm not convinced that my children will have the same standard of living as I have because it's so hard for them to get jobs ... So it is *so* important that we don't just sit quietly in our little corners ... So if I'm able to impact one person in the community then I think I've done something.

The power James feels he has is actually an extension of white institutional power, which he deploys through performances of a kind of dominant masculinity. Nevertheless, using white power to undermine white power is contradictory. Thus, while on an interpersonal level he circumvents the subordinating aspects of collaborating with white people by insisting on being in charge, he does not escape the contradictions, but rather internalizes them.

Maryam: Straight Talk

Maryam is a former teacher, an executive with a designated racial equity position in government, and has also worked in social service organizations. As someone who has migrated to Canada, Maryam comes to racial equity work out of a desire to address the stark contradictions between what she was led to believe of Canada as a "land of opportunity," and the marginalization and consequent high levels of frustration experienced by members of the community of people from her country in Canada. She feels that part of this frustration comes from a sense of not being able to openly talk about the injustices they experience. Determined not to be overwhelmed by frustration or to be muzzled at work, Maryam believes in being "open, honest, and direct," terms she uses repeatedly. She says:

> as a Black person, you have to – even if you know that you are a minority ... fill up the space of your body. You have to develop a strong effectiveness about your being and about your own self ... When you are yourself, you can cross the world! ... Be direct! You don't need to be aggressive. Be direct. That's it!

Maryam recognizes that the distribution of (in her opinion, mostly economic) power is racialized and seeks out collaborations with whites who will use that power to pursue racial equity. However, she is troubled by white colleagues who exercise power-over even in their supposed racial equity work. They work with Black people as long as that power dynamic is preserved, and offer "peanuts" to those Black people willing to subordinate themselves as supplicants towards them as benefactors. Maryam refuses this dynamic. "Filling up the space of her body" means asserting her humanity, refusing subordination, and affirming her own ways of being. For her, fitting in doesn't only mean cultural conformity, but also acquiescing to unequal power relations. She contends:

> It's a stress to live everyday life, OK? If you start to accommodate, "Oh I have to sit in that way" – it's inhuman! It's harassment! Why am I going to *fit*? ... No! I'm not a puppet.

Exercising her agency in this way, Maryam has been able to alter the anti-Black dynamics in her collaborative relationships. She says of one colleague:

> I was an insult because I couldn't fit in any box. So she hated me. But I left her [alone] and she was so tired of hating me that finally, OK, she overcame. We became friends ... she tells me that "you are so direct" ... it's so important to continue to be direct for us.

Maryam is also wary about unexpressed questions that her colleagues have of her community or other communities of Colour, usually based in racial stereotypes. She wants her white colleagues to also be "open, honest, and direct," asking her questions, and giving her the opportunity to address misconceptions, although she often finds their assumptions demeaning and insulting.

For Maryam, open and honest intercultural communication is the foundation for strong collaborative relationships, and her emotional labour comprises positioning herself as a teacher-mediator between Black and white people to foster intercultural understanding, while supressing her reactions to racist presumptions about her and her community. This approach seems largely consistent with an abstract individualist understanding of racism as cultural misunderstanding that is overcome through education. It does not account for the broader social and historical structures that mediate interpersonal relations. Nevertheless, Maryam's affirmation of Black people's right to "fill up the space of the body" represents her brand of resistance to subordinating aspects of her collaborative work.

Diane: Taking Stands, Facing Consequences

Diane works in a university setting, directing a program that addresses the needs of racialized students. Central to her approach is the sense of epistemic authority that she brings to her work based on her embodied experience of racial inequity. She feels that this epistemic authority extends to racialized people in general, and consequently, they should have "ownership" of the work – that is, leadership and the prerogative to decide on the direction and priorities of the work.

In her collaborative work, Diane requires that her white colleagues acknowledge her epistemic authority and "ownership" up front. She finds it disturbing when they exhibit what she calls a "take-over mentality" where they seize "ownership" of racial equity projects that serve communities/students of Colour. She sees this tendency to take over wherever white people become paternalistic (failing to take account of their own implication in relations of dominance), and where they dismiss Black perspectives as somehow biased (demonstrating their lack of understanding that whiteness is not disinterested). In those instances Diane takes firm stands to do what she feels is best:

> When I hit the wall of resistance, I just simply used my authority and did – ! ... at the end of the day, as director of the program, I was going to use my authority, and if you didn't think I had any, fire me! (*laughs*) But that takes courage!

Recognizing the wall of whiteness, Diane's agency is expressed in her willingness to charge headlong into it on the basis of principle in order to achieve racial equity ends. Diane is well aware of the consequences of taking such stands, and has suffered them repeatedly. Yet she accepts this as an occupational hazard:

> Oh there are *huge, huge* personal consequences for any of us who are doing [racial equity work]. In fact, I think there are huge health consequences just living Black in this world.

However, Diane also sees her embodied knowledge and authority as affording some measure of duty to teach about racism and to be there for white people who suffer consequences for standing up to racism:

> The advantages [of collaboration] are that you educate some white people who are open to being educated ... There have been a few [white] people

> that I've worked with that have really gone the distance ... I guess the down side is that when that happens and there are consequences to the white person ... then you have to do the nurturing ... So, in some senses I resent it, but I recognize the value of having to do it. But we have always, I think, always been nurturers as a people.

Unlike Sharon, Diane is willing to teach her white colleagues towards a critical race understanding, taking a more critical approach than Maryam's teaching for intercultural understanding. Where she will be heard, she prefers this hopeful, less painful way of working through the contradictions. Like Sharon, she recognizes that commiserating is emotional labour that positions her as caregiver and caters to privileged whiteness that does not face these consequences routinely. However, unlike Sharon she grudgingly accepts this role, hoping to strengthen collaborative relationships.

Keith: Strong Black Community Support

Keith leads institutional racial equity work in conjunction with his union, where he collaborates with white colleagues whom he finds largely critical and supportive. However, he also does community-building work in the Black community as part of the leadership of a local Black community organization. He refers to himself as a proud Black person who seeks the well-being of the entire community.

Keith values collaborative racial equity work with white people because he feels they have the "balance of power"; he believes the Black racial equity worker should engage with those white people who will offer financial and moral support. With his strong sense of working in the collective interest, he finds it problematic whenever racial equity workers – Black or otherwise – do the work seeking to address only their own equity priorities rather than the community's greater good, and, worse yet, when they do it for personal gain or recognition. Consequently, he is particularly wary when his white colleagues "push" him into prominent positions to be the "voice of the Black community" without its backing. This is not his model of leadership, and he actively refuses to be seduced into these precarious roles, regardless of the personal benefits:

> And if I was here to profile myself, who the hell knows where I would have been today? Because people are always trying to push you here, push you there ... The white folks is like, "Keith, oh we're trying to encourage you to move to a different level." And I say, "No. I ain't going there unless my people are behind me" ... I don't care how high it is. I'm not going there

> alone ... you have to be very cautions, because once you get a push, you're looking for support, there's nobody behind you to hold you up, right? (*laughs*) So you're down on your ass in no time.

Keith does not feel that his white colleagues mean him ill in encouraging him to be a Black "spokesperson"; however, he makes clear that white support is insufficient in a racial equity role. Rather, he believes strongly in being supported by the Black community, and in the need for consensus building within this collective:

> For a Black person doing race relations work in a white society, you have to have good foundations. And that good foundation means good strong Black support. So if you don't have that strong Black support behind the work that you are doing, you're destined to fail.

In fact, Keith makes it clear that the strength of the racial equity leader's community relationships determines the degree of political power that s/he is able to wield in their work: "You have to have community support, right? And that way you can move forwards in *any* environment and speak freely on any issue without fear of any reprisals from white folks." Thus, Keith resists the contradictions in racial equity collaborations by ensuring he is anchored in the Black community that will support him as necessary as he undertakes the risky work of challenging racial inequity. Any emotional labour he does seems restricted to managing his own ambitions with a view towards the greater good.

Terrence: Erasing His Own Agency

Terrence leads racial equity initiatives in the corporate sector as an executive with a racial equity portfolio. His interview is littered with sentinel statements foreshadowing his peculiar approach. For example, Terrence understands racial inequity as the effect of benign "cultural variability," and sees his goal as that of minimizing "cultural difference." He understands race as analogous to European ethnicity, and speaks about Black people needing to learn the "language" of the corporate environment. For him, white people no longer have any "intent or desire to exclude."

Terrence feels that racial equity work is impossible without white involvement, and he sees white men who have a sense of fairness and moral conviction as the source of all anti-racist change. He says:

> If the white male power structure is not behind you to make the change, the change will not happen! ... we never would have gotten this far in Canada if

> it wasn't for white males ... They sow the seed of major changes in Canada, and as much maligned as they are, the truth of the matter is they change the system.

Terrence overlooks the integral role of marginalized peoples' resistance in bringing about social change. In fact, he completely negates the idea that racialized communities might have any such power. His advice for Black racial equity leaders is:

> Please understand that despite how mighty you want your Blackness to be, you are not in a position of domination, of influence, of power ... The day that you believe that you're as powerful as the white person you're trying to get to champion the cause, you're gonna be ineffective!

This exaltation of white power and negation of Black agency informs his assessment of himself and his work. He expresses unreserved indebtedness to those who head-hunted him to manage employment equity in the corporation, while ignoring his own considerable professional reputation. For Terrence, a major component of his work is petitioning and teaching even more white people to support the cause.

Terrence ultimately erases his agency, seeing himself in terms of the power he does *not* have, saying: "I don't have the money. I cannot hire. I cannot fire. I cannot promote." Nevertheless, he understands his role of strategizing and giving direction to racial equity work, once white men have decided they want to see social change, as a vital one that white people cannot perform because they lack "the passion" that presumably comes from an embodied stake in racial equity. Yet, Terrence is so committed to the idea of white power and his powerlessness that he performs this racial equity work from a subordinate position:

> How do you mobilize the power structure? By affecting resources. And us [Blacks], it's to convince, it's to cajole, it's sometimes to profile, it's sometimes to beg. In my job in anti-racism, there is no low that I'm not gonna go to to get one visible minority hired.

Even when he is exercising agency, he works hard to disguise it while doing the emotional labour that allows white people to have an exaggerated sense of their agency. He says:

> So in any structure where one is powered, and one is somewhat powerless, you have to adapt a behaviour that somehow allows that to continue ... My biggest asset in the organization is to get people to do things, and for

> people to believe that it was their idea ... I never take credit. Technically speaking, I don't do anything ... I cannot appear that I am in control ... I need to walk a fine line where I must get people to do things, but they do it thinking that it was their idea.

Terrence is aware that his extreme deference is related to his lack of connectedness to a racialized community – exactly what Keith might predict – for Terrence has been recruited and promoted by white people, disconnected from his community, and works in isolation without community input.

In summary, Terrence's approach resolves the tensions of racial equity collaborations at the expense of Black agency and in favour of whiteness. However, it is worth noting that he does have considerable success in getting Black and other racialized persons hired and promoted within the organization, and where this is no longer possible, he too will leave the work. He says, "I do not want to be a figurehead. There's a million other things that I would like to do with my time."

Imani: Manipulating the System

Imani leads racial equity work at many levels within the public school system, and is also invited to sit on corporate boards based on her experience in racial equity work. She describes herself as outspoken, speaking out against the negation of human rights even in the face of potential reprisals.

Imani feels multiracial collaborations for racial equity are taken more seriously and are less easily opposed than other arrangements. She particularly values those white people who have "developed the intuition to read" racial dynamics. However, like James, she more frequently encounters white colleagues who stall racial equity work by prioritizing process over outcome. She sees them as roadblocks, and plays the "institutional plumbing" role (Ahmed, 2012, p. 186) of moving them out of the way. She understands the need to negotiate and compromise within any collaboration. However, where the success of the work is threatened, she resorts to other strategies. She is not reluctant to be crafty.

> I mean, let me not lie to you, one of the most important things for survival is being manipulative. Oh-ho-ho yes! ... You know, when you say, "Cheez. This roadblock is here, and it's *constantly* here, and he's it." How do we get rid of him? You can't get rid of him? ... [So] how do we give him something else to do ... something else that he's not going to realize is – ? [You might say,] "You work out the framework and we'll fit this workshop that we're planning into that framework." Now he might not even recognize the

> framework when you're through with it, but that's OK. I mean, you've gotta survive! You have to do the work!

Holding the racial equity objective as the highest priority, she cunningly undertakes a form of emotional labour:

> trying to give them meaningful opportunity and work and diversion while you get what you have to do done without demeaning them, without lessening them, but finding some very respectable appropriate way to move them out of the way. It requires some thinking. You could also look at it in a different way. You could look at it as being complimentary to them because you've given them something to do that is worthy of their talent and of their status, whatever the hell it is, and an opportunity not to butt heads with you.

While there seems to be a tongue-in-cheek aspect to this statement of respect, it is clear that unlike Sharon who refuses to engage, or Terrence who erases his agency, Imani remains engaged in the collaborative relationship without losing dignity:

> They do have the power to get rid of you if they're not comfortable ... But I mean, you have to decide. I mean you're not going out there to slap people in the head by rudeness and offensiveness, but nor are you there to shuffle ... Establish very quickly from your manner that you are selling the work, not yourself ... establish what that work is with your employers and with your colleagues so that when they know you're coming, they know what you're coming for ... so that you're not always having to sell out and back down.

Imani will also reluctantly teach, though she feels that doing so draws attention away from the lack of societal will to challenge racial inequity. But her outspokenness, commitment to the work, and refusal to "shuffle" mean that where teaching and "manipulation" will not work she will, like Diane, take unpopular stands, though she feels that this boldness has cost her promotions.

Discussion: The Contours of Agency and Resistance

The foregoing narratives demonstrate the ways that Black racial equity work is constrained and shaped within white institutions, and the various types of emotional labour that Black racial equity leaders get drawn into. As it is, collaborations between Black and white people in racial equity work exact inordinate amounts of laborious, subordinating emotional work for Black racial equity leaders, as they are implicitly expected to facilitate, or at least avoid disrupting, the terms upon which their white colleagues can come to know themselves as exceptional or "good" white people (Froyum, 2013, p. 1085).

However, the current work on racialized emotional labour does not adequately address issues of agency and resistance, and while Patton and Bondi (2015) consider the ways that interest convergence enters equity work, they do not attend to the related principle of racial fortuity – that is, the tactic of taking intentional advantage of interest convergences to advance racial justice (D.A. Bell, 2004) – that might reveal this agency. The site of collaborative institutional racial equity work opens up the opportunity to explore racial fortuity and thus leadership agency, since the emotional labour that Black racial equity leaders do is frequently an attempt to profit from interest convergence to further their work by playing to the deep psychic desires of white subjectivities. The idea of "forging fortuity" (D.A. Bell, 2004) itself speaks of agency and strategy. I propose, then, that rather than think about emotional labour solely as that which Black workers are forced to do against their will, we ought also to examine the ways racial equity leaders make choices about the kinds of emotional labour they will engage in, and to what extent, in the interest of forging fortuity and furthering their equity objectives.

We have seen that Terrence does the emotional labour of making his white colleagues feel effective and benevolent at the expense of his own agency to forge racial fortuity that gets Black people hired and promoted. Similarly, Diane reluctantly gets involved in the demeaning emotional labour of nurturing her white colleagues to forge fortuity that creates and maintains them as colleagues who sacrifice for racial equity work. Imani does the emotional labour of making white colleagues feel competent in the work where they are in fact hindering it, thereby forging fortuity to move the racial equity project ahead while avoiding confrontation.

However, from a critical race Africology perspective, we can see that achieving ostensible racial equity ends by subordinating the Black self and bolstering white subjectivities plays to anti-Blackness and makes for Pyrrhic victories. Thus, at strategic points we see Black racial equity leaders defying feeling rules, and flying in the face of racial fortuity, interest convergence, and their elusive promise in order to establish their dignity, equality, and full humanity: Keith resists being pushed into prominence without community backing, Maryam "fills up the space of her body" by being direct and refusing to "fit," Diane takes unpopular stands despite the consequences when teaching does not work, James "tells off" his colleagues, Imani will not shuffle, and Sharon absolutely rejects teaching and nurturing her colleagues by leaving the work altogether. Even Terrence will not be a "figurehead" by subordinating himself if there is no racial equity payoff. For all participants there is a limit to the amount of self-subordination they will allow.

Clearly there is a negotiable spectrum between forging racial fortuity to advance equity through subordinating emotional labour, and asserting one's full humanity at the potential risk of losing one's employment. For Black racial equity workers, navigating the contradictions of racial equity work with white colleagues seems to be precisely about the agency and resistance they exhibit in selecting a locus along this spectrum. At one end of this spectrum, Terrence fully subordinates himself while getting the work done, and at the other end Sharon refuses to be made into a mammy and abandons the work. The others fall somewhere in between. Their leadership agency is evident in the fact that, to the extent that they engage in emotional labour to forge racial fortuity, they are engaged in *self*-subordination – that is, subordination the degree of which, within constraints, they choose or refuse.

Perhaps some of their agency is also evident in the ways that they frame their choices. Thus, Terrence frames his emotional labour as a sacrifice for the greater good, Diane frames hers as part of her Black heritage ("we have always been nurturers"), and Imani frames her emotional labour as manipulation, putting her in the driver's seat. However, there can be no predetermined ideal place to strike the balance, for how can we dictate to someone that they should permit their own dehumanization? This must be a personal matter mediated by contextual specificities.

However, it is also worth considering the broader factors that might mediate these personal choices. One of these may be the gendered organization of work. Thus, while the participants do not constitute a representative sample of Black workers in Canada, the gendered organization of work is evident in the fact that all the women are or were educators, and none but Maryam have attained senior management levels. Consequently, we see all the women drawn into teaching and nurturing – to which they respond in various ways. The men are not asked to do so, and, in fact, all negotiate the expectation that they "take charge." This mediates the kinds of emotional labour expected of these racial equity leaders.

Related to the gendered organization of work is the impact of gendered controlling images of Blackness (Collins, 2000). Perhaps impacting the degree of forthrightness of the men's resistance are controlling images (Collins, 2000) of Black men as aggressive and threatening. Terrence mentions these stereotypes and his own juxtaposition against them in the eyes of white colleagues. In relation to his racial equity work, Keith also mentions the "angry Black man" stereotype through the ways in which icons Martin Luther King Jr and Malcolm X have been appropriated in mainstream discourse as, respectively, the "good," level-headed leader versus the dangerous, angry leader. These dichotomous images not only misrepresent the civil rights leaders' work, but attempt to domesticate Black resistance.

I suggest, then, that these controlling images mediate the men's racial equity work and resistance strategies as they engage in the emotional labour of managing public perceptions of themselves. Terrence and James, whose work and status are more dependent on colleagues' perceptions of them than are Keith's, use more attenuated strategies. All the men seem to risk less and seem to be less forthright than the women, who are more outspoken. Though Maryan is an executive like James and Terrence, she manages to be "direct," even winning over those with whom she disagrees through this strategy.

The women, on the other hand, evidently grapple with the mammy image, to which both Diane and Sharon refer. The mammy image portrays Black women as non-threatening, self-sacrificial caregivers to white people, and may represent a frame through which white allies see Black women's racial equity work, thus calling upon them to nurture. This gendered expectation of nurture cannot be separated from the history of Canadian slavery – more domestic than agricultural (Cooper, 2006, p. 77) – and the domestic workers' scheme under which many Black women entered Canada. Since the mammy image minimizes the threat of the Black female body (Collins, 2000), the women may have more leeway to be bold in their resistance than the men. The nurturing aspects of the mammy image may also converge with the climate of expectations set by these women's professional roles as educators and the prevailing liberal view of education as the solution to racism to mediate the choices that Diane, Maryam, and Imani make to take a pedagogical approach in their work, and Sharon's resistance to these gendered expectations.

Nevertheless, to say that Black women's racial equity leadership might be perceived as less threatening by their white colleagues is not to suggest that their work is any less forthright. Black feminist analyses have shown how, historically, Black women used their trusted positions as domestic servants to surreptitiously challenge their subordination (see, e.g., hooks, 1992). These have historically been quite successful ways of demonstrating agency and enacting resistance within the limits set up by white supremacy. Imani's strategy of covert manipulation perhaps best fits this pattern.

Conclusion: Maximizing Agency

This chapter has described the emotionally laborious work of being a racial equity leader in predominantly white institutions where one works in collaboration with white colleagues. It realizes the myriad contradictory forces that bring racial equity leaders to the work, and the consequences for the lives and work of Black racial equity leaders. The chapter identifies emotional labour as a both a subordinating phenomenon and a resource for forging racial fortuity. Within predominantly white institutions, and in the context of gendered and racialized patterns of employment and controlling images, ultimately Black racial equity leaders negotiate the tensions between advancing the work through self-subordinating emotional labour and resisting emotional labour to assert one's full humanity and dignity,

In light of these findings, I wish to underscore here that while it is always important to evaluate Black racial equity leadership in terms of the ways it serves Black communities, any attempt to frame Black racial equity leadership in binary terms such as "good" or "bad" is not helpful, and does not acknowledge the complexity of the social forces that mediate these leaders' decisions. The multiple competing forces and motivations that these leaders navigate must constantly be recognized when we consider how we might maximize agency and increase the effectiveness of resistance at these institutional sites.

Towards this end, there are some further broad lessons we can learn about leading racial equity work in white institutions, lessons that may serve to extend Black agency. First, there is a limit to the efficacy of white institutional power in/through the Black body. The Black body cannot become "the wall" to try to challenge "the wall," as James's situation shows us. This is a recipe for paralysis. Thus though James admonishes Black people to seek positions of power in white institutions, it matters what we aspire to do and who we aspire to be once we have achieved these positions.

Second, we should take seriously Imani's admonition to establish the terms of the racial equity project so as to "sell your work, and not yourself." This entails identifying the objectives of the work in advance, and one's commitment to it. It assists with navigating those difficult times when one has to take unpopular stands for the work. The leader can remain focused on the racial equity goals of the project rather than be seduced into image-managing emotional labour that seeks to maximize popularity. Further, these goals can operate as a benchmark for the work, such that when the work is no longer fulfilling its agreed-upon purpose there can be a reckoning. One might even call upon Black community support to help challenge this departure or to make sure the project is put back on track.

Third, learning from Diane, it is important to see Black embodied knowledge as a powerful resource in racial equity work – a point with which all participants agree. It is not necessary to see this knowledge as essentialist (Howard, 2009, p. 142), but simply to see it as salient knowledge that cannot be dismissed (Dei, 2006, p. 11). Claiming embodied knowledge is therefore a pragmatic response to the climate of appropriation and "takeover." It challenges white people's ability to claim authority in others' liberation struggles (see Lattas, 1993, p. 259). The salience of being anchored in the Black community, as Keith teaches us, as well as our insistence upon the salience of our embodied knowledge in racial equity work, remind us that we do not have to play the game fully on the terms of white institutions, but can sometimes "play by our own rules" (Dei, Karumanchery, & Karumanchery-Luik, 2004, p. 9). In so doing we affirm the resistance power that comes from asserting our humanity and refusing to be negated (Babbit, 1996, p. 50). If this is so, the agency spectrum between subordinating emotional labour and asserting humanity may be the tension between using white institutional power and using Black resistance power in the struggle against racial injustice.

Finally, the fourth lesson is to not, like Terrence, underestimate the importance of Black resistance power. Here, Keith's admonition to be anchored in the Black community resonates, and elsewhere I have noted the dynamic interplay between Black leaders within white institutions and the Black community outside of them in fostering agency at the centre (Howard, 2010). Instead of being limited to working with the institutional flows that Ahmed (2012) describes (p. 186) – either going with the flow or opposing it only to be seen as a lone obstruction to it – Black racial equity workers' engagement of Black community support introduces the considerable power of another flow altogether. Indeed, while this chapter might interest those who find themselves, and choose to stay, within predominantly white institutional contexts, these are not the only or best locations from which to do racial equity work. We must remain mindful of institutional racial equity work's dependence upon the indispensable work taking place beyond institutions that engages the powerful forces of Black resistance. For those who do the work from within, and who keep this crucial interdependence in mind, the reflections in this chapter open up space for agency and resistance in Black racial equity leadership that pushes back against the stifling effects of institutional whiteness.

NOTES

1 I use the terms "African" and "Black" interchangeably, and use "African Canadian" to refer to Black people in Canada.
2 I choose terms carefully here. I use the term "racial equity worker" instead of "anti-racist" deliberately. The term "anti-racist" implies an individual with a very specific politics and understanding of race and racialization. The term "racial equity worker" identifies individuals solely based upon the way their work is named, and does not presume any given politics.
3 It is understood that racial oppression is intersectional and interlocking, though this understanding is not necessarily evident in the work of the participants in the study.

REFERENCES

Ahmed, S. (2012). *On being included: Racism and diversity in institutional life.* Durham: Duke University Press.

Alexander, R., & Moore, S.E. (2008). The benefits, challenges, and strategies of African American faculty teaching at predominantly white institutions. *Journal of African American Studies, 12*(1), 4–18. https://doi.org/10.1007/s12111-007-9028-z

Asante, M.K. (1999). *The painful demise of Eurocentrism: An Afrocentric response to critics.* Trenton: Africa World Press.

Asante, M.K. (2002). Intellectual dislocation: Applying analytic Afrocentricity to narratives of identity. *Howard Journal of Communications, 13*, 97–110. https://doi.org/10.1080/106461702753555067

Asante, M.K. (2003). The Afrocentric idea. In A. Mazama (Ed.), *The Afrocentric paradigm* (pp. 37–53). Trenton: Africa World Press.

Babbitt, S.E. (1996). *Impossible dreams: Rationality, integrity, and moral imagination.* Boulder: Westview.

Bashi, V. (2004). Globalized anti-blackness: Transnationalizing Western immigration law, policy, and practice. *Ethnic and Racial Studies, 27*(4), 584–606. https://doi.org/10.1080/01491987042000216726

Bell, D.A. (1980). *Brown v. Board of Education* and the interest-convergence dilemma. *Harvard Law Review, 93*(3), 518–33. https://doi.org/10.2307/1340546

Bell, D.A. (2004). *Silent covenants:* Brown v. Board of Education *and the unfulfilled hopes for racial reform.* Oxford: Oxford University Press.

Bell, E.L. (1990). The bicultural life experience of career-oriented black women. *Journal of Organizational Behavior, 11*(6), 459–77.

Collins, P.H. (2000). *Black feminist thought: Knowledge, consciousness, and the politics of empowerment* (2nd ed.). New York: Routledge.

Cooper, A. (2006). *The hanging of Angélique: The untold story of Canadian slavery and the burning of Old Montréal.* Toronto: Harper Collins.

Dei, G.S. (2006). Introduction: Mapping the terrain – Towards a new politics of resistance. In G.J.S. Dei & A. Kempf (Eds.), *Anti-colonialism and education: The politics of resistance* (pp. 1–23). Rotterdam: Sense.

Dei, G.S., Karumanchery, L.L., & Karumanchery-Luik, N. (2004). *Playing the race card: Exposing white power and privilege.* New York: Peter Lang.

Durr, M., & Wingfield, A.M.H. (2011). Keep your "N" in check: African American women and the interactive effects of etiquette and emotional labor. *Critical Sociology, 37*(5), 557–71. https://doi.org/10.1177/0896920510380074

Essien, V. (2003). Visible and invisible barriers to the incorporation of faculty of color in predominantly white law schools. *Journal of Black Studies, 34*(1), 63–71. https://doi.org/10.1177/0021934703253687

Froyum, C. (2013). "For the betterment of kids who look like me": Professional emotional labour as a racial project. *Ethnic and Racial Studies, 36*(6), 1070–89. https://doi.org/10.1080/01419870.2011.644309

Goldberg, D.T. (2009). *The threat of race: Reflections on racial neoliberalism.* Malden: Blackwell.

Henry, A. (2015). "We especially welcome applications from members of visible minority groups": Reflections on race, gender and life at three universities. *Race, Ethnicity and Education, 18*(5), 589–610. https://doi.org/10.1080/13613324.2015.1023787

hooks, b. (1992). Representing whiteness in the black imagination. In L. Grossberg, C. Nelson, & P. Trichler (Eds.), *Cultural studies* (pp. 338–46). New York: Routledge.

Howard, P.S.S. (2008). Colliding positions on what counts as racially progressive: A critical race Africology of the film *Crash.* In P.S.S. Howard & G.S. Dei (Eds.), *Crash politics and antiracism: Interrogations of liberal race discourse* (pp. 25–47). New York: Peter Lang.

Howard, P.S.S. (2009). *The double-edged sword: A critical race Africology of collaborations between blacks and whites in racial equity work* (Doctoral dissertation). Ontario Institute for Studies in Education, University of Toronto, Toronto.

Howard, P.S.S. (2010). Turning out the centre: Racial politics and African agency in the Obama era. *Journal of Black Studies, 40*(3), 380–94. https://doi.org/10.1177/0021934709352990

James, C.E. (2012). Strategies of engagement: How racialized faculty negotiate the university system. *Canadian Ethnic Studies, 44*(2), pp. 133–52. https://doi.org/10.1353/ces.2012.0007

Kershaw, T. (1992). Afrocentrism and the Afrocentric method. *Western Journal of Black Studies, 16*(3), 160–8.

Lattas, A. (1993). Essentialism, memory and resistance: Aboriginality and the politics of authenticity. *Oceania, 63*(3), 240–67. https://doi.org/10.1002/j.1834-4461.1993.tb02420.x

Mahrouse, G. (2010). Questioning efforts that seek to "do good": Insights from transnational solidarity activism and socially responsible tourism. In S. Razack,

M. Smith, & S. Thobani (Eds.), *States of race: Critical race feminism for the 21st century* (pp. 169–90). Toronto: Between the Lines.

Martin, J.N., Hecht, M.L., & Larkey, L.K. (1994). Conversational improvement strategies for interethnic communication: African American and European American perspectives. *Communication Monographs, 61*(3), 236–55. https://doi.org/10.1080/03637759409376335

Mauthner, N., & Doucet, A. (1998). Reflections on a voice-centered relational method: Analysing maternal and domestic voices. In J. Ribbens & R. Edwards (Eds.), *Feminist dilemmas in qualitative research* (pp. 119–46). Thousand Oaks: Sage.

Maxwell, J.A., & Miller, B.A. (2008). Categorizing and connecting strategies in qualitative data analysis. In P. Leavy & S. Hesse-Biber (Eds.), *Handbook of emergent methods.* New York: Guilford Press.

Okolie, A.C. (2005). Toward an anti-racist research framework: The case for interventive in-depth interviewing. In G.J.S. Dei & G.S. Johal (Eds.), *Critical issues in anti-racist research methodologies* (pp. 241–67). New York: Peter Lang.

Patton, L.D., & Bondi, S. (2015) Nice white men or social justice allies?: Using critical race theory to examine how white male faculty and administrators engage in ally work. *Race, Ethnicity and Education, 18*(4), 488–514. https://doi.org/10.1080/13613324.2014.1000289

Payne, Y.A., & Suddler, C. (2014) Cope, conform, or resist? Functions of a black American identity at a predominantly white university. *Equity & Excellence in Education, 47*(3), 385–403. https://doi.org/10.1080/10665684.2014.933756

Picca, L., & Feagin, J. (2007) *Two-faced racism: Whites in the backstage and frontstage.* New York: Routledge.

Razack, S.H. (2004). *Dark threats and white knights: The Somali affair, peacekeeping, and the new imperialism.* Toronto: University of Toronto Press.

Thobani, S. (2007). *Exalted subjects: Studies in the making of race and nation in Canada.* Toronto: University of Toronto Press.

Thompson, A. (2003). Tiffany, friend of people of color: White investments in antiracism. *International Journal of Qualitative Studies in Education, 16*(1), 7–29. https://doi.org/10.1080/0951839032000033509

Westerman, M., & Huey, L. (2012). "Putting on band-aids": The contradictory roles and "small wins" of tempered campus radicals. *Discourse: Studies in the Cultural Politics of Education, 33*(2), 223–34. https://doi.org/10.1080/01596306.2012.666077

Wingfield, A.H. (2010). Are some emotions marked "whites only"? Racialized feeling rules in professional workplaces. *Social Problems, 57*(2), 251–68. https://doi.org/10.1525/sp.2010.57.2.251

Wingfield, A.H., & Alston, R.S. (2014) Maintaining hierarchies in predominantly white organizations: A theory of racial tasks. *American Behavioral Scientist, 58*(2), 274–87. https://doi.org/10.1177/0002764213503329

9 "Movin' On Up" in the Age of Neo-liberalism: Reflections on Black Middle-Class Consciousness and the Implications for Black Unity, Leadership, and Activism

KEVIN GOSINE

It can't speak English. It doesn't want to speak English. I can't even talk the way these people talk. "Why you ain't, where you is go, ra." I don't know who these people are. And I blamed the kid until I heard the mother talk ... And then I heard the father talk. This is all in the house ...

Everybody knows it's important to speak English except these knuckleheads ... You can't be a doctor with that kind of crap coming out of your mouth ... Where did these people get the idea that they're moving ahead with this? Well, they know they're not, they're just hanging out in the same place, five, six generations, sitting in the projects ... 50 percent dropout. Look, we're raising our own ingrown immigrants. These people are fighting hard to be ignorant.

Bill Cosby, 2004 (quoted in Dyson, 2005, pp. 57–8)

These words come from a meandering and confused yet controversial speech given by legendary entertainer and pop culture icon Bill Cosby. Cosby delivered this keynote address at an NAACP-sponsored 2004 event commemorating the fiftieth anniversary of the landmark *Brown v. Board of Education* US Supreme Court decision. Admittedly, this controversy might appear relatively innocuous in the wake of Cosby's multiple sexual assault allegations ten years after he made this speech, a scandal that exploded shortly after I (proverbially) penned a first draft of this chapter. Of relevance to my thesis, however, is Cosby's denigration and othering of Black Americans living in poverty, which took many Black North Americans aback (with a good number now highlighting the irony of Cosby's assertion of a dearth of moral and personal responsibility within low-income Black communities). The disappointment generated by Cosby's remarks is nicely captured in Michael Eric Dyson's 2005 book *Is Bill Cosby Right? Or Has the Black Middle Class Lost Its Mind?* In this book, Dyson retraces Cosby's life and career to contextualize his views and thoughtfully deconstructs Cosby's contentions with sociologically informed arguments highlighting broader social, political, and economic forces that generate racial inequality in America. While I will not go so far as to posit that the Black middle class has "lost its mind," I agree with Dyson that Cosby's views (his harsh sarcasm notwithstanding) reflect a growing class divide within Black North American populations, between middle-class Blacks socialized within a neo-liberal environment that purports to be colour-blind and privatizes racial inequality (what Cosby is clearly doing in his speech) and poor and working-class Blacks whose lives are disproportionately ravaged by neo-liberal economic restructuring, racism, and stigmatization (Galabuzi, 2005). Dyson (2005) suggested that Cosby's sanctimonious outlook, "widely held among a number of black constituencies," constitutes a vivid illustration of widespread fear on the part of middle-class Blacks and the Black elite of being stigmatized and socially damaged by the ignominious ways of poor Black Americans (p. xiii). Poor and working-class Blacks find themselves equally wary of Black people higher up on the socio-economic ladder who are heavily invested in the dominant meritocratic neo-liberal value system. In this chapter I consider the role neo-liberalism has played in fuelling this Black North American class divide and the resultant challenges activists face in promoting, to use the words of George Dei (2014), a "radical collective leadership with a shared vision, purpose and goal to contest and design our own futures" (p. 2).[1]

While university credentials and high socio-economic status are by no means mandatory prerequisites for taking on positions of leadership in social justice movements, it is difficult to deny that university-educated middle-class and upwardly mobile Blacks are, by virtue of their class location and resultant privilege, uniquely positioned to carve out pathways of opportunity for other Blacks and exert some degree of influence within the broader, White-dominated society. Indeed, given their access to social networks, education, facility with dominant modes of language, and experience navigating White-normed social structures, members of this population possess the social capital that can conceivably "translate into greater opportunity for their working- and lower-class counterparts" (Harris & Khanna, 2010, p. 641). Historically, Steve Biko, Aimé Césaire, Angela Davis, WEB DuBois, and Martin Luther King Jr are but a few of the highly educated Black figures who have been at the forefront of antiracist movements and struggles.

The question I explore in this chapter is twofold. First, in a neo-liberal context where inequality is highly racialized and educated middle-class and elite Blacks are viewed as a deviation from a normative (poor, academically disinclined, outcast, and oppositional) Blackness, how do members of this segment of Black diasporic populations experience the intersection of race and class? Second, how do they understand racial inequality and envision its amelioration? In short, drawing on existing scholarly research, I venture to paint a picture of what the Black middle-class experience might look like in Canada and the United States, highlighting tensions, complexities, ruptures, and contradictions that characterize the consciousness of this echelon of Black populations in global, neo-liberal times. I also consider theoretical approaches to Black leadership and activism that might resonate with members of this population and awaken within them a critical consciousness that enables them to recognize and resist the influence of neo-liberalism.

My central argument is that, in North America, neo-liberalism has played a significant role in exacerbating class divisions within Black populations and has socialized many successful Blacks towards individualistic solutions to combating racial inequality, thereby creating a divide between middle-class Blackness and race-centred social justice movements such as anti-racism. The remainder of this chapter consists of four sections. In the first section I describe neo-liberalism and detail the complex and conflicted ways in which it has influenced racialized subjectivities. In the second section I draw on existing scholarship to discuss the complexities and contradictions that permeate the lives of middle-class and upwardly mobile Black North Americans who reside in a contradictory space between racial stigmatization and class privilege (Benjamin, 2005; Cose, 1993; Gosine, 2008; Harris & Khanna, 2010). I highlight the conflicted relationship that members of this population share with both the dominant society and Blackness, and describe how, in the era of neo-liberalism, the juxtaposition between the individualistic disposition of "successful" Blacks and the collectivist and oppositional ethos of poor and working-class Black communities is rendered more pronounced than ever before.[2] That is, while racialized as Black, high-achieving and upwardly mobile Blacks find themselves "'cultured' as white" as a result of their internalization of neo-liberal values (Harris & Khanna, 2010, p. 640). In the third section I illustrate how neo-liberal discourses of individualism and meritocracy influence and inform the equity-promoting vision embraced by successful Blacks, who, by and large, appear out of touch with the transformative agenda advocated by anti-racist activists. In the concluding section, I consider the theoretical approach to Black leadership and activism that holds the greatest potential to cultivate a critical consciousness among middle-class and upwardly mobile Blacks. In this vein, I describe the limits of race-centred politics and elucidate the need for a theoretical framework that embraces intersectionality, specifically a version of intersectionality that acknowledges complex interactions between oppression and privilege in the lives of racialized individuals.

Neo-liberalism and Racialized Subjectivities

Neo-liberalism, with its pronounced emphasis on individualism and colour blindness, has fundamentally complicated the way in which racialized people of middle-class and elite status experience race in North America. In contrast to welfare state ideology, which recognizes the role of systemic discrimination in the perpetuation of inequality, neo-liberalism "promotes a form of market citizenship that is anathema to group claims and hence to equity as social justice" (Smith, 2010, p. 46). Some observers (e.g., Goldberg, 2009; Roberts & Mahtani, 2010) have gone so far as to elaborate the concept of "racial neo-liberalism" to signify the integral but obfuscated role played by race and racism within the neo-liberal ideology. These observers note that, while racism remains a systemically pervasive feature of North American society, neo-liberal discourse outwardly plays down the reality of race as a determinant of inequality, life chances, and opportunity by inculcating notions of individualism, neutrality, and meritocracy. In other words, racial inequality is portrayed as a function of individual or cultural deficiency rather than the result of structurally entrenched racism. Within the neo-liberal worldview, racism is relegated to the past, treated as a phenomenon historically mitigated via various liberal equity-promoting and diversity initiatives along with "cultural competency" models within education, health care, and the social services (Badwall, 2013; Goldberg, 2009). Hence, neo-liberalism and the equity-promoting measures that fit within this discourse work to mask colonial legacies and the resultant structural and endemic nature of present-day racial inequality. Neo-liberalism effectively "unburdens" Whiteness by evaluating diverse groups of people against supposedly neutral and universal standards, namely objectivity, meritocracy, and individualism (Badwall, 2013, p. 135).

Malinda Smith (2010) highlights the way in which neo-liberalism, alongside an emphasis on meritocracy and colour blindness, promotes a discourse of diversity that, on the surface, may appear progressive but ultimately reveals itself as self-serving and politically sterile. In a global age where capital is more mobile than ever, there is an increased emphasis on diversifying workplaces and courting international markets. As Smith (2010) observes, however, this emphasis on diversity is only useful "to the extent that a business case can be made that such diversities can be managed, marketed in branding exercises ... and made profitable in niche markets, as can be seen in the uses of diversity in internationalization strategies" (p. 46). In this way, the neo-liberal emphasis on diversity illustrates Derrick Bell's (1980) notion of interest convergence: it is a discourse engineered to serve the needs and organizational ideals of capital while ostensibly promoting equity (Smith, 2010).

Neo-liberalism, then, promotes discourses of individualism, meritocracy, and colour blindness and strategically emphasizes diversity, all of which work to conceal and reinforce the systemic basis of racism in Canada and the United States. Despite propagating the illusion of a post-racial world characterized by freedom and unbridled opportunity, neo-liberalism has in fact worked to proliferate class and racial inequalities. In the process it exacerbates class divisions within racialized populations as well as society at large. With the neo-liberal accentuation of individualism, colour blindness, and diversity, Sedef Arat-KoÇ (2010) argues that racialized people of higher socio-economic status have been lured into a sense of national belonging and universal subjectivity. At a point in history when the United States can boast of having had its first Black president (albeit in an era marked by deepening worldwide inequalities along class and racial lines), Arat-KoÇ contends that many non-European people have been "Whitened" via admission into the bourgeoisie. This phenomenon serves the "diversity" needs of global capital while propping up the meritocratic ethos that underpins a neo-liberal emphasis on the socio-economic achievements of "model minorities" (see also Pon, 2000). In the same moment, this hegemonic neo-liberal discourse works to further stigmatize the disproportionately racialized poor by portraying them as the unmeritorious and undisciplined architects of their plight, thereby accentuating socio-economic divisions within racialized populations.

There is research to suggest that, within Black populations, this neo-liberal phenomenon has exacerbated a clash of values between poor and working-class Black subcultures marked by a politics of resistance and relatively collectivist ethos, and middle-class Blacks who tend to adhere to neo-liberal, meritocratic ideals (Harris & Khanna, 2010; Lamont & Fleming, 2005). However, while elite and upwardly mobile racialized people throughout North America are afforded class privilege, many remain victims of subtle and, in the case of some, more salient forms of racism (Benjamin, 2005; Cose, 1993; Feagin & Sikes, 1994). Hence, for many racialized people who live between racial marginalization and class privilege, the neo-liberal moment is one of conflictedness and contradiction that, in many ways, works against intra-racial solidarity and mobilization.

Middle-Class Black Consciousness and the Class Divide

According to prevailing research, various globalizing forces, among which I argue neo-liberalism to be particularly influential, have fragmented and ruptured the consciousness, identities, and outlook of racialized people who have middle- and upper-class privilege (Gosine, 2008;

Harris & Khanna, 2010). In earlier eras, Du Bois (1997) and Fanon (1967) referred to this psychic splitting as a "double" or "dual" consciousness. Indeed, the lives of many high-achieving Blacks with elite or middle-class aspirations would appear to be characterized to a significant degree by conflictedness and contradiction, a condition that stems from residing in a space between racial exclusion and class privilege. Many members of this population struggle to balance a commitment to a Black "community" with the pursuit of individual goals. They also find themselves in the unique situation of simultaneously identifying with the cultural values and idioms of the White hegemonic society *and* a politically circumscribed Black identity. Many successful Blacks, however, occupy an insider-outsider status vis-à-vis the dominant society and Blackness in that they experience a degree of estrangement from *both* sociocultural entities. Middle-class and elite Blackness, then, can be characterized as a complex, perhaps even anomic, space (Gosine, 2012).

In previous research exploring social identity construction among highly educated and upwardly mobile Black Canadians, I documented some of the tensions and contradictions in the identities and lived experiences of the people studied (Gosine, 2008). Participants interviewed as part of this qualitative study were individuals who, at the time the research was conducted, were currently enrolled in or had recently completed high-profile university programs in law, business, medicine, and engineering as well as graduate programs in a range of fields. Most participants described a conflicted relationship with the White cultural ideal of Canada in that they felt a sense of belonging to and estrangement from the nation in which they resided. On the one hand, they expressed gratitude towards Canada for the opportunities they saw the society as offering them. They also acknowledged the advantages and privileges that their academic accomplishments and middle-class status often conferred upon them. Such feelings of belonging and appreciation make sense for racialized subjects socialized within a neo-liberal context that seduces accomplished non-White people into identifying with a universal Whiteness characterized by meritocratic ideals (Arat-KoÇ, 2010).

At the same time, most participants in my research experienced a degree of alienation from what they perceived to be an Anglo/White-normed and -dominated society that, in most realms, excludes and marginalizes Black people (Gosine, 2008; see also Feagin & Sikes, 1994; Lacy, 2004). While such individuals are shielded to some or maybe even a significant degree by their class position or aspirations, social scientists have employed the term "microaggression" to describe the subtle, covert, often unconscious everyday forms of racism that middle-class Blacks experience in White-dominated workplaces (Gosine & Pon, 2011; Sue et al, 2007).

Common examples of racial microaggression include conveying (often implicitly) stereotypical assumptions or making condescending allusions about members of a given racialized group (e.g., "all Black people are lazy," or "my Black colleague must have been an affirmative action hire") (Gosine & Pon, 2011). Microaggressions, observed Sue et al (2007), "are detrimental to persons of color because they impair performance in a multitude of settings by sapping the psychic and spiritual energy of recipients and by creating inequalities" (p. 273). The discourse of colour blindness inherent to neo-liberalism tends to conceal institutionalized racism of which prevalent and ongoing instances of microaggression represent manifestations.

Within Western contexts, a sense of alienation pushes a significant number of successful Blacks to identify with their transplanted ethnocultural heritage (e.g., a Caribbean or African identity), an identity that often intertwines with a transcendent Black, racially grounded disposition (Gosine, 2008; see also Edwards & Polite, 1992; Feagin & Sikes, 1994; Lacy, 2004; Lamont & Fleming, 2005). To be sure, I observed variation among participants in terms of the degree to which they centred Blackness in their identity negotiation work, with two of the sixteen study participants seemingly suppressing any notion of a Black racial identity (Gosine, 2008). In the case of these two participants, particular factors and experiences converged in their lives in a way that shaped a particular kind of Black consciousness – one where race is decentred and marginalized as a dimension of social identity. Hence, as I note elsewhere (Gosine, 2012), if one were to conceptualize a continuum where the left extreme represents a strong, critical Black consciousness and the right extreme represents little identification with being Black, high-achieving, middle-class Blacks would be scattered along *all* points of this continuum. Prevailing scholarship would indicate, however, that most high-achieving or upwardly mobile Blacks might be located to the left of the centrepoint along a continuum of this ilk (Gosine, 2008, 2012; see also Edwards & Polite, 1992; Lacy, 2004; Lamont & Fleming, 2005; Sampson & Milam, 1975).

Reconstructing one's "roots" and/or working to sustain an all-embracing Black identity that transcends class, religious, and ethnocultural differences can provide successful Blacks with a sense of empowerment and belonging that imbues their lives with meaning (Edwards & Polite, 1992; Gosine, 2008; James & Taylor, 2008; Lacy, 2004; Lamont & Fleming, 2005). Research conducted by Lacy (2004) demonstrates that many middle-class Black Americans with access to White neighbourhoods and White workplace settings possess a desire to remain connected to Black social networks in order to maintain a positive racial identity. "Black spaces and places," Lacy (2004) maintained, provide many native-born middle-class Black Americans with "a place to reconnect with other blacks after spending the bulk of the day in the white world, isolate middle-class blacks from ongoing discrimination, and constitute an important site for the construction of black racial identities" (p. 11). Encompassed within a pronounced and transcendent Black sense of self is a feeling of indebtedness to a politically defined Black community, that is, an inclination to in some way contribute to the cause of Black advancement (Edwards & Polite, 1992; Gosine, 2008; James, 1997; James & Taylor, 2008; Lamont & Fleming, 2005). "Successful African Americans," observed Edwards and Polite (1992), "are typically driven by both the desire and the need to give back – to reach back to help others of the race" (p. 265). To this end, we frequently see successful, upwardly mobile Blacks volunteering their time to mentor young people, participate in Black self-help organizations, and give their time and/or monetary resources to Black causes (Edwards & Polite, 1992; Gosine, 2008; James, 1997; James & Taylor, 2008).

While a transcendent Black identity can serve a protective and empowering function in the lives of successful Blacks living in a racially divided society, the relationship many successful Blacks share with "Blackness" can be complex and even conflicted. Edwards and Polite (1992) maintain that, in the decades following racial integration in the United States, many successful Blacks have endeavoured to take on a "pioneering" role, that is, to "function in an environment where no blacks have gone before – to be the first one or only one in a position or company previously populated by non-blacks" (p. 251). In this role they cultivate systems of support that make White-dominated contexts more hospitable for Black people, a responsibility that many successful Black people take on out of a sense of racial unity (Edwards & Polite, 1992; Gosine, 2008; James, 1997; James & Taylor, 2008).

As much as successful Blacks might take pride in serving as pioneers, however, the feeling that they are "representing" their race within White-dominated spaces – that is, the "burden of representation" – can result in considerable psychological strain. There is a persistent fear among many Black people in such settings that a failure to perform their role adequately will reinforce the demonization of Black people generally (Dyson, 2004; Gosine, 2008, 2012). In the context of describing football legend O.J. Simpson's inclination to play down his Blackness prior to his famous murder trial in the 1990s, Michael Eric Dyson (2004) eloquently explains the double-edged sword that is the burden of representation. According to Dyson, in a White-dominated society the positive actions and achievements of Black individuals are perceived as unique exceptions that do not atone for negative ones that inevitably inform hegemonic constructions of Blackness:

> Standing in for the group was a burden. It was also risky. You could never be sure that your efforts were taken seriously. In fact, a law of inversion seemed to apply. For most blacks, only the negative acts seemed to count. Even the positive became a negative good: it only counted as a credit against black liability, against all the wrong things black folk inevitably did. The good you did simply meant that you, and, by extension, all blacks, didn't mess up this time. When the good was allowed to count, it only underscored one's uniqueness, that one was not like other black folk. For many whites, excellence made blacks exceptions to, not examples of, their race. (p. 50)

Social psychologists Claude Steele and Joshua Aronson famously illuminated the psychological effects associated with the burden of representation in their empirical elucidation of the "stereotype threat," which refers to situations whereby members of marginalized groups have the opportunity to potentially reinforce or confirm stereotypes associated with the social group with which they identify (Steele & Aronson, 1995). Steele and Aronson vividly illustrated the stereotype threat in experiments that involved Black and White American college students taking a standardized test. Black students who were informed that the test measured intellectual aptitude performed significantly less well than White students given the same information *and* less well than Black test takers who were told that the test was "non-diagnostic" of intellectual ability. The researchers attributed this result to the stereotype threat impeding performance, as Black college students feared living up to and reinforcing Black racial stereotypes. In the case of professional and upwardly mobile Blacks, also psychologically draining is the balancing act associated with creating and sustaining racially hospitable educational and workplace environments while doing what is needed to succeed and advance in one's own career (Gosine, 2008, 2012).

Somewhat ironically, in addition to grappling with the burden of representation in academic and workplace settings, some successful Blacks experience a degree of disconnect from other people who identify as Black. Related to this, they also in many cases find themselves frustrated with the discursive boundaries that come with an essentializing and counter-hegemonic Black identity. Studies show poor and working-class Blacks tend to eschew dominant neo-liberal ideals, presenting a clash of values with upwardly mobile, middle-class Blacks. Their daily lives punctuated by the effects of interlocking racial and class oppression and their faith in the meritocracy permanently shaken, many such individuals respond by subscribing to an ethos that emphasizes the collective advancement of Black people and other marginalized folks within their low-income or working-class communities (as opposed to prioritizing individual mobility) (e.g., Fordham, 1988; Fordham & Ogbu, 1992; Gosine & Islam, 2014; James, 2012; Lamont & Fleming, 2005). While Canadian cities lack the Black-dominated inner-city communities found in large US urban centres, Black Canadians who reside in diverse, low-income neighbourhoods tend to possess a strong sense of communal identity that transcends Blackness (Gosine & Islam, 2014; James, 2012). With much of Black North America characterized to some degree by a relatively collectivist disposition, successful and upwardly mobile Blacks, owing largely to their academic and career accomplishments and resultant class identity, often find themselves defending or justifying their Blackness to Black peers who view such things as middle-class success ideals, certain political viewpoints, particular ways of speaking, and prominent middle-class values (e.g., meritocratic individualism, sacrifice, and delayed gratification) as inextricably linked to the dominant White society (Gosine, 2008; Harris & Khanna, 2010). In a qualitative study, Harris and Khanna (2010) explored class and racial cleavages within the Black American population by comparing the experiences, perceptions, and racial identities of middle-class Black Americans and Black-White mixed-race Americans.[3] Interestingly, they found that middle-class Blacks experienced a greater sense of ostracism from the larger Black "community" than mixed-race individuals, which "suggests that there may be greater acceptance of racial diversity in the black community than there is of class diversity" (p. 665). Their findings highlight divisions within the Black American community along cultural and, in particular, class lines that are to a large extent attributable "to the black mythical norm and the narrow construct of blackness" (p. 665).

As an oppositional disposition is fostered, Black communities tend to forge a dividing line between Black and White identities that constrains the individual agency of people who identify as Black. Dyer (1997) describes Whiteness as "a space for anything and nothing" (cited in Yon, 2000, p. 81), an insight that does not apply to Blackness. Constructed as a racialized digression from a normative and universal Whiteness, "Black," in the words of Dan Yon (2000), is "policed from the outside and inside" and therefore "denied the full range of human subjectivity opened to white" (p. 116). The degree to which a Black identity is conferred or denied is contingent on the extent to which people conform to shifting and contextual constructions of what Blackness encompasses (Gosine, 2008; Harris & Khanna, 2010; Yon, 2000). Hence, while many successful

Blacks derive a sense of empowerment and meaning from a pronounced sense of Blackness, they sometimes, if not frequently, find their Black identity being questioned by Black peers who cling to limiting conceptions of Blackness. Class divisions within Black populations are further exacerbated by a neo-liberal ideology that denigrates the racialized poor while accentuating the class privilege of those of middle-class and elite status. Within such a context, poor and working-class Blacks embrace, perhaps more tightly than ever, a collectivist and defensively situated outlook that stands in sharp contrast with the meritocratic values to which Blacks of higher socio-economic status subscribe.

It is clear, then, that high-achieving and upwardly mobile Blacks experience the intersection of race and class in unique and contradictory ways. This reality in turn results in multifaceted racial and class identities fraught with complexity and considerable conflictedness. While such individuals find themselves ensconced in the individualistic, career-driven ethos of the broader neo-liberal capitalist society, they tend to conceptualize such individually oriented, middle-class ideals as keys to uplifting the Black community as a whole (Edwards & Polite, 1992; Gosine, 2008, 2012; Lamont & Fleming, 2005). Indeed, research demonstrates that many successful Blacks perceive their educational and occupational success as enabling them to break down anti-Black stereotypes, serve as positive role models for Black youth, and empower Black people to traverse White-dominated environments (Edwards & Polite, 1992; Gosine, 2008, 2012; James, 1997; James & Taylor, 2008). In the case of high-achieving Black people, a group-based transcendent Black consciousness and the individualistic ethos of the wider neo-liberal society interlock in a distinctive way. Successful Blacks, many possessing a Black consciousness informed by the hegemonic neo-liberal discourse of meritocracy, confront racism and racial inequality through the dominant structures and ideological framework of capitalism (Edwards & Polite, 1992; Gosine, 2008, 2012; Lamont & Fleming, 2005). While successful Blacks chase their aspirations within a neo-liberal framework, this individualistic ethos is injected with meaning insofar as it correlates with a sense of commitment to a politically defined Black community (Gosine, 2008, 2012).

High-Achieving Blacks and the Quest for Racial Equality

While many high-achieving, upwardly mobile middle-class Black North Americans have been found to acknowledge racism and are generally inclined to confront it, research demonstrates that the ameliorative avenues emphasized fall within the parameters of neo-liberal middle-class individualism. In other words, the strategies championed and utilized by this population for mitigating inequalities and lifting the Black community (e.g., educational and occupational attainment, role modelling, building Black networks of support that enable Black people to negotiate White-dominated structures) are influenced to a significant degree by the dominant meritocratic, middle-class ideology.[4] Positive intent notwithstanding, such class-based strategies of resistance have seemingly widened the gulf between middle-class Blacks and poor and working-class Blacks, with the latter relatively disinclined towards individualism and who often find themselves challenged to acquire the cultural capital endorsed by the dominant neo-liberal society (not to mention Dr Cosby!) (Harris & Khanna, 2010; Lamont & Fleming, 2005). I have argued elsewhere (Gosine, 2012) that the tendency of highly educated Blacks with middle-class aspirations to formulate equity-seeking strategies through the framework of meritocratic individualism has created a seeming disconnect between successful Blacks and an anti-racist discourse that emphasizes the need to combat racism by way of structural change (see Dei, 2008).

James (1997) illustrated well the meritocratic disposition of upwardly mobile Blacks with middle-class aspirations in a study of Black Canadian teacher candidates enrolled in the faculty of education at a large Toronto university. These students entered the teaching program via a university access program that recruited students from traditionally disadvantaged communities. Participants in James's (1997) study experienced a significant degree of marginalization within the university environment, but still endorsed the system by attributing great importance to a university education for Black Canadians. Amidst prevailing systemic inequalities, these students emphasized a strong work ethic and individual initiative as a means of conquering obstacles. The chance to challenge negative Black stereotypes and serve as role models for Black youth furnished motivational fuel (James, 1997; see also Edwards & Polite, 1992; Gosine, 2008; Lamont & Fleming, 2005). Hence, James's (1997) study participants viewed academic achievement as a crucial means of improving the situation of the Black community (see also Gosine, 2008; Lamont & Fleming, 2005). A study carried out by James and Taylor (2008) found that a key survival strategy for Black Canadian university students is sustaining a belief in the meritocracy. That is, they hold dearly to the idea that "things are changing" in that individuals, increasingly, are being assessed based on their abilities and accomplishments rather than racialized identities (p. 571). Embracing this belief helps to reconcile "the conflict between their belief in meritocracy and their marginalized position" (p. 571). "To do otherwise," James and Taylor contend, "risks acknowledging that their own and/or their parents' immigrant dreams of success may not be realized" (p. 571).

Research demonstrates that, when traversing White, middle-class normed university settings distinguished all too often by Eurocentric curricula, a paucity of Black faculty, and a lack of effective anti-racist policies, procedures, and resources (Feagin, Vera, & Imani, 1996; James, 1997; Henry & Tator, 2007), Black students often find comfort, security, and belonging in Black peer networks as well as Black student organizations that provide support to current and prospective students (Feagin, Vera, & Imani, 1996; Gosine, 2008, 2012; James & Taylor, 2008). James and Taylor (2008), for instance, found Black Canadian university students worked hard to convince themselves that "through individual effort and willpower, their network of university colleagues, and their strong belief in education, they could successfully negotiate and attain their educational goals" (pp. 579–80). Rather than aggressively working to change structures of inequality within the university system, Black peer-support networks tend to focus on helping students to navigate existing structures (James, 1997; James & Taylor, 2008).

A neo-liberal disposition is further reflected in Black middle-class parenting. In his study of the attitudes and schooling experiences of Black middle-class male youth in the United States, Allen (2013) found that Black middle-class parents' expectations of their kids "included meritocratic approaches to school and using their high school experience as an explicit means to achieve a middle-class lifestyle through college attendance and a white-collar career" (p. 208). To cultivate academic opportunities for their children, parents frequently invoked their social networks (which often included their kids' teachers and highly educated family members and friends) and worked to make the home environment as congruent as possible with the school setting (e.g., by "replicating instructional techniques used in the school within their homes" [p. 208]). Allen found Black middle-class parents worked to instil a positive racial consciousness and sense of resiliency in their children. Rather than highlighting the need to challenge systems characterized by systemically embedded racism, however, parents emphasized to their children the importance of being able to navigate "different worlds," which entailed the ability to "adopt and perform the attitudes and preferences of the dominant group in situations that would provide economic and professional opportunities" (p. 209).

Allen's findings have been echoed by similarly themed Canadian research (e.g., Brown, 2003; James, 2013). James (2013), for example, documents the "costs" Black Toronto youth of Canadian Caribbean background incur when their parents migrate from the inner city to the (predominantly White) suburbs in hopes of providing their children with a "better life" (often making a profound financial sacrifice in doing so). Indeed, Caribbean parents viewed middle-class suburban communities as settings where their offspring could acquire the social and cultural capital necessary to realize socio-economic success in Canada. Their children, however, experienced a sense of alienation in a context that for them lacked community, socio-culturally relevant resources and supports, recreational and part-time employment opportunities, and peer groups that provided a viable sense of belonging. Moreover, many Black suburban youth found their lives violated by racial profiling, discrimination, and exclusion at the hands of teachers, the police, community stakeholders and residents, and peers. While cognizant of the racism that pervaded their lives, parents attempted to instill an individualistic resiliency in their kids by stressing the need to work hard (more so than their White counterparts), acquire the skills and accomplishments necessary for upward mobility, and demonstrate strength and aplomb when facing adversity. As far as these parents were concerned, "through these efforts [racist and exclusionary] structures could be sidestepped or surmounted" (James, 2013, p. 8).

Lamont and Fleming (2005) argue that the Black middle-class emphasis on educational and occupational attainment as a means of achieving equality works to estrange poor and working-class Blacks. The latter, as shown, have more of a collectivist orientation and often are not well positioned to attain such cultural capital.[5] By advocating equality-seeking strategies informed by neo-liberal individualism, successful Blacks unwittingly contribute to the continued demonization of the racialized poor by underestimating the effects of structural and interlocking racial and class oppression, thereby adding to the perception that Blacks of lower socio-economic status are unmeritorious (Lamont & Fleming, 2005). Lamont and Fleming (2005) assert the need to formulate a more inclusive vision for achieving racial equality, one that holds the potential to improve the plight of all Blacks without excluding poor and working-class Blacks from "membership in mainstream America" (p. 32).

Dei (2008) corroborates this problematization of human capital acquisition as a solution to racial inequality when he critiques the notion of "excellence" that is rooted in the discourse of meritocracy. While it is widely taken for granted that power, opportunities, rewards, and privileges are fairly and neutrally allocated by way of demonstrated individual excellence, Dei posits that "excellence" is actually an elitist concept that veils and enables systemic racism and resultant inequalities. Embedded within the meritocratic idea of "excellence" is the belief that equality of opportunity flourishes, an understanding that, in turn, underpins an ostensible colour-blind or "treat everyone the same" philosophy for creating an equitable society. This discourse fosters the belief that those who are not able to meet these meritocratic ideals – that is, people who do not possess or are unable to obtain the prescribed cultural capital – are somehow inadequate or deficient (Dei, 2008; Dyson, 2005). Nevertheless, it would appear that high-achieving and upwardly mobile Blacks in Canada and the United States tend to formulate oppositional strategies to combat racism through this neo-liberal prism of excellence (Gosine, 2012).

Conclusion: A Theoretical Basis for Black Leadership

I have argued that the prevailing discourse of neo-liberalism has played a profound role in fracturing and muddling the social identities and consciousness of upwardly mobile and middle-class Black people in Canada and the United States, in turn widening class cleavages within Black populations. Given that successful Blacks are socialized within a context that has complicated their relationship with both Blackness and the dominant society, and one in which they have been seemingly steered away from a transformative vision for ameliorating racial inequality, we must consider what theoretical approach to Black activism and leadership politics might resonate with successful Blacks and possibly help them to cultivate a "critical discourse of resistance" (Dei, 2008, p. 6). One framework that has historically informed Black leadership and activism is anti-racism, which has proven instrumental in highlighting institutionalized anti-Black racism, de-centring Whiteness, and challenging prevailing power relations (Dei, 2008). As I have illustrated elsewhere (Gosine, 2012), however, anti-racism has been critiqued for operating within a binary framework and a historical insistence on centring race as the overriding determinant of inequality and Black lived experience, thereby, in the eyes of some critics, creating a hierarchy of oppressions (see also Niemonen, 2007). The result of these tendencies has been a struggle to acknowledge, in a theoretically adequate and consistent way, intra-group differences, the contingent and complex ways in which different sources of oppression *and* privilege interlock, and the complicity of race-centred movements vis-à-vis other forms of oppression (see also Kumashiro, 2001; Niemonen, 2007). While there has been an increasing trend in anti-racist academic scholarship towards theorizing intersecting forms of oppression, the desire to centre race as the focal point through which we understand inequality remains quite salient within influential realms of anti-racist writing and activism (e.g., Dei, 2008; Goldberg, 2009; for critique see Gosine, 2012; Niemonen, 2007). When writing of Blacks with privileged social status(es), prominent Canadian anti-racist scholar George Dei (2008) notes that the "power of class, ability, gender, age and sexuality can afford some blacks a degree of respectability not accorded others of their kind" (p. 85). However, he appears to invoke a degree of racial reductionism when he states:

> While class and gender may allow some black males a certain degree of privilege, it must be noted, the all too frequent abhorrence or revulsion of blackness in the white imagination renders *any cushioning* by class, gender, [dis]ability and sexuality *insignificant.* (p. 85; emphasis added)

Indeed, the allure of race-centred politics is understandable. Activism and critique are much less complicated when people can take clearly bounded sides and pursue social transformation within a hierarchical "us versus them" binary framework (Kumashiro, 2001). As I have argued previously (Gosine, 2012), however, the insistence on centring race has created a seeming dissonance between anti-racism discourse and successful Black people who, in the neo-liberal context, share a conflicted relationship with the dominant society and may not always or necessarily experience their Blackness as the primary determinant of their everyday lived experience. Social identity is multifaceted, dynamic, fluid, and contingent; social categories are continually transgressed, resulting in intersection and overlap (Gosine, 2002; Kumashiro, 2001; Yon, 2000). Middle-class Blackness illustrates this point as it challenges the notion of clearly bounded racialized identities (or, more specifically, the idea of an easily characterized and neatly bounded Blackness) that anti-racist discourse has tended to reinforce (Gosine, 2002, 2012; Niemonen, 2007). Indeed, middle-class culture can be viewed as a sociocultural location where Blackness and the dominant White society overlap and intertwine insofar as it is a space where many Black and White people may share certain privileges, neo-liberal values, and meritocratic aspirations (Gosine, 2012). While something that resembles an inter-racial middle-class consciousness is fostered by the neo-liberal appeal to meritocracy, colour blindness, and diversity, racial divisions and hierarchies remain a reality. A race-centred social justice discourse is, however, inherently limited in its capacity to understand and viably address the contradictions and complexities generated by the intersection of race and class as influenced by neo-liberalism.

The key question becomes, then, what type of theoretical framework would resonate most profoundly with successful and upwardly mobile Blacks and possibly awaken their critical consciousness? A "critical consciousness," in this instance, means more than a desire to maintain communal ties as exhibited by many Black people of accomplishment and means. A critical consciousness entails the capacity to recognize how neo-liberalism masks systemic racial inequalities by, among other strategies, glorifying the socio-economic achievements of racialized elites via the discourse of meritocracy and, in the process, accentuating class-based cleavages within racialized populations. A critical consciousness also empowers successful Blacks to be conscious of how they might be implicated in perpetuating racial inequality and oppression, primarily through their investment in the meritocratic ideology. I maintain that a viable framework must take intersectionality seriously so as to address, in a theoretically satisfactory way, the unique and complex ways in which race, class, and other variables interlock in the lives of successful Black North Americans. When I note the need to take intersectionality seriously, I have two points in mind. First, the framework must enable us to account for the distinct ways in which various identities intersect in the lives of successful Blacks in the neo-liberal context to accentuate *or* mitigate the saliency of race at particular moments and in particular circumstances. Second, there must be recognition that we all (Black people included) have multiple social identities that privilege or oppress us depending on contexts and situations (Sakamoto & Pitner, 2005). As Black feminist scholars argue, analyses of inequality and oppression must account for, to modify slightly a well-known feminist concept, the "simultaneity of oppression *and privilege*" (Smith, 1983) to capture the complexities and contradictions in the lives of middle-class and upwardly mobile Blacks living in a neo-liberal context. As Zinn and Dill (1996) perceptively contend, "the idea of a matrix [of domination *and* privilege][6] is that several fundamental systems work with and through each other ... People experience race, class, gender, and sexuality differently depending upon their social location in the structures of race, class, gender, and sexuality" (pp. 326–7). Theoretical approaches to understanding inequality and oppression that emphasize intersectionality (without insisting that a particular source of oppression be perennially centred) are inherently more inclusive of successful Blacks whose lived experiences have been complicated by the simultaneity of racial oppression and class privilege as generated by neo-liberal and globalizing forces. In addition, acknowledging sources of privilege in the lives of Black people can highlight points of commonality with White society, thereby mitigating the divisiveness that frequently characterizes race-centred identity politics and heightening collaborative possibilities.

Acknowledgments

I am grateful to Dennis Soron and the editors of this volume for thoughtful and instructive feedback on previous drafts of this chapter. I hold sole responsibility for any mistakes that remain.

NOTES

1 For the purposes of this analysis, "successful" Blacks are those who hold an occupation or position that requires university qualifications and is financially lucrative and/or socially constructed as prestigious within the context of Western society, *or* those currently pursuing university credentials. I consider university students to possess a middle-class consciousness and to be upwardly mobile insofar as they have "assimilated middle-class norms and values" through their undergraduate training and actively aspire to middle-class careers (Cockerham, 1995, as cited in Beagan, 2001, p. 586).

2 I am aware of the theoretical dangers of creating an essentialist binary between Blacks of working-class status and middle-class and upwardly mobile Blacks (see Gosine, 2002). Indeed, as my colleague Erica Lawson has perceptively highlighted in reviewing an early version of this chapter, class lines within Black populations are often blurred, as Black people in Canada and the United States share interclass kinship ties and, in many instances, experience the social construction of Blackness in similar ways. That noted, there is scholarship to suggest that, relative to the broader, middle-class-oriented society, a collectivist disposition and oppositional outlook tend to prevail within Black working-class and low-income cultures (e.g., Fordham, 1988; Fordham & Ogbu, 1992; Gosine & Islam, 2014; James, 2012). By contrast, the research cited throughout this chapter suggests that highly educated and upwardly mobile Blacks who maintain a salient Black identity formulate strategies of resistance to racism that are informed by middle-class individualism, and as such emphasize educational and occupational attainment as important means of achieving racial equality. I discuss these class differences as general and emerging trends and tendencies that are inevitably fraught with complexities and contradictions.

3 While their research provides important insight into the class divide within the Black American population, a limitation of Harris and Khanna's (2010) study is that most of the mixed-race participants in their sample are classified as middle class according to the criteria they employ (possession of a college education and occupational status, e.g., white-collar position, entrepreneurs). This would seemingly complicate their effort to compare the experiences of middle-class Blacks and mixed-race Blacks, as race and class would inevitably interlock in the lives of members of the latter group, thereby making it difficult to disentangle which social status plays a more significant role in shaping their lived experiences. Moreover, given the middle-class identification of most mixed-race participants, it is unclear why they might report experiencing a lesser degree of ostracism from other Blacks than Black middle-class individuals who are not mixed-race. In accounting for this, the authors explain that where their mixed-race subsample is concerned, they "focus primarily on the ways in which being biracial has affected

these respondents' acceptance into the black fictive family. Nevertheless, where applicable, we discuss the intersections of race and class in the lives of both biracial and black middle-class respondents" (p. 648).

4 I am not characterizing the pursuit of academic qualifications as inherently wrong or neo-liberal. Educational attainment has long served as a vehicle by which members of Black diasporic communities achieve upward mobility. However, the tendency to view educational attainment in and of itself as an anti-racist strategy is problematic for many scholars (e.g., Dei, 2008; Lamont & Fleming, 2005) because it fails to account for (a) structural obstacles and discriminatory processes within schools that limit the success of Black students (a reality that prompts many Black students to opt out of the system), and (b) the unequal opportunities many Blacks face even after acquiring postsecondary academic qualifications.

5 Lamont and Fleming (2005) draw their conclusions from findings from an exploratory qualitative study of Black American elites. They conducted in-depth interviews with 10 professional and successful Black Americans selected from a larger random sample of 167 respondents that included Black politicians, executives, military officers, heads of philanthropic organizations, and media, entertainment, and sports figures. The researchers wanted to learn the "antiracist strategies" employed by highly successful Black Americans as well as "how they go about establishing their cultural membership in mainstream America" (p. 35).

6 Zinn and Dill borrow and employ Patricia Hill Collins's (1990) phrase "matrix of domination." I have augmented the phrase when I write "domination and privilege."

REFERENCES

Allen, Q. (2013). Balancing school and cool: Tactics of resistance and accommodation among black middle-class males. *Race, Ethnicity & Education, 16*(2), 203–24. https://doi.org/10.1080/13613324.2012.725041

Arat-KoÇ, S. (2010). New whiteness(es), beyond the colour line? Assessing the contradictions and complexities of "whiteness" in the (geo)political economy of capitalist globalism. In S. Thobani, S.H. Razack, & M.S. Smith (Eds.), *States of race: Critical race feminism for the 21st century* (pp. 147–68). Toronto: Between the Lines.

Badwall, H.K. (2013). *Can I be a good social worker? Racialized workers narrate their experiences with racism in everyday practice* (Doctoral dissertation). Ontario Institute for Studies in Education, University of Toronto, Toronto.

Beagan, B. (2001). Microinequalities and everyday inequalities: Race, gender, sexuality and class in medical school. *Canadian Journal of Sociology, 26*(4), 583–610. https://doi.org/10.2307/3341493

Bell, D.A. (1980). Brown v. Board of Education and the interest-convergence dilemma. *Harvard Law Review, 93*(3), 518–33. https://doi.org/10.2307/1340546

Benjamin, L. (2005). *The black elite: Still facing the color line in the twenty-first century.* New York: Rowman & Littlefield.

Brown, M. (2003). *Growing up black in Oakville: The impact of community on black youth identity formation and civic participation.* Oakville: Peel Social Planning Council.

Cose, E. (1993). *Rage of a privileged class.* New York: HarperCollins.

Dei, G.J.S. (2008). *Racists beware: Uncovering racial politics in the postmodern society.* Rotterdam: Sense.

Dei, G.J.S. (2014). *An indigenous Africentric perspective on black leadership.* Unpublished manuscript, Ontario Institute for Studies in Education, University of Toronto, Toronto.

Du Bois, W.E.B. (1997). *The souls of black folk.* Boston: Bedford.

Dyer, R. (1997). *White.* London: Routledge.

Dyson, M.E. (2004). *The Michael Eric Dyson reader.* Cambridge, MA: Basic.

Dyson, M.E. (2005). *Is Bill Cosby right? Or has the black middle class lost its mind?* Cambridge, MA: Basic.

Edwards, A., & Polite, C.K. (1992). *Children of the dream: The psychology of black success.* New York: Doubleday.

Fanon, F. (1967). *Black skin, white masks.* New York: Grove.

Feagin, J.R., & Sikes, M. (1994). *Living with racism: The black middle class experience.* Boston: Beacon.

Feagin, J.R., Vera, H., & Imani, N. (1996). *The agony of education: Black students at white colleges and universities.* New York: Routledge.

Fordham, S. (1988). Racelessness as a factor in black students' school success: Pragmatic strategy or Pyrrhic victory? *Harvard Educational Review, 58*(1), 54–84. https://doi.org/10.17763/haer.58.1.c5r77323145r7831

Fordham, S., & Ogbu, J.U. (1992). Black students' school success: Coping with the burden of "acting white." In J.J. Macionis & N.V. Benokraitis (Eds.), *Seeing ourselves: Classic, contemporary, and cross-cultural readings in sociology* (pp. 287–303). Englewood Cliffs: Prentice Hall.

Galabuzi, G.E. (2005). *The racialization of poverty in Canada: Implications for Section 15 Charter protection.* Paper presented at the National Antiracism Council of Canada Conference, Ottawa, 10–13 November.

Goldberg, D.T. (2009). *The threat of race: Reflections on racial neoliberalism.* Malden: Blackwell.

Gosine, K. (2002). Essentialism versus complexity: Conceptions of racial identity in educational scholarship. Canadian Journal of Education, *27*(1), 81–100. https://doi.org/10.2307/1602189

Gosine, K. (2008). Living between stigma and status: A qualitative study of the social identities of highly educated black Canadian adults. Identity: An

International Journal of Theory and Research, *8*(4), 307–33. https://doi.org/10.1080/15283480802365304

Gosine, K. (2012). Accomplished black North Americans and antiracism education: Towards bridging a seeming divide. *Critical Sociology, 38*(5), 707–21. https://doi.org/10.1177/0896920510380077

Gosine, K., & Islam, F. (2014). "It's like we're one big family": Marginalized young people, community, and the implications for urban schooling. *School Community Journal, 24*(2), 33–61.

Gosine, K., & Pon, G. (2011). On the front lines: The voices and experiences of racialized child welfare workers in Toronto, Canada. *Journal of Progressive Human Services, 22*(2), 135–59. https://doi.org/10.1080/10428232.2011.599280

Harris, C.A., & Khanna, N. (2010). Black is, black ain't: Biracials, middle-class blacks, and the social construction of blackness. *Sociological Spectrum, 30*(6), 639–70. https://doi.org/10.1080/02732173.2010.510057

Henry, F., & Tator, C. (2007, 24–5 February). Through a looking glass: Enduring racism on the university campus. *Academic Matters.*

Hill Collins, P. (1990). *Black feminist thought: Knowledge, consiousness, and the politics of empowerment.* Boston: Unwin Hyman.

James, C.E. (1997). Contradictory tensions in the experiences of African Canadians in a faculty of education with an access program. *Canadian Journal of Education, 22*(2), 158–74. https://doi.org/10.2307/1585905

James, C.E. (2012). *Life at the intersection: Community, class, and schooling.* Halifax: Fernwood.

James, C.E. (2013). *"Colour matters": Suburban life as social mobility and its high cost for black youth.* Paper presented at the 15th National Metropolis Conference, Ottawa, 14–16 March.

James, C.E., & Taylor, L. (2008). "Education will get you to the station": Marginalized students' experiences and perceptions of merit in accessing university. *Canadian Journal of Education, 31*(3), 567–90. https://doi.org/10.2307/1585905

Kumashiro, K.K. (2001). Queer students of color and antiracist, antiheterosexist education: Paradoxes of identity and activism. In K.K. Kumashiro (Ed.), *Troubling intersections of race & sexuality: Queer students of color & anti-oppressive education* (pp. 1–25). Lanham: Rowman & Littlefield.

Lacy, K.R. (2004). Black spaces, black places: Strategic assimilation and identity construction in middle-class suburbia. *Ethnic & Racial Studies, 27*(6), 908–30. https://doi.org/10.1080/0141987042000268521

Lamont, M., & Fleming, C.M. (2005). Everyday antiracism: Competence and religion in the cultural repertoire of the African American elite. *Du Bois Review: Social Science Research on Race, 2*(1), 29–43. https://doi.org/10.1017/S1742058X05050046

Niemonen, J. (2007). Antiracist education in theory and practice: A critical assessment. *American Sociologist, 38*(2), 159–77. https://doi.org/10.1007/s12108-007-9006-x

Pon, G. (2000). Importing the Asian model minority discourse into Canada: Implications for social work and education. *Canadian Social Work Review, 17*(2), 277–91.

Roberts, D.J., & Mahtani, M. (2010). Neoliberalizing race, racing neoliberalism: Placing "race" in neoliberal discourses. *Antipode, 42*(2), 248–57. https://doi.org/10.1111/j.1467-8330.2009.00747.x

Sakamoto, I., & Pitner, R.O. (2005). Use of critical consciousness in anti-oppressive social work practice: Disentangling power dynamics at personal and structural levels. *British Journal of Social Work, 35*(4), 435–52. https://doi.org/10.1093/bjsw/bch190

Sampson, W.A., & Milam, V. (1975). The interracial attitudes of the black middle class: Have they changed? *Social Problems, 23*(2), 153–65. https://doi.org/10.1525/sp.1975.23.2.03a00040

Smith, B. (Ed.). (1983). *Home girls: A black feminist anthology.* New York: Kitchen Table/Women of Color Press.

Smith, M.S. (2010). Gender, whiteness and the "other Others" in the academy. In S. Thobani, S.H. Razack, & M.S. Smith (Eds.), *States of race: Critical race feminism for the 21st century* (pp. 37–58). Toronto: Between the Lines.

Steele, C.M., & Aronson, J. (1995). Stereotype threat and the intellectual test performance of African Americans. *Journal of Personality and Social Psychology, 69*(5), 797–811. https://doi.org/10.1037/0022-3514.69.5.797

Sue, D.W., Capodilupo, C.M., Torino, G.C., Bucceri, J.M., Holder, A.M.B., Nadal, K.L., & Esquilin, M. (2007). Racial microaggressions in everyday life: Implications for clinical practice. *American Psychologist, 62*(4), 271–86. https://doi.org/10.1037/0003-066X.62.4.271

Yon, D.A. (2000). *Elusive culture: Race, identity and schooling in global times.* New York: SUNY Press.

Zinn, M.B., & Dill, B.T. (1996). Theorizing difference from multiracial feminism. *Feminist Studies, 22*(2), 321–31. https://doi.org/10.2307/3178416

10 Building Capacity and Making History: African Canadian Leadership in Ontario's HIV/AIDS Sector

SHAMARA BAIDOOBONSO

Within this chapter, I document the unique histories and shared experiences of four organizations focused on addressing HIV/AIDS in Ontario's African, Caribbean, and Black (ACB) communities. First, I provide the context underlying the ACB-specific response to HIV/AIDS and a brief description of each organization. Second, I fill a gap in knowledge by presenting new information I have collected from ACB community leaders who are intimately involved in the response to HIV/AIDS. Given the complete absence of information on this topic, original research was needed for this work. Third, in my analysis I focus on the ways in which ACB leaders are creating a movement to influence the HIV/AIDS agenda for the benefit of ACB communities.

At the outset, it is important to provide foundational information. I use a variety of terms specific to HIV/AIDS throughout, and these terms are important for understanding this work. They are defined below. Additionally, the importance of this work cannot be appreciated fully without an understanding of the epidemiological context that drove, and continues to drive, work on HIV/AIDS in ACB communities across Canada, which I also provide below.

Definitions

Canada has a "concentrated" HIV epidemic. This means that there are specific groups in which the prevalence of HIV infection and its risk factors are higher than in the broader Canadian population (Public Health Agency of Canada, 2012). Canada's epidemic is concentrated among vulnerable groups that face discrimination and stigma – men who have sex with men, injection drug users (IDUs), and non-IDU heterosexuals from countries where HIV is endemic. A growing proportion of new HIV infections are occurring among non-IDU heterosexuals born in HIV-endemic countries (Public Health Agency of Canada, 2009a).

I use the terms "ACB" and "HIV-endemic" interchangeably. The vast majority (92.7 per cent) of HIV-positive people in Canada who are from HIV-endemic countries are Black, and they tend to be from sub-Saharan Africa and the Caribbean (Public Health Agency of Canada, 2009a). HIV surveillance data also shows that 81 per cent of infections among ACB Ontarians fell within the HIV-endemic category (Liu & Remis, 2007). Since race-based data are not routinely collected, the HIV-endemic data provide the best available estimate of the impact of HIV on ACB communities (James, 2006). By including only foreign-born non-IDU heterosexuals, however, these data under-represent HIV among ACB people as a whole. Furthermore, to represent the diversity within the population, I use the term "ACB" in place of "Black."

Epidemiology of HIV in ACB Communities

At the national level, routinely collected public health data show that ACB are over-represented among the HIV-positive population. It was estimated that 71,300 Canadians were living with HIV at the end of 2011, and approximately 15 per cent of them were ACB people (Public Health Agency of Canada, 2012), although ACB people comprise approximately 2.2 per cent of Canada's population (Milan & Tran, 2004; Public Health Agency of Canada, 2009b).

The story of HIV's impact on ACB communities in Ontario is similar to that at the national level. From 2001 to 31 December 2006, the proportion of ACB heterosexuals who were living with HIV increased by 72 per cent (Remis, Swantee, Schiedel, & Liu, 2008). As of December 2009, the proportion of ACB Ontarians living with HIV (1.1 per cent) was nearly three times that of the broader Ontario population (0.4 per cent) (Remis, Swantee, & Liu, 2012).[1] Despite representing less than 4 per cent of Ontario's population, ACB people accounted for roughly 21 per cent of all new HIV diagnoses in Ontario in 2011 (Remis & Liu, 2013). Infections acquired in Canada are at least partially responsible for driving the epidemic in ACB communities (Remis & Liu, 2008). In fact, Ontario-based studies show that as many as 60 per cent of infections among ACB people occurred in Canada (Quorum Communications Inc., 2006; Remis & Merid, 2004; Williams, Newman, Sakamoto, & Massaquoi, 2009).

Description of Each Organization

In response to the growing burden of HIV/AIDS on their communities, ACB community members have formed community-based organizations to provide services and resources to ACB people living with and affected by HIV/AIDS. These community members are regular "every-day" people who recognize a need and collaborate to address a pressing health problem. They are not political leaders, and many of them will never be mentioned in history books. Nevertheless, their work is essential to Ontario's response to HIV/AIDS, especially in ACB communities. This chapter tells the stories of the seminal organizations involved in this response: the Black Coalition for AIDS Prevention (Black CAP), Women's Health in Women's Hands Community Health Centre (WHIWH), Africans in Partnership Against AIDS (APAA), and the African and Caribbean Council on HIV/AIDS in Ontario (ACCHO).[2]

Black Coalition for AIDS Prevention

Black CAP is a non-profit, charitable, community-based organization that works to create an inclusive space for ACB people who are living with HIV. It serves immigrants and refugees, straight men and women, and gay, lesbian, bisexual, and transsexual ACB people. Its mission is to "reduce the spread of HIV infection within Toronto's Black communities and to enhance the quality of life of people living with or affected by HIV/AIDS" (http://www.black-cap.com/index.php?option=com_content&view=article&id=1&Itemid=36). Black CAP's motto is: "Because All Black People's Lives Are Important."

Women's Health in Women's Hands

WHIWH is a community health centre that provides primary health care to immigrant, refugee, and racialized women (i.e., ACB, Latin American, and South Asian) ages sixteen years and over who live in the Greater Toronto Area. When providing its clients with access to care, WHIWH employs an "inclusive feminist, pro-choice, anti-racist, anti-oppression and multilingual participatory framework" that encompasses "gender, gender identity, race, class, violence, sexual orientation, religion, culture, language, disability, immigration status and socio-economic circumstances" (WHIWH, 2015). In addition to HIV/AIDS services, WHIWH offers programs for mental health support, self-advocacy, maternal health, health promotion and education, healthy living, diabetes, self-care, and food access.

Africans in Partnership Against AIDS

Like Black CAP, APAA is a non-profit, charitable, community-based organization. It provides linguistically and culturally sensitive HIV/AIDS education in the Greater Toronto Area. APAA is committed to providing a supportive environment to its clients and the communities it serves (see its website: http://www.apaa.ca/). Although APAA receives requests for support from diverse clientele, it predominantly serves African communities.

African and Caribbean Council on HIV/AIDS in Ontario

ACCHO is the newest of the four groups. It is mandated to coordinate and support the implementation, revision/renewal, monitoring and evaluation of the Ontario HIV/AIDS Strategy for African, Caribbean and Black Communities. ACCHO also advises and advocates on HIV/AIDS-related issues affecting ACB communities and promotes greater and meaningful involvement of ACB people living with HIV/AIDS. Not an organization in a legal sense, ACCHO is a network of organizations and individuals providing leadership in Ontario's response to HIV/AIDS in ACB communities. As one of its members described it: "I look at ACCHO as an octopus. The body is here, but the tentacles are all over the province."

Data Collection and Analysis

For this chapter, I interviewed six recognized leaders in the response to HIV/AIDS in ACB communities. These leaders were purposively selected on the following criteria: their affiliation with at least one of the four organizations, longstanding involvement in HIV/AIDS work, and ability to provide a unique point of view. The interviews were semi-structured and were conducted either in person or by phone. Following each interview, I sent the interviewee her/his interview summary, thereby enabling each to fact-check and revise it as s/he saw fit. The summary with the interviewee's revisions was used for the analysis.

I analysed the data from the interviews using qualitative content analysis, a valuable approach when analysing qualitative data gathered using purposive sampling and semi-structured interviews (Neergaard, Olesen, Andersen, & Sondergaard, 2009; Sandelowski, 2000). This is a particularly useful method of analysis when there is a dearth of information on a topic, as it does not rely on previous knowledge or theories but instead uses a grounded theory approach (Hsieh, 2005; Sandelowski, 2000).[3] The analysis followed six steps. First, I used summary coding to extract the points made during each interview. Second, I re-read interview summaries and recorded reflections and insights gained from the data. Third, I stratified the data by themes (i.e., history, mandate, research, political activity, challenges, and opportunities). Fourth, I stratified the data within each theme by organization and identified commonalities between interviewees' responses about each organization. Fifth, I made generalizations based on patterns observed in the data. Finally, I summarized the generalizations and shared them with the interviewees for validation purposes.

Documents and other information stored on the websites of the four organizations, documents shared by the interviewees, and documents I obtained independently served as sources of information for document review and analysis. These documents provided insight into the context for the founding, existence, work, and partnerships of each organization, while enabling me to cross-reference information gathered from interviews. In combining documents and interviews, this study employed triangulation of sources to ensure validity (Farmer, Robinson, Elliott, & Eyles, 2006; Patton, 1999). While performing triangulation, I identified areas of agreement and disagreement between the data from the interviews and that from the documents (Farmer et al., 2006; Leech & Onwuegbuzie, 2007).

Central Themes of ACB Leadership in HIV/AIDS

Seven themes were found to be central to understanding ACB leadership in the HIV sector. They are: having a mandate to serve ACB communities, unity and collaboration, the involvement of volunteers, demonstrating the value of their work before attracting funding, using research as a tool, advocating and engaging with policymakers, and being resourceful in the face of challenges. In the following pages, I will demonstrate the importance of each of these characteristics in the movement to make ACB communities a priority group within the HIV sector and attract resources to respond to HIV effectively.

Mandate to Serve ACB Communities

All four groups were formed specifically to meet the needs of ACB communities. For instance, although Black CAP was originally supported by a mainstream AIDS service organization, the AIDS Committee of Toronto, its mission was to unabashedly focus on HIV in ACB communities because mainstream organizations were not meeting ACB people's needs. WHIWH was originally intended as a multidisciplinary health centre for women, regardless of race or ethnicity. In 1991, however, ACB women held a sit-in at the centre to raise awareness about the significant marginalization and barriers they faced when accessing health care due to their race and immigrant identities. After that, the Ontario Ministry of Health and Long-Term Care agreed that WHIWH should serve only immigrant, refugee, and racialized women. In 1993, APAA was founded to provide much-needed services to continental African communities. Its founders first focused on translating materials from mainstream AIDS service organizations into culturally and linguistically appropriate content for Africans. Lastly, ACCHO was established in 2005 to oversee Ontario's newly created strategy for HIV in ACB communities. By the time ACCHO was founded, policymakers had already spent several years working with Black CAP, APAA, and WHIWH – organizations that were committed to ACB communities and their causes and were involved in actively discussing the effects of racism and other forms of discrimination and oppression. As one staff member noted of Black CAP's existence and mandate to serve: "There is value in our existence. There is more value in us coming together, running an organization, and serving the community. It is powerful that we exist."

In addition to serving ACB communities, each organization is mandated to respect the diversity among ACB people. Within each organization's mandate, there is explicit recognition of diversity related to language, culture, gender, sexual orientation, class, religion, physical and mental ability, immigration status, experience, and the list goes on. All four organizations are committed to operating within an anti-discrimination and anti-oppression framework. This orientation, while challenging, is foundational to the other characteristics that are essential to the response to HIV/AIDS. One APAA staff member noted: "It is not easy for one organization to serve every single country or community, because there is so much diversity."

These mandates pave the way for leadership that embodies the principles of social justice, anti-oppression, anti-discrimination, and inclusivity for all ACB people. With these mandates, these organizations and leaders within the HIV sector are granted the authority to fulfil their specific responsibilities to ACB communities, and they are expected to make ACB people their central focus. Using these mandates, organizations within the HIV sector have been able to collaborate, recruit leaders, and engage in activities that advance the interests of ACB people infected with, affected by, and interested in HIV/AIDS.

Unity and Collaboration

The organizations were created by people and groups working collaboratively and in unity towards a common cause: preventing HIV transmissions among ACB people and making sure that ACB people had access to good-quality HIV care. In the cases of Black CAP and ACCHO, their founding was the result of collaborative efforts between several existing community organizations. In the late 1980s, a group of volunteers from various ACB organizations formed the Black AIDS Project, which evolved into Black CAP, a group that wanted to provide culturally sensitive HIV/AIDS education to ACB communities. After its founding in 1991, Black CAP joined the mainstream HIV movement by obtaining membership in the Ontario AIDS Network and Canadian AIDS Society. Similarly, ACCHO was founded by volunteers from ACB organizations. In 1998, a volunteer working group was convened to chart Ontario's response to HIV/AIDS in ACB communities. The working group comprised APAA, African Community Health Services, Black CAP, WHIWH, Rexdale Community Health Centre, Toronto Public Health, Youth Clinical Services, Inc., the Ontario HIV Epidemiologic Monitoring Unit at the University of Toronto, Health Canada Ontario Region, and the AIDS Bureau of the Ontario Ministry of Health and Long-Term Care. Six members of this group formed the HIV-Endemic Task Force in 1999, which morphed into ACCHO in 2005.

In the cases of WHIWH and APAA, the organizations were largely formed by individuals working together to fill an identified community need. In 1987, WHIWH was formed by a group of women activists who recognized that women faced unique barriers to health care access. They held community consultations to form a health centre for women. Lastly, APAA was founded in 1993 when a collective of Africans collaborated to fill a gap in HIV services in African communities in Toronto. They recognized the need for an ethnically neutral organization that was nimble enough to provide culturally appropriate HIV services and messages that were respectful of the diversity among Africans.

Collaboration and unity have also been central to each organization's model for delivering HIV services to ACB people. WHIWH, for example, grew over the years to form partnerships with other organizations. In 1999, it hosted its first World AIDS Day event in collaboration with Black CAP, APAA, African Community Health Services, and Toronto Public Health. Since then, WHIWH has been collaborating with APAA and Black CAP to deliver HIV services to ACB women and their families. Additionally, in 2005, Black CAP became ACCHO's trustee and entered into a strategic partnership called Muungano (Swahili for "working together") with APAA and African Community Health Services. This partnership provided the framework for collaboration, which continues to this day, even though African Community Health Services no longer exists. Black CAP and APAA deliver several programs collaboratively with WHIWH, such as a holiday party and a forum for people living with HIV. They also support each other's funding applications.

This collaborative approach to service delivery and leadership enables each organization to move beyond its functional boundaries to provide more comprehensive, coordinated HIV services to ACB communities. As described above, collaborative leadership has resulted in these organizations providing value that extends beyond their formal roles within the health and HIV sectors. In addition, this approach has built trust across organizations and has facilitated the sharing of resources and information for the benefit of ACB communities.

Involvement of Volunteers

A third theme that was common across the organizations is that volunteers are an essential component of their existence and ability to serve ACB communities. As mentioned above, Black CAP was founded by volunteers representing various ACB organizations from around Toronto. It hired its first paid staff member in 1989 and then more staff in 1991. In those early days, the organization relied heavily on volunteers to implement its work. Today, Black CAP still relies on volunteers who help its staff with programs, outreach, and professional services. Similarly, the women who founded WHIWH did so as volunteers, and the organization hired its first three staff members in 1990 – three years after the women began holding consultations. Since then, the organization has not relied heavily on volunteers, based on the belief that women should be paid for their work. In 2015, it reversed this policy and hired a volunteer coordinator to build its volunteer program. However, prior to this hiring, WHIWH was using project-specific volunteers to support its HIV services. At the time of APAA's founding in 1993, all of its work was done by volunteers. The organization struggled to attract funding for many years. When it finally did, there was not enough money to fund all of the staff full time, so its staff often donated their time as volunteers. With hundreds of volunteers on its roster, APAA continues to use them to deliver a broad range of services, including outreach and event planning. Speaking of the experience of running APAA with little funding, a staff member commented: "I started afresh with a budget of $19,000 funded by the City. That was only able to cover rent. I worked three days per week and volunteered two to four days per week. I was working day and night." Lastly, many of ACCHO's members are volunteers; these include members of the council and various committees. An ACCHO member similarly noted:

> A lot of people have given of themselves to make ACCHO happen. Initially, it was just the council with no staff or workers. People had full-time jobs and

were volunteers. It is important to recognize the time and sacrifices people have made because they believed in ACCHO. It is important to acknowledge and recognize that.

Given the essential roles volunteers have played and the passion and knowledge they bring, it is not surprising that, where possible, the organizations have hired former volunteers as staff. For instance, APAA's first executive director started out as a volunteer while working full time at another AIDS service organization. Likewise, many of the organization's staff members were previously volunteers. As a Black CAP staff member noted: "I became the volunteer coordinator in a volunteer capacity, then I became a staff member." Also, several of Black CAP's staff members, including executive directors, were volunteers before joining the organization in a paid role.

The involvement of volunteers has been a means by which to fulfil important responsibilities of leadership. Unpaid positions attract individuals who want to build specific skills, gain certain experiences, and/or contribute to a cause dear to them. These people are essential to the continuity of movements, and have been of utmost importance to raising awareness and building support for HIV/AIDS, an issue that disproportionately affects very small, highly marginalized minority groups in Canada. Upon building the necessary skills, experience, and knowledge, volunteers have also transitioned into leadership roles, thus illustrating another important responsibility of leaders – building the leadership pipeline.

Demonstrating Value in the Absence of Funding

In every case, the organizations began executing their mandates before seeking funding. They were not created to respond to funding opportunities; they were created by passionate volunteers who wanted to make a difference. Once the organizations were formed, it often took several years to attract any funding and even longer to attract sustainable funding. While APAA was founded in 1993 and began operating shortly thereafter, it was not incorporated until 1994, and it did not attract funding for another several years. Despite its struggles, it still fulfilled its mission and provided valuable services to its clientele. Over the years, it has attracted support from a diverse group of funders, including municipal and provincial governments, businesses, research organizations, and foundations. The group that eventually formed ACCHO, the HIV Endemic Task Force, began meeting in 1998. The Ontario HIV Epidemiologic Monitoring Unit prepared a pivotal situational report about

HIV in Ontario's ACB communities. Following the report's release, the HIV Endemic Task Force conducted community consultations and held a forum to outline the development of a strategy to address HIV/AIDS within Ontario's ACB communities. The first strategy was completed in 2003 and launched in April 2005. ACCHO was created out of the need for an organization that would be responsible for the strategy and ensure its implementation; and it was fully funded from its inception. Years of work went into laying the foundation for ACCHO before the network was formed or funded. As an ACCHO member comments:

> We had individual consultations with organizations in Toronto to learn what their issues were, their challenges and successes, and how they worked with ACB people. We also did a provincial survey to mobilize, identify issues, and inform the strategy. We talked to people on the ground. We talked to the community and people living with HIV.

Likewise, much of the foundational work for WHIWH was completed between 1987 and 1989, and the organization did not receive funding until 1989. Since then, it has been fully funded as a community health centre, primarily by the Ontario Ministry of Health and Long-Term Care. Finally, the Black AIDS Project, which later became Black CAP, started meeting in the late 1980s. The group met for some time before Black CAP received funding in 1989. By 1991, Black CAP had secured funding from federal, provincial, and municipal governments that allowed it to hire more staff members; it became incorporated in March of that year. The work completed by the Black AIDS Project was essential for demonstrating need and the feasibility of the group's mandate.

By achieving goals in the absence of funding, each organization demonstrated another important responsibility of leadership: building and sustaining commitment. In so doing, the organizations gained credibility. The influence gained from this credibility helped them to secure funding and support from key players in the HIV and health sectors. As a result, they have gained continuity. Within the current fiscal climate, sustainability remains an ongoing challenge.

Using Research as a Tool

All four organizations have been involved in research out of a need for more information to better serve ACB communities. Aside from a study in the early 1990s for which Black CAP helped to recruit 358 people from the English-speaking Caribbean, and some work Black CAP had done with the Interagency Coalition on AIDS and Development, there was little research activity focused on ACB communities. Researchers did not have an appetite for or interest in conducting research with ACB people. Furthermore, since the City of Toronto had stopped collecting and reporting race-based statistics, there was little information to corroborate the need that Black CAP, WHIWH, and APAA were addressing. Without data, these organizations were unable to attract the level of support they needed. The situational report from the Ontario HIV Epidemiologic Monitoring Unit changed the tide. After that report, ACB people were recognized as a priority population for HIV prevention and care, and it became much easier for ACB organizations to access resources and funding. Citing the importance of demographic data, a Black CAP staff member observed that "you need to be counted to count." In addition, an ACCHO member noted that "Dr. Robert Remis produced the first status report that justified investment into strategies related to responding to HIV in ACB communities. Research is paramount. Anecdotal evidence is not enough for funders or the general public."

Research has also been used as a tool to organize the response to HIV in ACB communities in Ontario and worldwide. Since ACCHO's formation, research activities focused on HIV in ACB communities have become consolidated and knowledge generation has become streamlined. Black CAP, APAA, and WHIWH's involvement in research is now largely connected to the strategy for addressing HIV in Ontario's ACB communities and research priorities ACCHO has identified, in tandem with ACB people living with HIV, researchers, and other stakeholders. Some of the major research projects related to the strategy and research priorities are:

- The Black, African, and Caribbean Canadian Health (BLACCH) Study, a research project that used semi-structured interviews and a survey to gather information about general health, social determinants of health, health behaviours, HIV/AIDS, and health service use among ACB people in London, Ontario;
- The Stigma Study that used focus groups and semi-structured interviews to explore social, cultural, and structural dimensions of HIV stigma affecting ACB communities in Toronto;
- The MaBwana Black Men's Study, which explored HIV vulnerability among ACB gay and bisexual men in Toronto using one-on-one interviews and a survey;
- The East African Health Study in Toronto (EAST Study) that consisted of a survey about health-related beliefs, behaviours, knowledge, and attitudes among the five largest East African communities in Toronto (Ethiopians, Somalis, Kenyans, Tanzanians, and Ugandans);

- iSpeak, a study conducted in London, Ottawa, and Toronto that used focus groups and interviews to understand HIV-related needs, challenges, and priorities of heterosexual ACB men;
- weSpeak, a research program that built on iSpeak by bringing together researchers, service providers, policymakers, and community members in Toronto, London, Windsor, and Ottawa to enhance heterosexual ACB men's appreciation for the conditions that help HIV to spread, strengthen their commitment to HIV prevention, and strengthen community networks working to end HIV within ACB communities;
- The Promoting & Owning Empowerment & Resilience among African, Caribbean & Black Youth in Windsor project, which used surveys to identify factors that contribute to HIV infection and other sexual health outcomes among ACB youth and reduce their vulnerability to HIV and other sexually transmitted infections (STIs);
- The Co-infections Studies that used survey to look at HIV, STIs, and sexual practices among HIV-positive and HIV-negative ACB men and women in Toronto;
- The MSAFIRI Study, which consisted of questionnaires followed by in-depth interviews with ACB people in Ontario who became infected with HIV in Canada to provide rich descriptions of their perceptions of, and experiences with, HIV acquisition, diagnosis, disclosure, and sexual relationships subsequent to their arrival in Canada; and
- The A/C Track Study, which is a partnership between Toronto Public Health, Ottawa Public Health, and the Public Health Agency of Canada to collect information about HIV prevalence, behaviours associated with HIV vulnerability, HIV-related knowledge, community and structural factors (including discrimination), health care access, and health service utilization.

Each of these projects fills knowledge gaps and is of strategic importance to ACCHO, its members, ACB communities, and the HIV sector as a whole. Furthermore, research was the catalyst that led to the formation of the African Black Diaspora Global Network (ABDGN), an international collaboration to end the HIV epidemic in ACB communities worldwide. The group includes members from Canada, the United States, France, Jamaica, the United Kingdom, and Australia. ACCHO was a key player in forming the ABDGN, and WHIWH provides office space and resources to the group.

These organizations have also used research to support their requests for funding and to tailor their work – programs, services, strategies, etc. – to better meet clients' needs. Black CAP, for instance, has used research to support funding applications by demonstrating a need for its service offerings. Its research has also been used to demonstrate the effectiveness of its programs, like the "Many Men, Many Voices" HIV prevention intervention for ACB gay men. WHIWH's founders used research to demonstrate the need for the centre's existence, and its staff continues to use research to obtain funding from the City of Toronto for HIV prevention programs. WHIWH engages in research to inform its strategic plan, programs, and services; promote research capacity for its stakeholders; and build and promote mechanisms for knowledge translation and exchange. APAA started to become involved in research after realizing that researchers were not addressing the problems its clients faced. For instance, APAA serves linguistically diverse communities, but language issues were not being addressed in research or service delivery. To date, APAA's research projects have generated new knowledge about using immigrants/refugees living with HIV as knowledge transfer and exchange ambassadors; health and social service providers' knowledge and attitudes towards immigrants/refugees and non-status people living with HIV/AIDS; and barriers to accessing mental health services for immigrants/refugees and non-status people living with HIV/AIDS. In ACCHO's case, as remarked by one of its members, research provided the information it needed to secure funding to form and sustain the network: "Research is important and critical to ACCHO's work. The government rarely looks at anything not accompanied by a research component. Epi [epidemiological] data is very important."

The organizations have successfully convinced policymakers in Ontario to dedicate funds and resources to researching HIV in ACB communities. This has ignited researchers' interest in working with ACB communities and has created a feedback loop in which funds attract researchers and research, which in turn attract more funds. Relationships with researchers have not, however, always yielded the level of engagement the organizations expected. Consequently, Black CAP, APAA, and WHIWH have become more critical of the researchers with whom they work. As an ACCHO member observed:

> researchers tend to be very engaged in data collection but less engaged in knowledge translation. Many times, the objective is to research the community, not use knowledge to improve programming. There are issues on both sides, and there's room for improvement on both sides; both sides need to reach out.

The organizations are also working collectively to build, among ACB people who are meaningfully involved with them, the capacity to conduct research. For instance, through their advocacy, they have created positions to attract senior and junior scientists at the Ontario HIV Treatment Network. These scientists are responsible for conducting HIV research with ACB communities, creating training opportunities for aspiring ACB researchers, attracting funds for ACB-focused HIV public health surveillance projects, helping create an ACB research network, and advocating for additional funding for ACB research. Since funders do not always prioritize ACB research, there are structural barriers to realizing these initiatives.

Research involvement has also been used as a tool for capacity building. Through ACCHO, the organizations have collectively aimed to build and retain the capacity to engage in health research with ACB communities in Ontario, not just HIV research. Furthermore, the organizations specifically support research that has the potential to impact practice and policy in the short term, or in other words, research results that can be implemented. The growing involvement in research over time has resulted in funding success and the development of programs that better respond to the needs and realities of ACB Canadians. Finally, through research, these organizations have advocated for greater meaningful involvement of people living with HIV in the provincial response to the epidemic. This principle has led to the emphasis on community-based research, which facilitates capacity building around the generation and use of evidence in community settings. Emphasizing the importance of generating purposive research, an ACCHO member spoke to the wider benefit of research:

> It [research] benefits the entire province – Black CAP, APAA and all other ASOs [AIDS service organizations] that have strategy workers. Evidence-based knowledge allows us to craft programming specific for the ACB community. We are able to use research to look at programmatic things and address various areas of the HIV sector when it comes to the ACB community.

Research provides information that is useful for decision making, an important responsibility of leadership. Each organization has used research to determine priorities; hence, evidence has influenced planning and strategic decisions. Additionally, the organizations use research to demonstrate need and successfully influence funding decisions. By understanding and leveraging the power of research, these organizations have strategically built an evidence base to support and improve decision making as it pertains to the response to HIV in ACB communities.

Advocate and Engage with Policymakers

The four organizations advocate on the behalf of ACB communities and use shared strategies to engage with policymakers on common issues. They are all committed to attracting funds and resources to support HIV-related services for ACB communities. To accomplish this, they strategize and build alliances in order to raise issues collectively as a single, united voice. For example, APAA and Black CAP often represent each other's interests, because they coordinate efforts so that at least one organization is represented on each of the committees and working groups addressing HIV in Ontario. As expressed by a Black CAP staffer:

> We try to be at the tables we need to be at – on boards of the OHTN [Ontario HIV Treatment Network], OAN [Ontario AIDS Network], etc. We make sure that issues of racialized communities, Black or other, are addressed, and we make sure those organizations respond to issues of racialized communities. We are sometimes vocal, and sometimes we have been silenced. We recognize that to change issues and policies, we need to be sitting on those boards, even if we are ignored the first few times.

WHIWH became involved in HIV work when it realized that HIV disproportionately impacted ACB women. WHIWH's early work in the HIV sector included organizing the first forum on HIV and pregnancy in the early 2000s and bringing together more than one hundred stakeholders, including policymakers, to raise awareness about the issue. The organization has also used its involvement in research to generate data that can be used for advocacy when meeting with politicians, such as cabinet ministers. Policymakers have always been involved with ACCHO, but ACCHO also forms alliances and strategic partnerships with other stakeholders, like researchers. These relationships are instrumental, because they provide ACCHO with information and other resources.

Some of the organizations have overtly addressed political and social issues affecting ACB communities. For instance, Black CAP chooses to have "Black" in its name in order to recognize race and the impact of racism on Black people. As a Black CAP staff member noted: "Us existing is a political act." In a society where many people believe they live in a post-racial world, this is indeed a political and controversial act. Also, by explicitly and publicly speaking about taboo issues that are structural determinants of health, such as anti-Black racism, sexism, homophobia, transphobia, and biphobia, the organization is engaging in inherently political conversations. WHIWH has been overtly engaged in political activities since its founding. The organization's political activities have included campaigns focused on female genital mutilation, raising the national minimum wage, and educating women about their voting rights. The organization is nationally and internationally recognized for its political activism.

The organizations have also engaged in subtle forms of activism when engaging policymakers. Similarly to Black CAP, APAA proudly makes known its focus on Africans, and it usually works closely with Black CAP to show solidarity among ACB AIDS service organizations. For instance, as a united group, the organizations have approached funders to raise concerns about the lack of funding streams specific to ACB communities affected by HIV/AIDS.

As a result of the organizations' work over the years, the issues they address, and the strategies they have used, all of them are recognized by political leaders and policymakers. Many other ACB community organizations have not achieved such high levels of recognition. For example, the organizations have close relationships with the AIDS Bureau (part of the Ontario Ministry of Health and Long-Term Care) and the Public Health Agency of Canada, which have granted them a direct line to policymakers. The organizations' leaders have also met with politicians, like ministers of health and members of Parliament, to have conversations about issues related to HIV in ACB communities. On 7 and 17 February 2015, the Canadian HIV/AIDS Black, African and Caribbean Network – represented by Black CAP, ACCHO, and WHIWH – attended meetings at the Ontario legislature to mark African, Caribbean and Black Canadian HIV/AIDS Awareness Day (7 February) with the minister of health and other legislators. WHIWH has also received national recognition for its campaign against female genital mutilation. As a WHIWH member noted: "We supported women that were highly impacted by FGM [female genital mutilation] to take leadership and the front stage – they presented in Parliament in Ottawa to support criminalization of FGM."

The organizations face markedly different constraints on their political activities. As charitable organizations, Black CAP and APAA are barred from engaging in overtly political activities. Given that ACCHO is entirely funded by the provincial government to coordinate efforts at the provincial level, its funding prohibits it from engaging in any political activities. As a community health centre, WHIWH is far less politically constrained than the other organizations. Its funding allows for participation in community activities that create environmental and social conditions that promote women's health and wellness. As such, WHIWH is able to champion causes the others cannot.

Advocacy and meaningful engagement require courage and effective communication, two essential characteristics of leadership. Black CAP,

ACCHO, WHIWH, and APAA demonstrate courage when they name and directly challenge anti-Black racism, sexism, homophobia, transphobia, and biphobia in a society that shies away from fully acknowledging or tackling these issues. It takes courage to bring to the fore what makes people uncomfortable. Similarly, convincing policymakers to invest in race-based initiatives when there is a belief in post-racialism requires effective communication skills, which are foundational to persuasion and influence.

Resourcefulness in the Face of Challenges

Space, high staff turnover, lack of resources, HIV stigma, and discrimination were all common challenges for the organizations. Difficulty finding office space was a common theme, regardless of whether the underlying issue was unaffordable rents or HIV stigma and anti-Black racism. Additionally, the organizations expressed concern that staff retention was a problem, because a lack of resources means lower salaries and less attractive benefits. Many of the people who work in the sector are there, however, because of their passion for the work and commitment to community. HIV stigma and racial discrimination from the broader community also mean that ACB organizations lack the resources they require and do not receive the same levels of per-client support as mainstream organizations. Commenting on this difficult issue, a Black CAP member contended:

> Some funders say they will not fund "ethno-racial" organizations, just mainstream [White] organizations. Many funders are moving toward funding only mainstream organizations. The specificity and value of the work of ethno-racial organizations is diminished. We are up against mainstream organizations that we cannot win against.

As well, HIV stigma and discrimination from ACB communities create challenges in reaching out to ACB people and meeting their needs. It was remarked that "it is related to fear and denial about HIV. It's a challenge to engage people in conversations about HIV, sex, LGBT issues, risk, etc. There are people who will never have a conversation with us about HIV."

The most striking difference between the organizations is access to resources. Unlike APAA and Black CAP, ACCHO does not have to raise money through fundraising or grants; it is wholly funded by the Ontario Ministry of Health and Long-Term Care through the AIDS Bureau. On the other hand, unlike WHIWH, APAA, and Black CAP, ACCHO cannot raise funds. Both Black CAP and APAA have to compete with other organizations for funding, but they have more control over their budgets than ACCHO. There is also a difference in how resources are distributed between the three organizations, related to the size of their target populations and the points in their histories at which they started to receive funding (e.g., Black CAP started to receive funding before APAA). To illustrate this point, it is important to note that APAA's challenge with finding office space concerns affordability, but for Black CAP the main issues are HIV stigma and racial discrimination. Due to the close, collaborative relationship between the executives in both organizations, in recognition of this discrepancy, both organizations pool resources when possible to deliver programs and services.

Despite these challenges, however, the organizations continue to exist and achieve their goals. They have used research to access resources, and by participating in community-based research, they are able to offset costs by charging administrative fees when they are involved in research projects. Additionally, they have partnered with better-funded organizations to attract needed resources – like working with the Ontario HIV Treatment Network to attract researchers and funding. This has made HIV in ACB communities a "sexy" topic. Similarly, ACCHO works with strategy workers who are hired by AIDS service organizations and community health centres to implement the ACB strategy that it oversees. These strategy workers are used to reach ACB people and liaise between ACB communities and the broader HIV sector. Most importantly, though, each organization draws on the strength of its clients and the ACB community when it faces obstacles. As a Black CAP member mentions, this collaborative approach makes community stakeholders both creative and resilient:

> We overcome these challenges with tenacity, stubbornness and having confidence in our models and ways of working. We have our eyes on the prize. It can be very deflating working in a Black ASO [AIDS service organization] when it comes to funding and keeping our doors open, but we remember that we are here for our clients. There's nothing more energizing than witnessing growth in clients' lives – big and small. It makes us resilient against these systems and structures. It energizes and motivates us. Our motto is: "all Black people's lives are important." We are a strong community, and we believe in the strength of our community. What's out there, racism and homophobia, don't stand a chance against what we experience here.

In each case, the organizations have demonstrated resiliency, an important leadership characteristic. By using available resources creatively, they are able to meet the needs of ACB communities in the face of mounting challenges. Despite facing setbacks and adversity, these organizations continue to fulfil their missions to serve ACB communities. Their staff and volunteers unite to support each other and keep moving forward.

Conclusion: Impacts of ACB HIV/AIDS Leadership

The founders, leaders, and staff of APAA, Black CAP, WHIWH, and ACCHO stood up and led when no one else was leading and when HIV was still highly stigmatized. Rather than avoid the problem and view it as insurmountable, they formed organizations. Through these organizations, they mounted a collective response, and their efforts changed Ontario's response to HIV in ACB communities. APAA, Black CAP, WHIWH, and ACCHO created the province's first strategy for addressing HIV in ACB communities (HIV Endemic Task Force, 2003) and have been involved in all subsequent updates to that strategy (ACCHO, 2013). They have also set the agenda that should guide all research involving ACB people in Ontario (Ontario HIV Treatment Network, 2015; Patten, 2014) and have been involved in, or have inspired, many Canadian firsts. These include: the first social marketing campaign about HIV in ACB communities (Shimeles et al., 2012), the first study of Black men who have sex with men (George et al., 2012; Husbands et al., 2010), the first study about HIV stigma in Ontario's ACB communities (Gardezi et al., 2008; Lawson et al., 2006), the first socio-behavioural study about HIV in ACB communities (Gray, Calzavara, Tharao, & Johns, 2008), and the first study exploring HIV in ACB communities in London, Ontario (Baidoobonso et al., 2012; Baidoobonso, Bauer, Speechley, Lawson, & BLACCH Study Team, 2013).

Black CAP, APAA, ACCHO, and WHIWH have also been successful in effecting lasting policy changes. As a direct result of their work, the government of Ontario recognizes ACB communities as a priority population for HIV prevention and services (McGee, 2015). Beyond HIV, these organizations used their leadership to impact health care delivery in Ontario for ACB people in particular and the citizenry more generally. Drawing on their experience of successfully attracting funds and raising awareness about social and health issues facing ACB communities, they played an important role in creating TAIBU Community Health Centre. This was the first community health centre entirely dedicated to the health needs of ACB people (http://www.taibuchc.com/index.php?option=com_content&view=featured&Itemid=435&lang=en).

Despite the advances in research, advocacy, and service delivery, the full potential of this leadership has not been realized. Much of the research has not been translated into new programs or services for ACB people, and organizations within the HIV sector and funders are taking actions to address this. The gap between research and practice is not unique to ACB communities and ACB organizations, however. This gap is common in all areas of health research and in all communities, because it takes approximately seventeen years to translate scientific research into public health action (Brownson, Kreuter, Arrington, & True, 2006). Given that there was virtually no information about HIV in ACB communities in Ontario for many years, the effect of this lag is even more pronounced, especially when other priority populations are considered.

In closing, it is evident that ACB organizations have been leaders in Ontario's response to HIV/AIDS in ACB communities. They and the individuals affiliated with them were aware of when HIV started to enter the community and were poised to respond, even if that response had no financial resources to support it and was built on the human resources provided by volunteers. At its core, the leadership demonstrated by their response to HIV was based on raw passion, tenacity, persistence, and the ingenuity of ACB communities.

Acknowledgments

This chapter could not have been written without the assistance of Wangari Tharao, Trevor Grey, Dionne A. Falconer, Fanta Ongoiba, Valérie Pierre-Pierre, and Shannon Ryan, who freely shared their stories and their time. Their openness, trust, and honesty were greatly appreciated. Thanks also to Winston Husbands, who helped to identify potential interviewees. Finally, many thanks to Robert Remis and the staff and volunteers at Africans in Partnership Against AIDS, the Black Coalition for AIDS Prevention, Women's Health in Women's Hands Community Health Centre, the African and Caribbean Council on HIV/AIDS in Ontario, and the other AIDS service organizations within Ontario for their dedication to the province's response to HIV/AIDS in African, Caribbean, and Black communities.

NOTES

1 Figures for the ACB population might be greater than what is reported here, as only those who chose to report that they were born in a HIV-endemic country are included in this statistic, and race/ethnicity was only reported for about 60 per cent of all HIV cases identified in Ontario (HIV Endemic Task Force, 2003; Remis & Liu, 2006).

2 A fifth organization, African Community Health Services, was also a leader in this area, but this organization closed its doors circa 2008. Its clients and staff joined APAA and Black CAP.

3 As a descriptive method, qualitative content analysis is usually inappropriate for developing a full understanding of the concept being studied. Therefore, it relies on the quality of the underlying data, and steps must be taken to ensure the data's validity. Purposive sampling, asking open-ended questions, accurate recording of the interviews, member checking, and data-driven coding enhanced the data's authenticity (Neergaard et al., 2009). The credibility of the data was further enhanced by the focus on capturing participants' first-hand accounts of their experiences within the HIV/AIDS sector and with each organization (Neergaard et al., 2009).

REFERENCES

African and Caribbean Council on HIV/AIDS in Ontario. (2013). *Ontario HIV/AIDS strategy for African, Caribbean and black communities, 2013–2018.* Retrieved from http://www.accho.ca/Portals/3/documents/resources/ACB_Strategy_Web_Oct2013_En.pdf

Baidoobonso, S., Bauer, G.R., Speechley, K.N., Lawson, E., & BLACCH Study Team. (2013). HIV risk perception and distribution of HIV risk among African, Caribbean and other black people in a Canadian city: Mixed methods results from the BLACCH study. *BMC Public Health, 13*(1), 184. https://doi.org/10.1186/1471-2458-13-184

Baidoobonso, S., Mokanan, H., Meidinger, L., Pugh, D., Bauer, G., Nleya-Ncube, M., ... BLACCH Study Team. (2012). *Final report from the Black, African and Caribbean Canadian Health (BLACCH) Study.* London, ON: University of Western Ontario. Retrieved from http://works.bepress.com/shamara_baidoobonso/

Brownson, R.C., Kreuter, M.W., Arrington, B.A., & True, W.R. (2006). Translating scientific discoveries into public health action: How can schools of public health move us forward? *Public Health Reports, 121*(1), 97–103. https://doi.org/10.1177/003335490612100118

Farmer, T., Robinson, K., Elliott, S.J., & Eyles, J. (2006). Developing and implementing a triangulation protocol for qualitative health research. *Qualitative Health Research, 16*(3), 377–94. https://doi.org/10.1177/1049732305285708

Gardezi, F., Calzavara, L., Husbands, W., Tharao, W., Lawson, E., Myers, T., ... Adebajo, S. (2008). Experiences of and responses to HIV among African and Caribbean communities in Toronto, Canada. *AIDS Care, 20*(6), 718–25. https://doi.org/10.1080/09540120701693966

George, C., Adam, B., Read, S.E., Husbands, W., Remis, R.S., Makoroka, L., & Rourke, S. (2012). The MaBwana black men's study: Community and belonging in the lives of African, Caribbean and other black gay men in Toronto. *Culture, Health & Sexuality, 14,* 549–62. https://doi.org/10.1080/13691058.2012.674158

Gray, K., Calzavara, L., Tharao, W., & Johns, A. (2008). *The East African Health Study (EAST): Results from a survey of HIV and health-related behaviour, beliefs, attitudes and knowledge.* Toronto: HIV Social, Behavioural and Epidemiological Studies Unit, University of Toronto.

HIV Endemic Task Force. (2003). *Strategy to address issues related to HIV faced by people in Ontario from countries where HIV is endemic.* Toronto: ACCHO. Retrieved from http://www.accho.ca/index.aspx?page=resources

Hsieh, H.-F., & Shannon, S.E. (2005). Three approaches to qualitative content analysis. *Qualitative Health Research, 15*(9), 1277–88. https://doi.org/10.1177/1049732305276687

Husbands, W., Makoroka, L., George, C., Adam, B., Remis, R.S., Rourke, S., & Beyene, J. (2010). *MaBwana: Health, community and vulnerability to HIV among African, Caribbean and black gay and bisexual men in Toronto.* Toronto: CCHO and AIDS Committee of Toronto.

James, L. (2006). *HIV prevention guidelines and manual: A tool for service providers serving African and African Caribbean communities in Canada.* Retrieved from https://www.whiwh.com/sites/default/files/hiv_manual-part_1_ENGLISH.pdf

Lawson, E., Gardezi, F., Calzavara, L., Husbands, W., Myers, T., Tharao, W.E., ... & Department. of Public Health Sciences HIV Social Behavioural and Epidemiological Studies Unit. (2006). *HIV/AIDS stigma, denial, fear and discrimination: Experiences and responses of people from African and Caribbean communities in Toronto.* AACHO and HIV Social Behavioural and Epidemiological Studies Unit, Department of Public Health Sciences, Faculty of Medicine, University of Toronto. Retrieved from http://hdl.handle.net/1807/10304

Leech, N.L., & Onwuegbuzie, A.J. (2007). An array of qualitative data analysis tools: A call for data analysis triangulation. *School Psychology Quarterly, 22*(4), 557–84. https://doi.org/10.1037/1045-3830.22.4.557

Liu, J., & Remis, R.S. (2007). *Race/ethnicity among persons with HIV/AIDS in Ontario, 1981–2004.* Toronto: Ontario HIV Epidemiologic Monitoring Unit. Retrieved from http://www.ohemu.utoronto.ca/doc/Ethnicity_report_rev.pdf

McGee, F. (2015, March). *Proposed HIV/AIDS strategy to 2020: Changing the course of the HIV prevention, engagement and care cascade.* Paper presented at Ontario HIV Treatment Network staff meeting. Toronto.

Milan, A., & Tran, K. (2004). Blacks in Canada: A long history. *Canadian Social Trends, 72*(2), 2–7. Retrieved from https://www150.statcan.gc.ca/n1/en/catalogue/11-008-X20030046802

Neergaard, M.A., Olesen, F., Andersen, R.S., & Sondergaard, J. (2009). Qualitative description – The poor cousin of health research? *BMC Medical Research Methodology, 9*(1). https://doi.org/10.1186/1471-2288-9-52

Ontario HIV Treatment Network. (2015). *Priority populations.* Retrieved from http://www.ohtn.on.ca/otw-portfolio/priority-populations/

Patten, S. (2014). *Proceedings and evaluation report: 3rd Ontario African, Caribbean and Black Research Think Tank.* Toronto: ACCHO. Retrieved from http://www.accho.ca/Portals/3/documents/ACCHO_RTT3_Report_Final_Eng_Feb-27-2014.pdf

Patton, M.Q. (1999). Enhancing the quality and credibility of qualitative analysis. *Health Services Research, 34*(5, pt. 2), 1189–208.

Public Health Agency of Canada. (2009a). *Population-specific HIV/AIDS status report: People from countries where HIV is endemic: Black people of African and Caribbean descent living in Canada.* Ottawa: Surveillance and Risk Assessment Division, Centre for Infectious Disease Prevention and Control, Public Health Agency of Canada.

Public Health Agency of Canada. (2009b). *Summary: Estimates of HIV prevalence and incidence in Canada, 2008.* Retrieved from http://www.phac-aspc.gc.ca/aids-sida/publication/survreport/estimat08-eng.php

Public Health Agency of Canada. (2012, 29 November). *Summary: Estimates of HIV prevalence and incidence in Canada, 2011.* Retrieved from http://publications.gc.ca/collections/collection_2012/aspc-phac/HP37-16-2011-eng.pdf

Quorum Communications Inc. (2006). *HIV community plan: Southwestern Ontario.* London, ON: AIDS Committee of London.

Remis, R.S., & Liu, J. (2006, June). *Race/ethnicity among persons infected with HIV in Ontario.* Presented at the Provincial Community Planning Meeting, AIDS Bureau, Toronto. Retrieved from http://www.ohemu.utoronto.ca/doc/ethnicity2.pdf

Remis, R.S., & Liu, J. (2008, November). *Epidemiology of HIV infection in Ontario: Update to 2008.* Presented at the AIDS and Drug Prevention Community Investment Programs, Toronto Public Health, Toronto. Retrieved from http://www.ohemu.utoronto.ca/doc/HIV%20epi%20Ontario%202007_Nov212008.pdf

Remis, R.S., & Liu, J. (2013). *HIV/AIDS in Ontario: Preliminary report, 2011.* Toronto: Ontario HIV Epidemiologic Monitoring Unit. Retrieved from http://www.ohemu.utoronto.ca/doc/PHERO2011_report_preliminary.pdf

Remis, R.S., & Merid, M.F. (2004). *The HIV/AIDS epidemic among persons from HIV-endemic countries in Ontario: Update to December 2002.* Toronto: Ontario Ministry of Health and Long-Term Care.

Remis, R.S., Swantee, C., & Liu, J. (2012). *Report on HIV/AIDS in Ontario, 2009.* Toronto: Ontario HIV Epidemiologic Monitoring Unit. Retrieved from http://www.ohemu.utoronto.ca/doc/PHERO2009_report_final.pdf

Remis, R.S., Swantee, C., Schiedel, L., & Liu, J. (2008). *Report on HIV/AIDS in Ontario, 2006.* Toronto: Ontario HIV Epidemiologic Monitoring Unit. Retrieved from http://www.ohemu.utoronto.ca/doc/PHERO2006_report_final.pdf

Sandelowski, M. (2000). Whatever happened to qualitative description? *Research in Nursing and Health, 23*(4), 334–40. https://doi.org/10.1002/1098-240X(200008)23:4<334::AID-NUR9>3.0.CO;2-G

Shimeles, H., Husbands, W.C., George, C., Fenta, H., Afzal, A., Baidoobonso, S., & Mbulaheni, T. (2012). *Staying alive: Evaluation of the Keep It Alive! HIV awareness and prevention campaign for African, Caribbean and black communities in Ontario* (p. 44). Toronto: ACCHO. Retrieved from http://www.accho.ca/en/Links-Resources/Reports-and-Other-Materials

Williams, C.C., Newman, P.A., Sakamoto, I., & Massaquoi, N.A. (2009). HIV prevention risks for black women in Canada. *Social Science & Medicine, 68*(1), 12–20. https://doi.org/10.1016/j.socscimed.2008.09.043

Women's Health in Women's Hands. (2015). Mandate. Retrieved from http://www.whiwh.com/mandate

PART FOUR

The Politics of Black Ways of Life

11 Black Consciousness and the Heteronormative Sexual Politics of Black Leadership in Toronto: A Commentary

WESLEY CRICHLOW

No one colonizes innocently.

Aimé Césaire, *Discourse on Colonialism*

There is a distinct paucity of material, scholarly or otherwise, on Black gays and leadership within the Canadian landscape. Using critical autobiography to theorize Black leadership, I write from my own experience of leadership in Black consciousness movements and sexual politics. My personal vantage point serves as a point of departure for theorizing, concretizing, and developing Black Canadian leadership and Black critical LGBTQ theory. I also employ critical autoethnography to analyse my personal experiences in the specific context of organizing in the Black compulsory heteronormative culture that surrounds me.

Oral histories and self-reflexivity are imperative steps in advancing a methodology LGBTQ Black leadership praxis and Black leadership scholarship. I will draw on my past involvement with Zami,[1] the Biko-Rodney-Malcolm Coalition[2] (BRMC), and the Black Action Defense Committee (BADC) to illustrate my experience with the development of Black leadership. While Blackness is one of the key starting points for my social justice activism and leadership, Blackness by itself is not enough (Crichlow, 2003, p. 73). Key thinkers and activists drawing attention to the intersections of race, gender, sexuality, and class helped me to overcome my fear of rejection by the Black Nationalist movement and the Black community, to "come out" and engage in activist leadership (Crichlow, 2003, p. 73).

I am not interested in speaking about stories of pain, humiliation, alienation, suffering, or violence or the morbid pleasures their consumption might engender for some, nor do I want others to steal my pain and suffering. I do not want to contribute to the global shortage of love for

Black lives and Black people's bodies – mine included. I do want to be honest and acknowledge that there was and still is some exclusion, violence, and alienation experienced by Black LGBTQ persons even as they work to contribute to Black activist movements. Black heteronormative leadership, furthermore, does not make space for LGBTQ persons to see ourselves as leaders or contribute to thinking about Black leadership. We simply "get on with it" and do the work that needs to be done within Black community organizations. I write about Black leadership from a Black gay man's perspective because of a desire to serve the Black community and because I believe those who live in it understand its problems (Crichlow, 2003, p. 77). Given the lacuna of Black scholarship on Black community activism and leadership in Canada, my aim in this chapter is to make a theoretical contribution to activist community-university engagement and scholarship.

In this essay I focus on leadership models developed through Black consciousness, Black intersections with sexual politics and social activism within the Canadian/Toronto context, what some would call non-formal and biased learning, precisely because they are distanced from formal or state-based corporate and militarized schooling (Bingman, 1996; Finger, 1989; Holst, 2002, 2004). Spence (2012) reminds us that "while scholars and activists alike increasingly use the concept of neo-liberalism to explain rising levels of racial inequality they ... miss the way this dynamic is reproduced within, and not simply *on*, Black communities" (p. 140). It is this ideological reproduction within Black activist communities and leadership that I want to bring to the forefront even as I highlight the joys of finding community and mentorship from leaders within the BRMC, Zami, and the Black Action Defense Committee. Those connections developed despite the limitations imposed by the performance of Black heteronormativity on the formation of community.

I will also trace how race, class, gender, and sexual orientation have been explicitly incorporated into my activism as a Black gay man in heterocentric Black spaces without my having had to state "I am gay." These lines of reflection converge at the following points of enquiry: Can there be a praxis of and space for Black Canadian leadership towards liberation and resistance in Canadian society? What do we mean by Black leadership? Leadership, in my experience, results from the collective commitment of activists to social, sexual, and political wholeness. It means to subvert and displace pain in the psychology of Black people.

I stress the social justice of wholeness in and of leadership because I hope to ignite and inspire those who have thought about becoming more involved in social, cultural, or legal justice struggles at individual, organizational, communal, or policy levels. Those struggles collectively aim to eradicate structural and systemic biases, transform policies, and bring about social and legal change. Black leadership is also about service, volunteer work, and political engagement. An enquiry into Black leadership should accordingly encompass a multistranded, multitiered, triangulated set of approaches that addresses social justice intersections of community in terms of race, gender, class, sexuality, nationality, immigrant status, and so on. Black leadership in general has to make room to fulfil a *deep yearning for wholeness in a persistently alienating and anti-Black society.*

The Role of Autoethnography and Autobiography towards a Method of Leadership Praxis

Activism is the rent I pay for living on the planet.

Alice Walker in P. Parmar's film *Beauty in Truth*

Because I do not want to position myself as the single, authoritative, engendering voice of Black LGBTQ activism in the 1980s and 1990s, or of Black consciousness and its intersections with sexual politics, I take a critical autoethnographic approach towards the practice of remembering, narrativizing, and analysing (Crichlow, 2003, p. 44) my early days of activism and leadership. Autoethnography is "a text in which people undertake to describe themselves in ways that engage her presentations others have made of them" (Pratt, 1994, p. 28). It is an approach to research and writing that seeks to describe and systematically analyse ("graphy") personal experience ("auto") in order to understand cultural experience ("ethno") (Ellis, Adams, & Bochner, 2010).

Autoethnograpy is used as a self-referential tool to interpret previous experiences in order to understand socio-cultural positioning. This dialogic autoethnograpy, a critically responsive pedagogy, provides practical knowledge for living life dynamically and creatively (Visano, 2006). A critical autoethnography or self-study displays multiple layers of consciousness, connecting the personal to the political. Consistent with a methodology of uncovering organized ways of knowing or configuring race, sexuality, and self-identity "in terms of connectedness/embeddedness," this exercise asks us to make public our stories in an attempt to remind us of the impact of "being and belonging," which too many people, for far too long, have tried to erase (Visano, 2006, p. 244). Alexander (2012) writes that autoethnography is "a critical methodology or approach to doing critical cultural examinations that might shape the mode of investigating experience but not establish a standard of experience" (p. 141). While autoethnography has not lacked controversy as a method of research, its value as a corrective seems clear. Autoethnography can be seen as a powerful and radical method to disrupt normative systems of knowledge production and to investigate historically marginalized experiences (e.g., Boylorn & Orbe, 2014).

Autoethnography also serves as a political and intellectual move to call out taken-for-granted ideas and to diversify voices in the academy (e.g., Adams & Holman Jones, 2008; Calafell, 2012). The autobiographical approach is important to me because it authenticates and locates one's "organic" position. Location of the subject is crucial for any discussion of identity politics and crucial within the context of Black consciousness politics.

Locating myself within a particular set of experiences and social histories works to identify the sources outside "mainstream" academic literature that inform my theoretical framework. In representing myself and relating to similarly circumstanced others, interwoven fragments of biography facilitate an interrogation of dominant interpellations that have been integrated with and implicated in our daily lives. I am convinced that the autobiographical/autoethnographical is a self-reflective method of knowledge making and understanding of the everyday world that is compelling and valid. The autobiographic examination of my role as an intellectual and activist is multilayered by race, sexuality, gender, and class. I pay attention to the simultaneous functioning of what Yep (2010) would call my multiple identities and positionings that mirror macrostructural forces. The autobiographical/autoethnographical contributes to the struggle for freedom, which must begin with liberating the self. Struggles in the eighties and nineties were about freedom, and I could not help but get involved in the struggles against Black homoppression, white supremacy, colonization, and state-sanctioned police violence – now framed as "Black lives matter." That these struggles excluded LGBTQ bodies and had troubled gender relations was part of my early education in the field, all of which signified liberation from the internalized oppression of homoppression.

Early Influences and the Role of Black Canadian Feminism

Academic writers have an obligation to account for the framework they are using (Crichlow, 2003, p. 42). Autoethnography, being an elaboration of the forces and sources that constitute us, requires acknowledging those who helped shape our being. To this end I want to recognize the men and women who helped give my life substance during the formative period of my activist becoming. There was the joy of finding community and mentorship from the likes of leaders such as Makeda Silvera, Dionne

Brand, Lillian Allen, Debbie Douglas, Doug Stewart, Sherona Hall, and Akua Benjamin and brothers such Charles Roach, Dudley Laws, and Dari Meade. Works by African American LGBTQ scholars and activists. Tyson (2001), and McGuire (2010) complicate not only how sexism was understood by these activists, but also the relationship various actors and organizations had to Black women and the sexual orientation of gender-nonconforming Black men.

Black women, in particular, played a critical role in the development of my Black consciousness and sexual politics. Brand, Silvera, Douglas, and Hall were some of the early Black feminist *organic intellectuals* whose work and scholarship challenged state and male ideologues of the time; they argued for an intersectional, feminist, Black consciousness. Foregrounding the inequality between men and women, they also underscored the role of white women and racism in power relations. Black feminist work crucially analyses the intersections of sexuality, gender, race, and class. For example, Silvera's *Silenced: Talks with Working Class West Indian Women about Their Lives and Struggles as Domestic Workers in Canada* (1989) develops an understanding of the interconnectedness of racialized feminized domestic labour, political economy, family, and immigration. Silvera attends to the historically racialized pauperization and feminization of domestic work and the economic and political burdens borne by Black female domestic workers who migrated from the Caribbean to Canada. Silvera's analysis contributes to an understanding of the economic disadvantage experienced by Black families that places them outside access to wealth, due to colonization and white supremacy. As demonstrated by a number of authors in this collection, such as Gooden, Henry, hampton and Rochat, and Lawson, Black women have historically made a vast range of contributions to the cultural, economic, social, and political contributions of Black Canada.

Feminist Black consciousness in Canada finds an early inspiration in the actions of Halifax-born Viola Davis Desmond. In 1946, in New Glasgow, Nova Scotia, she challenged the Roseland Theatre's racial segregation policy, which restricted ground-floor seating to white people. As described by Jobb (2009), after being forcibly removed from the theatre, she was arrested, charged, found guilty, and fined. She subsequently sued the theatre manager, but did not have the law on her side, as Canada's first piece of general human rights legislation was not introduced until around 1969 (https://humanrights.novascotia.ca/content/about).[3] Viola Davis Desmond's revolutionary act of refusing to be put in her place, as she was tired of giving in to treatment as a second-class citizen, reflected what Black consciousness taught me: the revolution can sometimes be about ourselves and not necessarily a response to whiteness.

Black Consciousness Raising and Intersections with LGBTQ Activism

I became aware of the BRMC, BADC, and Zami upon entering university in the eighties. At that time of post-1960s and 1970s political ferment and growing reaction to Thatcherism and Reaganism, segments of the Black power (or militant Black) and anti-apartheid movements were active on campuses. They were joined by white LGBTQ activism and awareness of the national liberation struggles in Africa. There was a yearning for Black consciousness raising and politicization of the self. It found fruition not through the university curriculum but through the Black student associations that existed at almost every university and college in Toronto during the 1970s, 1980s, and 1990s. Through informal conversations within Black student unions/associations[4] at York University and the University of Toronto, I was introduced to the Zami and BRMC by Caribbean LGBTQ students, community elders, and fellow South African students and community activists. I embraced a Black consciousness that, as Biko (1978) describes it,

> seeks to show black people the value of their own standards and outlook. That urges black people to judge themselves according to these standards and not to be fooled by white society who [*sic*] have white-washed themselves and made white standards the yardstick by which even black people judge each other. (p. 30)

Black consciousness involves the substantive study of the conditions and quality of Black people's lives, which today continue to be marginalized and devalued by state violence, police killings, homicides, and socio-economic exclusion. It is an experience of daily vulnerability, where some lives matter more than others and are protected at all costs. The phrase and chant "Black Lives Matter" is one of outrage and a demand for equality, for the right to live free of criminal justice harassment and other forms of anti-Black racist assaults on the body. Black Lives Matter explains on their website: "When we say Black Lives Matter, we are broadening the conversation around state violence to include all of the ways in which Black people are intentionally left powerless at the hands of the state. We are talking about the ways in which Black lives are deprived of our basic human rights and dignity ... #Blacklivesmatter is working for a world where Black lives are no longer systematically and intentionally targeted for demise" (http://blacklivesmatter.com/about/). Black Lives Matter Toronto makes a unique contribution to the work started by Black Action Defense Committee, while making visible the intersections of Black activist work to include Black queer and trans folks, disabled folks, Black-undocumented folks, folks with records, women, and all Black lives along the gender spectrum.

Judith Butler, in an interview with George Yancy (Yancy & Butler, 2015), reframes the meaning of Black Lives Matter and state structural violence: "one reason the chant '#BlackLivesMatter' is so important is that it states the obvious but the obvious has not yet been historically realized. So it is a statement of outrage and a demand for equality, for the right to live free of constraint, neutralization and degradation of black lives, but also a police system that more and more easily, and often, takes away a black life in a flash all because some officer perceives them a threat" (p. 2). Blacklivesmatter has to some degree reframed the hegemonic traditional media gatekeeper's role, enabling Black click-activists (those who use social media platforms to organize and get their message out) to reach their audiences directly with their own message.

Alongside the meaning of Black life, so diminished by apartheid and racism in Toronto in the eighties and nineties, Black consciousness as an ideology compelled a self-criticism of my sexual and racial politics. In this regard, Black consciousness scholarship has the potential to make a healthy scholarly contribution to the debate on the relationship between Black radical social movements, Black consciousness, Black studies, and education more broadly. Zami and the BRMC were two groups of working-class organic intellectuals that aimed to fulfil their historic mission as revolutionaries. Gramsci (1971) wrote that "all men [*sic*] are intellectuals ... but not all men [*sic*] in society have the function of intellectuals or of qualified political intellectuals" (p. 16). BRMC's work was dedicated to fighting against white supremacy, capitalism, and racism. It forged ways to improve the living conditions of Blacks in Toronto specifically and Canada more generally. Organic intellectuals within Zami were deeply influenced by a Black consciousness critique of capitalism. The group made intelligible the functioning of racism and white supremacy as well as the new and emerging complexities of Black leadership, Black life, and Black intellectual freedom. I attended meetings organized by Zami and BRMC because they helped me develop a political point of departure regarding Black consciousness and sexual politics. Like in other activist groups, heteronormativity and patriarchal legacies were the flip side of a tradition of Black men fighting to secure a future for Black women and children. Furthermore, my own experience was marked by the violent silence around my sexual orientation and experience with heterosexism, homophobia, and the resulting exclusion and alienation felt within activist groups and the wider society. Black heterosexist exclusion and alienation is about the ways we Black LGBTQ persons are systematically made invisible within the Black community, and have silence forced upon Black queers and gender non-conforming persons.

It was within Zami, BADC, and the BRMC that I started speaking out against Black heterosexism and heteronormativity in Black social movements and the wider community. I slowly began to gain the support of their members (Crichlow, 2003, p. 209). With that support, we organized the first Black History Month panel – at the Jane and Finch community centre – entitled "Homophobia and Black Nationalism," at which Rozena Maart (a South African feminist, academic, and activist) and I were guest speakers. I spoke in a vacuum of silence with the support of my dear friend and sister professor Rozena. I came to realize that while fear can act as a kind of paralysis that immobilizes our thoughts and actions, fear can also be a great motivator and empowering experience. I no longer wanted to pluck out parts of my identity; rather, I wanted to be me – to be whole – and I did it by taking the risk at this event of rendering my dignity valuable. That day I wanted to begin my journey free from Black and societal homoppression and not ask the attendees for my freedom, upon which conditions will be set, even as we know one is never truly free, but rather always in (emphasis-added homoppressive) chains (Rousseau, 1968).

There is an assumption that economically less privileged Black people are more homophobic than Black people with education. My experience of coming out to roughly five hundred people at the Jane and Finch panel in 1990 saw room made for discussion and opened the opportunity to address the issue without facing humiliation. I no longer cared if I was out or outed at this event; rather, I was interested in the performance initiated by coming out and in seeing if my disclosure would get in the way of what Black folks came to hear: resistance to racism and indirectly to heterosexism. Black consciousness and gay activism confronted me with a deeply troubling dilemma, namely how to reconcile the deep yearning for love and acceptance from the Black community with the need to support the Black justice movement keeping our community alive. It was not easy: putting my sexual politics on the table within a Black community that had so many hardships to deal with meant that I risked being ostracized or taken less seriously. Interestingly, the shunning came from university-educated people rather than from the working-class Black people in the room. This was one of many dialectical situations where my Blackness and sexuality were in tension while I proclaimed the right to have ownership of my body and sexual imagination. The politics of sexuality has divided many communities, but I felt this was one occasion where the discussions of sexuality and racism converged in a liberating manner.

The powerful combining of gay activism with Black activism is evident in the history of the anti-apartheid movement. I had learnt about our gay South African anti-apartheid brother Simon Nkoli from my sister Rozena. Nkoli was arrested in South Africa for treason and tried in one of the most publicized trials of the apartheid era, the Delmas treason trials. I spoke about his arrest, incarceration, and trial with no resistance from the attendees at the Jane and Finch gathering. I was a member of the Canadian Simon Nkoli Anti-Apartheid Committee along with Rozena, who was conscious and critical of the treatment of both the gay and anti-apartheid movements. I will always remember that when I was a part of the anti-apartheid movement in Canada, there was no communal homophobia, silencing, or threats directed at me or any other gay people when we spoke against South Africa's apartheid or for gay rights for Nkoli. Gay rights organizations, Black activist organizations within Canada, and people around the world supported Nkoli. The ANC achieved its political power and goals with international support that included Black Canadian activism. Ironically, the Black community was fighting against South Africa's apartheid and for gay rights for Nkoli while Black LGBTQ Canadians were fighting against the homophobia within our various Black communities that persists even today. Like Judith Butler (1999), who insists upon the extension of legitimacy to bodies that have been regarded as false, unreal, and unintelligible (p. xxiii), I have always made it the goal of my work on and in Black leadership and Black LGBTQ leadership to challenge Black compulsory heteronormativity in all its forms while seeking the liberation of Black people.

Early Homoppression and Black Activism

> This is what I say to my comrades in the struggle who ask me why I waste time fighting for moffies and this is what I say to white gay men or women who ask me why I spend so much time talking about apartheid when I should be fighting for gay rights. I am black and I am gay. I cannot separate the two parts of me into secondary or primary struggle. They will be all one struggle.
>
> Tseko Simon Nkoli Nkoli in Beverley Ditsie's film *Simon and I*

In writing this piece from within, and not from without, I wanted to write with some mental freedom. My activism has been hugely impacted by witnessing and experiencing injustices in my youth and seeing the many Black organizations who stood up against racism, white supremacy, and homophobia. While Black consciousness was the foundation for my becoming an organic intellectual, it did not come without struggles against homophobic exclusion and alienation even as I strove to contribute, serve, and lead. The homophobic and patriarchal ideology of Black power movements from the 1960s and 1970s was still influencing Black activist leadership and struggles of the 1980s, 1990s, and 2000s. The Reverend Dr Martin Luther King Jr (1967) insisted on the importance of understanding power in context:

> Power properly understood is nothing but the ability to achieve purpose. It is the strength required to bring about social, political or economic changes. In this sense power is not only desirable but necessary in order to implement the demands of love and justice. One of the greatest problems of history is that the concepts of love and power are usually contrasted as polar opposites. Love is identified with a resignation of power and power with a denial of love ... What is needed is a realization that power without love is reckless and abusive, and that love without power is sentimental and anemic. Power at its best is love implementing the demands of justice. Justice at its best is love correcting everything that stands against love. (p. 37)

The power of hetero-hyper-masculinization of Black consciousness defined and policed the Other, thereby disciplining the political thinking of my early activist days as it does today. Though incomplete, sexual Othering within the Black community has significantly "flipped" from the long-standing historical fixation on the homosexual Other within Black nationalistic discursive formations that once championed Black heteronationalism. For example, during a Black History Month discussion on the Black family, Black consciousness, and Black nationalism at the University of Toronto in February 1989, a young Black woman bravely described herself as a Black lesbian and a woman who loves and sleeps with women. She challenged the heterosexist discourse and asked various communities to recognize same-sex relationships and families (Crichlow, 2003, p. 69). After she had posed her question, out and identified Black gays and lesbians in attendance were verbally and physically attacked by male and female Black nationalists, and some of us ran out of the room for our safety, literally and figuratively. In another example, when I published my book *Buller Men and Batty Bwoys: Hidden Men in Toronto and Halifax Black Communities* (2003), some community organizations to which I belonged received threatening phone calls about my involvement.

In Trinidad[5] and the Caribbean, where I am from, we all know about the harassment and oppression Black LGBTQ, gender nonbinary, and gender non-conforming persons face from some Black families and religious organizations that teach that homosexuality is immoral, sick, and an abomination. The expressed hatred and homophobia we have experienced after having been invited into organizations is simply horrifying. These experiences led me to ask myself: Why must Black LGBTQ people continue to experience discrimination and violence, suffer in silence, and experience abuse of their human rights and dignity simply for who they are and for refusing to live a life of lies? But it is equally important to note that Black LGBTQ and gender nonconforming and non-binary folks have always worked to challenge Black homoppression from within organizations and families in ways that have not been celebrated or made public. It is Black LGBTQ and Black non-binary folks who gave meaning to debates on gender from the point of view of the interlocking systems of oppression of race, gender, class, and sexuality. "Interlocking," today know as intersectionality, is a term coined by the Combahee River Collective in 1977 and elaborated upon in an edited collection by Cherrie Moraga and Gloria Anzaldua (1981), titled *This Bridge Called My Back.* Discussions about Black leadership and community must attend to the intersecting oppressions and gender spectrums of racism, sexuality, sexism, ableism, and homophobia, which are connected to combatting the extreme consequences of homophobic hyper- and para-masculinity. I have previously used the term *bionationalism* (Crichlow, 2003) to identify the ideological joining of religiously justified homophobia and racial reductionism.

Colonialism, the ROM, Black Consciousness, Sexual Politics, and State Violence

> We think that our fighting for Africa against colonialism and imperialism is proof of understanding your problem and also a contribution for the solution of your problems in the continent. Naturally the inverse is also true. All the achievements towards the solution of your problems here are real contributions to our own struggle. And we are very encouraged in our struggle by the fact that each day more of the African people born in America became conscious of their responsibilities to the struggle in Africa.
>
> Amílcar Cabral, "Connecting the Struggles"

The tendency of the state to usurp the leadership of sociopolitical movements at their peak is one that Black activists acknowledge and work against constantly (see James and Williams in this volume). The BRMC's road to critical consciousness included the recognition of how white domination works through colonizing methods of divide and conquer. Black consciousness mass-based political action, Biko (1978) notes, "is in essence the realization by the Black man [*sic*] of the need to rally together with his brothers [*sic*] around the cause of their operation – the Blackness of their skin – and to operate as a group in order to rid themselves of the shackles that bind them to perpetual servitude" (p. 49). My involvement in the 1980s with the BRMC saw the movement grow from meetings in kitchens to protest action on the streets. With it grew my critical understanding of the white supremacy diet of slavery and racism.

The Black consciousness leadership of the BRMC and other community groups was exemplified in two protest movements in particular. *Into the Heart of Africa* was an exhibition mounted by the Royal Ontario Museum (ROM) in 1989, consisting of about 375 artefacts from Central and West Africa that had been stored by the ROM for over one hundred years. It opened in November 1989 and closed in August 1990. Ostensibly, the theme of the exhibit was the impact of colonialism on Africa, particularly at the height of the colonial period (Henry & Tator, 2000, p. 91). Most demonstrations I, as a Black academic and activist, have been involved in dealt with human rights, bread-and-butter issues for the Black community such as under/unemployment of Black folks, their working conditions, immigration policies, police violence, and school retention issues. The ROM demonstration was intellectual in nature and about pedagogical praxis (teaching as activism) and working with others to transform education. Fanon (1963) reminds us that "for the colonizer to maintain his power over natives, he must constantly assert it through violent acts – not only physical, but through the infliction of the neuroses" (p. 1). The ROM demonstration was about reclaiming intellectual property and supporting Black scholarship. To some degree, one could argue that the activist leadership of the protests against the ROM and, later, *Show Boat*, were major impetus for the founding of the two Afrocentric schools in Toronto (see Gooden and James in this volume). The ROM demonstration influenced me to open a Black gay-owned bookstore, A Different Booklist, to create a visible critical cultural gay- and trans-positive place for Black LGBTQ people, due to our invisibility and lack of acknowledgment from heteronormative Black leadership. I saw opening the bookstore as a necessary tool for scholars and community activists to draw from each other's strengths while engaging in Black activism, inserting Black LGBTQ scholars and activists in the movement. The ROM demonstration taught me that we needed intellectual places to have conversations about decolonization, Black leadership, and community engagement. I saw my opening the bookstore as creating that space, as I was so deeply and personally involved in Black community activism. With the bookstore I wanted to politicize our sense of being and fight against injustices centred in Black Canadian leadership in Toronto.

The struggle over colonial representations of Black peoples includes not only the ways in which "white-supremacist ideas and practices have dehumanized and excluded black people from the human family" (West,

1993, p. 74), but also how Black people have been incorporated in a whitewashed fashion. *Show Boat*, a musical based on a 1926 novel by Edna Ferber, was staged in Toronto by Live Entertainment Productions in 1993 by now disgraced impresario Garth Drabinsky. Protests underscored the racist representations of the lives of Black performers who work on a boat that travels on the Mississippi River over four decades, entertaining white audiences in the American South (Henry & Tator, 2000, p. 92). Other putatively benevolent representations of Black people have also proven to be problematic. The immigrant, gay, Jamaican Canadian man, the Jamaican "gully queen" – rarely a lesbian in the discourses – serves an important symbolic function. He tends to be celebrated as a token of white Canadian gay beneficence, a symbol of Canada's status as a gay-friendly refuge, creating a LGBTQ Jamaican refugee poster children (Jackson, 2015) and stigmatizing the totality of Jamaican culture as an exemplar of homophobia.

Blackness as defined by Biko, Rodney, Malcom X, Memmi, Fanon, and others emerged as a direct response to dealing with colonial legacies such as those evident in the ROM's *Into the Heart of Africa* and the musical *Show Boat*. The protest movements engendered leadership in various forms. The BRMC was an excellent place for oral history, activism, and social justice work, with a unique Black consciousness and employing what is now called critical race theory. For example, Monifa Owosu and Akua Benjamin both espoused a Black feminist consciousness that relied on oral tradition and memory. They demonstrated the role played by memory in survival and continuity, with their storytelling of the impediments faced by Black women of their time and across the globe. There was great enjoyment in these storytelling moments with them, and the communication fostered a better understanding of everyday issues. My Black consciousness owes much to the Black feminist analysis of the hetero-hyper-masculinization of Black consciousness and the related impact of imperialism, colonialism, and racism in our lives.

Black leadership also grew out of demonstrations over the callous police killings of Black people (which today is encapsulated by the Black Lives Matter movement). Demonstrations expressed outrage, demanded social justice and equality for Black people, and specifically the right to a life free from police violence, racial profiling, carding, and state ratification of systemic anti-Black racism. As noted by the African Canadian Legal Clinic, Toronto (ACLC) at the Second African Canadian Summit (2015), "the African Canadian community in the GTA experiences markedly disproportionate rates of socio-economic disadvantage in a number of areas including, poverty, education, child welfare, employment, health and justice." My earliest experience of Black people expressing outrage against state and police violence was the Yonge Street disturbance of 1992, in reaction to the acquittal of four police officers caught on video beating black driver Rodney King in Los Angeles. On the same day of the trial verdict, Torontonians held a demonstration in solidarity with the people of LA, organized by BADC, protesting police violence and police brutality. The timing was ripe and ready for anger to spill into the streets of Toronto. I witnessed for the first time looting, fires, the smashing of storefront windows, and hurling of stones and bottles at Toronto riot police. I witnessed Toronto riot police arresting people, running their horses into the crowd. The protest was no longer one belonging to or organized by BDAC, as it was joined by youth from all walks of life: homeless youth, Indigenous youth, other racialized youth, white supremacist youth, and socialist/Stalinist youth. It was one of my most scary moments taking part in demonstrations – it stayed with me for months – I can safely say I was impacted by its violence and representation of difference.

Early experiences of activism and leadership within the BRMC and BADC were motivated by the paramilitary and war-zone-like thinking of police, its corrupt logic, and the ways in which racial inequality impacts the lives of Black people. The effects of racist policing and the manner in which the legal system punishes Black people's bodies also produces prisons as new forms of population control and a way of increasing the economic inequality that affects Black families disproportionately (Crichlow, 2014). BADC's demonstrations against police shootings of Black people highlighted public grieving through open protest. This form of leadership spoke back to the state, insisting on what should be obvious but is not: that the lost lives and broken bodies of Blacks are not acceptable losses.

Corporatization of the Black Professoriate

Despite the obstacles faced by Black LGBTQ persons within activist organizations, I look to the leadership models of those movements, as they stand in contrast to the limitations arising from the corporatization of academic institutions. If you are a Black consciousness scholar and revolutionary (or activist, if you feel the word best captures the Canadian sensibility) you face a dilemma in which university-educated people are expected not to address the Black masses but rather write about the corporatization and militarization of the Black masses. My own scholarship and that of others has resisted this tendency (Crichlow, 2014). Yet it is the corporatization and militarization of the curriculum that poses challenges for Black leadership, Black activism generally, and Black LGBTQ leadership specifically. Former Ontario premier Mike Harris's "common-sense revolution" ushered in a new era of attacks on the curriculum. After delivering a 25 per cent budget cut to Ontario universities in the 1990s, he called sociology a useless discipline that the universities might consider cutting. Former prime minister Stephen Harper, in addition to associating sociological thinking with committing suicide, said that criminologists "are not criminals themselves, but ... are always making excuses for them, and when they aren't making excuses, they are denying that crime is even a problem" (cited in Heath, 2013). He said this despite (or because of) the fact that the Black population in federal prisons is the fastest-growing incarcerated group. In response to a 2014 call for a national enquiry into missing and murdered aboriginal women, Harper urged Canadians to not frame it as a "sociological phenomenon" but rather "view it as a crime" (Kaye & Béland, 2014). These examples illustrate the politically hostile environment in which the sociological investigation of justice issues is dismissed in favour of a reductive, militarized response. At issue is how to maintain the dignity and integrity of Black leadership when corporatization and military colonization are already built into that leadership, the university curriculum, and the project of nation building.

Within the academy, one recent example of corporatization is the passage into law of Bill 100, the Universities Accountability and Sustainability Act, in the province of Nova Scotia. It threatens collective bargaining rights, most notably the right to strike and the right to file grievances, by allowing academic employers to invoke financial emergency. This is one kind of measure that works to deny Black folks tenure and promotion. The public and institutional backlash against newly appointed Boston University professor Saida Grundy, who was accused of anti-white racism on Twitter, illustrates another form of policing in the name of the corporate university's reputation (Nguyen, 2015). The corporatization and militarization of academic institutions puts Black academic leaders in a challenging position. Fanon, in *The Wretched of the Earth* (1963), suggests that "the unpreparedness of the educated classes, the lack of practical links between them and the mass of the people, their laziness, and, let it be said, their cowardice at the decisive moment of the struggle will give rise to tragic mishaps" (p. 148). Facing institutional aversion to challenges to the status quo, Black LGBTQ activists likewise face a lack of support from the broader LGBTQ community. In my estimation the LGBTQ movement at best abandoned its progressive left politics while fighting for white homohegemony, assimilation, and social acceptability. As a Black gay activist, I still have to address white homonormativity, white homohegemony, and white supremacy daily. In effect, the movement has failed to sustain a challenge to patriarchal and dominant heteronormative and racist assumptions, while granting LGBTQ white professors the privileges offered by the academy, thereby installing a new white homohegemony within academia.

Despite corporatization of the academy and the paucity of Black academics, Black leadership within universities has and is having great success. There has been a successful installation of deans, at least one president, and a number of Black research chairs committed to social justice agendas in education grounded in the lived experiences of Black community leadership. A common theme in all Black chairs is the role educational leaders can play in addressing the persistent inequalities and disparities for Black youth and the eradication of institutional disregard towards the Black professoriate, through advocacy and leadership in university education. The following chairs are great examples of Black leadership: Dalhousie University's James R. Johnston Chair in Black Studies; Queen's University's Robert Sutherland Endowment Chair; York University's Harriet Tubman Centre on the African Diaspora, Jean Augustine Chair in Education in the New Urban Environment, and Oscar Peterson Chair in Jazz Performance; and the University of Alberta's Michaëlle Jean Chair in Caribbean and African Diaspora Studies. These chairs reflect Black people's views of education as a tool for justice, equity, and upward mobility in the global educational economy. We can learn much from the leadership and inauguration of Black chairs in academia on how Black academic, LGBTQ, and political leaders have historically and successfully linked the causes of racial justice to education. Our challenge in these positions within the white academy is to change traditionally exclusive and exclusionary attitudes towards Black people in the academy – because we belong and have a place in the academy and have entered the academy to stay. The limitations of institutional assimilation if we buy into it completely may underscore the need for leadership developed in grass-roots, activist movements.

Conclusions and Future Action

> Solidarity does not mean that everyone thinks the same way; it begins when people have confidence to disagree over issues of fundamental importance precisely because they "care" about constructing common ground.
>
> Kobena Mercer, "Welcome to the Jungle"

I have attempted to expose Black political homophobia and hypocrisy in Black communities with respect to leadership and activism, while addressing some of the unspoken "truths" about silencing and violating Black LGBTQs activists and leaders. Each generation of Black leadership builds on the leadership of the previous generation. Black Lives Matter would not exist without historical ties to the Black power movements in the United States and the Black Action Defence Committee in Toronto, the Black power movement of the sixties. African History Month acknowledges this point in its celebration of the past, present, and future. So I don't want people to forget the mimesis of Black leadership, nor do I want any generation to forget the past in the name of "we were the first leadership." We live in a hegemonically heteronormative society. I would like to suggest that, in order to create common ground, Black leadership should aim to modernize the movement, to develop and include a more complex and fuller understanding of sexual identity and gender non-conformity alongside an acknowledgment of the role of critical autobiography and autoethnography to bring stories of inter/subjectivity and intersecting narratives of history. These steps are needed if Black leadership is to avoid replacing one form of heterocentric domination with another, and to accept new, intersectional cultural modes for educating, mobilizing, and organizing to achieve the best interests of the community.

In my Black activism I have always been cautious about making my sexual identity the locus of Black political struggles, not because I am ashamed or afraid, but because I strongly believe that one's coming out needs context to avoid reinforcing the hegemony of compulsory heterosexuality, as it only puts one body on the line. Coming out does not end one's relationship to the closet of sexuality, as every space we occupy is always assumed to be heterosexual and is fraught with its own capitalist heterocentric interests, values, issues, and struggles: no spaces are innocent or safe. Yet, despite the role that the performance of Black heteronormativity has played in restricting the formation of community, I choose to foreground race in my activism. I have learnt over the years not to seek anyone's approval – by extension I do not give them the right to reject me. As Silin (1995) reminds us, "the closet is a function not of homosexuality but of compulsory heterosexuality" (p. 166). He also reminds us that coming out can sometimes reproduce the same oppressive social categories from which we seek our liberation (1995, p. 57). LGBTQ Black leadership is similar to what Sue Golding calls *technique*: "an impossible geography – impossible not because it does not exist, but because it exists and does not exist exactly at the same time [as] Black heterocentric leadership" (cited in Britzman, 1998, p. 81). Our challenge as we work to advance Black Canadian leadership is to make it less despotic in its discursive renderings of sexual orientation, gender, and other sexual dynamics that currently produce a cavernous homophobic disconnection between people as they reinforce sexism and the masculinization of Black leadership. There must be a collective reflection on and opposition to the everyday ways in which Black heteronormativity takes hold of LGBTQ lives and the ways in which it supports homophobic violence as normal and obvious. This is not the only fragmentation of our community that we must be wary of. We also have to be cognizant of and remain critical of the corporatization, militarization, and military colonization of the academy as it impacts Black leadership. At issue is the potential for a kind of epistemological violence.

The challenge is to make Black organizations and families more accepting of LGBTQ persons – and I believe we could start with having established Black community organizations include LGBTQ services and support groups to make them more stable and integral to Black identity. It would be great to have our youth coming-out narratives tied to Black community organizations. It is not about community capacity: it is a lack of political will to commit to addressing what is seen as religiously and morally sinful, sick, and embarrassing. What is needed is to hire Black LGBTQ professionals to run programs under the same roof as other programs run by Black community organizations.

We are living within corrupt political systems vulnerable to bribery and corporate co-optation, nepotism, and propaganda. Black leadership must build alliances and coalitions with independent political parties and take non-compromising political actions, such as no corporate donations (cf. Scotiabank Carnival). This is politically important because corporate capitalism, imperialism, militarism, and globalization have normalized poverty. Further alliances are needed beyond Black organizational alliances and ones to political parties. Although the histories and constructions of our communities are different, we need active solidarities between Aboriginal, Brown, and Black communities precisely because the prison-militarization-surveillance industries strive to separate us. Also, we cannot afford to confine questions of gender to women as if Black men do not suffer from heteronormativity, nor can we isolate LGBTQ issues as the only ones in need of corrective action without attending to class differentials. True leadership needs to account for the causes of these different but intersecting phenomena or risk the erasure of the complexity of Black life.

Grass-roots activism will continue to be the vehicle by which Black youth develop leadership skills that influence their career choices later on in life (see Kitossa, this volume). Black activist leadership has produced some of the best Black leaders, who were not driven by celebrity or social media opportunism. Rather, they were and are leaders whose activism, sense of dignity, and values worked to raise the profile of social inequality and state violence inflicted upon members of the Black community. They created the space, place, and opportunity for Black Lives Matter, youth, and others to become leaders in social justice struggles. I do not envision Black leadership from a top-down approach, reinforcing the cult of the expert or celebrity. Academic institutions continue to fall short of socially transformative goals: just as Black Studies in general experiences lack of academic institutional support, so too have Black LGBTQ people felt excluded within the wider white homohegemony movement. There has never been a Black LGBTQ demonstration, conference, awards dinner recognition, scholarship, or institution named after one of its leaders. Black LGBTQ members are not voiceless, requiring Black heteronationalist leadership to speak for us. We are noble and courageous. I have never met any voiceless Black LGBTQ people in my community activism, only the deliberately silenced.

This chapter and the conference at which it was originally presented[6] are some of the very places we voice our politics. It is my hope that through the work presented here, we can see small and big ways that we can change society through Black LGBTQ community leadership and social justice activism. Black leadership must include a yearning for liberatory politics, not heterosexist homoppression. Finally, this paper contends that Black leadership cannot afford to sideline conversations around Black gender, sex, gender non-conformity, trans issues, and sexuality at the expense of dialogues on racial justice. When Black LGBTQ people are written out of conversations and disregarded in discussions on Black communities' leadership models, those efforts become not only complicit in our historical erasure but often are far weaker for not including us.

NOTES

1 Zami, a Toronto Black LGBTQ organization, was formed in 1984 as the first Black LGBTQ organization for people of Caribbean origin.

2 Named for South Africa's Stephen "Bantu" Biko, Guyana's Walter Rodney, and Afro-America's El-Hajj Malik El Shabazz (Malcolm X), the BRMC was formed in March 1983. I joined in 1989.

3 As John Cooper (2005) has shown, Black people in Dresden, Ontario, such as Hugh Barnett, played a pivotal role in the development of human rights legislation in Canada.

4 These Black student associations were often mentored by elders in the wider Black community. Elders Monifa Owsu, Sherona Hall, and Mitchel Holder attended some of the weekly meetings held on campus. In addition, African and Caribbean pan-African and Black consciousness scholars and activists were invited to assist in our politicization and consciousness raising.

5 Trinidad and Tobago, 12 April 2018: "The court declares that sections 13 and 16 of the [Sexual Offenses Act] are unconstitutional, illegal, null, void, invalid and of no effect to the extent that these laws criminalise any acts constituting consensual sexual conduct between adults," Justice Devindra Rampersad wrote in his ruling (https://www.nbcnews.com/feature/nbc-out/trinidad-tobago-set-decriminalize-homosexuality-n865511).

6 An earlier version of this chapter was presented as a keynote address at the Black Canadian Studies Association 2015 Conference in Halifax, NS.

REFERENCES

Adams, T.E., & Holman Jones, S. (2008). Autoethnography is queer. In N.K. Denzin, Y.S. Lincoln, & L.T. Smith (Eds.), *Handbook of critical and indigenous methodologies* (pp. 373–90). Thousand Oaks: Sage.

Alexander, B.K. (2012). *The performative sustainability of race: Reflections on black culture and the politics of identity.* New York: Peter Lang.

Biko, S. (1978). *I write what I like: A selection of his writings* (A. Stubbs, Ed.). New York: Harper & Row.

Bingman, B. (1996). Women learning in Appalachian grassroots organizations. In S. Walters & L. Manicom (Eds.), *Gender in popular education* (pp. 169–80). London: Zed.

Boylorn, R.M., & Orbe, M.P. (Eds.) (2014). *Critical autoethnography: Intersecting cultural identities in everyday life.* Walnut Creek: Left Coast.

Britzman, D.P. (1998). Queer pedagogy and its strange techniques. In *Lost subjects, contested objects: Toward a Psychoanalytic Inquiry of Learning* (pp. 79–96). New York: SUNY Press.

Calafell, B.M. (2012). Monstrous femininity: Constructions of women of color in the academy. *Journal of Communication Inquiry, 36*(2), 111–30. https://doi.org/10.1177/0196859912443382

Cooper, J. (2005). *Season of rage: Hugh Burnett and the struggle for civil rights.* Toronto; Plattsburg: Tundra.

Crichlow, W. (2003). *Buller men and batty bwoys: Hidden men in Toronto and Halifax black communities.* Toronto: University of Toronto Press.

Crichlow, W. (2014). Weaponization and prisonization of Toronto's black male youth. *International Journal for Crime, Justice and Social Democracy, 3*(3), 113–31. https://doi.org/10.5204/ijcjsd.v3i3.120

Ellis, C., Adams, T.E., & Bochner, A.P. (2010). Autoethnography: An overview. *Forum Qualitative Sozialforschung / Forum: Qualitative Social Research, 12*(1), art. 10. Retrieved from http://www.qualitative-research.net/index.php/fqs/article/view/1589/3095

Fanon, Frantz. (1963). *The wretched of the earth.* Trans. Constance Farrington. New York: Grove.

Finger, M. (1989). New social movements and their implications for adult education. *Adult Education Quarterly, 40*(1), 15–22. https://doi.org/10.1177/074171368904000102

Gramsci, A. (1971). *Selections from the prison notebooks* (Q. Hoare and G.N. Smith, Eds. and Trans.). New York: International.

Heath, J. (2013, 30 April). In defence of sociology. *Ottawa Citizen.* Retrieved from http://spon.ca/in-defence-of-sociology/2013/05/01

Henry, F., & Tator, C. (2000). *Racist discourse in Canada's English print media.* Toronto: Canadian Race Relations Foundation.

Holst, J.D. (2002). *Social movements, adult education, and civil society.* New York: Bergin and Garvin.

Holst, J.D. (2004). Globalization and education within two revolutionary organizations in the United States of America: A Gramscian analysis. *Adult Education Quarterly, 55*(1), 23–40. https://doi.org/10.1177/0741713604268895

Jackson, K. (2015) *Homohegemony and the Other: Canada and Jamaica* (Unpublished doctoral dissertation). Queen's University, Kingston.

Kaye, J., & Béland, D. (2014, 22 August). Stephen Harper's dangerous refusal to "commit sociology." *Toronto Star.* Retrieved from http://www.thestar.com/opinion/commentary/2014/08/22/stephen_harpers_dangerous_refusal_to_commit_sociology.html

King, M.L., Jr. (1967). *Where do we go from here: Chaos or community?* New York: Harper & Row.

Moraga, C., & Anzaldúa, G. (1981). *This bridge called my back: Writings by radical women of colour.* New York: Kitchen Table.

Nguyen, T. (2015). Boston U. professor under fire for "population problem" comment about white men. Mediaite News. Retrieved from https://www.mediaite.com/online/boston-u-professor-under-fire-for-population-problem-comment-about-white-men/

Pratt, M.L. (1994). Transculturation and autoethnography: Peru, 1615/1980. In F. Barker, P. Hulme, & M. Iverson (Eds.), *Colonial discourse/postcolonial theory* (pp. 24–46). New York: Manchester University Press.

Rousseau, J.J. (1968). *The social contract.* Harmondsworth: Penguin.

Second African Canadian Summit. (2015). Critical crossroad and the crisis in the African Canadian community [Conference abstract]. Retrieved from http://www.eventbrite.ca/e/the-2nd-african-canadian-summit-tickets-16383502497

Silin, J.G. (1995). *Sex, death, and the education of children: Our passion for ignorance in the age of AIDS.* New York: Teachers College Press.

Silvera, M. (1989). *Silenced: Talks with working-class Caribbean women about their lives and struggles as domestic workers in Canada* (2nd ed.). Toronto: Sister Vision Press.

Spence, L.K. (2012): The neoliberal turn in black politics. *Souls: A Critical Journal of Black Politics, Culture, and Society, 14*(3–4), 139–59. https://doi.org/10.1080/10999949.2012.763682

Visano, L. (2006). Class enriching the classroom: The "radical" as rooted pedagogic strengths. In S. Muzzatti & V. Samarco (Eds.), *Reflections from the wrong side of the tracks: Class, identity, and the working class experience in academe.* Lanham: Roman and Littlefield.

West, C. (1993). *Race matters.* Boston: Beacon.

Yancy, G., & Butler, J. (2015, 12 January). What's wrong with "All Lives Matter?" *New York Times.* Retrieved from http://opinionator.blogs.nytimes.com/2015/01/12/whats-wrong-with-all-lives-matter/?_r=0

Yep, G.A. (2010). Toward the de-subjugation of racially marked knowledges in communication. *Southern Communication Journal, 75*, 171–5.

12 "Is There No Balm in Gilead?": The Search for Radical Leadership in the Black Church of the Twenty-First Century

PAUL BANAHENE ADJEI

I am writing on a troublesome yet an important issue: contemporary leadership in the Black church. I am in a unique position of being a born-again Pentecostal Christian who has been an active church attender for at least the last thirty years. Thus, in writing about the issues of leadership in the Black church, I am also writing about something in which I am an active agent. I pose the question "Is there no balm in Gilead?" as a desperate search for answers concerning what is happening to the leadership of the Black church of the twenty-first century, many examples of which will be cited below.

In the Old Testament book, Jeremiah 8:22, the Prophet Jeremiah asks, "Is there no balm in Gilead; is there no physician there? Why then is not the health of the daughter of my people recovered?" The balm of Gilead is a medicinal salve. In the Old Testament, traders from neighbouring nations travelled frequently to Gilead to trade in balm. One of such examples is in Genesis 37:25, where the account describes the caravan that bought Joseph into slavery as Ishmaelite traders travelling to Egypt with trading goods (including balm) from Gilead. Also in Genesis 43:11, among precious goods that Jacob sent as gifts to Joseph in Egypt was the balm of Gilead. So in the midst of such famous healing medicine, how could the daughters of Israel be so sick with no hope for cure? The Prophet Jeremiah's questions may be a poetic search for hope and healing for the children of Israel, but they may also illustrate what could be described as an unnecessary and avoidable tragedy that has befallen the children of Israel.

In this chapter, I draw on Jeremiah's questions to ask if the Black church, one that has an enviable legacy of producing radical leaders that have created social transformations in Canada, the United States, and many parts of the globe, is today in need of radical leadership. Through personal communications with twelve active Christians belonging to different denominations (all part of the Black church) in selected cities in Canada and Ghana and a select review of the scholarly literature, this essay critically examines the current state of the Black church. Following the theologian Phillip Doddridge (1702–51), I assert that the Black church should live with heaven – and this world – in proper perspective. Ultimately, I investigate how changing social conditions continue to nuance the Black church's experience in contemporary times. In the face of radical social transformations presently under way, this essay ultimately calls for a radical renewal of leadership in the Black church. It calls for a reinvigoration of its radical response to addressing systemic inequities and injustices rather than accommodating, capitulating, compromising, and participating in them.

Writing about the Black church of the nineteenth and twentieth centuries in the United States, Franklin Frazier (1974) describes it as a nation within a nation, the centre of the Black community, and "a predominant venue of self-expression, recognition, and shelter from a cruel, hostile White world" (Perry, 1998, p. 33). In Canada James Walker, in series of publications (1979, 1992, 1995), describes the Black church of the nineteenth and twentieth centuries as the anchor that held the Black community together in the face of racist assaults in that country. Daniel Hill corroborates Walker's assertion and even describes the Black church as "the earliest and most important institutions in all Black Upper Canadian communities" (Hill, 1981, p. 130). Dorothy Shreve (1983) also describes the Black church in Canada as "a stabilizer," "a place where they [Blacks] could participate with dignity, pride and freedom" (p. 13). In his study of Union United Church (UUC), a Black church, and its influential role in developing the Black community in Montreal between 1907 and 1940, David Este (2004) describes how it provided for the needs of the Montreal Black community and became the voice of the community against racism and discrimination. One can also recall the important role of Toronto's British Methodist Episcopal Church and First Baptist Church in providing refuge and material support for fugitive slaves from the United States in the 1820s. Not surprisingly, though a tendency towards varieties of Islam was prominent from the 1930s onward, the Black community turned to the Black church for help to cope with everyday challenges of resettlement and integration in a racist and hostile environment (Smith 1978).

In spite of this enviable history of resistance against racism and injustices as well as producing radical leadership, attending the Black church in recent times has, arguably, become what Toni Morrison (1993) describes as "the process of entering what one is estranged from" (p. 4). In the past, one can say with conviction and evidence to support it that the Black church was the anchor that held the Black community together. Those were the days where the Black community could rely on the Black church to be its voice against social injustices, racism, and poverty targeting that community. Today, we are witnessing a different Black church that stands aloof and unconcerned as many people in the Black community, including some parishioners, wallow in poverty, social inequities, and oppression. In Canada, the social problems confronting the Black community are multiple and disturbing. There has been a 70 per cent increase in the incarceration rate of Black youth in the last ten years (Sapers, 2015). The economic and social exclusion of Blacks in Canada has reached such a disturbing level that it recently drew an open condemnation from the United Nations Working Groups (Keung, 2016). We are witnessing in Canada a copycatting of the anti-Black racism that exists in the United States to the point where Black Lives Matter rallies are being held in Montreal, Toronto, Calgary, and Vancouver (Saunders, 2016). In the face of these disturbing stories, we hear little responses from the majority of the Black churches in Canada.

On occasion such as the Black church's involvement in the gun-violence campaign in 2003, the church's role raised many critical questions about its ability to know and understand issues facing the Black community. In the midst of the crises of gun violence among Black youth in Toronto in 2006, the GTA Faith Alliance, a coalition of forty multifaith leaders chaired by Reverend Don Meredith, enlisted the services of Dr Eugene Rivers, a Black Pentecostal preacher from Boston, to assist with the analysis of youth violence in Toronto. Reverend Eugene Rivers identified absentee fathers in the Black community as well as dysfunctions within Black culture as the root cause of gun violence in the Black community. By the end of his campaign in Toronto, Reverend Rivers (2006), with the support of the GTA Faith Alliance, succeeded in depicting the Black community as a homogenous social group in which degeneracy, criminality, violence, and immorality are part of our normative culture and identity. Reverend Rivers and the GTA Faith alliance's prognosis of gun violence in Toronto runs contrary to numerous studies that associate gun violence in the Black community with systemic racism, poverty, and discrimination targeting that community in Canada (Chadwick-Parkes, 2012; Hulchanski, 2010; Lewis, 1992; McMurtry & Curling, 2008; Ontario Human Rights Commission, 2003; Walcott, Foster, Cambell, & Sealy, 2008).

As an analysis from Black preachers that dissociates Whiteness, anti-Black racism, and social inequities from the crises of gun violence, it was not surprising that Reverend Rivers and the GTA Faith Alliance's presentations received overwhelming approval from many White Torontonians. In the end, the church's role did not help the Black community; instead, it managed to shift the discussion of gun violence towards "the victim-blame game" and the usual conservative and liberal tongue-lashing of the Black community to accept responsibilities (Carnoil, 2006; Chong, 2006). This example and many more that will be mentioned below raise concern about the current state of the Black church, and especially its ability to respond to issues affecting the Black community.

I am an optimist and sincerely believe that all is not lost for the Black church. The church can claim its historical role as the beacon of hope in the fight against social injustice in the Black community. This, however, will only happen if it stops drawing on its historical currency to justify its continued relevance today, and realizes that its relevance to the Black community must be demonstrated through contemporary actions and not a nostalgic harking back to historical legacies. This essay critically examines the changing role of the Black church while identifying ways in which it can improve its relationship with the Black community. Given its inclusion within a volume that focuses on African Canadian leadership, it is expected that I draw only on examples and literature from the Canadian context. However, despite the burgeoning literature on the activities of the Black church in the United States, Africa, and the Caribbean, there is a dearth of writing on the Black church of Canada in the twenty-first century. In view of that, I will draw on literature from the United States and other parts of the globe to strengthen my analyses. Besides, the issues of the Black church are of global interest, and therefore drawing on a broader literature and set of examples can only strengthen the discussion and give the essay a global appeal. In the discussion that follows, I provide a brief history of the Black church in Canada.

History and Contemporary Experiences of the Black Church

The term "Black church" was coined by historians to discuss predominantly Black Christian congregations (Calhoun-Brown, 2000). The denominations that form the Black church operate with a high degree of ecclesiastical, theological, liturgical independence, marked by broad socio-economic and regional particularities. Although the origin of the Black church is not confined to a specific denomination or religious organization (Brown Spencer, 2009), the experiences of slavery and racist oppression in the United States and Canada arguably played influential roles in its formation (Perry, 1998). White racism, in a sense, created the Black church.

In his seminal text *The Blacks in Canada: A History*, Robin Winks notes that Blacks did not entertain any interest in establishing an independent Black church until the French territory of Acadia was handed over to the British after the Treaty of Utrecht (Alexander & Glaze, 1996). After the War of Independence in the United States, the Black Loyalists who arrived in Nova Scotia, Canada, were surprised to realize that baptism in the Anglican Church did not make them human enough to worship with White congregants. Instead, Black parishioners found themselves segregated from White parishioners (Boyd, 1976; Brown & Senior, 1984; Wetmore & Sellick, 1983; Winks, 1971). By 1815, the forced segregation and mistreatment of Black parishioners in the Anglican Church reached so intensive a hostile tenor that Blacks were told to meet in their own private homes instead of coming to the church (Brown & Senior, 1984; Wetmore & Sellick, 1983). The forced segregation, coupled with persistent racist attitudes of White congregants towards Black parishioners, led to the formation of what later became the Black church in Canada (Murphy & Perlin, 1996; Winks, 1971). James Walker (1992), using the experiences of the Black Loyalists of Nova Scotia, agrees with Winks and Perlin that the formation of the Black church was a direct reaction to the racist and exploitative nature of Canadian society (pp. 67–8). For example, the Cornwallis Street Baptist Church of Halifax, previously known as the African Chapel and the African Baptist Church, which was founded by Blacks in 1832, was the cultural centre for the Black community well into the 1900s (Riley, 2016). According to Clairmont and Magill (1970), the creation of a segregated Black church in Black communities actually laid the foundation for a Black Nova Scotian subculture. Israel (1928) describes the existence in Montreal of a de facto segregation: "It is rather the silent avoiding of contacts with Blacks as part of the process of preserving the status quo of the Canadian whites that he meets when he attempts to break away from his work on the railroads" (p. 81). Vipond (1976) agrees, stating that socializing between Blacks and Whites was virtually non-existent in Montreal. Describing the relationship between White and Black congregants, David Este (2004) writes:

> Religion was vital for the majority of African Americans who settled in Montreal. Although they initially sought religious salvation by attending the local White churches, they were not cordially received as the Whites would neither associate nor mingle with them. Blacks were often placed in the choir lofts or in the back pews where they could not be seen. In some instances, the pastors told the Blacks that they were not welcome and admittance was refused. (p. 10)

This de facto segregation in the White church and a sense of alienation and rejection coupled with White-centred church services that did not speak to the material, emotional, and spiritual needs of Black parishioners resulted in the formation of a Black church in Montreal (Este, 2004).

Given this historical social context of resistance to oppression, the theological orientation of the Black church focused on the needs of those seeking God's salvation as well as social liberation from systemic racism and social injustices. Sermons in the Black church were not only about personal salvation, but also about giving hope and liberation to those bruised by systemic racism and discrimination (Clairmont & Magill, 1970; Este, 2004; Shreve, 1983). David Este (2004) describes the activities of Union United Church of Montreal around two major goals: (1) to preserve the Black culture and (2) to address the injustices directed against Blacks. As Este (2004) writes:

> Once Union Church became relatively stable in terms of finances and direction, the leaders of the community recognized the need to confront the broader societal issues that were relegating Blacks to a marginal position within society. Hence, it can be maintained that rather than hindering the integration efforts of Blacks, Union Church played an extremely major role in breaking down barriers. (p. 21)

Put differently, the theologies of the Black church in Canada can be summed up as what Felder (1995), writing about the Black church in the United States, describes as "a process of critical reflection about God in the affairs of Black people, a story, and a contextual challenge to oppressive structures of racism and oppression" (p. 21). The same Bible White preachers used to justify slavery became the book Black preachers in the Canadian Black church used to express Black freedom and liberation (Brown Spencer, 2009). Dorothy Shadd Shreve (1983) describes the religious meetings of the Black church in Canada as an important spiritual and social outlet for dealing with everyday racist experience living in Canada:

> The cornerstones of their communities were the religious institutions, which ministered to their spiritual needs, performed social and educational functions and supplied most of the administrators. Religion, indeed, was fundamental to the Black experience: in slavery, it was the only consolation; in freedom, it inspired exultation and gratitude. When they were denied full participation in the regular churches, they were prepared to follow a separate path to Christian salvation. (p. 38)

Not surprisingly, the Black church also became the breeding ground for social and community activists as well as agents of the civil rights movement. Prominent Black leaders such as David George, Thomas Peters, Mary Ann Shadd, William Pearly Oliver, and Viola Davis Desmond were all products of the Black church. Unfortunately, these traditional roles of the church, as I mentioned above, appear lost in contemporary times.

Several reasons could account for the disappearance of the Black church's traditional role as the activist voice of the Black community in Canada. First, the Black community in its current form and structure is diverse, with many internal divisions. Not that this is a new phenomenon, but changes in the immigration patterns of Blacks in Canada over the last fifty years have accelerated these tendencies in the form and operations of the Black church. In the early church, most of the congregants were part of the free slaves and Black Loyalists from the United States (Winks, 1971). From the 1960s, Canadian immigration policy reforms eliminated preferences for immigrants of European ancestry, moving to a points-based system for economic immigrants. Consequently, the countries from which immigrants were drawn became increasingly diverse, with more Blacks coming from the Caribbean and the continent of Africa. In 1901, for example, there were only 17,400 Blacks in Canada; by 2011, the Black population had increased to 945,665, representing 3 per cent of the country's population (Statistics Canada, 2011). This figure is projected to increase to 1,809,000 by 2031 (Statistics Canada, 2012).

While the expanding presence of Blacks increased the number of parishioners of the Black church in Canada, it equally presented new challenges for the church. Many Black immigrants arriving in Canada in the 1980s and 1990s wanted to worship in churches similar to those that existed in their countries of origin. Mensah (2009) divides Christian religious groups in the African communities in Canada into two categories: the first group of Black churches are replicas or branches of mainstream mission churches like the Catholic, Methodist, Presbyterian, Anglican, and Seven-Day Adventists. The second group, which currently has the largest number of followers in Canada, consists of "what has become known on the African Continent and in diasporan settings as African Initiated Churches (AICs)" (Baffoe, 2013, p. 307). These AICs were established through the initiative of African immigrants rather than of foreign missionary organizations. AICs have multiple names across the globe. Gifford (2004) calls AICs in Ghana "New Christianity"; some call AICs"Charismatic and Pentecostals"; Barnes (2012), Bird (2007), Martin, Bowles, Adkins, & Leach (2011), and Putnam (2000) call those in the United States "Black Megachurches"; Soares (1992) calls those in Jamaica "New Churches"; and Phiri and Maxwell (2007) call those in Nigeria "Pentecostalism."

Currently, the number of AICs in Canada is becoming difficult to monitor, as more and new ones are established every day. For example, the Ghanaian community in Toronto, with an estimated population of seventy thousand, started with fewer than ten churches in the 1990s. By 2010 (less than twenty years), with breakaways from parent churches and new ones being established, the number had ballooned to one hundred churches (Baffoe, 2013). This is just one example; the figure is more likely to run into thousands if we factor in AICs formed by Ghanaian communities in other cities in Canada, African immigrants from the Caribbean living in Canada, and African immigrants from other sub-Saharan African countries in Canada. With such a growth trend in the Black church in Canada, coupled with the fact that these churches are the creations of individual initiatives, it has become difficult to identify the character and the nature of the Black church in Canada today.

Second, the emergence of AICs has made it difficult to identify a common theology that represents the Black church of the twenty-first century in Canada. In their studies of the Black church in the United States, Andrews (2002), Lincoln and Mamiya (1990), and Singleton (2002) identify two major theologies: "other-worldliness" and "this-worldliness." Other-worldliness theology focuses on building a spiritual path to heaven. Its theologians believe that "this world" is a transit place for Christians and heaven is the final destination. Thus, the responsibility of the Black church is to prepare parishioners for heaven, not to focus on parishioners' social struggles (Lincoln, 1999). By contrast, theologians of the this-worldliness branch of the Black church stress the importance of earthly matters to the Black community. Black preachers informed by this-worldliness encourage parishioners to pursue material wealth and live a flamboyant life on earth rather than waiting for riches in heaven (Martin et al., 2011). Although Andrews's (2002), Lincoln and Mamiya's (1990), and Singleton's (2002) typologies are heuristic and cannot be reified, they offer ideal types to help discuss the theologies of the Black church in the Canadian context.

In some sense, the theology of the Black church in Canada is structured broadly on a continuum spanning other-worldliness and this-worldliness, with some Black churches appearing to place more emphasis on this-worldliness. Arguably, this-worldliness theology appears to filter through the doctrines of almost all Black churches in Canada, but the situation seems to be excessive with African Initiated Churches. For this reason, my analyses and examples are draw from the activities of AICs. Further, my limited knowledge about the activities of AICs operated by African pastors who directly migrated to Canada from the Caribbean skews my examples and analyses towards AICs operated by African pastors who migrated to Canada from sub-Saharan Africa. This limitation,

I hope, does not discourage readers from seeing the relevance of the issues discussed below. In what follows, I briefly outline about how I collected, organized, and used the data I discuss.

Methods

The data of this essay were collected using a qualitative, in-depth, digitally recorded, semi-structured interview method. Since the study's focus is not to search for generalization but to identify participants' stories about their experience with the Black church, I opted for qualitative in-depth interviews, which, according to Hesse-Biber (2014), are relevant for assessing the "process" or "meaning" people assign to social situations and not for generalization purposes (p. 191; also see Mason, 2002). Twelve Christians who attend or had attended various denominations of AICs participated in the study. As already noted, I personally struggled while engaged in this study because I did not want it to feed into anti-Christian sentiments. It appears I was not the only one with this personal struggle. I noticed at the early stages of recruitment that not many Christians I approached to participate in the study were willing to talk openly about some of the issues in the Black church. Thus, I abandoned my initial plan of using purposive sampling to recruit participants and instead moved to snowball sampling. The limitation of this method is that I ended up with a majority of study participants who attend or had attended AICs. Only a few of the study participants attended other denominations (Presbyterian, Methodist, the Church of Pentecost, and Assemblies of God) of the Black church.

All study participants had at minimum obtained a bachelor's degree. In fact, one participant has a PhD, and another is in the closing stage of obtaining that degree. Four participants have master's degree. Five identified themselves as heterosexual males and seven as heterosexual females. The following questions guided the interview process: What is your current assessment of leadership in the Black church in your community? What do you make of the contemporary prosperity gospel preaching in some of the Black church? What do you see as important roles of the Black church in the Black community? Do you consider your church as a leading voice in the fight against social injustice and oppression facing the Black community? Do you have suggestions (if any) for ways to improve the existing relationship between the Black church and the Black community? I asked probing questions where necessary to gain further insights into what participants thought.

I collected the data between May 2014 and October 2015 in Toronto, Ottawa, and Ghana. Each individual interview lasted between thirty and forty minutes at places of participants' choosing and with the consent of each participant, I digitally recorded the interviews. I transcribed each interview and double-checked each transcription with the audio recording to ensure accuracy. Using NVivo 11 – a software program designed to sort qualitative data – as well as strategies suggested by Denzin and Lincoln (1994) for data organization and reduction, I coded and recoded transcripts according to the interview structure and emergent themes. With themes for the data formed, participants' responses were cross-referenced with interview notes and existing literature to tease out points of convergence and divergence, as well as sources of tension and pedagogic relevance. I relied on existing literature as a comparative base for interrogating and interpreting participants' responses. In order to protect the confidentiality and anonymity of participants, I gave each participant a pseudonym, as well as removed or modified any information that might reveal the identity of participants when reporting the findings. In addition, I edited each quote and statement of the participants to remove pause words (such as "like," "uh," and "um") and, where necessary, I corrected grammatical errors to make reading fluent. In editing the quotes, however, I was careful not to tamper with the substance of the conversation.

Given that the majority of study participants were drawn from AICs, the study findings are biased towards issues at the AICs. This suggests that not all findings in the study apply to other denominations in the Black church. However, some findings, such as the seemingly absent or diminished role of the Black church in community activism and the pursuit of social justice, are consistent within almost all denominations of the Black church. Further, as I have already mentioned, my lack of familiarity with the leadership activities in the Black church founded and operated by African Canadians originally from the Caribbean makes the analyses in this essay biased towards the operations and activities of the Black church as founded and operated by African Canadians from sub-Saharan Africa. Readers should therefore consider this when generalizing the findings of this essay. Despite the foregoing limitations, the study findings contribute to discussions about the role of the Black church in the twenty-first century.

The Study Findings

Commercialization and Commodification of Christianity

"Commercialism" refers to the syndromic tendency of people who are preoccupied with the desire to earn money or buy/sell goods rather than other values (Okoli, 2014). It also denotes an excessive emphasis on commercial profiteering. Commercialism in religious activities is a crude manifestation of commodification whereby every socio-religious/spiritual activity is commercialized for profit (Okoli, 2014, p. 78). Commodification is conceived as "the processes through which one or another aspect of material provisioning takes the form of commodity production and/or through which some economic agents seek to desire monetary revenues from material provisioning or immaterial activities that were not previously subject to monetary exchange" (Jessop, 2012, p. 17). Commodification and commercialism have been abiding features of the contemporary capitalist social formation, otherwise referred to as the market economy (Jessop, 2012; Okoli, 2014). Within neo-liberal corporate culture, commodification expands outside economic realms into the hitherto non-economic spheres that were exterior to the conventional realm of the market. Curiously, this trend of commodification is finding expression in the Black church of the twenty-first century. In what appears to be modern reformed Calvinistic principles, which exalt material success as a sign of one's spiritual state of grace (Weber, 1920), AICs have turned the Gospel of Christ into a multimillion-dollar industry in which spirituality is commodified and sold to the highest bidder.

In the interviews with the study participants, one of the emerging themes is commercialization and commodification of Christianity in the Black community. Preachers in this new brand of Black church teach their members to donate large sums of money, including tithing 10 per cent of their income to support church activities. Some of these denominations even sell prophylactic items, which preachers claim have performative and redemptive powers, to desperate and vulnerable members seeking answers to their varied problems. All Christian denominations, of course, engage in various methods to raise funds to support their activities; I do not critique that practice in itself. What is concerning, however, is that some of these fundraising methods are coded as a "transactional relationship" with God, in which God is "bound" by the principle of reciprocity to bless the donor in multiple forms. More troubling is the practice among some of the AICs where parishioners with no money are encouraged to borrow money to give as an offering.

Hannah, one of the study participants, recounted a statement made by a head pastor of an AIC in Canada:

> I recently heard a statement that a pastor had made and a very concerned church member called to talk to me about it, saying that "if you don't have money go and borrow and bring to the church." (Interview 12 December 2014)

Margaret, another study participant, also mentioned a case involving a friend who donated her college tuition fees to her church in Canada (Interview 17 June 2015). Andrew, a member of a traditional Black church – not an AIC – equally had something to say about the fundraising methods in the Black church. Although his pastor does not directly ask congregants to borrow money for donations, according to Andrew his pastor often invites congregants to donate a range of money (from one thousand to one hundred dollars) for special prayers:

> Money has become everything in the church today. When pastors call out members to donate specific funds in order to receive special prayers, those of us who have nothing to donate feel left out. This becomes more difficult when they start from $1,000 and come all the way to $100, and in each point, you are still sitting down with nothing to contribute. (Interview 14 July 2015)

Andrew's concern is not only that special prayers are tied to each level of donation – thereby creating an impression that a higher donation gives donors a chance for a greater blessing – but also that the manner of the fundraising prescribes a form of classism that makes those with nothing to contribute feel excluded and embarrassed.

Some preachers in AICs take fundraising to another level by selling prophylactic items such as blessed bottled water, handkerchiefs, olive oil, lime, and others spiritual props to congregants who are seeking prosperity and divine protection. Although this phenomenon of selling prophylactic items is not prevalent among AICs in Canada, it is popular in sub-Saharan Africa. In my conversation with study participants, almost all of them openly expressed concerns that the culture of selling prophylactic items is growing in AICs, especially in Africa. Abigail, a former congregant of AICs in Ghana and now a parishioner in a traditional Black church in Ghana, noted that she left her church because of the practice of selling prophylactics: "I left [that church] because of this practice of selling anointing oil, special water, and handkerchiefs" (Interview 9 June 2015).

Although Abigail believes in the "performative powers" of these prophylactic items, she felt those items should be free to members. Prince, a member of an AIC in Canada, shared the same view as Abigail. He too does not doubt the "divine powers" of these prophylactic items, but insisted that they ought to be free to church members (Interview 11 December 2014). Similar to study participants, some African clergy operating in sub-Saharan Africa – Reverend Dr Paul Frimpong Manso, the general superintendent of the Assemblies of God Church, Ghana;

and Dr Ezekiel Guti, the founder of Zimbabwe Assemblies of God – have strongly condemned the sale of prophylactic items and described it as excessive exploitation (Chakanyuka, 2015; Crentsil-Acquah, 2016).

The consensus from the study participants is that the Black church – whether traditional or AICs – overemphasizes money and is breeding new leaders who erroneously associate material possessions with godliness and a strong relationship with God. This quote from Johnson, a parishioner of a traditional Black church in Canada, best captures the general sentiment of participants about the culture of materialism creeping into the Black church:

> Most leaders today have missed the mandate of their calling and as a result they have come to a place whereby they believe that the portrayal of self-wealth gives them that leverage to portray it to people that they are called by God. They measure the level of their anointing or calling by the amount of wealth they are able to portray to the people and if I can show you this blessing, I can tell you do this and you would be blessed just as I am because I am talking to you from experience. (Interview 10 December 2014)

A closer look at the lifestyles of some pastors, in particular in the AICs, confirms Johnson's observation. Some of these pastors openly brag about their wealth and encourage their members not to see wealth and riches as the cornucopia of carnal indulgences, but instead as evidence of God's grace. In fact, some of the high-profile AIC preachers have their own private jets and fleet of luxury cars. This displayed wealth, unfortunately, does not trickle down to congregants. Congregants going through financial problems, misfortunes, and afflictions, in fact, are often told their problems are self-inflicted because they failed to pay tithes and free-will offerings (see Asamoah-Gyadu, 2014; Ashimolowo, 2006; Heward-Mills, 2009). Just as the early professional pardoners in the Catholic Church sold indulgence certificates to the highest bidders (Weber, 1920), some pastors of AICs are turning the gospel of Christ into a profit venture for themselves, their family members, and sycophants. The question is: How are these preachers able to get away with these practices given that some of their parishioners are highly educated?

Democracy, Transparency, and Accountability in the Black Church

Democracy is one system of governance that values and seeks to instantiate majority control, transparency, and accountability. In seeking a vibrant Black church to lead the Black community in the search for social justice and the protection of people's intrinsic rights, democracy must work and be seen to work within the church itself. Responses from study participants suggest that the attributes of democracy appear to be missing from the AICs. Hilda, a parishioner who previously attended an AIC in Canada, juxtaposes the decision-making process in the traditional Black church to that of the AICs. She concludes that the latter lacks democratic qualities. Whereas in the traditional Black church the board makes all-important decisions concerning the church's operation, including the salaries of pastors and when they should be transferred to other branches, Hilda does not see the same practice in the AICs. Hilda uses the term "one-man church" – a phrase that suggests one person alone makes all major decisions – to describe the lack of democracy in some AICs:

> My husband always refers to what he called "one-man church." In the more organized traditional churches like Catholic, Presbyterian, Pentecost, Methodist, Anglican and others, there are organized structure ways of accountability and decision-making process. Leadership does not evolve around one person. This is not the case of a one-man church. (Interview 12 December 2014)

Hilda further notes in the interview that she left her former church because the head pastor's salary was shrouded in secrecy. Nobody in the church knows the salary with the exception of two people in the church finance department. Pollock, also a parishioner of an AIC in Canada, has a slightly different story to tell about his former church. Although the church had an active board, the pastor did not subject himself to the board's authority. Instead, he took more salary than the amount the board had determined for him. He unilaterally put his family (wife and children) on the church payroll. When Pollock, as a board member, challenged this practice, he was branded an enemy of God's work (Interview 6 August 2015). Martin, a parishioner of an AIC in Canada, also spoke in general about the abuse of power and the lack of democracy in the AICs as a tradition borrowed from systems of government in some countries in Africa:

> Within the African context, leaders are dictators even in the church arena. Pastors want to be in full control because they want to control the people, dictate to the people. They don't want to be challenged. (Interview 8 December 2014)

Martin went on to explain that his pastor adopted a strategy of silencing dissent by claiming that all his decisions concerning the church's governance were informed by what he hears from God. By invoking

God's name, the pastor is able to justify his actions, because nobody in the church wants to challenge decisions that are coming from God (Interview 8 December 2014). Hilda further notes that there is a leadership crisis in many of the Black churches not only in Canada but also across the globe. She spoke about the role of Reverend Myles Munroe in responding to this global leadership crisis:

> The late Myles Munroe was doing a great work. God bless his soul and I know he is up there enjoying himself, but he was really concerned for this situation among people of African descent especially and the fact that there was a failure in leadership, and his last effort on this earth was all centred on this issue. He had such a sense of urgency, what he was doing was organizing a leadership forum for men of God to come and he was going from country to country talking about this, there are a lot of his videos online. His worry was the fact that African leaders both spiritually and secular lives did not want to pass on a baton of leadership, did not want to mentor others so that people will step in their shoes. Just wanted to keep everything for themselves, forgetting that the grave is waiting for them. (Interview 12 December 2014)

Although Hilda expressed her frustrations about the activities of the leaders of AICs in Canada, it is also interesting that she never hid her admiration for the leadership qualities of Myles Munroe, who is also the founder and leader of an AIC in the Bahamas, Bahamas Faith Ministries International. In a sense, Hilda was not against AICs in general, but only the activities of some AIC leaders who are abusing power and circumventing the democratic process in their churches.

The Pursuit of Social Justice in the Black Church

In his book *Prophesy Deliverance! An Afro-American Revolutionary Christianity*, Cornel West (1982) notes that Black theology has a unique opportunity to lead the liberation agenda of the Black community. Unfortunately, he writes, this has not been the case, because Black theologians have woefully failed to fully explore the relationship between oppression and the socio-economic order. From West's perspective, with the exception of Black theologian James Cone (see Cone, 1970), Black theologians in contemporary times have ignored the relationship between neo-liberal policies and practices and poverty and social needs in many parts of the world. Cone (1997) sees Black churches as silent community partners that have forgotten their liberating heritage. Silence in this context means that the Black churches have abandoned their social justice role. In my conversations with study participants, I asked them about the role of the contemporary Black church in the pursuit of social justice. Study participants were unanimous in responding that the Black church of today, whether traditional or AIC, has abandoned its historical social justice legacy. However, they gave different reasons for the church's lack of commitment to pursuing social justice for the Black community. Some suggested that Black preachers have focused so much on raising funds that they have no interest in matters of social justice. Hilda asked rhetorically: "If somebody is so interested in collecting the money for himself, how can he be capable of thinking of social justice" (Interview 12 December 2014)?

Others suggest that the seeming lack of interest in issues of social justice can be attributed to the lack of understanding and education among some of the contemporary Black preachers about social issues affecting the Black community. Even if preachers in the AICs are committed to talking about racism, sexism, and homophobia, they do not have any insightful knowledge about the subject matter. As Martin explained, many of the preachers in the AICs cannot lead the fight against social injustice because they themselves lack an explanation for or training on such issues:

> As we move from generation to generation, there are social changes and there are so many aspects of our community that unless you learn or you are taught you will not know, so the problem with our African leadership is that they spiritualized their calling to the extent that they believe that because they have been called by God the spirit of God will lead them, and therefore they fall short in the educational aspect of it. As a result of that they are misleading the people because their interpretation or explanation is out of context with our today's society and they are not able to stand up for any social cause or fight because they themselves have no training and the understanding to do so. (Interview 8 December 2014)

Another explanation offered is that some of the preachers in the Black Church – unlike activists such as Martin Luther King of the United States; David George, the Baptist preacher of Canada; and Reverend Charles Este of the United Church of Canada – have different understandings of their "calling." Those who see their calling as about serving the community will not hesitate to talk about issues that affect the community. This is how Johnson explained it:

> The leadership of people like Martin Luther King and the leaders of the past who stood up and fought for social injustices, the difference between them and today's leaders is that they saw their leadership as a mandate to

> serve the community, which involves fighting against racism and [other social ills] ... the position of today's leaders is more as a profession. (Interview 10 December 2014)

Martin agrees with Johnson's view about the connection between the pulpit and the fight against social issues affecting the community that preachers serve:

> If a leader is a servant leader that leader is a sacrificial leader, because the servant puts down his life for the flocks and the only one way you can see that is when you are able to ascribe everything within you as a leader to the one who called you, then you stand up for what the one who called talks against, you stand up when people are being maltreated, you stand up when people are being racially discriminated, you will stand up and voice because church leadership should not be limited to the church. It should be the community of worshippers and it includes everybody out there that we been mandated to bring to Christ that we have not even approached them yet ... But today because people are in leadership not to sacrifice but to gain and that is the centrality of our leaders today. (Interview 8 December 2014)

In his tribute to the leadership qualities of Reverend Charles Este, David Este (2004) notes that Reverend Este was once described as "the secular leader of the Black community" (p. 16) because in his ministry at the United Church of Canada in the 1920s, he did not separate his ecclesiastical duties from the social issues affecting the Black community. Instead, he used his platform as a Black preacher to remind the White society that "Blacks were the forgotten people" of Canada, and even "urged the local industries and businesses to hire Blacks" (p. 16). It appears both Martin and Johnson are expecting leaders of the contemporary Black church to make the Black community the centre of their ministries.

Discussion: Commercialization and Commodification of Christianity

The ascendancy of neo-liberal corporate culture within every aspect of human life has had harmful effects on the most vulnerable in our society (Brown, 2005; Giroux, 2008; Martin, 2007). According to the United Way of Toronto and the Canadian Council on Social Development (2004), the number of racialized families living in poverty increased 362 per cent between 1980 and 2000. This figure is likely to be higher when one narrows the parameters to the Black community (see Hum & Simpson 2007;

Li 2008; also see Block & Galabuzi 2011). In the case of sub-Saharan Africa, the figure is even more startling. Despite the Millennium Development Goals (MDGs) and other supporting programs from the global North, as many as 556 million people living in sub-Saharan Africa survive on less than (US) two dollars a day (World Bank, 2010).

In the midst of these economic uncertainties and social oppression, many people from the Black community are looking to the Black church to lead the fight against neo-liberalism and shield the Black community. The Black church has, unfortunately, been equally caught up in corporate greed and the culture of individualism and materialism associated with neo-liberalism. As became clear from the study's findings, the theology of prosperity has blunted the church's awareness of durable inequities within society. If wealth and aspiration to upward social mobility are connected to God's blessings just as poverty and social ills are connected to God's punishment, as prosperity theology suggests, then poverty and deprivation are not the creations of structural inequities but the creation of a divine power. In that case, those who seek upward mobility and wealth have to rely on the knowledge and wisdom of these preachers – whose flamboyant lifestyles suggest that they have found the solution to poverty and deprivation. As the study findings suggest, some within the Black church have adopted a mean-spirited competitiveness, selfishness, and greed to the point that even prayers for God's blessings are doled out in proportion to parishioners' ability to make big donations. Prayers that assure a twenty-hour-hour miracle are given only to those who can donate large sums of money. As Andrew, a study participant, suggested about his church: the poor and the needy are made to feel unwanted and underserving of God's grace and blessings. In the past, the Black church was a place of refuge for the Black community, a place where the poor, the needy, and the most vulnerable knew they would be accepted and treated as humans regardless of their socio-economic status. Today, the prosperity gospel theology running amok in the church has stripped off the caring content in the Black church. It has become numbed and less responsive to the scourges of racism, poverty, and social inequalities targeting members of the Black community, some of whom are parishioners of the Black church.

As I was writing this essay, a story broke that a Ghanaian-Canadian church in Toronto had bought a private jet as a birthday gift to their pastor. In an interview, the pastor who received the private jet noted, "Every church should do this for *their* pastors if *they* can" (Doe, 2016, para.7). Generally, there is nothing extraordinary about parishioners giving birthday gifts to pastors. However, a private jet as a birthday gift is extraordinary, and I, for example, would not associate such an ostentatious display of wealth with a church that operates 4.5 kilometres from Jane and Finch, a predominantly Black community known for its economic and social exclusion (see Opoku-Dapaah, 2006, 1993; Owusu, 1998, 1999; Wong, 2000; Zaami, 2012). The incident brings to mind what Hilda, a study participant, asked rhetorically: if Black preachers are so engrossed in raising funds, would they have time to care about social injustice issues affecting their parishioners?

More worryingly, the display of ostentatious lifestyles and the seemingly inadequate support for the Black community, including parishioners, is becoming a global trend. In his studies of African Canadian churches in four major cities in Canada, Baffoe (2013) observes that some pastors are using religion to exploit parishioners for their personal gain. Bonsu and Belk (2009, 2010) and Quayesi-Amakye (2011) alluded to similar exploitation in Ghana, where some pastors are using the gospel of prosperity to make themselves rich while leaving parishioners in poverty. In Nigeria, Phiri and Maxwell (2007) write about what they described as a growing "prosperity-tinged Pentecostalism" that opens the floodgates for exploitation in the Nigerian community. Maxwell (1998) makes similar observations about Zimbabwe, and Andersen (2005) about South Africa. Writing in general about the continent of Africa, Wariboko (2012) and Gifford (1990) have spoken against the prosperity gospel that has locked sub-Saharan Africa in economic exploitation. Chesnut (1997, 2012) and Soares (2008) have observed similar trends in Brazil and the Caribbean, respectively. Barnes (2012), Austin (2004), and Glaude (2015) have equally condemned a prosperity gospel ministry that has privatized social misery and encouraged a culture of mean-spiritedness that sanctions selfishness and greed in the United States. The situation is becoming so disturbing in the United States that Professor Eddie Glaude Jr (2012) titled his provocative article in *Huffington Post* "The Black Church Is Dead." The fear is that if this trend continues, the Black church will be dead to the Black community.

Further, as the study noted, the leaders of many Black churches escape the scrutiny of their parishioners because they use God's name to justify their autocratic decisions, a practice that is not common in the traditional denominations in the Black church. In my conversations with study participants, it became obvious that pastors in the AICs, in particular, get away with their autocratic leadership styles for several reasons. First, these preachers are blessed with oratory and specialize in entertaining people. This distracts parishioners from asking critical questions about church finances and undemocratic decisions. Second, if congregants do manage to see through these preachers' facades and demand accountability and transparency from them, the dissenters are quickly branded as the enemies of God's work. Third, the preachers intimidate congregants by presenting themselves as oracles of God; congregants thus become afraid to challenge their undemocratic decisions.

This finding about undemocratic leadership in the Black AICs is consistent with similar studies done by Bonsu and Belk (2010) in Ghana and Baffoe (2013) in Canada. In Bonsu and Belk's study (2010), they note that congregants who are independent thinkers, and whose views do not mesh with those of their pastor, are often encouraged to "bind the spirit of disloyalty" (p. 311) that creates such independent thoughts. In Baffoe (2013)'s study, some congregants accused their head pastors of running the church like their personal business:

> Our pastor ran the church as his private property. Although we had a Council of Deacons and Elders in the Church, the pastor always took unilateral decisions, announced them in the church and demanded total agreement and compliance from the membership. It became clearer and clearer that the so-called collective leadership we put in place in the church was a farce. He always appointed his cronies and those that never challenged his decisions to leadership positions, especially those that involved finances. Over time, he and his wife had total control of the church finances. (p. 311)

Obviously, the activities of the AICs as outlined in the essay complicate the social relevance of the Black church within the Black community, in many senses. For some in the United States, the Black church has lost its earthly relevance to the Black community (Glaude, 2012; West, 1999), and to others like the late Steve Bantu Biko of South Africa, the Black church has become "an *ivory tower*" to the Black community (Biko, 1987, para. 16). To my study participants, the message of freedom and hope for the oppressed and vulnerable has been replaced with a wealth workshop where Black preachers are doing the bidding of neo-liberalism and capitalism. The question of how the Black church can situate its historical and political role in today's context is a vital concern.

Although there are those asking the Black community in the United States to forget about the Black church and instead look to Black secular organizations in the fight against social injustice and racism in the Black community (Mukenge, 1983; Nelsen, 1988), I argue that this suggestion may be too hasty in the Canadian context. In spite of its contemporary challenges, the Black church remains a firm anchor that stabilizes the Black experience and gives it meaning in an era of uncertain but radical change and counter-change (Lincoln & Mamiya, 1990, p. 398). One only needs to travel to many parts of sub-Saharan Africa or any Black community in Canada and the United States on any given Sunday morning to appreciate the lasting effects of the Black church on the Black community. Thus the focus should be on ways in which the Black church can regain its important historical role as the voice of justice for the Black community. In the remaining pages of this essay, I offer some practical suggestions that can help improve the relationship between the Black church and the Black community.

Radical Leadership, a New Spiritual Direction for the Black Church: Final Thoughts

For a start, the Black church can restore its historical social justice legacy by first untangling itself from the theology of prosperity that offers false hope that poverty, unemployment, unaffordable housing, and other social issues affecting Black communities and society at large can be "cured" through prayers and healthy donations to the church. As a Christian, I know and understand the obligation of churches to raise funds to support their programs, and I hasten to say that I am not against fundraising in general. But turning the relationship between God and parishioners into a *quid pro quo* transaction (Jones, 1998), where God is "reduced to a kind of 'cosmic bellhop' attending to the needs and desires" of parishioners who give big donations to the church (Goff, 1990, p. 21) is a clear misapplication and misinterpretation of scriptures.

Second, the Black church must lead the crusade against poverty among its parishes, in the Black community and beyond to other races and religions. Dewi Hughes (2008) notes that the Old Testament laws restrain the rich and the powerful from exploiting the poor and the helpless in society. Taking cues from the Old Testament, the Black church must resist what Warren Gardner MacDonald (1981) describes as "the Gehazi-Simon syndrome"[1] (p. 33) – a practice where preachers put monetary value on the grace of God. Ronald Sider (1997) observes, "If centrality in Scripture is any criterion of doctrinal importance, the biblical teaching about God's concern for the poor ought to be an important doctrine for Christians" (p. 64). In this context, it is instructive for Black churches to draw some lessons from the Book of Acts, where the early church became a redistribution centre that shares wealth and resources among needy parishioners. As the author of Acts 4:34–35 describes it: "There was not a needy person among them, for as many as were owners of lands or houses sold them and brought the proceeds of what was sold and laid it at the apostles' feet, and it was distributed to each as any had need." Instead of pushing for new church buildings and an improved architectural design, the Black church must refocus its energy and resources on programs that support the poor and the disadvantaged in their parish.

Perhaps the time is overdue for Black churches to slow down on fund-raising programs that buy expensive gifts on "Pastors' appreciation day" and pastors' birthdays and rechannel those funds into effective programs that can eradicate poverty in church membership and the larger society. The Black churches need selfless leadership, leaders who are more driven by the collective interest of parishioners than their personal comfort. Some Black churches in Toronto – Christian Centre Church, Grant Church of African Methodist Episcopal (AME), and Metropolitan Community Centre of Toronto – who have programs such as "Inner City Outreach," "Soup Kitchen," and "Healing Racism" to support the Black community, set good examples for emulation. Although the activities of these churches may not be adequate in addressing the Black community's problems, they are steps in the right direction, and a far departure from those who want Black churches to buy private jets for their pastors.

Third, the Black church in the twenty-first century requires a theological balance between heavenly matters and earthly issues. As an African who grew up in a small community in Ghana, I have seen and heard things that cannot be explained rationally or scientifically. I am concerned, therefore, about those who dismiss people who cling to the theology of demonology as naïve and superstitious. Yet I am equally disturbed by pastors who attribute anything relating to human suffering to mystical powers. While under-application of the Bible as a book of metaphors with no relevance to contemporary issues is dangerous, over-application of the Bible to spiritualize and mystify everything is equally dangerous. The challenge is to create a balance of interpretation and application of the Bible. The Black church needs to create a balanced theology that warns followers of evils of this world while helping them to shift attention to God's grace, goodness, and promises to provide, even as believers take seriously the socially constructed sources of their individual problems.

Fourth, the Black church must become the catalyst to continue the quest for equity, fairness, and social justice within the Black community and the larger society. Sermons from the pulpit must synchronize the spiritual needs of the people with the general material conditions of the community. Archbishop Desmond Tutu of South Africa asked an important question about the Black church's post-apartheid era, and this question is equally relevant today:

> If [the Black Church] say[s] that religion cannot be concerned with politics, then we are really saying that there is a substantial part of human life in which God's writ does not run. Religion is not a form of escapism. Our God does not permit us to dwell in a kind of spiritual ghetto, insulated from the real life out there. Our God is not a God who sanctifies the status quo.

> He is a God of surprises, uprooting the powerful and unjust to establish His Kingdom. (cited in Sparks, 2006, p. 295)

Archbishop Tutu's words are a reminder that spirituality in the Black community has been the driving force through which many Blacks have situated their resistant projects against systemic racism and oppression (Cone, 1997, 1999; Stewart, 1999; West, 1999). It is not surprising that many civil/social rights activist icons from Black communities around the globe were spiritual leaders who practised God-centred spirituality. Space is not available to name and celebrate these heroes and heroines of faith, but I would be remiss to not mention a few: Harriet Tubman (nicknamed Black Moses), George Washington Carver, W.E.B. Du Bois, Martin Luther King Jr, Viola Desmond, Thomas Peters, Mary Ann Shadd, William Pearly Oliver, Nelson Mandela, Desmond Tutu, and Malcolm X. These individuals used their faith and spirituality as platforms to advance a social agenda to promote the virtues of love, peace, and reconciliation while openly confronting the tyrannies of racism, classism, and structural violence. These heroes and heroines of Black tradition did not concern themselves with religious ritualistic pedigrees that sometimes become camouflage for do-nothingism and holier-than-thou attitudes, but rather had unwavering commitment to the fight against social injustice regardless of what the issues were and who was affected.

Michael Dantley (2005) describes African American spirituality as an unassailable force that guards the people against the potential bondage of embracing the feeling of self-degradation, bitterness, and hopelessness due to systemic and institutional racism, sexism, and classism. He asserts:

> African American spirituality is critically creative in that it allows for Black citizens in the United States to envision life as it might be. Spirituality is a source of performative creativity in that spirituality prods many African Americans to not only dream but to also strategize. Dreaming and visioning is a spiritual matter that demands courage and great faith. To dream is courageous enough, but to blend dreaming with an agenda of expected change moves into the realm of a kind of active or militant faith. (p. 655)

In envisioning radical leadership for Black churches in the twenty-first century, the pulpit must be used to activate what Cornel West (1982, 1993) calls *aggressive* faith – internal belief that the *as is* of any given situation can be overcome for the better *not yet* (Dantley, 2005, p. 656). Aggressive faith dwells on possibilities and, ultimately, the hope of reclaiming social justice. Such faith produces actions and strategies that critically interrogate systemic inequalities while yearning for the better future.

In such radical spaces, Black church services not only become a litany of prayers, praises, and worship, offertory and tithing, sermons, announcements, and benedictions, but also become spaces for nurturing and constructing critically reflective citizens who are willing to hold their leaders (both spiritual and secular) accountable and responsible. These are not utopia ideas. David George, Reverend Charles Este, Thomas Peters, Mary Ann Shadd, William Pearly Oliver, Harriet Tubman, Martin Luther King, Nelson Mandela, and others, through their actions, showed that Christian living that aspires to God's grace, love, redemption, hope, and peace is not exclusive of the pursuit of a just society. These great heroes and heroines understood that their radical resistance to racism, poverty, sexism, and social oppression is their practical demonstration of the agapeistic love ethic of God. As Palmer (1999) astutely observes, "No punishment anyone might lay on us could possibly be worse than the punishment we lay on ourselves by conspiring in our own diminishment, by living a divided life, by failing to make that fundamental decision to act and speak on the outside in ways consonant with the truth we know on the inside" (p. 32). This must be the guiding principle and the rallying cry of the Black church in the twenty-first century. It must return to its first love: the social, compassionate, and liberating gospel of Jesus the Christ that did not shy away from the social and cultural realities of racism, classism, sexism, and neo-liberal policies that wreak havoc in the Black community as it does with others. There is balm after all in Gilead; all the Black church need do is to apply it to the Black community and the larger society.

NOTE

1 In 2 Kings 5:15–27 and Acts 8:9–24, respectively, Gehazi and Simon the Sorcerer in different ways attempted to place material value on the gifts of God, and in both cases they were punished severely – Gehazi with leprosy and Simon with blindness.

REFERENCES

Alexander, K., & Glaze, A. (1996). *Towards freedom: The African-Canadian experience.* Toronto: Umbrella.

Anderson, A. (2005). New African initiated pentecostalism and charismatics in South Africa. *Journal of Religion in Africa, 35*(1), 66–92. https://doi.org/10.1163/1570066052995843

Andrews, D.P. (2002). *Practical theology for black churches: Bridging black theology and African American folk religion.* Louisville: Westminster John Knox.

Asamoah-Gyadu, J.K. (2014). *Prosperity and poverty in the Bible: Search for balance.* Paper presented at the 2014 Lausanne Global Consultation on Prosperity Theology, Poverty, and the Gospel, São Paulo, Brazil.

Ashimolowo, M. (2006). *The coming wealth transfer.* London: Mattyson Media.

Austin, D. (2004). "In God we trust": The cultural and social impact of affinity fraud in the African American church. *University of Maryland Law Journal of Race, Religion, Gender and Class, 4,* 365–409.

Baffoe, M. (2013). Spiritual well-being and fulfilment, or exploitation by a few smart ones? The proliferation of Christian churches in West African immigrant communities in Canada. *Mediterranean Journal of Social Sciences, 4*(1), 305–16.

Barnes, S.L. (2012). *Live long and prosper: How black megachurches address HIV/AIDS and poverty in the age of prosperity theology.* New York: Oxford University Press.

Biko, S. (1987). The church as seen by a young layman. Retrieved 20 March 2016 from http://v1.sahistory.org.za/pages/library-resources/articles_papers/1987_biko_church_frank.html

Bird, W. (2007). *Megachurches as spectator religion: Using social network theory and free-rider theory to understand the spiritual vitality of America's largest-attendance churches* (Doctoral dissertation). Fordham University, New York.

Block, S., & Galabuzi, G.-E. (2011). *Canada's colour coded labour market: The gap for racialized workers.* Ottawa: Canadian Centre for Policy Alternatives.

Bonsu, S.K., & Belk, R.W. (2009). *Oh Lord, won't You buy me a Mercedes?: Materialism in the new African Pentecostalism.* Schulich School of Business, York University, Toronto.

Bonsu, S.K., & Belk, R.W. (2010). Marketing a new African God: Pentecostalism and material salvation in Ghana. *International Journal of Nonprofit and Voluntary Sector Marketing, 15*(4), 305–23. https://doi.org/10.1002/nvsm.398

Boyd, F.S., Jr. (1976). Introduction. In P.E. McKerrow (Ed.), *A brief history of the Coloured Baptists of Nova Scotia, 1785–1895* (pp. xiv). Halifax: Nova Scotia Department of Education.

Brown, W. (2005). *Edgework: Critical essays on knowledge and politics.* Princeton: Princeton University Press.

Brown, W., & Senior, H. (1984). *Victorious in defeat: The Loyalists in Canada.* Toronto: Methuen.

Brown Spencer, E.A. (2009). *The Black Oneness Church in perspective* (Doctoral dissertation). University of Toronto, Toronto.

Calhoun-Brown, A. (2000). Upon this rock: The black church, nonviolence, and the civil rights movement. *PS: Political Science & Politics, 33*(02), 169–74. https://doi.org/10.1017/S1049096500060911

Carniol, N. (2006, 12 January). Make children the bottom line; leaders urged to seize momentum: Pastor challenges politicians, churches. *Toronto Star,* p. E4.

Chadwick-Parkes, S. (2012). *Youth armed violence interventions: The Caribbean and its Toronto diaspora.* Retrieved from http://ploughshares.ca/wp-content/uploads/2012/08/youth-violence-manual-web-pdf.pdf.

Chakanyuka, T. (2015). Guti blasts new prophets, anointing oils. *Sunday News.* Retrieved from http://www.sundaynews.co.zw/guti-blasts-new-prophets-anointing-oils/

Chesnut, R.A. (1997). *Born again in Brazil: The Pentecostal boom and the pathogens of poverty.* New Brunswick: Rutgers University Press.

Chesnut, R.A. (2012). Prosperous prosperity: Why the health and wealth gospel is booming across the globe. In A. Attanasi & A. Young (Eds.), *Pentecostalism and prosperity: The socio-economics of the global charismatic movement* (pp. 215–24). New York: Palgrave Macmillan.

Chong, G. (2006, 19 January). Helping youth help themselves: Offer support but instill family values. *Toronto Star,* p. A18.

Clairmont, D., & Magill, D. (1970). *Nova Scotia blacks: An historical and structural overview* Halifax: Institute of Public Affairs, Dalhousie University.

Cone, J.H. (1970). *Black theology and black power.* New York: Orbis.

Cone, J.H. (1997). *God of the oppressed.* New York: Orbis.

Cone, J.H. (1999). Calling the oppressors to account: Justice, love and hope in Black religion. In Q.H. Dixie & C. West (Eds.), *Courage to hope: From Black suffering to human redemption* (pp. 74–85). Boston: Beacon.

Crentsil-Acquah, M. (Producer). (2016, 20 March). *Jesus never sold oils for miracles; ignore fake pastors – Head of Assemblies of God* [Video file]. Retrieved from http://www.myjoyonline.com/news/2016/february-6th/video-jesus-never-sold-oils-for-miracles-ignore-fake-pastors-head-of-assemblies-of-god.php

Dantley, M.E. (2005). African American spirituality and Cornel West's notions of prophetic pragmatism: Restructuring educational leadership in American urban schools. *Educational Administration Quarterly, 41*(4), 651–74. https://doi.org/10.1177/0013161X04274274

Denzin, N.K., & Lincoln, Y.S. (1994). *Handbook of qualitative research.* Thousand Oaks: Sage.

Doe, E.E. (2016, 10 June). *Church in Canada buys private jet for Ghanaian pastor.* Retrieved from https://yen.com.gh/44035-photos-see-church-canada-bought-pastor.html#44035

Este, D. (2004). The black church as a social welfare institution: Union United Church and the development of Montreal's black community, 1907–1940. *Journal of Black Studies, 35*(1), 3–22. https://doi.org/10.1177/0021934703261938

Felder, C. (1995). Biblical interpretation and black Christianity. In F.E. Harris, J.T. Roberson, & L.D. George (Eds.), *What does it mean to be black and Christian?: Pulpit, pew, and academy in dialogue* (pp. 19–38). Nashville: Townsend.

Frazier, E.F. (1974). *The Negro church in America.* New York: Schocken.

Gifford, P. (1990). Prosperity: A new and foreign element in African Christianity. *Religion, 20*(4), 373–88. https://doi.org/10.1016/0048-721X(90)90119-Q

Gifford, P. (2004). *Ghana's new Christianity: Pentecostalism in a globalizing African economy.* Bloomington.: Indiana University Press.

Giroux, H.A. (2008). Beyond the biopolitics of disposability: Rethinking neoliberalism in the new gilded age. *Social Identities, 14*(5), 587–620. https://doi.org/10.1080/13504630802343432

Glaude, S.E., Jr. (2012). The black church is dead. *Huffington Post.* Retrieved from http://www.huffingtonpost.com/eddie-glaude-jr-phd/the-black-church-is-dead_b_473815.html

Glaude, S.E., Jr. (2015). Too many black churches preach the gospel of greed. *New York Times.* Retrieved from https://www.nytimes.com/roomfordebate/2014/06/25/has-capitalism-become-incompatible-with-christianity/too-many-black-churches-preach-the-gospel-of-greed

Goff, J.J.R. (1990, 19 February). The faith that claims. *Christianity Today, 34,* 18–21.

Hesse-Biber, S.N. (Ed.) (2014). *Feminist research practice: A primer.* California: Sage.

Heward-Mills, D. (2009). *Why non-tithing Christians become poor and how tithing Christians become rich.* Wellington, South Africa: Lux Verbi BM.

Hill, D. (1981). *The freedom seekers: Blacks in early Canada.* Agincourt: Book Society of Canada.

Hughes, D.A. (2008). *Power and poverty: Divine and human rule in a world of need.* Nottingham: Intervarsity.

Hulchanski, J.D. (2010). *The three cities within Toronto.* Toronto: Cities Centre.

Hum, D., & Simpson, W. (2007). The legacy of immigration: Labour market performance and education in the second generation. *Applied Economics, 39*(15), 1985–2009. https://doi.org/10.1080/00036840600690223

Israel, W. (1928). *The Montreal negro community* (Master's thesis). McGill University, Montreal.

Jessop, B. (2012). Understanding the "economization" of social formations. In U. Schimank & U. Volkmann (Eds.), *The marketization of society: Economizing the non-economic* (pp. 5–36). Breman, Germany: Research Network "Welfare Societies," University of Bremen.

Jones, D.W. (1998). The bankruptcy of the prosperity gospel: An exercise in biblical and theological ethics. *Faith and Mission, 16*(1), 79–85.

Keung, N. (2016). Canada chided for treatment of black people by UN group. Retrieved from https://www.thestar.com/news/immigration/2016/11/02/canada-chided-for-treatment-of-black-people-by-un-group.html

Lewis, S. (1992). *Report of the race relations and policing task force.* Toronto: Government of Ontario.

Li, P.S. (2008). *The market value and social value of race.* Toronto: Canadian Scholars' Press.

Lincoln, C.E. (1999). Introduction. In A. Billingsley (Ed.), *Mighty like a river: The Black church and social reform* (pp. xix–xxiv). New York: Oxford University Press.

Lincoln, C.E., & Mamiya, L.H. (1990). *The black church in the African American experience.* Durham: Duke University Press.

MacDonald, W.G. (1981). The cross versus personal kingdoms. *Pneuma, 3*(1), 26–37. https://doi.org/10.1163/157007481X00106

Martin, P.P., Bowles, T.A., Adkins, L., & Leach, M.T. (2011). Black mega-churches in the internet age: Exploring theological teachings and social outreach efforts. *Journal of African American Studies, 15*(2), 155–76. https://doi.org/10.1007/s12111-011-9181-2

Martin, R. (2007). *An empire of indifference: American war and the financial logic of risk management.* Durham: Duke University Press.

Mason, G. (2002). *The spectacle of violence: Homophobia, gender, and knowledge.* New York: Routledge.

Maxwell, D. (1998). "Delivered from the spirit of poverty?": Pentecostalism, prosperity and modernity in Zimbabwe. *Journal of Religion in Africa, 28*(3), 350–73. https://doi.org/10.1163/157006698X00053

McMurtry, R., & Curling, A. (2008). *The review of the root cause of youth violence.* Toronto: Queen's Printer for Ontario.

Mensah, J. (2009). "Doing religion" overseas: The characteristics and functions of Ghanaian immigrant churches in Toronto, Canada. *Societies Without Borders,* 4(1), 21–44. https://doi.org/10.1163/187219108X300037

Morrison, T. (1993). *Playing in the dark: Whiteness and the literary imagination.* New York: Vintage.

Mukenge, I.R. (1983). *The black church in urban America: A case study in political economy.* New York: University Press of American.

Murphy, T., & Perlin, R. (1996). *A concise history of Christianity in Canada.* Toronto: Oxford University Press.

Nelsen, H.M. (1988). Unchurched black Americans: Patterns of religiosity and affiliation. *Review of religious research, 29*(4), 398–412. https://doi.org/10.2307/3511578

Okoli, A.C. (2014). Commercialism and commodification of illicity: A political economy of baby buying/selling in south east of Nigeria. *International Journal of Liberal Arts and Social Science, 2*(2), 77–85. Retrieved from https://www.ijlass.org/data/frontImages/gallery/Vol._2_No._2/8.pdf

Ontario Human Rights Commission. (2003). *Paying the price: The human cost of racial profiling: Inquiry report* Toronto: Government of Ontario.

Opoku-Dapaah, E. (1993). *Inventory of African community groups in Metropolitan Toronto.* North York: York Lanes.

Opoku-Dapaah, E. (2006). African immigrants in Canada: Trends, socio-demographic and spatial aspects. In K. Konadu-Agyemang, B.K. Takyi, & J.A.

Arthur (Eds.), *The new African diaspora in North America: Trends, community building and adaption* (pp. 69–93). New York: Rowman and Littlefield.

Owusu, T.Y. (1998). To buy or not to buy: Determinants of home ownership among Ghanaian immigrants in Toronto. *Canadian Geographer, 42*(1), 40–52. https://doi.org/10.1111/j.1541-0064.1998.tb01551.x

Owusu, T.Y. (1999). Residential patterns and housing choices of Ghanaian immigrants in Toronto, Canada. *Housing Studies, 14*(1), 77–97. https://doi.org/10.1080/02673039983019

Palmer, P. (1999). The grace of great things: Reclaiming the sacred in knowing, teaching and learning. In S. Glazer (Ed.), *The heart of learning: Spirituality in education* (pp. 15–32). New York: Jeremey P. Tarcher/Putnam.

Perry, D. (1998). *Breaking down barriers: A black evangelical explains the black church.* Grand Rapids: Baker.

Phiri, I., & Maxwell, J. (2007). Gospel riches: Africa's rapid embrace of prosperity pentecostalism provokes concern and hope. *Christianity Today.* Retrieved from http://www.christianitytoday.com/ct/2007/july/12.22.html

Putnam, R.D. (2000). *Bowling alone: The collapse and revival of American community.* New York: Simon and Schuster.

Quayesi-Amakye, J. (2011). Prosperity and prophecy in African Pentecostalism. *Journal of Pentecostal Theology, 20*(2), 291–305. https://doi.org/10.1163/174552511X597161

Riley, R. (2016, 3 July). The forgotten exodus: 7 facts about the Black Loyalists and 3,600 refugee Negroes escaping American Wars to Canada. Retrieved from http://www.africanamerica.org/topic/the-forgotten-exodus-7-facts-about-the-black-loyalists-and-3-600-refugee-negroes-escaping-american-wars-to-canada#lastReply

Rivers, E. (2006). Growing up without men [Radio broadcast]. *Metro Morning,* CBC Radio, Toronto.

Sapers, H. (2015). *Annual report of the Office of the Correctional Investigator 2014–2015.* Retrieved from http://www.oci-bec.gc.ca/cnt/rpt/annrpt/annrpt20142015-eng.aspx

Saunders, D. (2016). Why black Canadians are facing U.S.-style problems. *Globe and Mail.* Retrieved from https://www.theglobeandmail.com/opinion/why-black-canadians-are-facing-us-style-problems/article30939514/

Shreve, D.S. (1983). *The African Canadian church: A stabilizer.* Jordan Station: Paideia.

Sider, R.J. (1997). *Rich Christians in an age of hunger: A biblical study.* London: Hodder and Stoughton.

Singleton, H.H. (2002). *Black theology and ideology: Deideological dimensions in the theology of James H. Cone.* Collegeville: Liturgical Press.

Smith, T.L. (1978). Religion and ethnicity in America. *American Historical Review, 83*(5) 1155–85. https://doi.org/10.2307/1854689

Soares, J. (1992). *New churches, old ideology: The role of fundamentalism in Jamaican politics, 1980–1988* (Doctoral dissertation). Queen's University, Kingston.

Soares, J. (2008). Religion and poverty in the Caribbean. *Peace Review, 20*(2), 226–34. https://doi.org/10.1080/10402650802068242

Sparks, A. (2006). *The mind of South Africa: The story of the rise and fall of apartheid.* Johannesburg: Jonathan Ball.

Statistics Canada. (2011). *2011 national household survey: Data tables: Immigration and ethnocultural diversity.* Ottawa: Statistics Canada.

Statistics Canada. (2012). Population. Retrieved from http://www.statcan.gc.ca/pub/12-581-x/2012000/pop-eng.htm

Stewart, C.F. (1999). *Black spirituality and black consciousness: Soul force, culture, and freedom in the African-American experience.* Trenton: Africa World Press.

United Way of Toronto and the Canadian Council on Social Development. (2004). *Poverty by postal code: The geography of neighbourhood poverty, 1981–2001.* Toronto: United Way of Toronto.

Vipond, P. (1976). The road to now: Retired community worker and shipbuilder Charles Ashby recalls five decades of life for Montreal's blacks. *Spear Magazine, 5*, p. 14.

Walcott, R., Foster, C., Campbell, M., & Sealy, D. (2008). *Racial minority perspectives on violence: A report prepared for the review of the roots of youth violence.* Toronto: Ministry of Children and Youth Services.

Walker, J. (1979). *The black experience in Canada.* Toronto: Ontario Educational Communications Authority.

Walker, J. (1992). *The Black Loyalists: The search for a promised land in Nova Scotia and Sierra Leone 1783–1870.* Toronto: University of Toronto Press.

Walker, J. (1995). African Canadians. In M. Magocsi (Ed.), *Encyclopedia of Canada's people* (pp. 139–76). Toronto: University of Toronto Press.

Wariboko, N. (2012). Pentecostal paradigms of national economic prosperity in Africa. In A. Attanasi & A. Yong (Eds.), *Pentecostalism and prosperity: The socio-economics of the global charismatic movement* (pp. 35–62). New York: Palgrave Macmillan.

Weber, M. (1920). *The Protestant ethic and the spirit of capitalism.* London: Unwin Hyman.

West, C. (1982). *Prophesy deliverance: An Afro-American revolutionary Christianity.* Philadelphia: Westminster John Knox.

West, C. (1993). *Keeping faith: Philosophy and race in America*: New York: Routledge.

West, C. (1999). *The Cornel West reader.* New York: Civitas.

Wetmore, D., & Sellick, L.B. (Eds.). (1983). *Loyalist in Nova Scotia.* Hantsport: Lancelot.

Winks, R.W. (1971). *The blacks in Canada: A history.* New Haven: Yale University Press.

Wong, M. (2000). Ghanaian women in Toronto's labour market: Negotiating gendered roles and transnational household strategies. *Canadian Ethnic Studies, 2,* 45–74.

World Bank. (2010). *World development indicators.* Washington, DC: International Bank for Reconstruction and Development/World Bank.

Zaami, M. (2012). *Experiences of socio-spatial exclusion among Ghanaian immigrant youth in Toronto: A case study of the Jane-Finch neighbourhood* (Master's thesis). University of Western Ontario, London, ON.

PART FIVE

Black Intellectuals

13 An Indigenous Africentric Perspective on Black Leadership

GEORGE J. SEFA DEI

This chapter presents a vision and a theoretical framework for thinking about leadership in the African Canadian community. It does so at a critical juncture in history when anti-Blackness, anti-Black racism, and state-sanctioned violence against Black bodies are daily occurrences. In particular, the chapter argues *for* African Canadian leadership *from* African Canadian intellectuals, a form of leadership that acknowledges membership in, and indebtedness to, the Black community across space and time, as well as leadership that is not inhibited by what I call the intellectual gymnastics of poststructuralism and postmodernism. Clearly, these are ongoing intellectual trends that complicate the possibilities of such leadership. They cannot be divorced from the Eurocentric academy and political and social climate in which they are formed, and mitigate against and impinge upon Black intellectual involvement in Black resistance and community interests, broadly conceived. I assert that a theorization of the leadership responsibilities of Black academics must confront these challenges in relation to an African-centred vision and set of principles to guide Black academic leadership. Black intellectual leadership must identify and understand the nature and complexity of the challenges our varied communities face today. Consequently, an effective discussion of Black intellectual leadership must also highlight specific social issues over which African Canadian academics can assert our cultural and scholarly "capital" to provide our communities with knowledge resources as the means for socially transformative struggles.

In the current climate of anti-Blackness, the mere presence of progressive Black leadership is an important intervention. Such leadership must seek ethical and active participation in anti-racist, anti-colonial struggles from the standpoint of Black selfhood, collective identification, and the well-being of communities. It must offer a vision of how we might resist the normal economic, cultural, social, and political workings of white supremacy and consciousness (see also Mutua, 2006, in another context).

Right from the outset, let me be clear about what this chapter is attempting to communicate. This work speaks to how leadership might be informed by an African Indigenous knowledge and sense of community. It raises key issues and questions in imagining pan-African Indigenous leadership in ways that have not been seriously theorized since the formal closure of "decolonization" and abolition of apartheid. Contestations against claims of "community," "Africanness," and the like, while relevant, are not my intellectual concern, though I do not dismiss these conversations. Instead my main argument, as is supported by the various contributions to this book, is that there is a problem with Western conceptions of leadership, and with leadership in our educational institutions. Counter-hegemonic definitions of leadership are necessary. Western conceptions of leadership are about individual attributes, skills, and capabilities and the manner in which these are marshalled in the service of a purpose or objective. While such an understanding of leadership is important and relevant, I argue it is inadequate. I am proposing that leadership be framed for Black intellectuals from an Indigenous sense of African awareness. Clearly, in the Euro-American context, we cannot speak about leadership without also recognizing migrations, and the effects of a politics of place. We also need an "essential anti-essentialist" stance in articulating Indigenous Black leadership.

I do not say all this to deny Black agency and resistance. Everywhere we have exemplary Black leadership from within local communities worthy of mention. For example, in contemporary Black politics the Black Lives Matter movement, led by Black feminist and queer women, has brought to public consciousness the issue of police brutality and anti-Black racism while simultaneously focusing on education, health, Black children in state care, and social issues that affect Black lives. This movement has shown how Black/African survival in the diaspora goes beyond extrajudicial killings of Black people by police and vigilantes and other forms of state-sanctioned violence. The persistent and escalating problem of anti-Black racism and state-sanctioned violence against Blacks in the Americas presents unique challenges to the discourse of race and national belonging. Race continues to define not only *expressions* of citizenship and the kind of citizenship we practise, but also the extent to which we are recognized as citizens-subjects at all, or even as worthy to live. In effect, it is argued that the way Euro-North American society was founded all but guarantees that race will always be at the centre of politics no matter how one defines race (see also Lindsey 2015; Sexton 2015; Smith, 2015).

My analysis centres African/Black leadership in African Indigenous knowledges as a philosophy that leads one to being critical. There exist important works of Black scholars, developed from the interests of the community and which are informed by a critique of Black intellectuals that emerges from the community itself. As Black intellectuals aspiring to be part of pioneering new systems for understanding our communities, we need to heed existing critiques made by our intellectuals and communities. For many our scholarship alone is insufficient if it is not imbued with a vision addressing the needs of the Black community.

Intellectual African leadership or leadership in the Black community should not be inordinately focused on critiquing the West, as important as that might be. Such a narrow focus or preoccupation only serves to solidify racist, oppressive, and unfounded charges of African intellectual immaturity or mediocrity. But any attempt to offer a counter-hegemonic discourse is, of its nature, a critique of dominant, hegemonic discourse. There are no two ways around this. While there is a need for critiques of a racialist African-centred politics, we must also avoid being distracted from a collectivist politics that an Indigenous leadership project entails. My arguments, while resisting hegemonic, Eurocentric conceptions, are predicated on the clear premise that "Black Lives Matter" and should be lived to the fullest expression of that humanity. A focus on African Indigenous knowledge is a promising start for this consideration.

The Intellectual Politics of Claiming "Community" and "Collective Leadership"

African Leadership and Indigenous Knowledge: Identity Intersections and the Politics of Community

There is an urgent a need to look back to African Indigenous knowledge, and engage in a community politics that eschews individualism and the sense that the community is simply a "sea of individuals." On the other hand, to the extent that individual freedoms and liberties are important, the idea of subordination to the dictates of a mass can be equally problematic, and I do not want to downplay this. Yet here, what I offer (and what many others have offered) is a particular way of knowing that must be evaluated on its own merits for empowerment, as well as disempowerment.

In the contemporary world, where class, gender, race, sexuality, and other cleavages are important dimensions of identity, it is important for us to be critical of evocations of "community" that erase these differences. The lens through which we view the Black/African world and ourselves is enshrouded with these identity markers and contingencies. These myriad identities embodied in the self and collective render any single account of the Black/African experience impossible (see also Johnson, 2003, 2005). Unfortunately, the articulation of Black/African Indigenous leadership, while conveyed as collective knowledge, is in fact sometimes simply an assemblage of Black knowledges coming from a heterosexual, masculine, male, able-bodied membership, while posing as representative of Blackness in its entirety. We cannot equate the Black male condition with the condition of the entire Black community/ies (Mutua, 2006, p. xiii). A search for a genuinely Black/African-centred Indigenous leadership must be an anti-domination project, one committed to the existential wholeness and well-being of Black/African peoples and our varied communities, expressive of our material, emotional, cultural, and spiritual well-being. In speaking of Black leadership that is collective and community driven, we must exercise care and caution, not foreclose on possibilities. For example, how is the local cultural resource base engaging with knowledge of Black womanist, feminist, queer, gay, and transgendered and disabled bodies? In complicating what African-centred leadership might look like, we must ask key questions so as to address emerging challenges such as the implications of imagining gender, sexuality, and class in terms of Indigenous knowledges and the politics of Black leadership. We must in particular assess the roles African women have played as Black communities engage in reclamation and transformation. African Canadian male scholars need to deconstruct the masculine culture and self. This means that we have to enter a moment of decolonizing our exclusive value systems. It is only through this act of revisioning that we can invite new discussions that enrich and empower the course of our history.

Yet, we must keep in mind that often in attempts to understand the complexities of the Black community and Black leadership, the resonances depend on who is conducting the conversation and analysis. Social difference has always been a site of contestation when speaking about local knowledge. In the case of claiming African-centred knowledges, the question of gender and the patriarchal nature of knowledge always emerge as if Africa and African peoples have a monopoly on patriarchal relations. The ways that gender, class, sexuality, and ethnicity intersperse and intersect discussions of a collective African Indigenous leadership are crucial to broach, while we also critically assess the ways that these critiques are sometimes leveraged by the dominant to derail the core issues of anti-Black racism and Black resistance. When we speak of "minority experiences" and we use voices of particular bodies to articulate these experiences, we are routinely confronted with the questions:

Who speaks for whom, and how, and why? How do we know if these voices are representative of the broader community? And who comprises this community? These questions are legitimate, especially if they are meant to trouble taken-for-granted assumptions. But we must also attend to who is asking what. Usually it is dominant bodies who lead the charge in raising these questions. Yet these same bodies refuse a corresponding gaze on other related questions such as: Who wields power and privilege? Who is in positions of authority? Who determines how we can claim community? Who gets to conscript the idea of a fractured community, and how does it deny accountability and responsibility? Put bluntly, there is some hypocrisy at play here. I am not interested in the Eurocentric-gaze on the Black/African experience and our narrating of our social, political, spiritual, and cultural circumstances to the extent that it is validating knowledge using Western positivist standards and procedures. We need to reclaim our experiences and relearn how we think. We need the Black/African community in general, including Black/African scholars, to become our own intellectual agents taking up responsibilities as thinkers of Black/African experience, however complex, diverse, and contradictory. For the purposes of this chapter it is critical to ask: How do we come to understand Black/African leadership from an African-centred or "Indigenist/anti-colonial" African perspective (Dei, 2014b)?

African-Canadian Leadership: Mobility, Indigeneity, and the Politics of Place

Mobile subjects have always travelled across borders, boundaries, and spaces. The experience of the mobile subject is one of fluidity of identity, displacement, and the pain of not always belonging to a new place. But Africans in the diaspora everywhere are mobile subjects, and as such also live a very fluid and contested existence. It is interesting that some mobile subjects are questioned about their travels more than others. The presence of racialized bodies in global spaces is always under close scrutiny, and globally, the Black existence is continually questioned. As African peoples we are continually asked to justify our existence in particular places; this is not a safe experience for any of us. "No One Is Illegal – Toronto" uses the catchy slogan "We didn't cross the border, the border crossed us" (http://toronto.nooneisillegal.org/node/284). The ways that this phrase has been taken up in the Canadian context speak to the global reach and the entrapments of globalization. African peoples have historically had to deal with dehumanization of our existence through "common-sense" knowledge about our movements. This dehumanization knows no borders or boundaries.

Take, for example, the case of our supposed complicities in colonial settlerhood. Everywhere we need to trouble our conceptions of settlement in a place and the contradictions of claiming spaces and ownership of lands using our Indigenous identities and prisms. Elsewhere (Dei, 2016), I have argued that our settlement in Canada does not make us "settlers" like Europeans who annexed Aboriginal lands. Some of us are Indigenous to the land and others have come through the global migration processes resulting from geopolitical, economic relations. Effective Black/African leadership should be able to negotiate the politics of place and displacement and address the question of how to make the spaces in which we live safer for all. My interrogations of Black and Indigenous relations in Canada have been constructed (misconstructed) as futuristic in terms of anti-colonial solidarity. Claims of African Indigeneity must be read as broadening the meaning of Indigeneity while also acknowledging the rights of those indigenous to Turtle Island, as well as the realities and impacts of Canadian settler-colonialism. Race and Indigeneity are intertwined, not just for African bodies but for all colonized, racialized, and Indigenous bodies. Some of us have been psychologically deported from our cultures, histories, traditions, and cultural knowledge systems. We need a return. We need to (re)claim our rich intellectual heritage in which we have always devised solutions to our own problems. What we have in common as African peoples is a relation to ancestral lands. This relation requires that as African people we do not relinquish our ties with the Mother Land, Africa, and that we join our common forces to advance our welfare and dignity as peoples. African education for progressive leadership must be rooted in the land and soil (earth and land teachings) if it is to be sustainable and relevant.

Some have suggested that the reality of African dispersal through diasporas undermines any realistic notion of African community. I would insist that the African diaspora can express a common African intellectual character rooted in a set of clear principles. In such a reading there is no requirement for a shared physical space as a precondition. As with Rasta, which took up their enslaved forbears' chants of "back to Africa," the centring of Africa need not imply a physical return to the source, since as Amilcar Cabral (1974) notes, we must "bloom where we are planted." To belong to a community is not about physical residence. It is about a shared history and affinity, however fictive the relationships arising from the slave ships, plantation slavery, colonialism, and the oppression of late-day anti-African racism. It is about claims of membership. This membership comes with entitlements and responsibilities. It is in meeting these responsibilities and securing our entitlements that we come to belong. How are we able to understand the procedures that enhance everyone's well-being?

I see a discussion about African leadership for social change as a project for the re-education of the African mind, soul, body, and spirit. What good are our ideas if they fail to bring about social change? We can survive as a collective only by holding fast to a vision for designing our own futures and setting our own agendas. This realization clearly has implications for how we talk about African leadership.

The Lure of the Academy and the Debt to the African Canadian Community

I single out Black intellectual leadership for the simple reason that it implicates me. Elsewhere (Dei, forthcoming) I point out the continuing "deep cynicism and alienation" of Black intellectual politics from our communities, that is, the legitimate question the community keeps asking: "Who speaks for and with us?" For as Black/African scholars we live with the unpleasant truth that our communities have increasingly been sceptical of our academic achievements simply because either our work has either been distant from the community or we have not been a major force in the transformation of these communities. There is a feeling in our communities that they can do without Black/African intellectuals. For some time now questions of why we do our intellectual work, and on behalf of whom, have been very germane to my scholarship (Dei, 2014a).

Despite claims to the contrary, there is a troubling assimilation of many of us Black intellectuals into Western academic culture, and we have been intoxicated by the ways this culture pursues intellectuality. What I refer to here are the ways we seek legitimation, validation, and acceptance in white colonial spaces, competing and putting our own colleagues down so that we are deemed more "intellectual"; the unilateral fragmentation around difference – as if our world is all about accentuating our differences; a failure to read between the lines when dominant discourse conscripts the idea of a fractured community in order to deny responsibility and accountability; mimicry of Eurocentric theories that, for the most part, hardly speak to the complexity of Black/African lived experiences. While we have not collectively been duped, we have not always fully resisted the ways Black radical politics and scholarship has been co-opted by capitalist bourgeois culture within a corporate modernity, embracing such things as individualism, competition, greed, hierarchies of knowing, or the deceptions of individual excellence and meritocracy. Today many forms and aspects of Black resistance are themselves commodified by the economic, cultural power of neo-liberalism. Black complicities in hegemonic, anti-Black knowledge production, including the simplistic discourse of Blacks as "settlers" and the seductiveness of inserting the Black experience into white colonial settlerhood, have gained traction and, in the process, marginalized the African genocide, enslavement, mass incarceration, school "push outs," and the tenuousness of Black citizenship in the nation state.

I also want to raise the issue of whether Black academics owe a debt to Black communities to produce work that is relevant to the community. Clearly, both the issue of "relevance" and the concept of "debt" to community are contested. And many who reject this critique point to a certain extortionate and rejectionist criticism of those Black scholars who do not perform a hegemonic mode of what it means to be Black. I agree with this position. I am not interested in presenting a hegemonic discourse or prescribing what we must all do. I am, however, also not interested in supporting the idea that Black scholars may concentrate solely on advancing an intellectual agenda. My own intellectual work has a politics with no apologies, and I do not want to be silenced with postmodernist/Eurocentrically-informed charges of "Black essentialism." The power of community leadership is to me a strongly held belief about possibilities of working for effective social change. Articulating new ideas and believing in the power of ideas to bring about change has its merits and social power. Long ago African philosopher Paulin Hountondji (1997), in his ideas on "scientific extroversion," called on African intellectuals not to spend time critiquing the West but rather working on the need to understand the mechanisms of our intellectual dependence on the West, its knowledge systems, science and technology, theories and perspectives. The challenge is that we build, develop, and centre our own cultural knowings, ideas, and philosophies in producing knowledge about African reality and the human condition: "To become ourselves again is one of the major tasks prescribed by History" (Hountondji, 1997, p. 12). This is a collective task and requires collective leadership. But above all else we need an epistemological shift beyond the self to an organized political collective for change.

So, must every single Black scholar devote all his or her scholarship to studying the Black community, which is not itself a monolith? No. Yet I would maintain that for Black intellectuals, academic excellence as defined by the West is not enough for our Black communities. This kind of "excellence" at one's craft as a scholar is not enough, and debates about what is enough, when, and on whose terms/standards miss a critical point. There are some luxuries and privileges of academic grandstanding in the West that Black scholars cannot afford. Our work must always be in the service of the community, bearing in mind that we need to recognize the richness of cultures in our community. This will allow us to serve our communities without being paternalistic. It is a reflexive exercise that recognizes the existing knowledge and power within communities. It could be asked: While race-based organizing has paved the way for Black intellectuals to hold the positions they do, can such organizing be abstracted from the influence of other forces and factors that are themselves independent of the intentions of Black political practice? But why is this question being asked in the first place? We may ask: When will our requisite "debt" be paid? This is a seriously flawed question. We can never really repay our debt to the community, given the historical legacies we have dealt with. Thus, the question is not *when* but *how*. And at the end of the day if we feel we are benefitting the community, it is enough.

Reconceptualizing African Leadership as Collective Leadership

The question of leadership has received much attention in the academic literature. In the field of education, there is a general agreement that "leadership matters" (Kramer & Swing, 2010). It is argued that a strong leader with a vision-setting agenda and well-defined goals is one that builds relationships and collaborative cultures and secures accountability. Such a leader can successfully ensure school/academic results and community achievements (see Fullan, 2001; Hargreaves & Fink, 2006; Leithwood, Jantzi, & Steinbach, 1999; Leithwood, Louis, Anderson, & Wahlstrom, 2004). The problem, however, is that dominant conceptions of leadership are mired in liberal and neo-liberal agendas that assert ideas of quality, competencies, standards, accountability, and transparency without any critical engagement with equity, social justice, and diverse local and cultural knowings about leadership from the perspective of marginalized and oppressed communities (Dei, 2015; Logan, 2013; Portelli & Campbell-Stephens, 2009;). While these are significant, they do not help us understand the varied conceptions that different communities have of leadership.

Opening up space for critical reflection on leadership, Portelli & Campbell-Stephens (2009) propose alternative ways to represent leadership. These include representations of leadership in the form of a "community of leaders," principally about equity, centred on spirituality, and community driven. These forms of leadership are bottom-up and emerging. In accessing the potential for African leadership to transform our communities, we must focus on a key question: Are there Indigenous, anti-colonial patterns of leadership we could be exploring and building to foster shared responsibility and meet social expectations?

In writing about Black leadership I engage with the ideas and ideals of African local cultural knowledge while acknowledging the differences between Eurocentric leadership and leadership inspired by African Indigenous cultural knowledges. In engaging multiple knowledges, there are points of divergence and convergence. For example, Indigenous African cultural knowledge rewards the values of community, social responsibility, collective belonging, mutual interdependence, and seeking the welfare and well-being of the group. These values are not the sole ownership of African peoples. They are values that local communities through time have cherished. Nevertheless, in the present circumstances there is a corruption by individualism, self-aggrandizement, personal greed, and lust for power and authority – values that have become much embedded in today's society. Dominant, white Eurocentric leadership rooted in contemporary whiteness is very power driven. Today such Eurocentric leadership has been embraced (to a large extent) to foster relationships of domination even within African communities and on the African continent itself. It is often rooted in the ongoing historical unfolding of colonial relationships between Africa, Europe, and the Americas. Colonization subverted African conceptions of leadership to serve the interests of dominant powers.

The particular meanings we bring to our concepts of leadership are therefore important. In traditional Indigenous and African communities, leadership is less about individual attributes and skills than shared community expectations and roles. An African-centred/Indigenous perspective sees leadership as not about a romantic or charismatic persona. Leadership is not about the individual. African leadership signifies the heroics of collectivities to resist domination, colonization, and oppression and to ensure that local peoples design their own futures and agenda. It is a leadership based on serving the community rather than the other way around. It is a leadership meant to involve the community in such a way that power relations are spread out to all. This is manifested in decision-making processes where everyone is considered an important player at the table. It is a kind of leadership where everyone has something to contribute and participates in without being victimized. In traditional African communities (Asante, Zulus, etc.) we know that great leaders have been acknowledged as those able to lead their communities collectively in battles against colonization and oppression. African peoples have for long held their own conceptions of leadership, which do not imply any "absolute interiority." African Indigenous leadership recognizes the agency and power of the Indigene to name what constitutes leadership in cultural contexts (see also Hountondji, 1997, p. 18 in a related context). An African conception of leadership is spiritually informed and spiritually based. It is about developing ethical and social responsibility to all humans and non-humans as sharing the Earth. It is leadership that is nurtured by the land and the teachings of Mother Earth. It is leadership that we each live and breathe. It is possessed by all. It is about the ethics of caring for everyone, including the non-human. African leadership is about respecting the sanctity of life and developing interpersonal relations that affirm the bond of the individual, the group, and the community. Such leadership works with consensual decision making and upholds the integrity of the group.

Amid current neo-colonial and re-colonial relations, Africans are generally punished for naming Indigeneity and colonialism and for remembering our histories (see hooks, 1989). However, to reclaim indigenous understandings of African leadership we must be willing to embrace African Indigeneity notwithstanding colonial resistance. What is needed is a return to African Indigenous leadership rooted in local cultural knowledge, shunning rugged and competitive individualism as well as relations of domination and power and instead fostering shared collective understandings and community aspirations. African peoples must reclaim the power of cultural memory, resisting the temptation to forget and to erase our history and knowledge systems due to colonial occupation and white colonial settlerhood. Kiti (2013) speaks of a physical and psychological deportation of bodies and minds. I will add that as Africans we are confronted with a mental and intellectual deportation and the need to affirm our Indigenous knowledge systems as a necessary step in our own decolonization and return to an African mental universe or intellectual (home)land. Kiti (2013) asserts that "in spite of our openness to exteriority ... the African home will always be where we belong." This is not an exercise in romanticism. It is a realization that something else, something different, is possible. It is imperative, however, to recognise the therotetical, political, and pragmatic Afrocentric and Eurocentric form of leadership as contributing to the complex, overlapping, and intertwined relationships involving the interface of cultural imperialism, African-centredness, and local Indigeneity, and ongoing colonial relations of racial domination, inequity, and injustice. This is the nature of contemporary (Euro)modernity.

Consequently, throughout African histories there have been some disappointments of individual leadership. I highlight the importance of resurrecting the ideas of C.L.R. James in terms of the implications for critical dimensions of African leadership (see Dei, 2009). Collective leadership and (small-group) organization is critical to the success of struggles for change. It has been noted that C.L.R. James bestowed too much faith on personalities and leadership (e.g., Nkrumah and Nyerere in the African contexts) only to be disappointed. We cannot repeat this mistake. It is only a collective leadership that can remain true to principles of social change. Therefore, we must be wary of placing all our eggs in the basket of personalities that sometimes betray larger causes. We need to rethink African leadership in contemporary contexts. We must also rethink Black/African solidarity for contemporary times through a re-examination of ongoing calls for unifying causes around the lines of social identities, politics, economics, and the environment as well as emotional, cultural, and symbolic solidarity. This calls for a reclaiming and affirming of African past intellectual traditions, knowledge, and contributions in world history, as a necessary exercise in our decolonization, that is, an engagement with the rich intellectual African traditions helps us examine contemporary issues facing local communities, particularly the project of decolonization. It also demands that we reflect on the present in order to theorize Africa beyond its boundaries and, of course, on the big question of Black consciousness, that is, for us to understand the pursuit of a critical reflection about our collective existence as about consciousness of our interconnected realities and social well-being as racialized, gendered, classed, sexualized, (dis)abled bodies/groups towards an agenda of justice.

Let me be clear on one thing because sometimes the idea of "speaking differently" can be and is misunderstood. I do not acknowledge the claims of any scholar who does *not* see "Black communities." We may be heterogeneous, complex, and competing communities, but we are still "Black communities." In claiming, insisting on, and working with the notion of "Black community/ies" I am not being defensive but, rather, am speaking clearly in a political and resistant tone. It is indeed limiting and, in fact, a luxury for us to always think strictly in terms of our individualities and individual agencies. There is a particular responsibility of Black/African intellectuals and a particular direction for our collective Black/African scholarship today. We must confront some questions: What are our roles and responsibilities as Black scholars? How do we deal with the "knowledge crisis" and the "cultural crisis" in our communities (see Dei, 2014a) so as to engage at the collective level? From an African-centred perspective rooted in the philosophy of Indigenous knowledges, it is simply not enough for the African/Black body to be present in the space of academic scholarship. We can insist on our presence, and both our presence and absence in the academy can be understood differentially. It is significant when we come to legitimately occupy the academic space. Our collective intellectual engagements must allow us to take up different strategic positions of power and influence in the economic/social order so as to transform our social existence. For Black intellectuals today, the imperative is to rewrite knowledge and our histories as a necessary exercise in our own decolonization (see also Diawara, 1996; Du Bois, 1947, 1969). The expertise and knowledge of local communities make it imperative for us as Black scholars to tap those communities for an understanding of their challenges and problems and what ought to be done to address them. There is also the opportunity for us to build local capacity to articulate our issues, undertake our own research, and search for genuine home-grown solutions to our problems. We need to reclaim what colonialism interfered with: the knowledge embedded in our bodies and cultural memories. The African idea of community is knowledge that is embedded in us. We can retrieve it even in the highly individualistic context of the academy through collective exercises. For example, there are philosophical principles of African Indigenous knowledges (community building, sharing, reciprocity, social relevance, etc.) that invite us to "return to the source" in terms of articulating values of harmony in society and with the environment.

We need Black intellectuals and the Black middle class to assist the wider African family and community in the areas of collective social existence such as education. For example, we need to help to address what I have called the "economics of schooling," and specifically the issue of educational access (Dei, 2013). The high cost of schooling and ever-increasing tuition costs require strategic responses from the institutions offering grants, scholarships, and bursaries to help struggling communities. For the Black intelligentsia this may mean owning up to our responsibilities. We must recognize the sacrifices that others made to pave the way for us. We have reached the top on the back of community struggles. Clearly our achievements do not mean the "end of history" for us, and neither are these achievements attained solely in isolation from larger forces of class solidarity and broader processes in capitalist and liberal societies that are part of the dialectic of Black economic and political struggles. It is not all about our race and racial identity as Black people. However, a remembering of historic sacrifice requires that we do not lose sight of what it means to be Black in white spaces irrespective of our status in the society. We can highlight our intellectual voices so as to understand the realities of African peoples in the diaspora. What is required is a holistic approach – one that considers the diverse social processes that each African community faces, based on its socio-economic and political positioning, nationalist affiliations, and access to state resources. African scholars everywhere have a responsibility to document the differential impact of contemporary national economic and social turmoil on our community, including highlighting the gender differences of policy impact. A new vision of Indigenous African leadership is meaningful only if it is applied to the concrete problems and realities of African and oppressed peoples in the struggle for political, cultural, spiritual, social, and educational liberation. This will be a pan-African vision that borrows from the ideas of old but adds new meanings and confronts challenges – starting at the source, grassroots, local community organizing provides a healthy ideological frame to diagnose problems and offering African solutions. This will be an approach that is not ashamed of our culture, histories, and identities as peoples of African descent. We need to challenge ongoing manifestations of Eurocentric visions of the world as articulated through understandings of "communism," "scientific socialism," "governance," and "democracy." African Indigeneity is always interwoven in the history of Black struggles. However, we need a new Indigenous African ideology that shifts a centring on materialist social thought onto African Indigenous concepts, spiritual ontology, and knowledge principles.

Confronting Contemporary Challenges

In this section of the chapter I highlight specific social issues over which Black/African-Canadian academics can employ cultural and scholarly "capital" to provide our communities with cultural knowledge resources as "ammunition" for social transformative struggles. Notwithstanding our resistance and survival struggles, Black life is always in danger. As has been noted, we live in an era of Black "violability," defined as "a construct that attempts to encapsulate both the lived and historical experiences of Black people with state-initiated and state-sanctioned violence," including the perniciousness of everyday anti-Black racism (Lindsey, 2015, p. 234). It is this human condition that makes a resurgence of critical Black/African Indigenous leadership imperative at this juncture. We must understand and appreciate the unique relationships between Black peoples and the Canadian nation state, and the negotiation processes in which Black/African peoples engage in order to navigate our community belonging and social existence. This calls for Black/African intellectuals to understand the particular challenges our communities face in order to be a key part of a collective Black leadership. Notwithstanding our long presence, successes, and achievements, the Black/African community in Canada continually faces challenges in education, employment, health, law, and the justice system. The institutionalized nature of these challenges shows that it is limiting to simply blame African Canadians for a lack of critically conscious leadership in our varied communities. Still, it is important that we think through ways of promoting radical collective leadership with a shared vision, purpose, and goal to design our own futures

Questions of Citizenship and Belonging

There is a hegemonic threat to Africanism. There is a sense of belonging in this country and yet not being fully accepted. The community has long-standing issues regarding the education of our children. We are concerned about the prison system targeting black males. Similarly, the child welfare system particularly scrutinizes Black mothers and their children. These are all part of the ways in which the Black/African in Canada is being cut off at the knees. We must be at the forefront in redefining the sense of belonging in the Canadian nation state. There are pressing issues of rights and responsibilities, access to health, education, jobs, and housing, immigration and family re/unification, and so on for most Africans in a diasporic context. The problem of youth alienation, violence, and incarceration is real for our communities. In fact, despite some successes that we can all be proud of, there are mounting challenges involving pessimism among youth, their sense of hopelessness and despair, and their feelings of living a dead-end existence. We need to give hope to our youth, and this requires collective efforts. Intellectuals and community leaders can play a key role in identifying and generating the sorts of knowledge that enable collectivist responses to social problems (Kitossa, 2012).

The Under-Utilization of African Knowledge and Expertise

The non-recognition of continental African education and credentials is a major barrier to accessing employment and developing a sense of belonging. African communities in Canada possess a wealth of local cultural resource knowledge. What is frustrating is that highly developed skills for nation and community building are going untapped. It is common knowledge that many trained professionals are either unemployed or underemployed, and in some cases medical doctors, engineers, and technologists are driving taxi cabs or the like in Canadian cities such as Toronto, Montreal, and Vancouver ("Overqualified immigrants," 2012). There is a frequent cry for Canadian experience, which has restricted the employment opportunities of otherwise highly qualified personnel in the Canadian labour force.

A Growing Disintegration of the African Family Unit

Employment and immigration woes and protracted family reunification challenges continue to create loneliness and family disunity. There appears to be a weakening of the traditionally closely knit African family (e.g., divorce, separation, other disruptions). This is common where men of African descent find it hard to get a job in Canada. Black women are accommodated only in precarious service industries. This can create discord within a family, bearing in mind that such families, while resilient, confront serious challenges in sustaining themselves. Economic hardship has tested the solidarity of African families, resulting in frequent marriage breakdowns and the inability of breadwinners to support the large extended family that has been a feature of Black/African families. Our challenge is how we build institutions and support structures that strengthen the African social unit (e.g., families, communities, males, and youth, including role models and authority figures). Without strongly supported families, community solidarity is threatened, posing serious challenges for our ability to provide a united front in seeking redress to state- and private-sector-sponsored "structural violence" (Crichlow, 2014; Galtung, 1990; Kitossa, 2012). We also need to fuse such understandings of the Black family with critical gender analysis that explain some of the forces that shape the family (Oyewumi, 1999).

Divisions in Community

With the manufactured scarcity of resources, local communities find themselves struggling with each other to compete for attention and a fair share of state resources. This, naturally, has not bolstered group unity; it has intensified divisions among Black/African communities. The welfare state, as it currently stands, makes us both protective of our resources (worthy versus unworthy) and gives the privileged a sense of entitlement to resources. The nation state creates an "us/them" dichotomy that breeds racism and favouritism. Recourse to history as a site of privilege is twisted into claims of being more deserving by accident of history and having arrived here earlier. Rather than histories being intertwined and connected, history has become a flashpoint for asserting privilege, leading to mistrust among communities and groups within and outside the broader African community. Consequently, those who arrived earlier claim community power, prestige, and privilege to the detriment of newcomers. This has led to mistrust amongst the African population in diaspora.

African Youth Education

Education is crucial for community development. But we know schools provide differential access to education because of class and economics, geography, history, and politics. Study upon study reveals the

Black/African community is poorly served by the school system. Yet we need our young learners to be at the centre of knowledge production for the twenty-first century. We need to equip young learners with multiple, counter, and oppositional knowledges to challenge and resist the dominance of Western knowledge. Dropping out of school is very much linked with hegemonic knowledge forms operating in our school systems. The problem of "push out" and/or disengagement from school (e.g., low teacher expectations, lack of curricular sophistication, absence of African teachers, racism, language and integration issues) (see Dei, 2010; Dei, Mazzuca, McIsaac, & Zine, 1997) is in large part a knowledge question. African Canadian youth in Canadian schools have to contend with the problem of "racialized streaming." Some may deny it, but the problem is not going away. Research has long shown there is a strong correlation between race and academic streaming (see Brown, 1993; Cheng, 2002; Dei, 2010; Dei et al., 1997; Toronto District School Board, 2009). This is not a dated research finding.

Rather than question this fact, it is important for us to ask: How are the different stakeholders participating in the institutional and "unconscious" racism leading to this effect? There is the old issue of "special education." Similar to the operation of "racialized streaming," Black boys and working-class youth are being pathologized as mentally and behaviourally defective and deficient (see Baldridge, 2014). Similarly, the impact of systemic racism on Black girls and the struggles of Black women suggests a gender, class, and racial dynamic or perspective on the issue. How are the different stakeholders participating in the institutional and "unconscious" racism leading to this effect? What is the responsibility of schools and the African community in taking concrete measures to address the problem? There is also a need to redefine "safety in schools" broadly to ensure all our students have a sense of belonging, connectedness, and identification with our schools. We need to initiate discussions in schools as to what safety means beyond policing and surveillance. How do our schools become "safer" spaces for all? How are we able to understand the procedures that enhance all students' success? "Safety" issues include the violence of school curricula, and a failure to address questions of who gets hired and who is criminalized and/or overly policed. How do we facilitate spaces to learn, share, and discuss the meaning and importance of discipline rather than simply enforcing discipline? These are tough questions that responsible educational leadership is best positioned to ask (see also Dei, 2015). Teaching discipline requires an understanding of community claiming, engagement, boding, mutual interdependence, sharing, and reciprocity, as well as respect for community history, leadership, and welfare.

Employment

There is a grim picture of (un)employment among the African community in Canada. According to a study carried out by Laryea and Hayfron (2005), labour market performance (earnings and occupational attainments) reveal that the average annual earnings for African men ($30,828.70) was lower than that for Canadian-born men ($33,119.50). The average annual earnings for African women ($25,274.80) was greater than that of Canadian-born women ($24,471.10). Without separating average annual earnings by gender, average annual earnings for Canadian born ($29,461.30) was slightly greater than the average annual income for African immigrants ($28,750.50). African immigrant women with any level of education (except those with post-secondary education) were likely to have lower annual earnings than their Canadian-born counterparts. African immigrant women with post-secondary education were likely to have higher annual earnings (0.9 per cent) than Canadian-born women with post-secondary education. African immigrant men with a PhD were 61 per cent less likely and those with anMA degree were 71 per cent less likely to be employed in high-skill occupations than their Canadian-born counterparts. African immigrant women with PhDs and MAs are, respectively, 85 per cent and 37 per cent less likely to be employed in skilled professional occupations than their Canadian-born counterparts.

Going Forwards with a Collective African Leadership

If we take collective leadership as involving everyone going forwards, we have to think through, relate, and work with radical ideas for our collective survival and advancement. First, we need to develop a strong, vocal African presence through collective leadership. There are some pressing questions as we engage collective leadership: Who speaks for us, how, and when? How are we understood in the larger realm of Canadian public policy and discourse? How does the media engage African communities and their issues? How do we tap the available skills and resources that these communities bring to the Canadian context? How is Africa registered in the Canadian public consciousness? We need an intellectual and social leadership to help us tap the wide expertise and knowledge of our local communities both to understand challenges and problems and to develop unique and effective African-centred solutions to them. Such leadership is vital in helping build and develop local capacities to articulate our issues, undertake research, and offer home-grown solutions to problems. There is a strong need for political involvement, such as seeking political representation at various levels of government. It is imperative to intensify political advocacy that will ensure the acceptance of the international educational backgrounds and professional credentials of Africans new in Canada.

Second, we must build strong, healthy, sustainable local African communities in which we each have access to the valued goods and services of the wider society. In order to be a "responsible community" we must have access to available resources. We need to call on a collective leadership to ensure that issues of access to housing, good health, education, immigration and integration of families, and unemployment that stand in the way of building strong, healthy African communities are addressed. Education, retraining, and employment are all key to the success of our African communities. We must be generating self-employment opportunities and not always rely on the Canadian state. We must be able to use the privilege of history when we network. This means that those who have been there before should work with newcomers in a way meant to empower them. This empowerment should be informed by the two parties rather than being paternalistic. It is an empowerment of mutual understanding and respect.

Third, community leadership is about coming up with communities of differences with a shared purpose and destiny. Communities are not formed without human agency: we collectively create communities, and any community is as good as we collectively work to make it. Communities are also about differences and sameness. Shared experiences are never singular. The nation state often homogenizes "communities" and attempts to pit communities against each other in the distribution of social rewards and benefits. We need strong community leadership that counters divisive strategies and builds the community as a site and place of learning and healing. Strong community leadership is vital to inculcating in African youth an understanding that the perceived tensions between the "individual" and "community" are false. The individual is part of the community, not an island unto him or herself. The Western liberal notions of the individual can be limiting when they encourage rugged individualism and competitiveness. In Indigenous African knowledge the individual makes sense only in relation to the community he or she is part of. The African worldview makes the important and necessary distinction between the competitive individual who is not afraid of those around her or him, and the cooperative individual who sees herself or himself as enriched by the community s/he is part of.

Fourth is the need for a strong collective pan-African/Indigenous and anti-colonial leadership to address the perennial question of African unity. Unity is only a means to an end, in this case African power. As a community we can have collective power when we discharge collective responsibilities, for example, the role of the African middle class in investing in our families and communities. Similarly, the African intelligentsia must own up to our responsibilities and begin to put our scholarly work, research, and knowledge into the service of our communities. We must become part of the community that seeks trust and support by making our work relevant to them. We cannot study our communities from a distance. Unity as a means to African power also requires that we connect the African diasporas in general in joint struggles and historic implications. We must begin to relearn and to earn each other's trust. The lessons of the past, present, and future must help us reinvent our Africanness in a diasporic context such as by teaching about African traditional values of family, community, and ethical and social responsibility for the young, our elders, and identity differences. This is the exercise of African collective leadership. We must teach our youth not to forget who they are as African peoples and the sacrifices that brought us to where we collectively find ourselves now. We must remember the old African adage "When lost go back to the departure point"! We must teach ourselves and our children not to forget our African ancestral roots as well as what is included and excluded from our claims of Africanness.

Fifth, collective African leadership must shape debates about our membership in a "global citizenship." Elsewhere, I have critiqued the notion of "global citizenship," but my critique is intended to ask about its redemptive qualities rather than as an abrogation or disavowal (see also Charania, 2011; Golmohamad, 2008, Spina, 2012). Moving forwards, we need to focus less on the question "At what point does one move from immigrant to Canadian?" and instead to value our "global citizenship" by asking critical questions. For example, how do global communities define their responsibilities to each other? How do we address power and inequities? How do we share resources among communities, and how do we create a sense of welcoming and belonging for all? We must begin to honour diverse skills and knowledges, and consider experience gleaned from other places of origin as relevant to the varied nature of our realities and the composition of the global community. We must ask new questions as a responsible global leadership. There is an need to continuously clarify, challenge, and define the type of global relations we want both as an African/Black collective in Canada and in our relations with the African continent, the Caribbean, and other African diasporas globally. These prospects/opportunities/challenges of making connections should be addressed within a specific understanding of this global relation. There is a need for an alignment in strategic global economic presence. For example, given our numbers in the African diaspora, can we facilitate alliances – such as technological, economic, and institutional – that allow us to serve current needs on the continent and also enable us to build our capacity over time here in Canada? How can we shape ongoing social and technological transfers to ensure they are more culturally relevant and beneficial for the critical mass of Africans (born and unborn)? How do we ensure any new and emerging global relations do not perpetuate structures that repress us and future generations of African peoples? We must move forwards envisioning a collective resolution without illusion. I emphasize "we" as a collective vision and a global effort. The future of the human world has a lot to do with the prospect of African peoples. We, the people from and in Africa and the diaspora, are an integral part of the global future. We have been told our success closely hinges on global development. To the same extent, our future is also a global future. Having overcome centuries-long extreme oppression and exploitation through our resilience and resistance, it is time we centre our leadership role in human civilization.

"Moving forward" is a global vision with responsible leadership. We should be there to shape the future of the world, and we should do our best, both locally and globally, to define the collective resolution for our future. To move forwards, we need to get beyond a few common illusions. We must get beyond the temptation of "moving on," so that we do not forget our past. Moving forwards is about making advances; however, making advances does not mean we have to move on without our past and our identities. History has to be told, and those who forget our common history are destined to fail. As Confucius reminds the Chinese, "Study the past if you would define the future." We must see beyond the success of only a few. This means moving forwards with no one left behind. Moving forwards is a collective vision – towards a future that we not only dare to dream together, we work on together, and more importantly, we share the outcome together. Moving forwards is not about getting the elite, the rich and the leaders, to the top while leaving the poor and underprivileged behind. No one should be left behind.

For those of us fortunate enough to get a good education, even at considerable personal expense, great jobs and desirable positions, we must not forget to give back to the community. We must go beyond the optical illusion and not be fooled by the sensation of moving forwards while everything in fact remains stationary. Looking at our school system in Canada, for example, there seem to be new policies and programs being introduced to address historical and current socio-economic disparity. And yet report after report reminds us things have not changed a bit. African Canadians are still suffering from racial profiling in policing, suspension and expulsion in schools, chronic unemployment, and extreme poverty. So let us not be misguided by those elusive political discourses, and make sure any ideas of moving forwards will bring tangible results.

We must go beyond the myth of "one world, one dream." While striving for a better future for our collective, the continent, our people, and the world, we have to ask whose dream it is and in whose interests. Moving forwards is a collective resolution, a call for collective efforts, a reminder of collective responsibilities. Globally, we have to insert ourselves in every platform and every forum to make sure African heritage and wisdom will be there; we have to rectify biases and systemic barriers that have been silencing us for a very long time. Locally, we need women and our youth to take central positions in this discussion. It is a question of taking space at the decision-making table. More fundamentally, moving forwards involves an ongoing double consciousness of who we are as African-Canadians and who we are as members of a global citizenry. As much as we love to be equal global citizens, we also have to realize that this does not mean we have to seek conformity (whether in thought processes, schooling and education, business pursuits, or anything else) and become what we are not. Our African heritage has as much to contribute to the world as the rest of the world has to offer us.

Conclusion

We need to create an environment that facilitates growth by moving from dependence on state support to a place of self-governance and community advancement. We need to empower ourselves not only mentally, but also spiritually. We need to use all aspects of our "humanness." We have to move away from the materialistic/Eurocentric ideology to a more communal paradigm. We need to decolonize our minds and not continue to seek divisions among ourselves. This does not mean we sweep differences under the carpet. We see our differences as interconnected to what make us a collective as African peoples, or peoples of African descent. We need to be accountable and recognize how we are implicated in maintaining colonial divisions and hierarchies, not supporting one another, and exploiting each other. We need to empower our youth to become self-reliant and self-employed. In the coming years we will still have to grapple with challenges (such as the criminalization of Black/Africans in Canada, cultural changes that impede one's identity, disempowerment as immigrant/racialized bodies, racism, and lack of access to knowledge). But it is an important step towards resiliency and resolutions when we realized that our destiny lies in developing collective leadership.

Acknowledgments

I thank Rick Sin, Camille Logan, Yumiko Kawano, and Dionisio Nyaga of the Department of Social Justice Education, Ontario Institute for Studies in Education of the University of Toronto (OISE/UT) for comments, notes, and suggestions that have helped shaped my thoughts and ideas in this chapter. I also thank the editors and reviewers of this volume for their critical reviews and comments, which helped strengthen my arguments.

REFERENCES

Baldridge, B.J. (2014). Relocating the deficit: Reimagining black youth in neoliberal times. *American Educational Research Journal*, 51(3), 440–72. https://doi.org/10.3102/0002831214532514

Brown, R. (1993). *A follow-up on the grade 9 cohort of 1987 Every Secondary Student Survey participants.* Research report no. 207. Toronto: Toronto Board of Education.

Cabral, A. (1974). National liberation and culture. *Transition*, 45, 12–17. https://doi.org/10.2307/2935020

Charania, G. (2011). Grounding the global: A call for more situated practices of pedagogical and political engagement. *ACME: An International Journal for Critical Geographies, 10*(3), 351–71. Retrieved from https://acme-journal.org/index.php/acme/article/view/902

Cheng, M. 2002.Factors that *affect the decisions of racial/ethnic minorities to enter and stay in teaching and their implications for school board's teacher recruitment and retention policies* (Unpublished doctoral dissertation). Ontario Institute for Studies in Education, University of Toronto, Toronto.

Crichlow, W. (2014). Carceral geography & the prisonization of Toronto black youth. *International Journal for Crime, Justice and Social Democracy, 3*(3), 113–31. https://doi.org/10.5204/ijcjsd.v3i3.120

Dei, G.J.S. (2009, October). Racial politics and the question of black unity. Paper presented at the conference Re-Imagining Western Civilization: On the 60th Anniversary of the Writing of C.L.R. James's *American Civilization*, Faculty of Law, University of Ottawa.

Dei, G.J.S. (2010). *Learning to succeed: The challenges and possibilities of educational development for all* (with A. Butler, G. Charamia, A. Kola-Olusanya, B. Opini, R. Thomas, & A. Wagner). New York: Teneo.

Dei, G.J.S. (2013, April). The global "economics of schooling" in the context of Africa and the Caribbean. Keynote address presented at AERA Caribbean and African Studies in Education (CASE) Special Interest Group (SIG), San Francisco.

Dei, G.J.S. (2014a). The African scholar in the Western academy. *Journal of Black Studies, 45*(3), 167–79. https://doi.org/10.1177/0021934714525198

Dei, G.J.S. (2014b). Global education from an "Indigenist anti-colonial" perspective. *Journal of Contemporary Issues in Education, 9*(2): 4–23. https://doi.org/10.20355/c53g6b

Dei, G.J.S. (2015). Anti-racist educational leadership. In D. Griffiths & J.P. Portelli (Eds.), *Key questions for educational leaders* (pp. 99–103). Burlington: Word & Deed & Edphil Books.

Dei, G.J.S. (2016). *Reframing blackness and anti-blackness through anti-colonial and decolonial prisms.* New York: Springer.

Dei, G.J.S. (Forthcoming). Teaching race and African indigeneity: Personal reflections of a black scholar. In G. Dei, A. Vasquez, & E. Odozor (Eds.), *Cartographies of blackness and black indigeneities.* Gorham: Myers.

Dei, G.J.S., Mazzuca, M., McIsaac, E., & Zine, J. (1997). *Reconstructing "drop-out": A critical ethnography of the dynamics of black students' disengagement from school.* Toronto: University of Toronto Press.

Diawara, M. (1996). Pan-Africanism and pedagogy. Retrieved from http://www.blackculturalstudies.org/m_diawar/panafr.html

Du Bois, W.E.B. (1947). *The world and Africa.* New York: Viking.

Du Bois, W.E.B. (1969 [1903]). *The souls of black folk.* New York: Penguin.

Fullan, M. (2001). *Leadership in a culture of change.* San Francisco: Jossey-Bass.

Galtung, J. (1990). Cultural violence. *Journal of Peace Research, 27*(3), 291–305. https://doi.org/10.1177/0022343390027003005

Golmohamad, M. (2008). Global citizenship: From theory to practice, unlocking hearts and minds. M.A. Peters, A. Britton, & H. Blee (Eds.), *Global citizenship education: Philosophy, theory and pedagogy* (pp. 519–33). Rotterdam: Sense.

Hargreaves, A., & Fink, D. (2006). *Sustainable leadership.* San Francisco: Jossey-Bass.

hooks, b. (1989). *Talking back: Thinking feminist, thinking black.* Boston: South End.

Hountondji, P. (1997). *Endogenous knowledge: Research trails.* Dakar: Codesria.

Johnson, E.P. (2003). *Appropriating blackness: Performance and the politics of authenticity.* Durham: Duke University Press.

Johnson, E.P. (2005). The pot calling the kettle "black." *Theatre Journal, 57*(4), 605–8. https://doi.org/10.1353/tj.2006.0025

Kiti, P.C. (2013, October). *Recentering Africa: From Paulin Hountondji to Meinrad Hebga.* Paper presented at the Fourth International Conference of the Science & Indigenous Knowledge Systems Project/South African-Mozambican Collaborative Project, University of Western Cape, Capetown, South Africa.

Kitossa, T. (2012). Black Canadian studies and the resurgence of the insurgent African Canadian intelligentsia. *Southern Journal of Canadian Studies, 5*(1): 255–84. https://doi.org/10.22215/sjcs.v5i1.298

Kramer, G.L., & Swing, R.L. (Eds.). (2010). *Higher education assessments: Leadership matters.* Lanham: Rowman & Littlefield.

Laryea, S.A., & Heyfron, J.E. (2005) African immigrants & the labour market: Exploring career opportunities, earning differentials, & job satisfaction. In W. Tettey & K. Puplampu (Eds.), *The African diaspora in Canada: Negotiating identity and belonging* (pp. 94–113). Calgary: University of Calgary Press.

Leithwood, K., Jantzi, D., & Steinbach, R. (1999). *Changing leadership for changing times.* Buckingham: Open University Press.

Leithwood, K., Louis, K.S., Anderson, S., & Wahlstrom, K. (2004). *How leadership influences student learning.* New York: Wallace Foundation.

Lindsey, T.B. (2015). Post-Ferguson: A "herstorical" approach to black violability. *Feminist Studies, 41*(1), 232–7. https://doi.org/10.15767/feministstudies.41.1.232

Logan, C. (2013). School leadership (Unpublished PhD proposal). Ontario Institute for Studies in Education, University of Toronto, Toronto.

Mutua, A. (2006). *Progressive black masculinities.* New York: Routledge.

Overqualified immigrants really are driving taxis in Canada. (2012, 10 May). *Globe and Mail.* Retrieved from http://www.theglobeandmail.com/globe-debate/editorials/overqualified-immigrants-really-are-driving-taxis-in-canada/article4106352/

Oyewumi, O. (1999). Multiculturalism or multibodism: On the impossible intersections of race and gender in American white feminist and black nationalist discourses. *Western Journal of Black Studies, 23*(3), 182–9.

Portelli, J.P., & Campbell-Stephenes, R. (2009). *Leading for equity: The investing in diversity approach.* Toronto: Edphil.

Sexton, J. (2015). Unbearable blackness. *Cultural Critique, 90*(1), 159–78. https://doi.org/10.5749/culturalcritique.90.2015.0159

Smith, C.A. (2015). Blackness, citizenship, and the transnational vertigo of violence in the Americas, *American Anthropologist, 117*(2), 384–92. https://doi.org/10.1111/aman.12242

Spina, N. (2012). *Overcoming anxiety: Global citizenship education and the crisis of the white subject.* Paper presented at the Annual Conference of Sociology and Equity Studies, Ontario Institute for Studies in Education, University of Toronto, Toronto.

Toronto District School Board. 2009. *2008 parent census, kindergarten–grade 6: System overview and detailed findings – Executive summary* (J. O'Reilly & M. Yau, research coordinators). Toronto: Organizational Development Department, Research and Information Services, TDSB.

14 Just Below the Threshold: A Conversation with David Austin on Black Leadership

SAM TECLE AND DAVID AUSTIN

In this chapter, I present my conversation with writer, scholar, and historian David Austin on the state of Black leadership in Canada and the role of intellectuals in that regard. At the time of our conversation (mid-2016) the issues pervading Black Canadian life – premature Black death, police brutality, streaming in education, discrimination in employment and social services, as well as an unprecedented disproportionate growth in the Black prison population – were all coming to the forefront of Canadian consciousness. A vital part of this emergent consciousness was the constant contrasts and comparisons with the United States, which made glaring the absented presence Black Canadian intellectuals occupy due to erasure by an uninterested and dismissive Canadian media. This absenting of Black (intellectual) leadership specifically, and Black life generally, makes the question of the role Black Canadian intellectuals play a prescient if not multifaceted one. Interestingly, a hidden dimension of the erasure of Black intellectuals is that Canada has long been a transnational space for Black leadership and collective organizing. For instance, nineteenth-century African abolitionists, Garvey's Universal Negro Improvement Association (UNIA), the 1968 Montreal Congress of Black Writers, the Sir George Williams affair, the Black United Front in Nova Scotia, the Congress of Black Women, Toronto's Black Education Project in the 1970s, to Black Lives Matter among others: all represent the long and braided history of Black leadership in Canada. This history is only now being appropriately studied and placed in proper historical context.

Much in the way that Harold Cruse's 1967 landmark study *Crisis of the Negro Intellectual* signalled a crisis in Black American leadership during the civil rights era, a similar crisis frames the perceived dearth of Black Canadian leadership. As the editors of this volume indicate in the Introduction, the current perception of crisis has more to do with conventional and outdated parameters informing the search for Black Canadian leadership than the actual state of Black leadership in Canada. Those suggesting that Black Canadian leadership is in crisis assume leadership is wholly contained in the form and substance of notable individuals. Very often in the search for leadership, conventional thinking directs us to those charismatic, larger-than-life figures of history who seem exceptional for their time, and who did extraordinary things associated with single-handedly steering the course of major events of their period. Those working within the Black radical tradition, as David Austin does, see the issues confronting Black Canada as long-standing, and as such requiring rigorous examination, especially to demonstrate the ways that leadership in Black Canada has responded and continues to respond.

These sets of factors make it an apt time to sit down with David Austin, who is one of Canada's foremost experts in the emergence, growth, and diffusion of Black political expression in the Americas. His work is in the Black radical scholarly tradition that unabashedly looks beyond the present context of anti-Blackness in the Americas in ways that radically imagine Black life as free and in full expression. Many of these sentiments – found in Austin's work – are at the heart of the Black Lives Matter movement, and have ignited newfound critical awareness across the Americas both within and outside sites of higher learning. This is the backdrop to the discussion that follows.

Rather than examining leadership through the prism of the individual, we sought in our conversation to consider how the practice of leadership is mediated by organized collectives. With specific attention to C.L.R James, Sylvia Wynter, and Linton Kwesi Johnson among others, we suggest that Black leadership and movements in Canada are always enriched by diasporic and transnational sentiments and that leadership emerges through the self-organizing activities of people. Finally, we explore the inherent difficulties, critical care, and precision needed when gauging Black Canadian leadership in the context of a society premised on what Carl James in this volume describes as "white logic." Our conversation centres on the core idea that *contention* – the holding together of various struggles, oppositions, and duelling tensions – is the basis of leadership, it establishes the terrain for forging complex unities, and is a necessary and vital space where the open and ongoing struggle for change can take place. When we think of it in this way, we move from leadership in the singular to *leaderships* in the contingent, dialogic, and plural. This perspective, we believe, opens up many possibilities for radical thinking, political action, and social change. The break from hagiography towards historicizing a people's movements opens the possibility of conceiving of Black leadership in its fullest, most creative and imaginative sense, none of which signals dearth or crisis.

Our Conversation

ST: Let's start with some of your general thoughts on Black leadership?

DA: Leadership from below is a profoundly important idea for me. It is a way of understanding how power works, who is invested with power, and how to challenge and transform master-slave dynamics. Leadership with the ultimate goal of genuine social transformation is, for me, the way to think about this; or at least a major part of that dynamic is intricately related to how people organize from below. Increasingly I find myself returning to C.L.R. James. I say "returning" because I needed to take some critical distance from him over the past six or seven years or so, but now that I have "returned" I have greater appreciation of the importance of his work. There isn't anyone else I can think of who spent more time thinking about how to organize for change. In the history of the Haitian Revolution we can think about those leaders who led the Haitian Revolution: Toussaint L'Ouverture, Dessalines, Christophe. In James's classic study of the Haitian Revolution, *The Black Jacobins* (2001), Toussaint L'Ouverture becomes the voice through which James narrates that history. It is through L'Ouverture's eyes that we see the Haitian Revolution unfold as a historical process. He wrote that book in 1938 and by the 1970s he was encouraging one of his students, Carolyn Fick (1990), to rethink the Revolution and she eventually wrote a very different book (based on her PhD dissertation) on the Haitian Revolution.

What she did was to look at the Haitian Revolution from down below. Who were the unnamed slaves that sustained the Haitian Revolution, even when many of the "official" leaders were willing to betray the revolution? Who were these leaders? For me, history is a methodology, a way of gaining insight into the present. Let us think for example about the implications of the Haitian Revolution for the unfolding of events leading to the present day. These former slaves were put in positions where they had to challenge the leadership of Toussaint, Dessalines, and other leaders because there were times when the leadership were willing to compromise with the French in ways that would undermine the autonomy of those we might call maroon leaders – that is, autonomous slaves who challenged the authority of the slave regime. They confronted the decisions of the revolutionary "leadership" and ultimately questioned the revolutionary leadership's entitlements and the presumption that their authority did not depend on consent from below. So if we think about that in relation to today, there is always that fundamental question: there are those that lead and expect others to follow, but what happens when we flip that and those who are presumed to be followers assume the role of leaders in a more generalized, more collective, and a more self-organized way?

The question of leadership is central to *The Black Jacobins*, but it is also important to state here that the Haitian Revolution is not only a foundational, inaugural moment of the Black radical tradition, but also the first universal breach within what was a plantation-capitalist global system. Why? Because unlike the American and the French revolutions, which proclaimed universal rights but maintained a slave regime, the Haitian Revolution represents the abolition of the genuine slaves through their own self-activity. If, as Carole Boyce Davies suggests, the Trinidadian-born communist and feminist Claudia Jones was left of Karl Marx because of her combined analysis of class, gender, and race, then it might be argued that the former Haitian slaves and their revolution were in front of G.W.F. Hegel.

While the contemporary Western conception of the dialectic is owed to Hegel, he is neither the first nor last word on this point, as there are also African expressions of the dialectic in Akan philosophy, among others (see Gyeke, 1995; Henry, 2000). But as Susan Buck-Morss in *Hegel, Haiti and Universal History* (2009) as well as others before her have hinted, Hegel owes his conception of the master-slave dialectic to his bearing witness to the Haitian Revolution, in which genuine slaves staked and risked their lives in a life-and-death struggle against real masters. It is the Haitian, then, not the French Revolution, which inaugurates not only the first fully fledged political breach against slavery in world history, but also the first truly philosophical breach in terms of the modern world that was shaped by slavery, colonialism, and mercantile capitalism. The Haitian Revolution influenced the development of Hegel's dialectic, which is also the precursor to Marx's conception of class struggle, which of course ideologically shaped the Bolshevik Revolution without which the Cold War – which dramatically shaped Black lives in North America and the Caribbean – does not happen; without the Cold War, the Russian intervention in Afghanistan and opposition to Russia in the form of the Pakistani ISI, Sunni Gulf states, and the Carter-administration-backed Mujahedeen in Afghanistan with Osama Bin Laden playing a key role, does not occur, and Al-Qaeda perhaps does not come into being. The rest, as they say, is history and speculation, but what I am trying to suggest is that when we put the Haitian Revolution, a seminal moment in the history of humankind, at the centre of our consciousness, strange things happen to the historical trajectory that we have inherited. It begins to look very different, and becomes one other example of how the Black experience in the Americas has been a central leading component in the shaping of the modern world.

ST: *Black Jacobins* seems mostly to have been read from the vantage point of labour, colonialism, imperialism, and the cultures of capitalism and white supremacy that enveloped it, but in your opinion are hidden aspects of the social dynamics of the Revolution.

DA: James is attempting to work something out in *The Black Jacobins.* He is obviously on the side of those who are fighting for liberation, but he is struggling with the dynamic between the official leaders who represent a "modern" challenge to the slave regime and colonization, and the leaders from below who are not interested in or at least less preoccupied with the trappings of modernity and ties to colonial France. They were the Haitians who were born in Africa and who represented the majority of the population, with their own worldview and military techniques. Their conception of leadership and freedom is very different from that of the official, creolized leaders. And it is to James's credit that he, in a sense, works out this dynamic in detail through someone else's work – that of Carolyn Fick – after realizing that he had missed something. He talks about this in one of his lectures published in *Small Axe,* "How I Would Rewrite *The Black Jacobins*" (James, 2000).

This question of how to represent from below surfaces in the poetry of Black British poet Linton Kwesi Johnson (LKJ), whom I am currently writing about in relation to the dynamic that exists between poetry, the human imagination, and social change (Austin 2018). Borrowing from (not surprisingly) C.L.R. James's conception of self-organization as expressed in *Notes on Dialectics,* "Di Good Life" as well as "Di Anfinish Revalueshan," "Tings an Times," and "Mi Revalueshanary Fren," LKJ meditates on the meaning of social transformation and socialism in the post-Soviet Union and the post-apartheid world. In "Di Good Life," the poet-persona tells us that while the flock has historically followed the shepherd, it is now time for the shepherd to follow the flock, which is a way of saying that the time of the shepherd, that moment, has passed because shepherds are following their flock, therefore they are no longer shepherds. LKJ's vision of the new society, couched in biblical lore and metaphor, is principally shaped by James's almost life-long preoccupation with the notion of self-organizing.

The question for LKJ and James is, how do you capture those human possibilities in any given society at a given time? If you are looking at the conventional leaders, historically that is not where the creativity is. It is where a certain notion of leadership evolves and unfolds in practice, but it is not, historically, the place where the creative possibilities for re-imagining change occur. And of course this again raises the question, "change for what purpose?" If we are talking about change in terms of representation – where we see more Black faces in powerful places – I don't think we should dismiss that outright. That is a form of change and we know that. For example, Black students and students of colour benefit from having Black teachers and professors of colour in the classroom at all levels, but there is obviously a caveat. If these teachers and professors are conservative, what does this mean? What does it add or model in terms of the kind of society we want to create?

ST: Interestingly, there is a strong possibility of Black conservative leadership taking place under the guise of increased diversity, which to a significant extent is relished by a broad cross-section of people. But as with Haiti's revolutionary leaders who were willing to compromise with France, what are the risks of compromise that comes with representation of Black faces in high places?

DA: Right. Here we can think of Obama, while linking him to an example in the Canadian context. In the last chapter of *Fear of a Black Nation* I begin by talking about a young man that used to spend time in a youth centre where I once worked in Montreal. I ran into him in 2008 right after Obama's democratic nomination, before he was elected president. By then many people believed Obama was going to be the next president. I ran into Jason on the corner of my street and he was over the moon: "*We* are going to have a Black man in the White House." And he goes on to say: "now that we know there can be a Black president, no Black person has any excuse to say that we can't achieve anything." That's exactly what he said to me, and I listened very calmly and attentively. I'm saying to myself as I listened: "This is interesting. He's all fired up about Obama, which demonstrates the symbolic importance of Blacks in positions of leadership and power," but there's something missing – not from him; it's not his lack or inadequacy.

ST: Do you think Jason's response reflects our collective inadequacy in terms of how we think about politics, leadership, and representation? For example, Obama once represented Illinois, but what did his presence mean in terms of the conditions under which people in the South Side of Chicago live?

DA: On the day of Obama's first election, I was teaching a course at Concordia University here in Montreal, and I remember talking about the election with some friends who were white and on the left who were completely dismissive of the significance of his election. And I could see that, as the conversation unfolded, another friend, who is Black, was feeling uneasy and uncomfortable with the conversation, and I understood where she was coming from right away. You cannot dismiss the symbolic significance of Obama's presence and what that meant for Black people and many people of colour, particularly in this case where we're talking about, at least in theory, holding the most powerful position in the world – a Black man in the White House. The symbolism could not be more poignant or real. The problems occur when the conversation stops at that point and we don't pose the questions: "What kind of leadership? How is that power going to be exercised, and on behalf of whom?" When we pose these questions it becomes obvious that as a member of the power elite, Obama's chief preoccupation was not with the working class or the US's permanent Black underclass who languish in public housing and behind prison bars, or with those, including many Black folks, who lost their homes in sub-prime mortgage schemes only to see the big banks being bailed out by his government.

ST: Just to return to something you said about the narratives of leadership from below and history from below. There is a dialectic and tension between dominant and repressed that is captured in Fick's work. It's interesting the way in which we think about leadership in the Black radical tradition as being very patriarchal and very male – Angela Davis and other scholars remind us that there were a whole number of Black women who were always holding the movements up. What do you think about this tension and dialectic of history that has operated like this: these narratives are, at first, mostly written from the Black male patriarchal perspective, and then in turn provide the points of entry for other narratives to emerge? What do you think about that dialectic and tension as you write and work in this field?

DA: When James writes *The Black Jacobins* in 1938, his preoccupations leave little space for reflections on gender. So he can't write the book that Carolyn Fick writes, because what she does, among other things, is bring women into the narrative, unnamed women who played active roles in the revolution. But again, it is to James's credit that he realizes that fact later – that there's a need for the discourse to be in concert with and also supersede the apparent possibilities and dominant ideas of the moment. He later embraces the work of writers such as Toni Morrison, Alice Walker, and Ntozake Shange, and of course his wife, Selma James, was very active in the international feminist movement. If he was saying the same things in 1970 and in the 1980s and thinking that the book is perfect and that he didn't need to change anything, then that would be a problem.

For my part, the ideas, theory, of Sadiyya Hartman, were profoundly important as I was writing *Fear of a Black Nation*, particularly *Scenes of Subjection* and *Lose Your Mother*. I was also influenced by the work of Carole Boyce Davies's *Black Women, Writing and Identity* (and more recently her biography of Claudia Jones), Belinda Edmonson's *Making Men: Gender, Literary Authority* in *Women's Writing in Caribbean Narrative*, Hazel Carby's *Race Men*, and also Katherine Mckittrick's *Demonic Grounds: Black Women and the Cartographies of Struggle*. And of course there's Afua Cooper's *The*

Hanging of Angelique, which is absolutely about a Black women's agency and desire for freedom.

I had to think about gender and agency quite a bit when I was writing *Fear of a Black Nation.* In interviewing women over the years, they would defer to the men. And then I realized the role that they played was clearly understated on their part, and definitely by their male counterparts (the work of Saba Mahmood, *The Politics of Piety: The Islamic Revival and the Feminist Subject,* was very helpful in thinking this through). Part of this might be due to not trying to overemphasize their role, as they always brought their involvement back to the group. And yet, when you dig deeper you find that they played profoundly significant roles both in terms of organizing in the community, organizing events, and in the cases of Anne Cools and Brenda Dash, were in the public and in the forefront, and not only working in the background (although the work in the background is also fundamentally important). So there is a question – when thinking about Black leadership – to what extent do we valorize the public leaders and the spokespersons? And then we ask about representation and who determines who the spokespersons are? We de-valorize the important leadership work that is done quietly – overemphasizing one at the expense of the other.

Kathleen Cleaver has talked about this. The work of women becomes invisible because they are not working at the forefront. It is another way of saying we have to challenge that conception of who the leader is and what leadership is, as in many instances of the sixties and seventies, women were doing much of the actual organizing work – and often less glamorous work, the kind of work without which a movement, organization, or institution cannot be sustained. In many respects, the same can be said today. This is clearly what has happened historically in the Haitian community in Montreal, as Sean Mills's recent book *A Place in the Sun: Haiti, Haitians, and the Remaking of Quebec* makes clear, along with the forthcoming work of Desirée Rochat. I think that that work has to be elevated because, while individual leaders come and go, that work continues through institutions that continue to meet the needs of their communities for decades, although it is also true that, while many organizations survive, time often passes them by and they often become ossified and prove no longer capable of meeting the needs of the community they purport to serve.

Generally speaking, the leadership and self-organization of people who are on the margins, those who are not perceived as having the capacity to lead or to organize, is always there, and people are always organizing in order to humanize their existence; it's just that we often don't look to those places. I think that we can't be oblivious to the world around us. It doesn't mean that we cannot have particular preoccupations. In my case, I see myself as part of several communities. My background is partly centred in England and I try to keep in tune with what is happening there. I lived in Montreal before attending high school and junior high school in Toronto, so I still feel a strong connection to that city and I have close family ties there. And I have been living in Montreal for more than twenty-eight years consecutively, almost thirty in total. These are all my communities in one sense or another.

As someone born to Jamaican parents, I feel a strong connection to being Jamaican and of the Caribbean, I have close ties to Cuba (my wife and adopted family are Cuban), and I try to pay attention to what transpires on the African continent, not because I initially studied African studies alongside anthropology, but because, at least initially, growing up listening to reggae music, being attuned to the ideas of Marcus Garvey as a child, all while living in London, England, and then reading Fanon, Walter Rodney, James, and Cheikh Anta Diop as a teenager in Toronto – and here again I cannot overstate the importance of Third World Bookstore on Bathurst Street in this process: all of this happened before moving to Montreal to attend university as an undergraduate and it is all part of a very typical, and atypical, Black diasporic experience.

Many of us occupy multiple worlds, in a sense, and we underestimate the transgressive political potential of being part of a diaspora whose affiliations cross porous boundaries. This is part of what the late Richard Iton thinks about in his fantastic book *In Search for the Black Fantastic: Politics and Popular Culture in the Post-Civil Rights Era.* I am – and I think we should all be – preoccupied with the incarceration rate of Blacks in this country, which has risen *50 per cent* since 2000 in Canada. But we need to see this rise within the context of this current stage of capitalism and neo-liberalism that we are experiencing in which Black labourers who used to produce surplus labour have now become surplus labourers.

This is what we can refer to as the plantation-to-plant-to-prison pipeline, and it is an unabated international phenomenon. The idea of inserting the plant into this syllogism came to me after watching the film *Finally Got the News* (1970) a few years ago. The film was produced in association with the League of Revolutionary Black Workers (LRBW) in Detroit, and it demonstrates in graphic detail why Black labour and organizers were not only shunned by the auto industry in Detroit, but by the broad labour movement as well. They were too militant for the presumably militant AFL-CIO, which was supposed to represent all workers in the industry, but failed to represent the most vulnerable workers, who were Black, so the LRBW created its own autonomous organization to represent its concerns without being mediated by the labour bureaucracy. That's leadership. I think we have to be able to make those links. We are part of those links, and I think they are important to our analysis of the world in which we live today, and our place in it.

ST: When you say we need discourse in concert with the moment, and James needing to acknowledge Fick's work in moving forwards, it reminds me of Aimé Césaire's quote about a "true humanism – a humanism made to the measure of the world." In that moment, he is critiquing humanism as it has heretofore existed, while calling on it to be reformulated, perhaps recalibrated is the better word, to the measure of a profoundly dehumanizing world. I think that's an interesting thing to think about in a conversation around Black leadership, we should not only examine it historically – as in the archive – but in the now, paying attention to what is going on in the moment.

DA: I was recently reading Katherine McKittrick's interview with Sylvia Wynter in which Wynter makes precisely this point: that we are stuck in a biocentric moment, a biocentric discourse or understanding of humanity, but our historical moment warrants a shift towards a more poetic concept of humanity that allows us to break with those concepts of the human and the sociological and ecological devastation that the logic of modernity, this false notion of progress, has brought to bear on the world. We need to be able to speak about Black self-organization in view of social transformation in ways that acknowledge the particular circumstances that confront Black peoples while simultaneously recognizing that the system is ethically, economically, and politically unsustainable, but has been buttressed by credits and deficits, and that historical political experience, past and present, has a great deal to contribute in terms of thinking about transforming the world in which we live, and that there is an urgent need to do so. We cannot afford to delve into simple essentialism that limits our capacity to think transgressively about the break that we need to make with this current socio-economic course.

ST: That's interesting because I remember a quote; I think it is from Ralph Nader, that "the best leader produces the most leaders." But I think that might still look through the lens of the leader, the particularity and exceptionality of the leader. But also I think what is in your last comment is the question of what does it mean to do the work that seems less glamorous – to give the appearance of being led. There is something more that needs to be said, if you're talking about leadership of those that give off the appearance of being led, because in some situations it's practical to have just one spokesperson. That might be linked to James's idea of self-organizing, where we see in his work that there is something historical about the way in which we have conceived of group and leader discussions in which we do not acknowledge the potency and immediacy of the collective. That said, what is the role of the Black intellectual as interlocutor, as framer of discourses, and as leaders?

DA: We need to push the boundaries and to create a space for these kinds of conversations, which as Tapo Chimbganda wrote in her PhD dissertation (now published as *The Classroom as Privileged Space: Psychoanalytic Paradigms for Social Justice in Pedagogy* [2017]), means taking the risk, the all-important risk, of stepping outside the bubble and comfort of our "safe spaces" sometimes. We are clearly in the moment of post-911, post-apartheid – that is to say, official South African apartheid – post-socialist (in terms of the former Soviet Union and its allies) era, etc. – but not postcolonial – in which the world is in need of dramatic change, and we have, should have something to say about our place in this world as intellectuals of African descent, and about the world itself.

The big question in the case of Obama was, should Black people be critical of this Black head of state? For many, if not most, it was a difficult question, but ultimately the answer is, "of course!" What else is the role of the "revolutionary intellectual" that Walter Rodney so eloquently spoke of? We are in a post-racial context, not in the literal sense, but in the sense that, as populations in African and Caribbean states know well, a leader is not essentially good by virtue of being Black, and as people know too well in the Middle East, smart bombs have no colour. The myth that we can enter a post-racial and more egalitarian society simply by replacing the white power-elite with Black surrogates has, I think, been dispelled. In other words, we should now know that a purely racial politics is antithetical to a politics that is anti-racial, and is antithetical to politics in general.

ST: It's the ethical necessity of an intellectual, I think.

DA: It's an ethical necessity to be critical, but it is also a political necessity. Walter Rodney was always clear on this issue and it was central to his early work and writing, and I don't think he has been taken as seriously as he should be as a theorist, a thinker on race, class, and revolutionary change. What sides are we on? Yes, we have an appreciation for all the machinations of politics and what that means for a Black person in relation to white counterparts in the White House and how the established leadership, including members of his own party, responded to him as a Black being, including Hillary Clinton's attempts to undermine him (see Goldberg, 2016). But even after we account for that, there's power at work there, both global and local, and there are Black folks in the US who live in war zones too, as they do in Jamaica, and almost in the same manner as people do in Africa and the Middle East, and if political representation is not addressing this, then what is it doing?

ST: We don't know which way our struggles for freedom will go. History is our teacher. Much is expected of Black academics, who by default are expected to be public intellectuals. And for Black people in positions of visibility and power, leadership is expected. Said another way, those assumed to be Black leaders are not always the best fit for the role of leading Black people. That might be a good opening for some thoughts in Carl James's chapter in this volume:

> Last November Barack Obama was elected for a second term as US president. And while his leadership has been welcomed by the Black community, it's made the absence of a similar strong Black presence in Canada all too evident ... Is Black leadership lacking in this country? Is it hard to find?

And though Carl James gets into how problematic it is in always comparing ourselves – the Canadian context – to the US, I wanted to ask: what are some of your thoughts on Black leadership in Canada past and present?

DA: For geographical reasons it is hard for us to sincerely talk about Canada in the broad sense of the word.

ST: As a cohesive nation, and as a cohesive Black community within a nation.

DA: I live in Montreal, and this is the city I know best. I have delved into portions of its history, I feel I can write and think through this city with some degree of competency. I am familiar with Toronto but I can't speak about Toronto in the same specific terms. Vancouver is another world, Ottawa is around the corner from Montreal, but it is a different kind of place; that is the nature of Canada, and probably of any big country. And it is true that there is an overarching narrative of the US that doesn't exist in Canada in the same way (the fact that overarching narrative overlooks very important specificities is also an important conversation). Los Angeles, Oakland, New York, Chicago – we think we know those places because they are represented to us through the media. But then there are a whole lot of other places we rarely see or have reason to talk about.

ST: The American South, Washington, Baltimore ...

DA: Yes, and Black people in Seattle, Portland. What's going on in those places? And in what forms? What I can say in terms of the trajectory within this context here in Montreal, Canada, is that there was a moment in the sixties and seventies that represented a turning point, as the moment did in terms of anti-colonial movements, in terms of gay rights, women's rights, civil rights, and Black Power. All of this, in all of its various forms, permutations, and contexts has been part and parcel of what George Kastsiaficas refers to as the eros effect. It is his way of trying to characterize what it was that bound all of these people and movements in many different parts of the world together despite the differences, and Blacks in Canada were also part of that.

ST: That which binds the communities of Blacks is often overlooked.

DA: Very much so. There is a kind of "contrapuntalism," to borrow from Said. There are forces at play that link Black struggles with larger and more global struggles. There is this thing working itself out, whether it is conscious or unconscious – or both at times – with what's happening in the rest of the world. And the state has its response to this. The state attempts to disrupt these substantive connections from being made, and destroy them before they take form, and one of the ways this is achieved is by using provocateurs. We're talking about Canada and people like Warren Hart and all those unknown and unnamed people that were embedded in groups and organizations, spying on them and providing intelligence to state security forces.

ST: Warren Hart as provocateur was borrowed from the US. When it comes to anti-Blackness, nations form partnerships (and work together) quite easily and swiftly.

DA: The same applies to the sharing of intelligence in the case of Jamaica, the US, and Canada in relation to Walter Rodney when he visited Canada in 1968. And intelligence sharing in relation to C.L.R. James, members of the Caribbean left, or Black Power figures like Robert Hill, Franklyn Harvey, Stokely Carmichael, and Rodney during their sojourns or visits to Canada were also shared. And for me, we live in the Americas, and Canada is part of the Americas – even though there are certain specificities that define Canada as a state as well as provinces and municipalities within this state. So it is important to situate ourselves within this broader context that extends beyond the national boundaries that at times hem us in historically (in terms of narratives), geographically, and politically, when in actual fact the lived history and experiences is both trans-Atlantic and trans-Pacific, and also inter-Atlantic in the Gilroy Black Atlantic sense of the word.

ST: So anti-Blackness in Canada as compared to the US is not to a lesser degree. Just different degrees.

DA: Yes, and it's tied to a particular set of experiences that go beyond the Canadian border. When I travelled to Haiti, Cuba, or other parts of the Caribbean, I am thinking about Canada. There is a historical relationship and a colonial relationship between Canada and the Caribbean, and it becomes obvious when you examine the role of Canadian banks and mining companies, and particularly in the bauxite-aluminium industry that has historically been tied to the city of Saguenay, Quebec, for example, where aluminium is produced. Alissa Trotz, professor of Caribbean studies at the University of Toronto, is currently doing work on this, and Peter Hudson has done important work on the role of Canadian as well as American banks in the Caribbean.

ST: Colonial logic and the discourse of anti-Blackness have no borders in the Americas.

DA: Right. And Canada is in Haiti, and evidence suggests that it was involved in the overthrow of President Jean-Bertrand Aristide in 2004, and the former mayor of Montreal was apparently an advisor to former prime minister Paul Martin, and is said to have advised Martin's government in its role in the removal of Aristide from office. And yet the mayor openly described himself as the city's first Haitian mayor (he's French Canadian), and is not shy about caricaturing a few words of Haitian Creole in public. So there are all these connections that remind us that we live in this complex of territories called the Americas. And there was a wave – the Sir George Williams affair was part of it, the Congress of Black Writers was part of it and, of course, related to that is the presence in Montreal of the Guyanese historian Walter Rodney, one of the most important figures in the history of Caribbean, African, and Black politics and thought. Rodney was a political organizer, intellectual, pan-Africanist, and Marxist who became an important figure among Jamaica's dispossessed. Moreover, mobilizations in response to his expulsion from Jamaica helped breathe life into the array of left movements that emerged in the Caribbean in the late 1960s. But in addition to these events, there were protests and sit-ins, the development of community and educational institutions, research and cultural centres, and, importantly, study circles in which people would read and reflect on the meaning of social change. These were all central to that historical moment and, in various forms, this tradition has morphed and continues in various guises today. Everything that happened in and around, before, between, and shortly after those important events speaks to the experiential and experimental nature of that moment and how people were changed by them on the level of consciousness. The state responded to that moment with repression, and then grants. Repression, we know what that means, but grant money created an opening, financially, probably tied to Trudeau's multiculturalism policy at that time, and in response to Sir George and other events and the fear of the occurrence of similar types of events. But at the same time, this opening also represented a closure as it tied the hands of organizations in terms of the kind of advocacy they could do as a result of receiving government funds and charitable status.

ST: Perhaps used as a means to appease to a certain degree? Or quell more radical sentiments?

DA: I'm avoiding using the word "appease," but ultimately that's what I'm suggesting. So the money is there, and I'm not saying that the money was received in the cynical sense because the grant money is used to build institutions, and it all comes out of the moment ... It works for a moment because there were programs that were needed, that did not exist before: there were after-school programs, access programs for colleges and universities, cultural programs, a Black studies centre here in Montreal, which is now defunct. All of this was happening, and there's a sense of movement, and of possibilities ...

ST: An optimism?

DA: Yes, optimism. And there were also folks who were working through these organizations and who were connected to Caribbean Liberation movements, groups like the Caribbean International Service Bureau, which I hope to write more about at some point soon. That's also happening. But at a certain moment, a divide occurs and this kind of liberatory politics becomes largely only tied to the Caribbean. The local institutions here in Montreal are providing programs, which are necessary, but as you know, once you become a registered institution that offers programs and services and receives government funding, once you have charitable status, you are no longer in a position to do politics, or to express those politics in public ways. It becomes subterranean and kind of clandestine if it happens at all. So you can organize programs to meet the day-to-day needs of the community, but that's essentially it, at least in public. I'm generalizing and there are many exceptions to this rule, but this becomes the overarching trend.

ST: That makes me think about a group in California – INCITE! Women of Color Against Violence Collective that is connected to UC Santa Barbara. They collectively put out a book titled *The Revolution Will Not Be Funded: Beyond the Non Profit Industrial Complex* (2009) that speaks directly to the dynamic we're discussing. I think you mention this in your last book. You discuss the plantation-to-plant-to-prison pipeline, which locks us into a certain logic that is not about freedom, that is not about structural change, or to be honest, about changing the world. We don't dream about that anymore when we get locked into these systems. We get mortgages, and as Thatcher told us, "people with mortgages don't go on strike." In a way, we're in it but we're not free.

DA: This is definitely not about criticizing people that work for community organizations, which is the work I did for many years as a youth worker and a community organizer. But it is easy to get caught up in that dynamic in which, to the extent that you talk about survival, the conversation is often more about the survival of the institutions or organizations, and less about the survival of the community.

ST: No, it is definitely not about criticizing, but about the real concerns of those working in community organizations. At a very material level, they are thinking about the survival, maintenance, and reproduction of their families, which are of course vital concerns. And that's important to think about when we're talking about Black leadership. Sometimes the Crown, or the media, or institutions that report on Black collectives look to these organizations and the people running them as the Black leaders. This is sometimes misplaced and unfair, in the sense of expecting – and sometimes demanding – a radical politics be produced out of the complex combination of institutional and political restraints within which they exist, as we are discussing here. An example of this for me is the segment on *Canada AM* that Carl James takes up in his chapter of this book. The show had Don Meredith on a panel about Black leadership. Meredith, a Black Conservative senator, sitting on a panel about Black leadership, to me, speaks to the way in which it is the institution that constantly survives and reproduces itself; the body in there doesn't matter, neither does the politics of that person because they usually don't have any that can be radical or reproduced. So that's an interesting thing to think about when it comes to Black leadership.

DA: So then the question becomes how did people organize for change before those grants?

ST: Self-organize? Resources? Collective economics?

DA: What resources did they draw on? We're not simply talking about money, but what was available to them that allowed people to organize even if they had full-time jobs and other responsibilities. I think we need to go back and really think about that, to understand how we might have arrived at this point today, at this critical juncture, or to at least understand what has changed since then.

ST: That's a perfect segue to the next question. I remember reading Althea Prince's book of essays *Being Black*, in which she expressed her dismay when sitting at a conference in the mid-nineties at York University hearing of the efforts of faculty and students pushing for a Black Studies department. If successful, it would have been the first of its kind in Canada. According to Prince, what she was hearing echoed sentiments of her generation of university students. They too sought to address the needs of Black students – something about which my generation were unaware. To my mind, that is one of the too few instances of Black collective organizing recounted in print in Toronto, especially on university campuses. I bring this up because I am part of a collective of Black graduate students at York University who in 2015 came together to address the dearth of departmental support for Black graduate students at the university. A group of us Black students organized and formed the Black Graduate Student Collective (BGSC), designed to, among other core demands, increase the number of Black Studies course offerings, hire more Black faculty members, and put in place specific supports for Black students at an institution that touts ideals of diversity, social justice, and multiculturalism. During the course of BGSC's work, many stories of similar efforts came to light. These past collectives pushed to have the university direct institutional attention to the nurturing of Black students and they pressured the university, as we were, to be more attentive and responsive to its Black student population. The issues we were addressing in 2015 existed in the 1970s, 1980s, and 1990s – meaning that they were structurally embedded in our institution. Our efforts were not isolated, but rather part of a long historical trajectory of organizing and leadership long in the making. In doing this work, we learnt of strategies, tactics, and resources that were used in the past; this knowledge was vital to us in the work in which we were engaged. We had questions: How might we link to past collectives and those who have also struggled to do similar work? How do we access the experiences of earlier activists – experiences that need to be archived? What forces were – and perhaps currently still are – at work to maintain these silences?

I raise these questions with a broader horizon in mind: which is that in the Canadian context there is an absence of documentation on these experiences, tactics, and strategies of Black organizing and leadership in the recent past. Growing up and studying the Black radical tradition, I have noticed that there is considerably more literature that comes out of the US and the UK about how Black organizing was done in those contexts. Black organizing in the US and the UK boasts a rich and deep literature. So, do you have some thoughts on why there's a dearth of that literature in the Canadian context? Unless I have direct conversations with you or others who have worked for change in person, that information is difficult to come by. I know we spoke about the difficulty in Canada in terms of geography and organizing, but what do you think about the dearth of literature on what was happening in Montreal, Toronto, Vancouver in the seventies, eighties, and nineties around Black organizing and Black leadership?

DA: I think we are in a moment now where there's a different kind of revisiting of the past. If we think about the past, present, and the future as a continuum, the past can be the 1980s or 1990s or even the 2000s. I do not mean the past in the grand sense. I think about conversations we've had about popular culture in the 1990s. I think about Much Music and the program *Soul in the City*, and the role that it and host Michael Williams played for an entire generation in Canada. That's now history, in the sense that we can look back at what it meant for that moment and what it means for us now as we look back. I think a narrative or narratives are working themselves out in Canada. This is relatively new; people have been writing for a long time, but there is now a congealing of multiple generations.

(I made the mistake of naming a few authors in another interview, but of course, by doing that it serves to create the impression that that list can be exhaustive when in actual fact, so many people are now doing this work in Canada in the areas of history, education, sociology, philosophy, politics, critical race theory, etc.). You have a generation that experienced the 1960s and 1970s, and before, who are in a position to share their experiences; you have professors and academics who are researching in this area and there are now people who are doing master's and PhDs on these topics. In this case, they/we are two ore more generations removed from how a similar process unfolded in England, for example, and a few generations behind how it unfolded in the United States.

There's nothing problematic about this apparent late entry into "history." It is what it is and has to do with scale and the demographic growth of the Black population in Canada and the consolidation of a generation or two that were born and/or raised in Canada, and of course the pre-existing Black population in Canada. I think there are more parallels that can be drawn between Canada and the UK, even though we are much more closely connected to the US economically and, to a large degree, culturally and socially. There are similar patterns happening in different moments and there are also cross-patterns that happen simultaneously in some respects if we think about the processes that brought large numbers of people from the Caribbean in the fifties, sixties, and seventies to Canada. At a certain moment, Anglo Caribbean and African women and men were now coming to Canada instead of the UK or, in the case of Haiti, Martinique, Guadeloupe, Senegal, the Congo, and Guinea, and other countries – they were migrating here instead of to France. There is a dynamic of doors being closed on one side of the Atlantic (in the UK) only to be opened, though not necessarily with open arms, on the other. And while it might feel as though we are "behind" in relation to the UK, it seems as though the time is now right to reflect and write about the past in relation to the present and it is now possible to write about the sixties, seventies, and eighties in a way that was not even possible in Canada ten or twenty years ago, and in this sense, Canada becomes an important political-intellectual site that has the potential to renew the body of ideas that have emerged from the US and the UK in relation to transgressive Black thought and politics.

ST: It is interesting, I never thought about that. As a graduate student, I always approached that absence in the Canadian literature of Black organizing as a lack. I've always just wanted more to read and consume. But the students have entered the institutions at the same time that some of these people have found positions in the university, so that cross-pollination and that congealing is a strong place from which to now think about that absence as merely temporary – as narratives working themselves out. Everything is, as you said, of its time.

DA: "Nothing comes before time," as my late grandmother used to philosophically say. Some of the work is now being done, and by people like you. Fortunately, we still have people around who were an integral part of the historical moments and movements that we are referring to – the 1950s, and before, through to the 1970s, and even now the 1980s and 1990s, which is also now "history" – although clearly we are not simply talking about history in the historical sense, but of history as continuity in which the past is very much about and part of the present, not because we want to repeat the past, but because we can learn from it without being burdened by it. It is still experiential for those who lived it, the service of social transformation towards better futures.

Postscript

Having worked on and thought through many revisions of this chapter, David Austin and I began to reflect on how the histories we pointed to in our conversation applied to the contemporary dimensions of Black leadership in Canada, in particular the leadership and advocacy role that Black Lives Matter Toronto (BLM-TO) is playing in Canada's Black political culture, but especially in Toronto. As Austin said to me:

> You can't help but be impressed by BLM-TO's level of analysis of race in relation to gender, sexuality, class, neo-liberalism, imperialism, etc. There is a level of praxis, and a point of departure, that is assumed and taken for granted within the movement that is new, particularly in terms of gender and sexuality in relation to other forms of oppression, even as it draws on the past of other movements from other contexts; and there are important experiences that the movement can draw upon. For example, how the state responds to public protests, in this case public protests by young Black women and men, can provide important lessons. This is part of what I tried to get into when I assessed some of the RCMP's files on Black groups in Canada in the sixties. It's not about being paranoid that groups and movements can be infiltrated and manipulated, but about not being naive. Even as we criticize the myth of Canadian innocence, there are parts of that narrative that are so deeply ingrained in our minds that we tend to be shocked when the narrative is breached by the police or the state. We cannot afford to be naive when there is so much at stake.

What is evident here is that Black leadership, in all its fluidity, creativity, and malleability, is difficult to capture when framed through conventional constructs. There is no crisis or dearth of Black leadership; rather, there exists substantive living archives waiting to be explored – leaderships from below that are only now beginning to be chronicled. In as much as Black leadership in Canada remains always in motion, a terrain filled with imagination and dynamism, so too are the forces at play that operate to suppress its existence and fullest expression. The forces in play – anti-Black in nature – are also constantly reformulating to repress Black leadership and organizing in new and novel ways. These attempts actively seek to negate the linking of Black struggles across space and time, but also and perhaps more so a linking to broader global struggles – a Black contrapuntalism of struggle is at once an exciting and dangerous thought.

With regard to Black organizing and leadership for change, it is paramount to link the past with the present. The past is important, as more than just an indexing of accumulated events, but part of a historical context that when theorized and contextualized with care demonstrates new trajectories and movements that tell different stories. Rather than simply dispossession and marginalization – for those engaged on the forefront of organizing and leadership work – these alternate trajectories provide the zeal to envision different futures. In Canada particularly, there is an integral necessity for articulations of the past in the service of those future efforts. Towards that end, David Austin's work details insights into how we might engage in pulling Canada into the orbit of the Black radical tradition.

This chapter highlights the need to conceptualize leadership as the coalescing of thinking and action – as a praxis that reflects on a present while preparing for a different future. Theory and practice go hand in hand, ideas represent congealed experience, and when we draw out and on ideas that are shaped by social and historical contexts, we are benefitting from concentrated experiences that have accumulated over space and time. Theory and history, combined, open a window into experiences that allow us to see human possibilities beyond the here and now and, in terms of strategies and tactics, prepare us to avoid potential pitfalls by learning from the mistakes of the past. For those dissatisfied with the state of the world as it is – in particular the state of Black life – leadership is encapsulating the organization, vision, and audacity to tackle head on the reality of those who yearn for change in a context of what Gramsci framed as "the old is dying and the new cannot be born." Present efforts of leadership or otherwise are built upon the histories and past activities that others have mounted. An integral role for academics and intellectuals is to layer these histories, to theorize and contextualize them usefully and tangibly – for as Austin reminds us, "there is much at stake."

REFERENCES

Austin, D. (2013). *Fear of a black nation: Race, sex, and security in sixties Montreal.* Toronto: Between the Lines.

Austin, D. (2017). *The Black Jacobins*: A revolutionary study of revolution, and of a Caribbean revolution. In C. Forsdick & C. Hogsbjerg (Eds.), *The Black Jacobins Reader* (pp. 256–77). Durham: Duke University Press.

Austin, D. (2018). *Dread poetry and freedom: Linton Kwesi Johnson and the unfinished revolution.* London: Pluto.

Buck-Morss, S. (2009). *Hegel, Haiti and universal history.* Pittsburgh: University of Pittsburgh Press.

Chimbganda, T. (2017). *The classroom as privileged space: Psychoanalytic paradigms for social justice in pedagogy.* Lanham: Lexington Books.

Fick, C. (1990). *The making of Haiti: Saint Domingue revolution from below.* Knoxville: University of Tennessee Press.

Goldberg, J. (2016, April). The Obama doctrine. *Atlantic Monthly.* Retrieved from http://www.theatlantic.com/magazine/archive/2016/04/the-obama-doctrine/471525/

Gyeke, G. (1995). *An essay on African philosophy: The Akan conceptual scheme.* Philadelphia: Temple University Press.

Henry, P. (2000). *Caliban's reason: Introducing Afro-Caribbean philosophy.* New York: Routledge.

James, C.L.R. (2000). Lectures on the Black Jacobins. *Small Axe: A Caribbean Journal of Criticism, 8*, 65–112.

James, C.L.R. (2001). *The Black Jacobins: Toussaint L'Ouverture and the San Domingo Revolution.* New York: Penguin.

Contributors

Dr Paul Banahene Adjei is an assistant professor at the School of Social Work, Memorial University of Newfoundland. He holds a PhD and a master's degree from the University of Toronto and a bachelor's degree in social work from the University of Ghana. Paul's teaching and research interests are in the areas of adaptation and integration processes and challenges that new and old immigrants of African descent face in Canada and the United States.

David Austin is the author of *Fear of a Black Nation: Race, Sex, and Security in Sixties Montreal* (Between The Lines, 2013; winner of the 2014 Casa de las Americas Prize) and *Dread, Poetry and Freedom: Linton Kwesi Johnson and the Unfinished Revolution* (Pluto, 2018); he is the editor of *You Don't Play with Revolution: The Montreal Lectures of C.L.R. James* (AK Press, 2010) and editor/author of *Moving Against the System: The 1968 Congress of Black Writers and the Making of Global Consciousness* (Pluto, 2018). He teaches in the Department of Humanities, Philosophy, and Religion at John Abbott College.

Dr Shamara Baidoobonso in a researcher and public health epidemiologist. Her areas of expertise include community-based research, quantitative-qualitative mixed methods, and moving research evidence into action within communities and governments. She is keenly interested in engaging diverse stakeholders (including marginalized communities) to produce meaningful, actionable information and positive results.

Dr Wesley Crichlow is a professor in the Faculty of Social Science and Humanities at the University of Ontario Institute of Technology (UOIT), and is associate dean of equity, chair of the President's Equity Taskforce, and director for Youth in Foster Care Pathways to University at UOIT. He is committed to working across borders, connecting the spaces between the Caribbean and Canada as well as unsettling the uneven terrain. This is evident in his groundbreaking book *Buller Men & Batty Bwoys: Hidden Men in Toronto and Halifax's Black Communities* (University of Toronto Press, 2003). He is currently investigating the experiences of LGTBQ incarceration, victimization, and reintegration. Dr Crichlow's work is dedicated to community-university collaborations, and his many years of scholarly and community engagement have engendered trust, credibility, and respect.

George J. Sefa Dei is professor of social justice education and director of the Centre for Integrative Anti-Racism Studies at the Ontario Institute for Studies in Education of the University of Toronto (OISE/UT). He is a 2015, 2016, and 2018 Carnegie African Diaspora Fellow (International Institute of Education/ISIU-Africa). In June 2007, Professor Dei was installed as a traditional chief in Ghana, specifically as the Gyaasehene of the town of Asokore, Koforidua, in the New Juaben Traditional Area of Ghana. His stool name is Nana Adusei Sefa Tweneboah.

Amoaba Gooden is an associate professor, scholar, and researcher at Kent State University. Her ongoing research includes the study of African Canadian organizing and community building, and decolonizing teaching and research practices. Dr Gooden is the editor of a special edition of the *Southern Journal of Canadian Studies* on the theme "Constructing Black Canada: Becoming Canadian." Her other publications can be found in *S'TEṈISTOLW_ – Moving Forward in Indigenous Higher Education*, the *Journal of Black Studies, Journal of Pan-African Studies,* and *Wagadu: Journal of Transnational Women's and Gender Studies.*

Kevin Gosine is an associate professor of sociology at Brock University. He specializes in the areas of racial identity construction, the critical study of race and racialization, youth studies, and the sociology of education. His work has appeared in such journals as the *Canadian Journal of Education*; *Identity: An International Journal of Theory & Research*; the *Journal of Progressive Human Services*; *Critical Sociology*; the *Review of Education, Pedagogy & Cultural Studies*; and *The School-Community Journal.*

rosalind hampton is an assistant professor of Black studies in education in the Ontario Institute for Studies in Education at the University of Toronto. Her areas of teaching and research include Black radical thinkers and artists, Black studies in Canada, visual culture, anti-colonialism, and racialized social relations in higher education.

Annette Henry holds the David Lam Chair in Multicultural Education in the Faculty of Education at the University of British Columbia. She is a professor in the Department of Language and Literacy Education and is cross-appointed to the Institute for Gender, Race, Sexuality, and Social Justice.

Philip Howard is an assistant professor in the Department of Integrated Studies in Education at McGill University. His work focuses on how relations of race and anti-Blackness mediate the ways we come to know ourselves, create community, and exercise agency in the Canadian settler-colonial context. He has published in such journals as *Ethnicities; Social Identities: Journal for the Study of Race, Nation and Culture;* and *Race Ethnicity and Education* and is co-editor of the collection *Crash Politics and Antiracism: Interrogations of Liberal Race Discourse* (Peter Lang, 2008).

Carl E. James holds the Jean Augustine Chair in Education, Community, and Diaspora in the Faculty of Education at York University, Toronto, where he is also the affirmative action, equity, and inclusivity officer. He teaches in the Faculty of Education and in the graduate programs in sociology and social and political thought. James's research includes examination of the lives and experiences of racialized people, and of African Canadians in particular. He is a fellow of the Royal Society of Canada and was awarded an honorary doctorate from Uppsala University, Sweden, where he also taught for many years in the Faculty of Education. James holds numerous scholarly and community awards for his equity, social justice, and community work. He holds a PhD in sociology and has authored, co-authored, edited, or co-edited several books, book chapters, and journal articles seeking to move us beyond essentialist, universalizing, and homogenizing representations of Black people.

Tamari Kitossa is associate professor in the Department of Sociology at Brock University. Research interests include race and criminalization, criminology and the sociology of knowledge, anti-Blackness, racism and racialization, and interracial unions. He contributed a chapter to the edited volume *Habitus of the Hood* (Intellect, 2012) and has published articles in the *African Journal of Criminology and Justice Studies*; *International Journal of Canadian Studies*; *International Journal of Criminology and Sociological Theory*; *Journal of Black Studies*; *Critical Race Inquiry*; *Journal of Pan African Studies*; and *Southern Journal of Canadian Studies.*

Erica S. Lawson is an associate professor in the Department of Women's Studies and Feminist Research at the University of Western Ontario. She teaches in the areas of feminist and critical race studies. Her research interests include the politics of maternal activism and leadership.

Désirée Rochat is a community worker and educator, and a PhD candidate in the Department of Integrated Studies in Education at McGill University. She currently works for the preservation and promotion of archives in Montreal community-based organizations, especially those of Caribbean communities, and has worked on various research and educational projects connecting the community and university sectors.

Sam Tecle is a PhD candidate in the Department of Sociology at York University. His areas of focus include Black and diaspora studies, urban studies, and sociology of education.

Christopher J. Williams is a Toronto-based activist and scholar specializing in issues of criminal justice and racial marginality. Williams worked with a team of *Toronto Star* journalists to generate multimedia material for the widely read "Known to Police" investigative series, winner of a National Newspaper Award in 2014. He is a member of the Toronto Police Accountability Coalition (Toronto) and, with Joseph Mensah, is co-author of *Boomerang Ethics: How Racism Affects Us All* (Fernwood, 2017).

Index

www.ingramcontent.com/pod-product-compliance
Lightning Source LLC
LaVergne TN
LVHW090800070826
844660LV00022B/1046

* 9 7 8 1 4 8 7 5 2 3 6 6 4 *